DISCARD

NABOKOV AT CORNELL

NABOKOV AT CORNELL

EDITED BY GAVRIEL SHAPIRO

Cornell University Press   Ithaca & London

Copyright © 2003 by Cornell University

Chapter 8 copyright © 1999 by Brian Boyd. Reprinted
by permission of Princeton University Press.

"On Returning to Cornell" by Dmitri Nabokov copyright © 2003
by Dmitri Nabokov. Reprinted by courtesy of Dmitri Nabokov.
All rights reserved, including the right of reproduction
in whole or in part in any form.

Extracts from the works and correspondence of Vladimir Nabokov
are published by arrangement with the Estate of Vladimir Nabokov.

All rights reserved. Except for brief quotations in a review,
this book, or parts thereof, must not be reproduced in any
form without permission in writing from the publisher. For
information, address Cornell University Press, Sage House,
512 East State Street, Ithaca, New York 14850.

First published 2003 by Cornell University Press
Printed in the United States of America

Library of Congress Cataloging in Publication Data

Nabokov at Cornell / edited by Gavriel Shapiro.
    p. cm.
Includes bibliographical references and index.
    ISBN 0-8014-3909-4 (acid-free paper)
    1. Nabokov, Vladimir Vladimirovich, 1899–
1977—Criticism and interpretation.   I. Shapiro,
Gavriel.   II. Title.

PG3476.N3 Z777 2003
813'.54—dc21   2002013923

Cornell University Press strives to use environmentally
responsible suppliers and materials to the fullest extent possible
in the publishing of its books. Such materials include vegetable-
based, low-VOC inks and acid-free papers that are recycled, totally
chlorine-free, or partly composed of nonwood fibers. For further
information, visit our website at www.cornellpress.cornell.edu.

Cloth printing   10 9 8 7 6 5 4 3 2 1

Frontispiece: Vladimir Nabokov in his Cornell office, 278 Goldwin Smith Hall, 1958.
Courtesy Division of Rare and Manuscript Collections. Carl A. Kroch Library,
Cornell University. Photo: Robert L. Wegryn '59.

TO THE MEMORY OF GEORGE GIBIAN

{ CONTENTS }

Preface *Gavriel Shapiro* xi
Abbreviations xiii

I. THE RUSSIAN YEARS

1. The Fourth Dimension of Nabokov's *Laughter in the Dark* 3
   Vladimir E. Alexandrov
2. Sources of Nabokov's *Despair* 10
   D. Barton Johnson
3. The Semiotic Validity of the Mirror Image in Nabokov's *Despair* 20
   Marina Kanevskaya
4. *The Enchanter* and the Beauties of Sleeping 30
   Susan Elizabeth Sweeney

II. THE AMERICAN YEARS

5. Suffer the Little Children 49
   Zoran Kuzmanovich
6. "Signs and Symbols" and Silentology 58
   Joanna Trzeciak
7. Reinventing Nabokov: Lyne and Kubrick Parse *Lolita* 68
   Ellen Pifer
8. *Pale Fire*: The *Vanessa atalanta* 78
   Brian Boyd
9. Buzzwords and Dorophonemes:
   How Words Proliferate and Things Decay in *Ada* 91
   Charles Nicol

III. THE MIRACULOUS AMPHORA

10. Metapoetics and Metaphysics: Pushkin and Nabokov, 1799–1899 103
    Sergei Davydov
11. Nabokov the Pushkinian 114
    Irena Ronen
12. Nabokov and Tiutchev 123
    Christine A. Rydel
13. Nabokov's *Nikolai Gogol*: Doing Things in Style 136
    Leona Toker

IV. THE GLORIOUS OUTPUT

14. The Daedalus–Icarus Theme in Nabokov's Fiction 151
    Julian W. Connolly
15. Vladimir Nabokov and the Scriblerians 161
    Lisa Zunshine
16. The Triple Anniversary of World Literature: Goethe, Pushkin, Nabokov 172
    Omry Ronen
17. Vladimir Nabokov, Translator of Lewis Carroll's *Alice in Wonderland* 182
    Nina Demurova
18. Nabokov on Malraux's *La Condition humaine*: A Franco-Russian Crisscross 192
    John Burt Foster, Jr.

V. THE THRILL OF SCIENCE AND THE PLEASURE OF ART

19. Theme in Blue: Vladimir Nabokov's Endangered Butterfly 205
    Robert Dirig
20. The Evolution of Nabokov's Evolution 219
    John M. Kopper
21. Toward a Theory of Negative Pattern in Nabokov 231
    Stephen H. Blackwell

22. Nabokov and Early Netherlandish Art   241
    Gavriel Shapiro
23. Krazy, Ignatz, and Vladimir: Nabokov and the Comic Strip   251
    Clarence Brown

Afterword   265
Nabokov Studies: The State of the Art Revisited
    Stephen Jan Parker

Postscript   277
On Returning to Ithaca
    Dmitri Nabokov

About the Contributors   285

{ Preface }

GAVRIEL SHAPIRO

Vladimir Nabokov (1899-1977), whose centenary was recently celebrated all around the globe, occupies a towering position in Russian and world literature. An inexhaustible subject of research for several generations of literary scholars, widely taught and extensively translated, Nabokov and his creative legacy have a large and continuously growing audience.

The occasion for this volume was the Cornell Nabokov Centenary Festival, held in Ithaca, New York, on September 10-12, 1998, to mark the jubilee of Nabokov's advent at Cornell and his then approaching centenary. By coming to Ithaca in 1948, Nabokov provided Cornell University with an excellent "excuse" for inaugurating his centenary celebrations. With this fatidic occurrence, Nabokov rewarded his favorite academic institution, where he taught for more than a decade—the longest at any one place in the United States—and where he enjoyed the heights of his creativity.

It is at Cornell that Nabokov composed the English and Russian versions of his autobiography, *Conclusive Evidence* and *Drugie berega*, the novels *Lolita* and *Pnin*, and numerous poems and short stories; translated and annotated two works at the pinnacle of Russian literature, its medieval epic *The Song of Igor's Campaign* and Alexander Pushkin's *Eugene Onegin*; prepared and delivered in the classroom his now highly acclaimed lectures on Russian and Western European literature; and began to conceive *Pale Fire*. In addition, following his summer butterfly-hunting trips across America, Nabokov wrote at Cornell a number of scientific papers on lepidoptera—his great lifelong passion, second only to literature.

Nabokov at Cornell is divided into five parts. The titles of parts I and II allude to the magisterial biography by Brian Boyd, who used "the Russian years" and "the American years" to represent the linguistic periods of Nabokov's writing. The titles for parts III, IV, and V fittingly refer to Nabokov's

Cornell lectures, "Lectures on Russian Literature" and "Lectures on Literature," respectively. All together, the volume reflects the great diversity of the interests of Nabokov—perhaps the last Renaissance man—from poetry to prose, from original fiction to translation and to literary scholarship, from literature to visual art, and from humanities at large to natural science.

The Cornell Nabokov Centenary Festival, and this volume, would not have been possible without the spirited participation of Cornell's administration, faculty, and staff. I am grateful to President Hunter R. Rawlings III, Provost Don M. Randel, and Vice President Ingeborg T. Reichenbach; Deans Walter I. Cohen, Peter J. Kahn, Philip E. Lewis, and Carolyn A. (Biddy) Martin; Patricia Haugen, Carol True Palmer, Laurie A. Robinson, and Clare Ulrich of the Cornell Development Office; Ross Atkinson, H. Thomas Hickerson, Katherine Reagan, and Sarah E. Thomas of Cornell Library; Paul Cody, Linda Grace-Kobas, and Simeon F. Moss of Cornell News Service; Anna D. Geske and Pamela M. Lafayette of Cornell Council for the Arts; Abby H. Eller of Cornell School of Continuing Education and Summer Sessions; Catherine A. Carlson and Mary K. Fessenden of Cornell Cinema; Warren M. Bunn II and Franklin W. Robinson of the Herbert F. Johnson Museum of Art; Henry W. Crans and Charles Eric Fields of Cornell Facilities; Xak Bjerken, Judith G. Kellock, Loralyn Light, Mark D. Scatterday, and Stephen E. Stucky of the Department of Music; Anne E. Berger of the Department of Romance Studies; David M. Feldshuh, Thomas E. Scharff, and Leah Shafer of the Department of Theatre, Film, and Dance; and Patricia J. Carden, Jenka T. Fyfe, George Gibian, Slava Paperno, Nancy Pollak, and Diane D. Williams of the Department of Russian. Among the last group, Jenka T. Fyfe, who did so much to make the Festival a success and this volume a reality, deserves the highest praise.

Special thanks go to Jon A. Lindseth '56, Joseph F. Martino Jr. '53, and many other Cornell alumni for their generous support of the Festival. I express my great appreciation to William F. Buckley Jr., Leslie Carrère, Kathryn Jacobi, and Terry Quinn, whose invaluable contribution to this celebration helped to turn it into genuine festivity.

Most of all, my immense gratitude goes to Dmitri Nabokov, whose participation in almost every facet of the Festival, in the remarkable spirit of his family's legendary versatility, left an indelible, truly Nabokovian mark on this unforgettable event.

{ ABBREVIATIONS }

All references are to these editions, except as otherwise noted.

Ada   *Ada, or Ardor: A Family Chronicle.* 1969; New York: Vintage International, 1990.
AnL   *The Annotated Lolita.* Ed. with preface, introduction, and notes by Alfred Appel, Jr. 1970; revised and updated edition, New York: Vintage International, 1991.
BS   *Bend Sinister.* 1947; New York: Vintage International, 1990.
CE   *Conclusive Evidence: A Memoir.* New York: Harper, 1951.
Def   *The Defense.* Trans. Michael Scammell in collaboration with the author. 1964; New York: Vintage International, 1990.
Des   *Despair.* 1966; New York: Vintage International, 1989.
En   *The Enchanter.* Trans. Dmitri Nabokov. 1986. New York: Vintage International, 1991.
EO   *Eugene Onegin: A Novel in Verse by Aleksandr Pushkin.* Trans. with commentary by Vladimir Nabokov, 4 vols., Bollingen Series 72. 1964; revised edition, Princeton University Press, 1975.
Eye   *The Eye.* Trans. Dmitri Nabokov in collaboration with the author. 1965; New York: Vintage International, 1990.
IB   *Invitation to a Beheading.* Trans. Dmitri Nabokov in collaboration with the author. 1959; New York: Vintage International, 1989.
Gift   *The Gift.* Trans. Michael Scammell with the collaboration of the author. 1963; New York: Vintage International, 1991.
Glory *Glory.* Trans. Dmitri Nabokov in collaboration with the author. 1971; New York: Vintage International, 1991.
KQK   *King, Queen, Knave.* Trans. Dmitri Nabokov in collaboration with the author. 1968; New York: Vintage International, 1989.
Laugh *Laughter in the Dark.* 1938; New York: Vintage International, 1989.

LATH	*Look at the Harlequins!* 1974; New York: Vintage International, 1990.
LDQ	*Lectures on* Don Quixote. Ed. Fredson Bowers. New York: Harcourt Brace Jovanovich/Bruccoli Clark, 1983.
LL	*Lectures on Literature.* Ed. Fredson Bowers. New York: Harcourt Brace Jovanovich/Bruccoli Clark, 1980.
Lo	*Lolita.* 1955; New York: Vintage International, 1989.
LoR	*Lolita.* New York: Phaedra, 1967.
LoScreen	*Lolita: A Screenplay.* 1974; New York: Vintage International, 1997.
LRL	*Lectures on Russian Literature.* Ed. Fredson Bowers. New York: Harcourt Brace Jovanovich/Bruccoli Clark, 1981.
Mary	*Mary.* Trans. Michael Glenny in collaboration with the author. 1970; New York: Vintage International, 1989.
NWL	*The Nabokov–Wilson Letters, 1940-1971.* Ed., annotated and with an introductory essay by Simon Karlinsky. New York: Colophon, 1980 (corrected edition with same pagination as Harper and Row, 1979).
NG	*Nikolai Gogol.* 1944; New York: New Directions, 1961 (corrected edition).
PF	*Pale Fire.* 1962; New York: Vintage International, 1989.
Pnin	*Pnin.* 1957; New York: Vintage International, 1989.
PP	*Poems and Problems.* New York: McGraw-Hill, 1970.
RLSK	*The Real Life of Sebastian Knight.* 1941; New York: Vintage International, 1992.
SL	*Selected Letters, 1940-1977.* Ed. Dmitri Nabokov and Matthew J. Bruccoli. New York: Harcourt Brace Jovanovich/Bruccoli Clark Layman, 1989.
SM	*Speak, Memory.* 1967; New York: Vintage International, 1989.
SO	*Strong Opinions.* 1973; New York: Vintage International, 1990.
Song	*The Song of Igor's Campaign.* Trans. Vladimir Nabokov. 1960. New York: McGraw-Hill, 1975.
Stikhi	*Stikhi.* Ann Arbor: Ardis, 1979.
Stories	*The Stories of Vladimir Nabokov.* 1995; New York: Vintage International, 1997.
TT	*Transparent Things.* 1972; New York: Vintage International, 1989.
USSR	*The Man from the U.S.S.R. and Other Plays.* Trans. and introductions by Dmitri Nabokov. New York: Harcourt Brace Jovanovich/Bruccoli Clark, 1984.

{ PART I }
THE RUSSIAN YEARS

{ 1 }

The Fourth Dimension of Nabokov's *Laughter in the Dark*

VLADIMIR E. ALEXANDROV

I suggested in publications in 1988 and 1991 that Nabokov may have been influenced by the Russian occultist Petr Dem'ianovich Uspenskii (1878–1947), better known in English as P. D. Ouspensky, or even as Fourth Dimension Ouspensky.[1] Uspenskii's role in the history of culture is that of a thinker who influenced a surprisingly wide range of major figures in Russia and Europe during the first decades of this century.[2] In the simplest terms, he can be seen as belonging to the broad stream of syncretic mysticism that appeared in Europe during the last quarter of the nineteenth century with the "theosophy" of Elena Petrovna Blavatskaia (also known as Madame Blavatsky). This stream fed into the revival of religious, philosophical, and mystical thought in Russia around the turn of the previous century, where it left a profound influence on many major writers, artists, and musicians. Uspenskii's ideas, like all branches of this broad trend, centered on the nature of the relationship between the material world and "higher dimensions" of being, and the consequence this has, or should have, for human existence. More specifically, Uspenskii argued that by cultivating a higher form of consciousness that gives insight into the "fourth dimension," man can transcend his state and thereby also serve a realm higher than his own.

---

1. See Vladimir E. Alexandrov, "Nabokov's Metaphysics of Artifice: Uspenskij's 'Fourth Dimension' and Evreinov's 'Theatrarch,'" *Rossija/Russia* (Venice) 6, no. 1–2 (1988): 131–44; idem, *Nabokov's Otherworld* (Princeton, N.J.: Princeton University Press, 1991), 227–34.

2. The following summary is based on Alexandrov, *Nabokov's Otherworld*, 227–29.

The connection between Nabokov and Uspenskii remains speculative because Nabokov appears to have left no testimony suggesting that he had any interest in, or knowledge of, Uspenskii's ideas. What warrants speaking of a possible influence, however, is that Nabokov shared with Uspenskii several unusual viewpoints, including the seminal redefinition of "artifice" and "nature" as synonyms on the basis of mimicry among insects. As I suggested in my earlier publications, the high degree of congruence between Nabokov's and Uspenskii's formulations is what prompts the inference that Nabokov's thinking about mimicry among lepidoptera may have been derived from— or, at least, influenced by—Uspenskii's. The specific arguments Uspenskii made are apparently unique and had not appeared previously in the history of speculation about mimicry in nature. However, this claim needs to be tempered by the caveat that, because Nabokov had been passionately interested in lepidoptera since boyhood and because the polemics surrounding Darwinian interpretations of mimicry began very shortly after the publication of *The Origin of Species* in 1859, Nabokov could have developed his views about the metaphysical implications of mimicry entirely or largely on his own.

Be that as it may, there are three parallels between Uspenskii's and Nabokov's conceptions of insect mimicry: (1) both dismiss the Darwinian principle of utilitarianism—that is, that mimicry is camouflage whose primary effect is the survival of the fittest; (2) both insist that it is artistic deception that operates throughout nature; and (3) both conclude that the mimetic patterning found among insects implies the role of a transcendent *maker*. The metaphysical implications of insect mimicry are central to Nabokov's conception of the "otherworld," and because they also motivate his making "nature" and "artifice" into synonyms, they undergird many of the characteristic themes and stylistic features of his art.[3] A major difference between Nabokov and Uspenskii is that Nabokov was, of course, always far more circumspect in his speculations about matters otherworldy than was Uspenskii, who wrote entire books on the subject.

Laughter in the Dark (1938) contains additional evidence suggesting—albeit not necessarily proving definitively—Uspenskii's influence on Nabokov. In

---

3. See Vladimir E. Alexandrov, "Nature and Artifice," in *The Garland Companion to Vladimir Nabokov*, ed. Vladimir E. Alexandrov (New York: Garland, 1995), 553–56; idem, "The Otherworld," in ibid., 566–71.

chapter 32 of the English translation—or revision—of the novel (chapter 29 in the Russian original), the narrator presents a series of elevated perspectives onto the road along which Albinus's car is speeding toward the fateful accident that will literally blind him, then associates these perspectives with Albinus's abandoned wife, Elisabeth, in distant Berlin. These descriptions—which are very similar, but not identical, in the Russian (1933) and English versions of the novel—resemble closely passages in Uspenskii's well-known treatise *Tertium Organum*.[4]

Here is Nabokov's English translation, into which I have inserted the few details from the Russian original that differ from the English and that are significant for my purpose:

> The old woman gathering herbs on the hillside saw the car and the two cyclists approaching the sharp bend from opposite directions. From a mail plane flying coastward through the sparkling blue dust of the sky [the Russian has "Iz liul'ki iaichno-zheltogo pochtovogo dirizhablia"—lit., "From the cradle of an egg-yellow postal dirigible"], the pilot could see the loops of the road, the shadow of its wings . . . and two villages twelve miles distant from one another. Perhaps by rising still higher it would be possible to see simultaneously the mountains of Provence, and a distant town in another country—let us say, Berlin—where the weather was hot too. . . .
>
> In Berlin, on this particular day, a great many ices were sold. Irma [Albinus's young daughter, in whose death he is obliquely implicated] had once used to look on with the gravity of greed when the ice-cream man smeared a thin wafer with the thick yellowish substance which, when tasted, made one's tongue dance and one's front teeth ache deliciously. So that, when Elisabeth stepped onto the balcony and noticed one of these ice-cream vendors, it seemed strange to her that he should be dressed all in white and she all in black.
>
> She had awakened feeling very restless, and now she realized with a strange dismay that, for the first time, she had emerged from that state of dull torpor to which she had grown accustomed of late, and she could not

---

4. P. D. Ouspensky, *Tertium Organum: A Key to the Enigmas of the World*, trans. E. Kadloubovsky and P. D. Ouspensky (New York: Vintage, 1982). This is probably Uspenskii's best-known and most influential work, which was first published in Russia in 1912 and in 1916; the first two English translations appeared in 1920. Vladimir Nabokov, *Kamera obskura* (1932; repr. Ann Arbor: Ardis, 1978).

understand why she felt so strangely uncomfortable. She lingered on the balcony and thought of the day before, on which nothing special had happened: the usual drive to the churchyard, bees settling on her flowers, the damp glitter of the box hedge round the grave [of Irma]; the stillness and the soft earth.

"What can it be?" she wondered. "Why am I all a-tingle?"

From the balcony she could see the ice-cream vendor.... The balcony seemed to soar higher, higher [this phrase does not appear in the Russian]. The sun threw a dazzling light on the tiles—in Berlin, in Brussels, in Paris and farther toward the South. The mail plane was flying to St. Cassien [in the Russian, we still have "zheltyi dirizhabl' plyl v Tulon"—lit., "the yellow dirigible floated toward Toulon"]. (*Laugh* 237–38)

Now for Uspenskii. In the fourth chapter of *Tertium Organum*, he speculates about time as the "fourth dimension of space," and about what would happen if human beings were able to transcend the everyday plane of being that is defined by three spatial dimensions and by time understood as linear and irreversible:

> If our perception could rise above this [mundane] plane, it would most certainly see below *simultaneously* a far greater number of events than it usually sees from its position on the plane. If a man *climbs a mountain* [italics added] or *goes up in a balloon* [italics added] he sees *simultaneously* and *at once* a great many things that it is impossible to see simultaneously and at once when on earth—the movement of two trains towards one another which must result in *a head-on collision* [italics added]; the approach of an enemy detachment to a sleeping camp; two towns separated by a mountain ridge and so on....
>
> With this ascent the *angle of vision will widen* [italics added], the *moment* will expand....
>
> But for this to take place it is necessary for us to be able *to free ourselves from matter* [italics added], because matter is nothing other than the conditions of time and space in which we live.[5]

The similarities between these passages from Nabokov and Uspenskii include elevated perspectives from similar vantage points: a mountain and a balloon (as we have seen, in the English translation Nabokov modernizes the "diri-

---

5. Ouspensky, *Tertium Organum*, 33–34.

gible," or kind of "balloon," into a "mail plane"); we also have Uspenskii's imminent "head-on collision" of "two trains" translated into the image of Albinus's car and two cyclists heading for a collision. Perhaps most interesting is that the implied perspective from the non-material fourth dimension that Uspenskii strives to describe appears associated with Elisabeth and her soaring balcony. What is the function of this association? There is reason to infer that it may be an evocation of the dead Irma's otherworldy presence or influence in her mother's—and, possibly, her father's—life. This is, incidentally, an interpretation that William W. Rowe suggested in 1981, albeit without relying on evidence extrinsic to Nabokov's novel.[6]

Uspenskii makes the elevated, fourth-dimensional perspective, such as the one he describes in the passage quoted earlier, contingent on transcending the material plane of being. It is tempting to conclude, therefore, that this is in fact the state that Irma's spirit achieves when she dies. This possibility appears to be suggested in several ways. When Elisabeth first thinks of Irma in chapter 32, it is in connection not with the girl's sad death but with her delight in the sensuous pleasures of ice cream—a perfectly normal recollection under the circumstances, of course, but one that also subtly sidesteps the seeming facticity of the girl's demise. Indeed, the mother's position on the balcony, her line of sight, and her mental state in this scene are a kind of parodic echo of Irma's, because the girl had caught her fatal chill while looking down at a man in the street who she hoped might be her father. And although Irma is dead, the mother nevertheless feels that she has herself now "emerged from that state of dull torpor" to which she had become accustomed after her daughter's death, a development that can be understood as a kind of revivification of the mother under the influence of some mysterious cause. We are also told several times in chapter 32 about the mother's inexplicable restlessness and about a visit to Irma's grave, during which, as the narrator puts it, "nothing special had happened"—which may be an instance of Nabokovian indirection. Finally, there is the all-important soaring balcony on which Elisabeth is standing—a detail Nabokov added to the English translation—and the dissolution of Elisabeth's rising perspective in that of the omniscient narrator, which, in turn, rises still higher. The passages from Uspenskii support reading this as Elisabeth's being vouchsafed a perspective that can be achieved only by someone who has escaped "this

---

6. William W. Rowe, *Nabokov's Spectral Dimension* (Ann Arbor: Ardis, 1981), 88–91.

mortal coil"—namely, Irma (and the narrator, with what can be taken as his "otherworldy" omniscience).

Perhaps relevant here as well is the detail that, in the English translation, the mail plane was flying to St. Cassien; in the Russian original, the dirigible was flying to Toulon. St. Cassian, spelled with an "-ian," is the name of a town in southeastern France, and St. Cassien, with an "-ien," is the name of a lake in the same part of the country (Lac de St. Cassien). Whether Nabokov really meant the lake rather than the town is less important than the fact that he chose a relatively obscure, albeit *saintly,* toponym to replace the well-known city of Toulon. "Toulon" has various associations, but primary among these is naval warfare and an important early Napoleonic victory, neither of which appears relevant to the occult experience that Elisabeth has. By contrast, the most obvious meaning of St. Cassie/an is that this recalls the fourth- and fifth-century monk and theologian John Cassian, who established monasteries in Marseilles, wrote treatises based on Eastern Christian practices that influenced all subsequent monasticism in the West, and is venerated as a saint in both the Roman Catholic and Russian Orthodox churches. Particularly noteworthy is that he was also associated with a heretical teaching known as Semi-Pelagianism, which argued against what it saw as St. Augustine's inclination toward fatalism, and for the view that humankind does not need to rely on divine grace for salvation and that children are born innocent of the sin of Adam.[7] This last point may in fact be specifically relevant for *Laughter in the Dark,* because not only do we have the death of the innocent Irma as a central event in the novel, but Axel Rex is overtly identified with "Adam after the Fall" (*Laugh* 278), as the narrator puts it, when Uncle Paul thrashes him for his sins later in the novel. In short, the change to St. Cassien, even without all these esoteric resonances, can be seen as buttressing the otherworldy associations in chapter 32 that appear to be derived from Uspenskii.

    7. See *The New Columbia Encyclopedia* (New York: Columbia University Press, 1975), 472, s.v. "Cassian, John"; Carl J. Peter, *Encyclopedia Americana* (Danbury, Conn.: Grolier, 1997), 21:608, s.v. "Pelagianism"; *Polnyi pravoslavnyi bogoslovskii entsiklopedicheskii slovar'* (St. Petersburg: Izdatel'stvo P. P. Soikina, n.d.; Moscow: Vozrozhdenie, 1992), 1:1101–2, s.v. "Ioann Kassian." I am grateful to Professor Gennady Barabtarlo for pointing out that Saint John Cassian is venerated in the Russian Orthodox church and that his Saint's Day is February 29. Saint John Cassian's association with leap years is the kind of calendrical oddity that might have appealed to Nabokov.

I might mention in conclusion that Uspenskii was not only an original thinker within his occult realm but also a popularizer of views that he borrowed from others. Uspenskii's speculations about the fourth dimension, and about how higher dimensions relate to lower ones, owe a great deal to the turn-of-the-century English mathematician, writer, and inventor Charles H. Hinton, to whom Uspenskii refers often in his treatise. Moreover, some of Hinton's own attempts to popularize his ideas about the relationships among worlds with different numbers of dimensions also recall Edwin A. Abbott's well-known romance *Flatland* (1884), which is part of the same speculative nineteenth-century, quasi-mathematical stream. In fact, the way all these writers conceived of the relations among such worlds may be reflected in the description of the realm into which Albinus passes when he is blinded and in how he appears to transcend it in the novel's final scenes. It is therefore also possible that Uspenskii was more of a mediating than a direct influence on Nabokov.

… { 2 }

Sources of Nabokov's *Despair*

D. BARTON JOHNSON

Nabokov began his novel *Despair* (*Otchaianie*) a "month before moving into Nestorstrasse on July 31, 1932.... By September 10, worn out, he had finished the first draft."[1] *Despair*'s story is a hackneyed one. The protagonist-narrator Hermann, owner of a failing Berlin chocolate business, perceives himself as a creative artist. On a business trip, he encounters a vagrant whom he believes is his exact double. Following an elaborate plan, Hermann kills his double after switching clothes and identities, leaving the body near his car in a deserted wood. Hermann's wife is to identify the body as his, collect the insurance money, and later join him (under his new identity) in France.

But the scheme goes awry. First, the vagrant, Felix, does not resemble Hermann; and second, Hermann inadvertently leaves the tramp's name-incised walking stick in the car, revealing the victim's and his own newly assumed identity. At the end of the story, the shattered Hermann writes his account while awaiting the arrival of the French police.

Much of the criticism of *Despair* has focused on Nabokov's reworking of the doubles theme—especially that in Dostoevsky's *The Double*.[2] Far less attention has been paid to the crime itself, which Nabokov reshaped from

---

1. Brian Boyd, *Vladimir Nabokov: The Russian Years* (Princeton, N.J.: Princeton University Press, 1990), 382.

2. Julian W. Connolly, "Dostoevsky and Vladimir Nabokov: The Case of *Despair*," in *Dostoevsky and the Human Condition after a Century*, ed. A. Ugrinsky and V. Ozolins (New York: Greenwood Press, 1986), 155–62; Alexander Dolinin, "The Caning of Modernist Profaners: Parody in *Despair*." Available from http://www.libraries.psu.edu/iasweb/nabokov/forians.htm.

contemporary newspaper accounts. Hermann obliquely refers to these cases. After the failure of his plan, Hermann, who has no emotional reaction to the murder itself, is distraught only because the world has failed to notice the master stroke in his scheme—Felix's perfect resemblance to himself. He berates the press in particular:

> I make no mention here of the monstrous epithets which those irresponsible scribblers, those purveyors of thrills, those villainous quacks who set up their stalls where blood has been spilt, consider it necessary to award me.... All that drivel and dirt incensed me at the outset, especially the fact of my being associated with this or that oaf with vampirish tastes.... There was, for instance, that fellow who burned his car with his victim's body inside, after having wisely sawed off part of the feet, as the corpse had turned out to exceed in length his, the car owner's, measure. They and I have nothing in common.[3]

Hermann's real anguish comes from being lumped with "ordinary" criminals. Both of the murderers he cites are real. Although the first, the vampire, does not appear to resemble Hermann's case, the second—which involves a murder, an identity switch, and a car—does, although the gruesome particulars differ. A close look shows marked similarities to Hermann's crime.[4]

---

3. Vladimir Nabokov, *Despair* (New York: Vintage International, 1989), 203. Page citations are to this edition, unless noted otherwise. Other citations in English are to Vladimir Nabokov, *Despair* (London: John Long, 1937); citations to the original Russian text are to Vladimir Nabokov, *Otchaianie* (Ann Arbor: Ardis, 1978). I thank the Nabokov bibliographer Michael Juliar for making parts of the rare 1937 version available to me.

4. This paper owes its genesis to Judge Philip Howerton, of Charlotte, North Carolina, who noticed the similarity of Hermann's crime to the 1930 British Rouse case. After an exchange of information among the author, Howerton, and the Moscow Nabokov aficionado Peter Kartsev, Howerton and Kartsev collaborated on an unpublished paper, "A Source for *Otchaianie*?" In the investigation, the German Tetzner case, which proved to be a closer fit, surfaced. Dieter Zimmer, who was preparing his editor's essay for the *Despair* volume of Nabokov's collected works, located the original German press reports and kindly summarized them in "Facts of the Tetzner Case" (unpublished ms., December 23, 1997). In addition, he summarizes the Rouse–Tetzner investigation in "Nachwort des Herausgebers," in *Vladimir Nabokov, Gelächter im Dunkel. Verzweiflung. Camera obscura*, Vladimir Nabokov Gesammelte Werke, vol. 3, ed. Dieter Zimmer (Hamburg: Rowohlt, 1997), 555–81. I later learned that Nikolai Mel'nikov had stumbled on the Tetzner case in *Rul'* and recognized its relationship to *Despair* in "Kriminal'nyi shedevr Vladimira Vladimirovicha i Germana Karlovicha (o tvorcheskoi istorii romana V. Nabokova *Otchaianie*)," in *Volshebnaia gora* 2 (Moscow, 1994): 150–65. I am greatly indebted to Howerton, Kartsev, and especially Zimmer.

On November 28, 1929, the *Leipziger Volkszeitung* reported that a burned-out car had been found on a rural road. The driver's mangled, badly burned body was unrecognizable, but according to the license plate the vehicle belonged to Erich Kurt Tetzner, a twenty-five-year-old employee of a Leipzig publisher.[5] On December 4, it was reported that Tetzner's insurance company suspected fraud and insisted on an autopsy, which was performed at the chapel just before the interment ceremony. The autopsy showed "a badly charred trunk to which were still attached the cervical segment of the vertebral column together with the base of the skull, the upper halves of both thighs, the lower articular extremity of the right femur, and parts of the arms."[6] The medical examiner concluded that the charred torso was too young and too slight to have been Tetzner. A wanted poster was circulated for Tetzner, who had fled to France. Having seen only the initial November report in a German paper, Tetzner assumed that all was well, and on the morning of December 4 phoned his wife, Emma, from the Strasbourg Post Office. The police had already tapped the phone (which belonged to a neighbor). Tetzner, who called under an assumed name, was told that Emma was out and that he should call back around 6 P.M. The French police arrested Tetzner as he made his phone call. He had recently taken out three insurance policies, with his wife as beneficiary. The German press provided major coverage, and their reports were summarized the next day in the Berlin Russian émigré newspaper *Rul'* under the headline "Corpse in Automobile."[7] A few days later, *Rul'* ran a photo of Tetzner with a brief recap.[8]

The publicity frenzy flared up again when Tetzner's trial was held on March 17–18, 1931. Tetzner, a petty criminal from youth, by chance or foresight had taken out an insurance policy on his cancer-ridden mother-in-law shortly before she had unsuccessful surgery. With the proceeds, he had bought a green, two-seat Opel. Soon short of cash, he mulled over insuring and poisoning his own mother but decided on bigger prospects. Having insured himself, he set about finding a hitchhiker whom he could kill and burn beyond recognition in his car. After two false starts, he picked up an itinerant—a sawmill worker

---

5. Zimmer, "Facts."

6. Jürgen Thorwald, *The Century of the Detective*, trans. Richard and Clara Winston (New York: Harcourt, Brace and World, 1965), 222.

7. "Trup v avtomobil'," *Rul'*, no. 2745, December 5, 1929, 3.

8. Ibid., no. 2749, December 10, 1929, 4.

from Czechoslovakia, whose identity was never established. Tetzner bought his passenger dinner at the same restaurant to which he had taken a previous candidate, who had escaped. (He had even given the earlier man money for a shave, a new collar, and a tie, as well as for dinner and drink.) This time, Tetzner had sought out a less muscular adversary. To obscure the disparity in their builds and height, Tetzner, after killing his victim, had severed the legs, arms, and head. When asked by the judge about the death torment of his victim, Tetzner replied: "Mir erschien es gar nicht so schlimm [It didn't seem so bad to me]."[9] Tetzner was sentenced to death.

If Nabokov did not know of the case from the German press, he certainly would have from the detailed account that appeared in *Rul'* the day after the trial. In a further item in the November 27 issue, *Rul'* reported that Tetzner had confessed to the prison authorities that the passenger had complained about being cold. After solicitously cocooning him in a blanket, Tetzner strangled him with a rope. The May 3, 1931, edition of the paper reported that Tetzner had been guillotined the day before at Regensburg Prison.[10]

Insurance fraud with switched bodies was not an unknown crime even in the 1920s, although the use of a car as crematorium was a novelty. The evidence linking Nabokov's *Despair* to the Tetzner case rests on a handful of details: the car; the tramp as substitute victim; the vagrant's nationality (like Felix, he was from Czechoslovakia); the killer's hospitable purchase of food and drink, shave, and a collar for the victim; the killer's flight to France to await his wife with the insurance money; and so on. Although the match is convincing, the differences should not be ignored. Hermann does not burn the car; nor does he mutilate his victim.

In his closing speech in the Tetzner trial, the prosecutor noted that the crime had already been imitated abroad and that there, the killer had been executed.[11] There can be little question that he was referring to the Rouse case in England. Alfred Rouse, born London in 1894, did well in school and later worked in an office. He married early and, in 1914, was sent to fight in France,

9. Zimmer, "Nachwort," 576.
10. In "Suicide as Literary Fact in the 1920s" (*Slavic Review* 50, no. 4 [1991]: 827–35), Anne Nesbet describes another example of Nabokov's incorporation of material from *Rul'* into his fiction: the Grunewald suicide pact. Reported in the April 19, 1928, edition of *Rul'*, the suicides provoked much discussion as a sign of the times. Nabokov drew on the story for the suicide pact among Yasha, Olia, and Rudol'f in *The Gift*.
11. Zimmer, "Facts."

where he suffered head and leg wounds, spending a year in hospitals. He appeared to undergo a change of personality, becoming a liar of heroic proportions and a great seducer of women as he made rounds as a sales representative for a firm selling menswear accessories, such as suspenders and garters. He seduced dozens of women, impregnating several. Rouse, whose marriage was childless, welcomed the children and even tried to support them, albeit sometimes under court order. Matters came to a head in late 1930, when two new children were in the offing. Financial affairs were desperate, and, as Rouse said in his confession, "I wanted to start afresh.... I tried to hit on something new. I did not want to do murder just for the sake of it."[12]

Rouse took out several insurance policies. By chance, he encountered a down-and-outer at a pub and bought him a beer while he, a non-drinker, had lemonade. Rouse arranged to give his victim a lift to Leicester on the night of November 5-6—a date he picked because it was Bonfire Night, the popular holiday when Guy Fawkes is burned in effigy to celebrate a failed Catholic attempt to blow up the King and House of Lords in 1605. Rouse's own bonfire would be less conspicuous. Before setting out, he once again treated his passenger to beer (while he drank lemonade) and, on departing the pub, bought a bottle of whiskey for his victim. Pulling off on a side road, Rouse strangled his passenger, poured gasoline over the car, and set it ablaze. Rouse never asked his victim's name, later saying, "I did not care." The body remained unidentified. On November 7, London's *Daily Sketch* published a picture of the burned-out hulk of Rouse's Morris Minor two-seater under the headline, "Riddle of Body Found in Blazing Car." Rouse was arrested on his return to London. Although Rouse's lurid personal life came to light in the initial hearings, the information was not admitted at his trial, which took place on January 26-31, 1931.[13] He was hanged on March 10, 1931.

I have not uncovered evidence that Rouse knew about the Tetzner case, although he very well may have. Nor is there irrefutable evidence that Nabokov knew about the Rouse case before he started *Despair*. There is, however, reason to suspect that Nabokov learned about the case before he made his En-

---

12. Helena Normanton, ed., *The Trial of Alfred Arthur Rouse* (London: Hodge, 1931), 295-96.

13. The London *Daily Sketch* provided extensive, detailed coverage. J. C. Cannell, who covered the case as "special correspondent," included much additional information in his book *New Light on the Rouse Case* (London: John Long, 1931). Rouse had a considerable history of automobile-insurance fraud.

glish translation. Howerton and Kartsev point to the telling detail that Hermann, like Rouse, ordered lemonade while "a tankard of beer" was served to Felix (*Des* 82). An examination of the three versions of *Despair* shows some curious, if minor, discrepancies. In the pre-Rouse Russian edition, both men drink beer before and after dinner during their meeting at a Tarnitz tavern (*Otchaianie* 75, 79, 86). In the post-Rouse English edition (*Des* [1937] 112, 122) and in the 1966 revision (*Des* 78, 82, 89), only Felix drinks beer, while Hermann has lemonade. There is one other discrepancy. In his vituperative letter to Hermann (*Otchaianie* 197; *Des* [1937] 280), Adalion asserts, "You are wonderfully like a great grisly wild boar with putrid tusks—pity you did not put one into that suit of yours." The 1966 version reads: ".... pity you did not put a *roasted* one into that suit of yours" (*Des* 206; emphasis added). The insertion of "roasted" is odd because Hermann, unlike Tetzner and Rouse, did not set his car ablaze. The image of the "roast boar" is undeniably toothsome but counter to Hermann's version of the events.

Tetzner and Rouse were not alone in using fire to cover up the substitution of bodies in insurance-fraud schemes. While Tetzner was awaiting trial, Fritz Saffran, age thirty, devised a somewhat similar scheme.[14] Saffran was the manager of a provincial furniture store owned by his father-in-law. Apparently a successful businessman, Saffran, with help from his young mistress, the company's bookkeeper, and the assistant manager, had embezzled the firm to the point of bankruptcy. One day, Saffran approached his mistress and asked whether she had read about the Tetzner affair. He proposed to solve their problems in the same way. The trio cruised back roads in search of suitable candidates. At length, the deed was done, and the corpse was placed in the

---

14. Unless noted otherwise, information about the Saffran case is from E. Liebermann von Sonnenberg and O. Trettin, *Continental Crimes*, trans. Winifred Ray (London: Geoffrey Bles, 1935). Liebermann von Sonnenberg and Trettin were directors of the Berlin Detective Bureau; Ray, the translator, is very possibly Winifred Roy, who, much to Nabokov's dissatisfaction, translated *Kamera obskura* into English for John Long in 1936. The on-line World Catalogue (http://www.oclc.org/worldcat) does not mention a "Winifred Roy" but says that Winifred Ray was active as a translator from German and French in the 1930s. At least one of her translations was published by John Long, making it not unlikely that Nabokov's *Laughter in the Dark* was also Ray's work. There is no evidence that Ray knew Russian, so if she was the translator, she must have worked from Doussia Ergaz's French version (V. Nabokov-Sirine, *Chambre obscure* [Paris: Bernard Grasset, 1934]).

office wearing Saffran's ring and watch. Saffran then torched the place on the night of September 15, 1930. His male accomplice reported that Saffran (who had five insurance policies) had run into the flaming building to recover the company books and perished. The body substitution was unsuccessful, and Saffran, who had planned to flee to Brazil, was apprehended. Tried with great fanfare, he and his colleague were condemned to death on March 25, 1931, only a few days after Tetzner's trial. The case was widely reported in the German press and in *Rul'*.[15] Because the trial stories ran almost concurrently, it is very likely that Nabokov was aware of the Saffran case.

Hermann's diatribe against the press for linking him with "ordinary" criminals (*Des* 202) more vaguely alludes to a second example. He is especially incensed at being associated with "this or that oaf with vampirish tastes" (*Des* 193). The "oaf" was Peter Kürten, known as "the Düsseldorf Vampire." Mild-mannered, polite, forty-eight-year-old Peter Kürten—with sleek, neatly parted blond hair; cloud of eau de cologne; immaculate suit, and polished shoes—resembled "a prim shopkeeper or minor civil servant."[16] When Kürten's attorney argued insanity—given the horrors committed by his client—a medical specialist responded: "And [he] was at the same time a clever man and quite a nice one."[17] Former employers testified to his honesty and reliability. One of his surviving victims described him as "a rather sedate man." So innocuous did Kürten appear that a former girlfriend was fined for making a malicious allegation when she told the police early on that Kürten might be the killer.

Kürten, who had spent twenty years in prison, launched a rampage of terror that extended from February 1929 to May 24, 1930, when he was apprehended. One of thirteen children, Kürten was raised in a one-room flat by a drunken father and abused mother. The father was sentenced to three years for incest with a thirteen-year-old daughter. Kürten was apprenticed to a dog-catcher, who taught him to torture and sexually abuse animals. While stabbing sheep and goats, he discovered that the sight of blood could bring him to orgasm. On one occasion, he beheaded a park swan and placed his mouth over the severed neck. Kürten committed his first sex murder during a bur-

15. *Rul'*, no. 3031, November 11, 1930; ibid., no. 3140–42, March 25–27, 1931.

16. *Crimes and Punishment: The Illustrated Crime Encyclopedia* (Westport, Conn.: H. S. Stuttman, 1984), vol. 8, s.v. "Peter Kürten: The Düsseldorf Vampire," 986. See also Margaret Seaton Wagner, *The Monster of Düsseldorf: The Life and Trial of Peter Kürten* (London: Faber and Faber, 1932).

17. *Crimes and Punishment*, 988.

glary in 1913 in which he cut the throat of a sleeping thirteen-year-old girl and relished the spurting blood.[18] At his trial (where he was caged), he was charged with nine murders and seven attempted murders and calmly recounted the details. He also admitted drinking the blood from his victims' throats—in one case, gulping so much that he vomited. He also told of mass-murder fantasies. At his trial, he expressed bitterness at his fate compared with that of two socialist doctors who had performed abortions on five hundred working-class women. "I have no remorse," he said. "As to whether recollection of my deeds makes me feel ashamed, I will tell you. Thinking back to all the details is not at all unpleasant. I rather enjoy it."[19]

The Düsseldorf Vampire's career came to an end when he took a young woman to his room and gave her a glass of milk and a ham sandwich. Afterward, in a wooded area, he attempted to strangle and rape her. Unaccountably, he released the girl, who later led the police to his empty room. As the girl and the police were leaving, Kürten glimpsed them. Realizing he was on the verge of capture, he encouraged his unsuspecting wife to turn him in so that she could collect the reward. The sensational trial was held on April 13–22, 1931. Before Kürten was guillotined, he hopefully inquired about whether he might, at least for a moment, hear the sound of the blood gushing from his severed neck. "That would be for him, he said, the pleasure to end all pleasures."[20]

We now come to the question of why Nabokov and Hermann chose to allude, albeit obscurely, to the Düsseldorf Vampire. Kürten's trial was the culmination of a sensational and heavily publicized series: Tetzner, the first killer, was tried in mid-March 1931 and beheaded on May 2; Rouse (who committed his deed a year later) had been tried in January 1931 and was hanged on March 10; Saffran was condemned in March 1931. Kürten was tried in mid-April 1931. His notoriety in the public eye was doubtless enhanced by the May

18. Ibid.
19. Karl Berg, "Kürten—The Vampire of Düsseldorf," in *Monsters of Weimar: Comprising the Classic Case Histories: Haarmann—The Story of a Werewolf. Kürten—The Vampire of Düsseldorf* (London: Nemesis, 1993), 159–289. Professor Berg, the chief expert witness in forensic medicine at the trial, wrote the monograph on Kürten after working with him for more than a year. Kürten's image as evil incarnate lingers. Lisa Erdman, the heroine of D. M. Thomas's *The White Hotel* (in which she is a patient of Sigmund Freud), is deeply troubled by the Kürten case: D. M. Thomas, *The White Hotel* (New York: Viking, 1981), 177–79, 262–63. My thanks to Susan Sweeney.
20. Berg, "Kürten," 247.

premiere of Fritz Lang's now classic film "*M*," starring Peter Lorre, which was loosely based on the Kürten case.[21]

In the 1920s and early '30s, Nabokov was writing two kinds of novels: those with chiefly Russian characters, and those with German characters. The Russian novels, such as *Mary, The Defense, The Eye,* and *Glory,* are concerned with the themes of nostalgia and identity. The German novels, such as *King, Queen, Knave, Laughter in the Dark,* and *Despair* are crime stories in which Nabokov investigates the nature of evil. Dieter Zimmer is undoubtedly correct in seeing the German triptych as Nabokov's attempt to utilize genre literature and film as modes for the stark exploration of the moral dementia he saw around him. His protagonists do not merely lack feeling; they have no sense of the pain inflicted on others.[22] They display a "passive" moral dementia exceeded in evil only by human monsters who do recognize the suffering of others but regard it as a source of pleasure. According to Zimmer, only Axel Rex falls in the latter category; Hermann's late comment, "What on earth have I done?" (*Des* 210), suggests some degree of empathy.[23] Zimmer may be too harsh on Axel Rex, who is not even a murderer, and too lenient on Hermann, who carefully premeditates a murder that troubles him not in the slightest.

The series of highly publicized trials in March–April 1931 probably planted the seeds for Nabokov's *Despair.* The rationale for his allusion to Tetzner is obvious: the similarity of Hermann's and Tetzner's crime. This similarity provided the nucleus of the plot. Nabokov discarded the mutilation and car-burning not from any sense of fastidiousness, but because they would have "interfered" with his one novel idea in the plot—Hermann's fixation on the idea that he and Felix are identical. The rationale for the second allusion—to Peter Kürten, the Düsseldorf Vampire—is less apparent. Kürten's crimes bore no similarity to Hermann's, apart perhaps from Kürten's willingness to share a cozy meal with his intended victim. Sedate, prim Kürten, the very paradigm of evil, had no compassion for others—the same lack that Hermann displays

---

21. Paul Anthony Woods, "The Silver Screen Shadows of Weimar," in *Monsters of Weimar,* 293.

22. Zimmer, "Nachwort," 579.

23. Examination of the Russian text shows that Hermann's cri de coeur does not arise from compassion. He is, rather, brooding on that fatal stick. His "Chego ia, sobstvenno govoria, natvoril?" (*Otchaianie* 201) is more, "What a mess I made of it." Hermann is mourning his fatal error and its implications for his genius, not his victim.

for Felix and even his wife. Note Nabokov's remark in his foreword to the 1966 translation of *Despair:* "Hell shall never parole Hermann" (*Des* xiii).

More than a year passed between the March–April 1931 trials and Nabokov's beginning *Despair* around July 1, 1932. Fading interest? Indecision? Gestation? One thing is certain: Peter Kürten, the Düsseldorf Vampire, was guillotined on July 2, 1932.

{ 3 }

The Semiotic Validity of the Mirror Image in Nabokov's *Despair*

MARINA KANEVSKAYA

The mirror's entrenchment in culture cannot be without influence on its validity as a symbol and semiotic sign.[1] However, the placement of the reflection in the mirror, or the mirror image, in a system of semiotic signs certainly presents a problem. In his article "Mirrors," Umberto Eco excludes the mirror image from the class of semiotic signs.[2] This chapter will use Eco's approach in order to analyze Vladimir Nabokov's novel *Despair* (1932) and prove that the narrator's attempt to deal with the mirror image as if it were a semiotic sign serves as the main clue of his insanity.[3]

In Nabokov's novel, the mirror reflections (and the objects comparable to them, such as portraits and photographs) orchestrate the plot structure.[4] The contents of *Despair* can be summarized as follows: Hermann, an émigré businessman from Russia, lives in Berlin in the mid-1920s. He has an affectionate

---

1. On the symbolic value of the mirror and the mirror image in human culture, see *Zerkalo: Semiotika zerkal'nosti* (special issue, Tartu series on semiotics), *Trudy po znakovym sistemam*, vol. 22 (1988).

2. Umberto Eco, "Mirrors," in *Semiotics and the Philosophy of Language* (Bloomington: Indiana University Press, 1983), 202–26. Eco talks about the mirror image only as an optical phenomenon. He does not touch on the mythology or the symbolism of the mirror, in which "the mirror is a threshold phenomenon marking the boundaries between the *imagery* and the *symbolic*" (Eco, "Mirrors," 203).

3. Vladimir Nabokov, *Despair* (New York: Vintage International, 1989).

4. The novel's mirror structure is analyzed in Sergei Davydov, "Teksty-matreshki" *Vladimira Nabokova* (Munich: Otto Sagner, 1982), 52–59.

(if empty-headed) wife. Suddenly, his business fails. During a business trip, on a stroll in the country one day, he stumbles on a sleeping vagrant named Felix. The sleeping man strikes Hermann as his exact double. Hermann conceives a plan to kill Felix after dressing him up in his own clothes, in order to make it look as if it is Hermann who has been murdered. He plans to retire with his wife after collecting the insurance money. After coaching his wife to tell the police that it was really her husband who was killed, Hermann hides in a small French town, using Felix's identity. There he intends to wait until the inquiry has been closed and his wife joins him with the money. His plan fails, because the supposed resemblance between him and Felix is the product of Hermann's own sick imagination.

Before analyzing Nabokov's text, let us review what Eco perceives as a semiotic sign. According to Eco, one can call a sign any phenomenon that is capable of conveying information—ranging from the elementary, such as a traffic signal, to the complex, such as a myth. Interaction becomes possible when the information is expressed in a code that is subject to decoding by the receptor. The transfer of information consists of a series of coding and decoding processes in which all of the participants must be aware of the significance attached to (the majority of) the signs transmitted.

Eco points out that the mirror image does not present the iconic image of the reflected object, because the mirror reflects the object without communicating its significance: "A mirror does not 'translate'; it records what struck it just as it is struck. It tells the truth to an inhuman extent."[5] Although a mirror must be considered as a mere prosthesis, according to Eco, "A mirror is an absolutely neutral prosthesis.... We trust mirrors just as, under *normal* conditions, we trust our organs of perception."[6] Here, the illusive concept of *normality* plays a role that is impossible to overstate.

In Nabokov's novel, the conditions are not normal. However, because of the peculiar point of view (the first-person narrative), one realizes this abnormality rather late in the text: It is made clear only by the discrepancy between the narrator's and the other characters' different perceptions of the same objects. Through the narrator's interpretative explanations, Nabokov informs the reader that Hermann's understanding of what he sees in the mirror is wrong—that is, that he does not see what the mirror shows. If we assume that

---

5. Eco, "Mirrors," 207–8.
6. Ibid., 208; emphasis added.

nothing is wrong with Hermann's physical vision, and if the mirrors in the novel are "plain," the misperception must arise at the stage of the narrator's interpretation of the mirror image.

The main theme of *Despair* is the reading of a mirror image as if it were a text rather than an icon. Nabokov highlights the importance of this misreading. Hermann thinks that the mirror image is subject to interpretation (that the details can be ignored or altered, that they can be classified as more or less important, or that they can be defined as more or less visible). This selective vision limits his perception. Nabokov pursues Hermann's distorted subjective point of view in several stages:

1. The first view of Felix's body lying on the ground introduces the idea of death into Hermann's mind. The predominant impression is one of immobility: "I was about to pass, but something in his attitude cast a queer spell over me: the emphasis of that immobility, the lifelessness of those widespread legs, the stiffness of that half-bent arm" (*Des* 7). In Hermann's mind, the idea of death precedes the idea of resemblance. To this extent, he conceives the crime before the plan to use the resemblance of the alleged double to obtain money through the murder. In that sense, therefore, his crime is "art for art's sake." The recognition of the resemblance in the immobile reflection alludes to the myth of Narcissus—a subtext that is reinforced throughout the novel by the main character's self-adoration: "I approached, and with the toe of my elegant shoe flicked the cap off his face" (*Des* 7). At this point, Herman (subconsciously) compares the memory of his own face with the face of Felix, finding the faces identical.[7]

2. Felix wakes up. That motion, in Hermann's opinion, slightly distorts the similarity between them. The smile on the vagrant's face is different from Hermann's. The reader may presume that the "inspection of his ear and hollow temple," as well as Felix's "blue-black, square fingernails," also did not give the observer the desired result. But "by this time I was loath to part with the marvel," the narrator admits (*Des* 10). Throughout the novel, Hermann deliber-

---

7. The theme of narcissism carries a warning to the reader about the accurateness of Hermann's recollections: "Frolics of the intuition, artistic vision, inspiration, all the grand things which have lent my life such beauty.... My health is perfect, my body both clean within and without, my gait easy; I neither drink, nor smoke excessively, nor do I live in riot. Thus, in the pink of health, well-dressed and young looking ..." (*Des* 8–9).

ately overlooks details that do not fit his plan. Nabokov refers several times to Hermann's inattentiveness to certain details. This contrasts with his minute care for hitherto nonexistent details—details that he himself creates (for example, by clipping Felix's nails and toenails during their final encounter). My argument here is that the details do not objectively inform Hermann about the adequacy of his impressions; rather, he views them as subservient to his plan.[8]

3. Felix wakes up and looks at Hermann but does not share the latter's astonishment, because he does not share Hermann's strong impression that they look alike. Hermann attributes this apparent lack of perceptiveness to Felix's stupidity.

4. After accusing Felix of blindness, Hermann offers him a pocket mirror: "He looked at himself in the sky-blue glass [from Hermann's position]. . . . I drew his head sideways to mine, so that our temples touched; in the glass two pairs of eyes danced and swam" (*Des* 12). Still, having refused to acknowledge the resemblance, Felix even mocks Hermann's idea by telling him a silly anecdote about some twins he saw at a fair. Later, Felix turns out to be left-handed, which Hermann believes stems from the reciprocity of the mirror image.

5. Back in his room, Hermann looks in the mirror and perceives its reflection as an object (Felix). From the point at which he sees Felix as an equivalent of the reflection, Hermann starts to be interested in the object from a pragmatic point of view. He becomes interested in the question of whether what he sees in the mirror is equally identical to his face and to Felix's face: "When at last I got back to my hotel room, I found there, amid mercurial shadow and framed in frenzy bronze, Felix awaiting me. Pale-faced and solemn he drew near. . . . I took out my handkerchief; he drew out his handkerchief too" (*Des* 14). Again, the real dissimilarities of details are replaced by the forced similarities in Hermann's imagination. Apart from everything else, the real Felix cannot

---

8. One can risk the supposition that Nabokov was familiar with Giovanni Morelli's writings, in which a new method for correctly attributing old masterpieces was proposed. Carlo Ginzburg summarizes Morelli's method: "[O]ne should concentrate on minor details . . . : earlobes, fingernails, shapes of fingers and toes." See Carlo Ginzburg, "Morelli, Freud, and Sherlock Holmes: Clues and Scientific Method," in *The Sign of Three: Dupin, Holmes, Peirce*, ed. U. Eco and T. A. Sebeok (Bloomington: Indiana University Press, 1983), 81–82.

possibly possess a handkerchief. Hermann proves that his optical vision is not marred. He can see the differences but considers them to be of no importance:

> You now see both of us, reader. Two, but with a single face. You must not suppose, however, that I am ashamed of possible slips and type errors in the book of nature. Look nearer: I possess large yellowish teeth; his are whiter and set more closely together, but is that really important? On my forehead a vein stands out like a capital M imperfectly drawn, but when I sleep my brow is as smooth as that of my double. (*Des* 17)

6. One example of a third person's impression of Hermann's face is the portrait of Hermann painted by his wife's lover. Nabokov increases our uncertainty about the resemblance of the portrait by making the painting modernistic (presumably cubist). In comparison, Eco defines a painting as a production of the iconic similarities: "This is why men draw (and produce the signs which are precisely defined as iconic): they draw to achieve without mirrors what mirrors allow them to achieve."[9] Unlike Eco, Nabokov explains painting as the striving to express a *subjective* view of reality. In Nabokov's novel, the portrait shows the difference in opinion between Hermann and the artist regarding Hermann's face: "Look as one might, none could see the ghost of a likeness!" says Herman about the portrait (*Des* 56). Indeed, the nature of the painting is different from that of the mirror image in that the latter cannot contain any expression of opinion. The main feature of the portrait in the novel is the lack of eyes on Hermann's face, which expresses the third person's judgment of Hermann's ability to see reality and, in particular, to objectify his own appearance.

7. One of the most important episodes in the novel is the second meeting between Hermann and Felix. This meeting turns out to be especially discouraging for Hermann's plan. Throughout his encounter with Felix, Hermann takes unneeded precautions to conceal their similarity. He is so absorbed with artificial details (such as growing a mustache) that he remains inattentive to the fact that his and Felix's appearance together in public does not stir up curiosity among onlookers. In fact, nobody besides Hermann perceives that the two look alike:

> There were only three people and these paid no attention to us whatever....
> While awaiting our order he [the waiter] looked at me, then at Felix. Nat-

---

9. Eco, "Mirrors," 210.

urally, owing to my mustache, our likeness did not leap to the eyes; and indeed, I had let my mustache grow with the special purpose of not attracting undue attention when appearing together with Felix. (*Des* 79)

Thus, instead of reading the objective reaction of a third person, Hermann reads his own meaning into the situation. He sees the world as a projection of himself, as a reflection. In several studies, Hermann's eyes have been compared to a mirror's inverted surface, which does not allow light—or impressions from the outside—to penetrate; it merely reflects the character's inner world. Hermann has no disagreement with this inner, imaginary mirror image, but his insanity becomes increasingly obvious to the reader through his efforts to bring his interpretations into agreement with a real mirror, a mirror that is not "a sheer illusion or a hallucinatory experience."[10]

8. The culmination of the novel is Felix's murder. As noted earlier, Hermann states that the money is of "secondary importance" and that the main objective in killing his quasi-double can be found in some elusive aesthetic harmony. Thus, the greatest harmony of Felix's face, in Hermann's perception, is stillness. When Hermann kills Felix, Felix's face bears a maximum resemblance to the reflection of Hermann's face in the mirror during those moments in which he was studying his own appearance. The dead Felix's face must have reminded him of the sleeping Felix's face at their first meeting. It is surprising that Nabokov does not mention the main detail—that is, whether the murdered Felix's eyes were closed (as must have been the case when Felix was asleep) or open (as happens when one is looking at one's own face in the mirror):

> Like an author reading his work over a thousand times, probing and testing every syllable ... so it happened to me, so it happened.... At that moment when all the required features were fixed and frozen, our likeness was such that really I could not say who had been killed, I or he. And while I looked ... with that face before me slowly dissolving, vibrating fainter and fainter, it seemed as if I were looking at my image in a stagnant pool. (*Des* 171–172)

The dead face, like the face of a sleeping person, and the mirror image are ideal objects of interpretation for the insane Hermann. When life is absent and

---

10. Ibid., 207.

no unexpected changes can occur, Hermann's power of interpretation is total. He scans the mirror image for elements of information that he selects according to their conformity with the matrices he has planned. Those elements that do not fit (ears, eyes, shape of the fingernails, and so on) are ignored. Actually, any process of verification of a resemblance—unless one is talking about ideally identical objects—consists in the selection (and discarding) of relevant elements. The critical problem lies in the relative proportion of those elements. Hermann invariably pays the most attention to the elements that he can change at will—he clips Felix's fingernails and toenails, for example, and shaves him with his own hands. At the same time, the unchangeable elements, such as the eyes and ears, are pronounced to be unimportant. It seems as if, for Hermann, life and death turn out to be changeable details, too: In this case, Hermann changes life to death by murdering Felix. By committing murder, Hermann transfers his plan from the plane of his imagination to the "real" and objective world of others' judgment: "I longed, to the point of pain, for that masterpiece of mine ... to be appreciated by men" (*Des* 178).

9. While looking at Felix's passport photograph, Hermann notices that Felix's face does not resemble the Felix he saw earlier in the mirror while scrutinizing his own face; nor does it resemble the Felix he remembers, alive or dead. "Oddly enough, his pictured face did not resemble mine closely; it could easily pass for my photo—still it made an odd impression upon me" (*Des* 173). Hermann's reaction to this is characteristic: He does not realize that he is dealing with a photograph that is devoid of referential meaning. In other words, Hermann does not realize that he is dealing with a variation of a mirror image. Hermann perceives the photograph as an expression of someone's opinion—an opinion that disagrees with his own. Hermann even explains Felix's lack of awareness of their resemblance by saying that Felix knew his own face from this photograph. Hermann switches to the passport's verbal description of Felix without realizing that he is exchanging iconic language for verbal language. The fact that the verbal description of Felix's face does not correspond to what he would be able to say about his own face brings Hermann to a convenient conclusion about human obtuseness and "fatheadedness": "Human fatheadedness, carelessness, slackness of senses, all this was revealed by the fact that even the official definitions in the brief list of personal features did not quite correspond with the epithets in my own passport" (*Des* 173).

10. Most important to this discussion is the gradual change in Hermann's relationship with mirrors after the murder has been committed and his plan enters the passive phase of waiting for his wife and the money. As soon as the situation begins to slip out of Hermann's control, the mirror image acquires independence. At that point, the mirrors start to forward to Hermann's mind the "objective" message that tells him that he does not look like Felix, dead or alive:

> Far worse was my failure to put up with mirrors. In fact, the beard I started growing was meant to hide me not so much from others as from my own self. So it is quite easy to understand that a man endowed with my acute sensitiveness gets into the devil of state about such trifles as a reflection in a dark looking glass, or his own shadow, falling dead at his feet. (*Des* 177)

In the last phrase, the allusion to the dying Narcissus is obvious. At this point, Hermann is unable to tell whether the resemblance is present or absent. His clinging to his aesthetically perfect plan grows into plain stubbornness. The information derived from the mirror image undermines his confidence even before the newspapers break the truth to him about his "aesthetic solecism."

11. The last "encounter" with the outside world's view of Felix's appearance, and therefore with Hermann's own interpretation of the mirror image's meaning, is presented in Hermann's rendition of a newspaper article:

> Not a word was there about our resemblance; not only was it not criticized (for instance, they might have said, at least: "Yes, an admirable resemblance, yet such and such markings show it to be not his body") but it was not mentioned at all—which left one with impression that it was some wretch whose appearance was quite different from mine.... [After death] his countenance ought to have acquired a marble quality, making our likeness still more sharply chiseled. (*Des* 186)

When his "marvelous" plan is ignored by the police, Hermann accuses mankind of inattentiveness and insensitivity. In that way, Nabokov conclusively admits his narrator's insanity.

Conclusions

In *Despair*, Nabokov creates a model of an individual's interaction with his own reflection in the mirror. What later became Eco's thesis about the failure of the mirror image to comply with the requirements of a semiotic sign is applied in *Despair* to verify human (in)sanity. The question, then, is: Why does the mirror image provoke such an ambivalent perception? By nature, the mirror image is situated between sign and image, or between sign and signal.[11]

According to Eco's definition of a semiotic sign, the sign is a meaningful phenomenon that can be included in a meaningful system of the same cognitive nature. In this capacity, Eco considers the sign as a paradigmatic element of a given code. The mirror image is unique because it is neither a signified (for it does not need representation through another sign) nor a signifier (because it is iconically equal to the reflected object and, in most cases, to the observer—that is, the recipient of the information). The most characteristic feature of the mirror image as a sign is its instability and virtual unrepeatability.

The plot of Nabokov's novel is built around Hermann's willful interpretation of his mirror image and, consequently, his erroneous belief that his face is identical to Felix's. The reader receives the negative answer from the *fabula* level of the novel, while the narrator tries to impose a positive answer through the *sujet plain*. In describing his psychopathological case, Nabokov uses Hermann's attempts to submit the mirror image to a reading process as the main devise to expose his "unreliable narrator." Hermann projects his willful interpretation on different objects around him, not only on mirrors. The novel contains many examples of this, the most striking being Felix's cane, into which his name and address are carved, which Hermann carelessly forgets at the scene of the crime. When Hermann describes the cane, he indicates that his physical vision is intact but that his evaluation of reality is relative and arbitrary. The main clue to understanding Hermann's insanity lies in his conviction that the "third party," the world at large, must know the code for his individual interpretations, such as his interpretation of the mirror image. This

---

11. Consider, for example, the myth of Narcissus; fairy tales about falling into wells; Lewis Carrol's *Through the Looking-Glass;* and Jean Cocteau's film *Orphée.*

conviction makes him immune to assimilating concepts that do not correspond to his own interpretations. In this way, Nabokov alludes to a symbolical meaning of the mirror image, its function as an instrument of self-study, and even of self-consciousness. These meanings of the mirror image remain closed for Hermann, and he remains confined to the reflecting surface of his own misconceptions.

{ 4 }

The Enchanter and the Beauties of Sleeping

SUSAN ELIZABETH SWEENEY

The Enchanter alludes to folktales about "enchanted slumber" (*En* 87, 91), such as "Sleeping Beauty," in order to depict a middle-aged man's longing for his stepdaughter. Nabokov composed this novella—entitled "Volshebnik" in the original Russian—in 1939, but it did not appear in print until 1986, after his son, Dmitri Nabokov, translated it into English as *The Enchanter*.[1] The unnamed protagonist dreams about fondling a drowsy child in a fantasy that recurs throughout the novella and becomes more elaborate with each repetition. He imagines himself, more specifically, as an "enchanter" who can maintain the child's "enchanted innocence"—which he thinks of as a blissfully unconscious state, like a storybook princess's magic sleep—in order to suspend time and possess her sexually without her knowledge or consent (*En* 92, 73).

The Enchanter's erotic of sleep is reflected in the narrative's plot, narration, and imagery. Nabokov's novella thus demonstrates close connections with two of his other fictions—the early story "A Nursery Tale" and his most famous

---

1. Vladimir Nabokov, "Volshebnik," *Russian Literature Triquarterly* 24 (1991): 9–41. Nabokov wrote "Volshebnik" in Paris in 1939 and later identified it, in his 1956 essay "On a Book Entitled *Lolita*," as "a prototype of my present novel" (*AnL* 311). He believed that this prototype had been destroyed (*AnL* 312); three years later, however, Nabokov told his editor at Putnam's that he had found it, decided it was "precise and lucid," and thought it should be translated and published (*SL* 283). Other projects prevented him from doing this, although he allowed Andrew Field to include two passages from the manuscript in his *Nabokov: His Life in Art* (Boston: Little, Brown, 1967), 328–29. The novella was published only after Nabokov's death, first in Dmitri Nabokov's English translation, *The Enchanter* (1986), then in the original Russian (1991). Page citations are to the 1986 edition, unless noted otherwise.

novel, *Lolita* (1955)—which also use tales of enchanted slumber as a model for the protagonist's erotic fantasies and for the narrative itself.[2]

Fairy-Tale Sublimation

The handful of Nabokov scholars who have discussed *The Enchanter* in any detail note its intimations of fairyland. Dmitri Nabokov praises its "surreal, enchanted aura" and "eerie humor";[3] Brian Boyd finds its "fairy-tale wish fulfillment" theme less satisfying than that of *Lolita*;[4] and Tony Sharpe remarks that it has "the generalized feel of a fairy tale."[5] In the first extensive analysis of the novella's narrative poetics, Gennady Barabtarlo identifies some specific folkloristic overtones, such as the echo of "a Russian fairy-tale refrain" in one passage, the "faintly but inescapably familiar fairy-tale intonation" in another, and the fantastic complications that hinder the protagonist, "as in a good fairy tale," when he comes close to attaining his goal.[6]

Nabokov embedded such allusions to folklore in his novella to reflect the Enchanter's own unreliable, romantic, immature, self-deceiving perspective, which shapes the entire novella because the third-person narration provides access to only his thoughts. The Enchanter longs for a twelve-year-old girl whom

---

2. Vladimir Nabokov, "A Nursery Tale [translation of "Skazka" (1926)]," in *Tyrants Destroyed and Other Stories,* trans. with Dmitri Nabokov (New York: McGraw-Hill, 1975), 40–58. See also Susan Elizabeth Sweeney, "'Ballet Attitudes': Nabokov's *Lolita* and Petipa's *Sleeping Beauty,*" in *Nabokov at the Limits: Redrawing Critical Boundaries,* ed. Lisa Zunshine (New York: Garland, 1999), 111–26, repr. Ellen Pifer, ed., *Vladimir Nabokov's* Lolita: *A Casebook* (New York: Oxford University Press, in press); and idem, "Fantasy, Folklore, and Finite Numbers in Nabokov's 'Nursery Tale,'" *Slavic and East European Journal* 43, no. 3 (1999): 511–29, repr. in *Twentieth-Century Literary Criticism* (Detroit: Gale Research, 2001), 108:205–15. Those essays, like the present essay, are part of a broader study of Nabokov's fictions about pedophilia, in which I analyze the plot, narration, and imagery of *The Enchanter* in more detail.

3. Dmitri Nabokov, "On a Book Entitled *The Enchanter*" (*En* 121, 124).

4. Brian Boyd, *Vladimir Nabokov: The Russian Years* (Princeton, N.J.: Princeton University Press, 1990), 513.

5. Tony Sharpe, *Vladimir Nabokov* (London: Edwin Arnold, 1991), 53.

6. Gennady Barabtarlo, "Those Who Favor Fire (on *The Enchanter*)," *Russian Literature Triquarterly* 24 (1991): 94, 99. Barabtarlo adds that the hidden storyline he finds in *The Enchanter*—a dead mother's efforts to protect her daughter from an evil stepfather by means of a magic charm—is reminiscent of folklore (ibid., 108).

he meets in the park in a scene that echoes Erwin's encounter with his first choice in "A Nursery Tale" and foreshadows Humbert Humbert's first glimpse of Dolly Haze in *Lolita*. Like those other protagonists, moreover, the Enchanter expresses his desire for the girl in fairy-tale terms. He thinks of the coin that he finds only moments before he first sees the little girl as a magic "talisman" (*En* 70). He has already thought to himself, at the beginning of the novella, that "he would have paid anything for any one of" the few brief encounters that he has enjoyed, over the years, with other little girls (*En* 25). He now muses—as in the folktales of "Rapunzel" and "Rumpelstiltskin," in which food and gold are bartered for children—that he would give "a sack of rubies, a bucket of blood, anything he was asked" to possess this little girl in particular (*En* 37). The price for possessing the child, apparently, is marrying her mother; however, when it comes to consummating his marriage to "this cumbersome behemoth," this "monstrous bride," this "giantess" (*En* 48, 49, 58), he hesitates and briefly considers returning to the "fairyland obscurity" from which he himself has emerged (*En* 57).[7]

The Enchanter's erotic fantasies about the child, moreover—as in "A Nursery Tale"—are couched in the plots, devices, and images of folklore. Dmitri Nabokov called this practice "fairy-tale sublimation" and listed it among those aspects of the novella that he expected future readers to identify and document.[8] In one instance, the Enchanter, speculating about ways to maintain the child's innocence even after he has introduced her to sex, decides that he should explain his genitalia in terms of "storybook images"—"the pet giant, the fairy-tale forest, the sack with its treasure" (*En* 72)—that recall actual elements of the old English children's story "Jack and the Beanstalk."[9]

---

7. Nabokov also alludes to folklore and fantasy in describing his protagonist's anxiety about performing sexually with his new wife. The Enchanter thinks of himself as a "little Gulliver," confronted with her "broad bones," "multiple caverns," and "bulky velvet" (*En* 55). This emphasis on extreme differences in scale, which is also characteristic of the Enchanter's erotic fantasies, no doubt reflects his pedophilia—as do his musings on "the arithmetic of Oriental debauchery" and his "measuring" the little girl with his "enchanted yardstick" (*En* 21, 91). In the larger project from which this essay is drawn, I discuss the Enchanter's preoccupation with differences in size more fully.

8. Dmitri Nabokov, "On a Book Entitled *The Enchanter*," 120.

9. "Jack and the Beanstalk" and many of the other tales mentioned in this chapter are cited from Opie and Opie's wonderful edition, which features the earliest English version of each tale, as well as extensive commentary on it: See "Jack and the Beanstalk [1807]," retold by William Godwin in *The Classic Fairy Tales*, ed. Iona Opie and Peter Opie (London: Oxford University Press, 1974), 162–74.

But the clearest example of such fairy-tale sublimation is found in a series of references to "Little Red Riding Hood" that has been briefly mentioned by both Dmitri Nabokov and Barabtarlo.[10] At first, the novella alludes to "Little Red Riding Hood" only indirectly, when the Enchanter identifies an "old crone" as the child's "inevitable companion" and resolves to keep his lupine intentions secret, lest he "fall prey to a chance hunter in these populated valleys" (*En* 50, 47, 49). But after the child's mother dies, such allusions become more explicit and more frequent. Planning his wife's funeral, the Enchanter happily thinks of himself as a "lone wolf" about to "don Granny's nightcap" and lure Little Red Riding Hood into bed with him (*En* 67). Later, at a hotel, he "lick[s] his chops" as he prepares to enter the room where the girl is sleeping (*En* 85). The Enchanter fails in his secret attempt to fondle the child, however, and after he wakes her, he knocks over a lamp with a "reddish" shade on the night table, barely noticing when, as in "Little Red Riding Hood," it "scamper[s] off with its red cowl" (*En* 87, 92). Overcome with fear and shame, he rushes into the hotel corridor, where he overhears, from behind a nearby door, "a melodious voice [that seems] to be finishing a nursery tale (Mr. White-Tooth in the bed, the hoodlum brothers with their little red rifles)" (*En* 93). The image of "Mr. White-Tooth in the bed" refers to the disguised wolf's climactic encounter with Little Red Riding Hood, in which, having explained to the child why his arms are so large, his legs so long, his ears so enormous, and his eyes so big, he finally reveals his identity as well as his intentions: "'Grandmamma, what great teeth you have got!' ... 'It is to eat thee up!'" And the phrase "hoodlum brothers with their little red rifles," which Dmitri Nabokov identifies as one of several "telescoped Little Red Riding Hood wordplays," clearly alludes to the folktale's title character. This pun, in Dmitri Nabokov's English translation, echoes the multilingual wordplay in the original Russian, in which the corresponding phrase—"brat'ia s shapron-ruzh'iami" (brothers with shotguns)—puns on the French title of the tale's earliest printed version, Charles Perrault's "Le Chaperon Rouge."[11] What the Enchanter overhears, then, is the very ending of "Little Red Riding Hood," which usually concludes with the wolf's slaughter at the hands of a

---

10. "Little Red Riding Hood [1697]," retold by Charles Perrault, trans. Robert Samber, in Opie and Opie, *Classic Fairy Tales,* 93–97; Dmitri Nabokov, "On a Book Entitled *The Enchanter,*" 116; Barabtarlo, "Those Who Favor Fire," 94.

11. "Little Red Riding Hood," 97; Dmitri Nabokov, "On a Book Entitled *The Enchanter,*" 100; Vladimir Nabokov, "Volshebnik," 41 (emphasis added).

hunter—thus foreshadowing the death of the Enchanter, who explicitly identifies himself with the wolf.

The phrase "hoodlum brothers with their little red rifles," however, also suggests that, in his panic, the Enchanter may have conflated the single avenging huntsman of "Little Red Riding Hood" with the multiple miniature brothers of "Snow White and the Seven Dwarves." The dwarves are also hunters, and they wear hoods and carry tiny weapons in most illustrated editions of that story. Of course, "Snow White" is not the tale of a child being lured into bed, as "Little Red Riding Hood" is; rather, it describes a child being cast into a deep sleep. For the Enchanter, such bedtime stories always seem to get mixed up with bedrooms, beds, and the bewitching thought of a nodding, heavy-eyed little girl.

An Erotic of Sleep

Nabokov's other fictions also link drowsiness and eroticism, but they do so to a lesser extent.[12] The Enchanter seems to fantasize about sleep, in particular, because it epitomizes a little girl's purity, passivity, and powerlessness. The first child he remembers finding attractive was "a sleepy wan girl with a velvety gaze" (*En* 24). And his daydreams about his stepdaughter revolve obsessively around her slumber, as shown by such recurrent motifs as tightly shut eyes; "lolling on the bed"; "warm, cosy closeness" at night; and "kisses, tussles on the shared bed" in the morning (*En* 37, 66, 72). When his new wife goes to the hospital, for example, the Enchanter anticipates being able to fondle the drowsy little girl that very evening: "[B]y nightfall we'll be back here, the two of us, in utter seclusion, the little thing will be tired and sleepy, get your clothes off quick, I'll rock you to sleep—that's all, just some cosy cuddling... the stillness, her naked clavicles, the little straps, the buttons in back, the foxlike silk between her shoulder blades, her sleepy yawns, her hot armpit, her legs, her tenderness—mustn't lose my head" (*En* 65). This passage, which uses free

---

12. *Glory*, for example, features a romantic interlude in which Sonia—grief-stricken, sleepy, barefoot, and pajamaed, her eyes blinking and her lashes matted—crawls into Martin's bed. When Martin tries to embrace her, she bursts into tears. He does not dare "touch her, losing his head at the thought that she might start screaming and awake the entire household" (*Glory* 95). *Glory* often alludes to fairy tales (see, for example, *Glory* 19, 45, 61, 158) and even uses the prince's entry into the enchanted wood in "Sleeping Beauty" as its central conceit.

indirect discourse to narrate the Enchanter's thoughts in the first person, constitutes a sort of inventory of the child's drowsiness and the access that it might give him to different parts of her body. Indeed, the rhythmic parallel clauses imply that merely conjuring up this scene has lulled the protagonist himself into such a state of enchantment that he must be careful not to "lose [his] head."

The Enchanter mentally rehearses this imaginary scenario in more and more elaborate detail as the narrative progresses. The child's sleep is essential to his fantasy because it mitigates his fear, guilt, and shame. He believes that his caresses are not wrong if she is not aware of them. As he inwardly remarks, in another lullaby of parallel clauses, "[Y]ou're asleep, you're extraneous, don't interfere with grownups, this is how it must be, it's my night, it's my business" (*En* 88). Indeed, the Enchanter is aroused by the thought of her obliviousness to his arousal. He imagines himself as an "incubus"—a male demon who seduces sleeping women—who can possess the girl's body without her knowledge or consent (*En* 25). More precisely, as the novella's title indicates, he thinks of himself as an "enchanter" who can prolong the girl's innocence indefinitely, as if inducing a suspended state in which to caress her to his heart's content.

The Enchanter's reveries about fondling a sleeping child are juxtaposed, moreover, with his own insomnia and "nocturnal despairs" (*En* 50). He spends a sleepless night after meeting the little girl, and "at daybreak ... drowsily la[ys] down his book" to scold himself for not having befriended her chaperone, which would have made establishing contact with the child easier (*En* 30). The next day in the park, when the child holds his wrist to examine his marvelous watch,[13] he notices a leaf in her hair—"and during his next spell of

---

13. The Enchanter's watch is "a rarity," he explains, because it displays only the tips of its hands, thus appearing not to measure time at all (*En* 33). The timepiece reveals the Enchanter's attitude toward temporal progress, which is also shown when he calls the "seaside sand," where he has ogled one little girl, "useful only as food for an hourglass" (*En* 25) and when he describes his stepdaughter's necklace as being "thin, golden, fluid as time itself" (*En* 59). This attitude, in turn, reflects a resistance to aging and maturity that is characteristic of pedophiles: Margaret Morganroth Gullette, "The Exile of Adulthood: Pedophilia in the Midlife Novel," *Novel* 17, no. 3 (1984): 215-16. The Enchanter's wristwatch also anticipates an important detail in *Lolita*: the waterproof watch that Humbert wears at the aptly named Hourglass Lake (*AnL* 89, 272). I analyze descriptions of the Enchanter's watch and other temporal images in more detail in the larger project from which this essay is drawn.

insomnia he kept yanking off the ghost of that leaf, grasping and yanking, with two fingers, with three, then with all five" (*En* 33). Later, he thinks of his infatuation as the "many-ringed dream with which he was already so indistinctly but so firmly entwined that, for instance, he no longer knew what this thing was, or whose: part of his own leg or part of an octopus" (*En* 35). The Enchanter's nightly encounters with the little girl's image continue after his marriage to her mother (which in various ways reinforces the association between sleep and sex). After the wedding, his fantasies elaborate even further on the implicit correlation between his imagined possession of the child and the grasping, clasping physical movements with which, once everyone else is asleep, he satisfies himself: "And sometimes, at night . . . when it had all grown totally still, he would lie supine and evoke the one and only image, entwine his smiling victim with eight hands, which turned into eight tentacles affixed to every detail of her nudity, and at last he would dissolve in a black mist and lose her in the blackness, and the blackness spread everywhere, and was but the blackness of the night in his solitary bedroom" (*En* 61–62). As these fantasies progress, the number and size of the Enchanter's apparent appendages magically increase—from two or three fingers to eight tentacles—in an arithmetical feat that conveys his growing desire and sense of fabulous potency. These magnifying, multiplying appendages also emphasize, again, his preoccupation with the difference in scale between himself and the little girl. Indeed, the Enchanter's swarming tentacles stress the contrast that appears in all of his fantasies between his obsessive, wakeful actions and the child's helplessness and passivity.

Because the Enchanter's erotic fantasies focus in particular on his stepdaughter's drowsiness, it is not surprising that they often allude to "nursery tale[s]" that lull a child to sleep (*En* 93)—especially tales of enchanted slumber, which may have been intended for that very purpose.[14] All folktales take place in a timeless realm, as indicated by such repeated phrases as "once upon a time," "happily ever after," and "if he was there once, he is there still," but tales of enchanted slumber heighten this sense of fantastic perpetuity even further, because they depict a sleep that defies the passage of years, and even death itself. Two such tales, "Sleeping Beauty" and "Snow White," are especially appropriate models for the Enchanter's imaginary scenarios. Each tale features a young girl—Beauty is fifteen, and Snow White is only seven years old—who falls into a deep, deep sleep. The young girl remains in this state of suspended

---

14. Macleod Yearsley, *The Folklore of Fairy-tale* (London: Watts, 1924), 68.

animation, imprisoned within her castle ("Sleeping Beauty") or her crystal casket ("Snow White"), until Prince Charming arrives. He falls in love with her unconscious form; indeed, he seems to be attracted by her very immobility and helplessness.[15] The prince becomes so aroused by her sleeping body, in both tales, that he wants it for himself. He commandeers the coffin; he wakes her with an unwanted kiss; or, in some versions of "Sleeping Beauty"—Princess Zellandine's story in the fourteenth-century romance *Perceforest;* "Sole, Luna, e Talia" in the *Pentamerone;* and "The Queen of Tubber Tintye" from Irish folklore[16]—he rapes her in her sleep. Because "Sleeping Beauty" and "Snow White" both focus on the abduction or rape of a young girl's sleeping body, these folktales provide an ideal pretext for the Enchanter's fantasies.

When the Enchanter's sickly wife dies, his daydreams about fondling an oblivious little girl grow more detailed, and their fairy-tale sublimation becomes more pronounced. At his wife's funeral, he thinks of himself as "floating on featherbeds of happiness"—an image that could allude to "Sleeping Beauty" as well as to other tales—now that he knows his wishes may finally come true (*En* 69). And after the funeral, as he travels by train to fetch his stepdaughter from the home of family friends, he conjures up an elaborate scenario based on several folktales, especially "Sleeping Beauty."

Sitting in the railway compartment, the Enchanter decides to take his orphaned stepdaughter to the seashore, where he will begin the process of lulling her into such a state of "enchanted innocence" that his caresses will literally seem like child's play (*En* 73). He knows, of course, that she will eventually grow up, but even then "her present image [will] always transpire through her metamorphoses, nourishing their translucent strata from its internal fountainhead," as if she were Snow White asleep in her coffin (*En* 74). The Enchanter believes, in fact, that if he maintains his enchantment until the

---

15. "Sleeping Beauty [1697]," retold by Charles Perrault, trans. Robert Samber, in Opie and Opie, *Classic Fairy Tales,* 81–92; "Snow White and the Seven Dwarfs [1823]," retold by Jacob Grimm and Wilhelm Grimm, in ibid., 175–82. See Ruth B. Bottigheimer, *Grimms' Bad Girls and Bold Boys: The Moral and Social Vision of the Tales* (New Haven, Conn.: Yale University Press, 1987), 164; Maria Tatar, *The Hard Facts of the Grimms' Fairy Tales* (Princeton, N.J.: Princeton University Press, 1987), 446.

16. *Perceforest,* quoted in Opie and Opie, *Classic Fairy Tales,* 83; "Sole, Luna, e Talia [1636]," retold by Giambattista Basile, trans. N. M. Penzer, in P. L. Travers, *About the Sleeping Beauty* (New York: McGraw-Hill, 1975), 85–91; "The Queen of Tubber Tintye [n.d.]," retold by Jeremiah Curtin, in ibid., 93–107.

little girl becomes "delineated and elongated into womanhood," then she will never be able to distinguish "her own development from that of their love" (*En* 75)—just as, in some variants of "Snow White," the heroine's crystal casket magically grows as she does. The Enchanter compares this state of protracted innocence to an "eternal nursery" set within a fairy-tale fortress (*En* 72). His plan to keep his stepdaughter there recalls yet another tale: that of Rapunzel, a young girl who is taken from her parents by an enchantress and confined to a high tower, with no means of entry but a window, until a prince eventually rescues her. The Enchanter's scheme also alludes to "Sleeping Beauty," in which another enchantress plots to keep a young girl hidden from the world, also in a fortified building—although for different reasons—until a prince is able to penetrate that structure, too.

Following the lead of his fairy-tale predecessors, the Enchanter thinks that a contemporary version of Rapunzel's tower or Sleeping Beauty's castle—"a mini-villa in a blind garden" (*En* 73)—would be the ideal setting for his enchantment of the little girl. This proposed domicile reinforces his resolve not to "push his way too insistently into some little blind alley," lest he break the enchanted spell too soon (*En* 74). The Enchanter's identification of constriction and enclosure with sightlessness—the blind garden, the blind alley—underscores his fixation on the child's innocence as well as his wish that she remain oblivious to his desire. He decides that, whether or not he finds such a secluded mansion in which to live with the little girl, he will figuratively confine her until she is ready for her prince, keeping her within the psychological equivalent of a fortified, closely guarded palace and "[r]aising drawbridges . . . until such time as the flowering chasm itself reached up to the chamber with a robust young branch" (*En* 73). This image of an enchanted castle, surrounded by a blossoming hedge that grows higher each year until the time comes for a prince to break the spell, specifically refers to "Little Briar-Rose," the German variant of "Sleeping Beauty." Waiting until the time is ripe is, of course, the major theme of that tale. In some variants of "Sleeping Beauty," suitors who try to wake the sleeping princess too soon die as a result. P. L. Travers even suggests that the prince's timeliness is his single heroic quality.[17] Accordingly, the Enchanter promises himself that he will not "disenchant [the child] prematurely"; that he will "make no attempt on her virginity in the tightest and pinkest sense of the term"; that he will "hold back

---

17. Travers, *About the Sleeping Beauty*, 69.

until that morning when, still laughing, she would hearken to her own responsiveness" (*En* 74). He dreams that if he waits for the right moment, as the prince in the folktale does, then he, too, will live happily ever after with his princess—and no longer in a figurative castle surrounded by rose briars, but in "the flowering walled prison of the world." Meanwhile, as the Enchanter becomes engrossed in this newly refined version of the familiar fantasy, his state of rapture grows so manifestly apparent that a woman sitting near him on the train decides, "for some reason," to move to another compartment (*En* 75).

The Realm of Her Repose

After fetching his stepdaughter, the Enchanter plans to wait until they arrive at the seashore before he begins to enact his fantasy. But he cannot wait. When they stop on the way for dinner, he is already rehearsing, in yet another lullaby of first-person parallel clauses, his imaginary vision of the child's drowsiness: "My darling is tired and flushed from the trip, the rich meat course, the drop of wine. The sleepless night with the rosy glow of the fire in the darkness is taking its toll, her napkin is slipping off the soft hollow of her skirt" (*En* 80). He becomes so aroused, in fact, that he foolishly asks whether the restaurant has any bedrooms available.

As they drive on, the Enchanter continues to note each stage of the little girl's "increasing lassitude"—which in turn corresponds to each stage of his own mounting excitement. By the time he finds a hotel, which anticipates The Enchanted Hunters Hotel in *Lolita,* the little girl has fallen "half asleep." She "crawl[s]" out of the car and "halt[s] numbly" on the sidewalk (*En* 80); she blinks drowsily, "trying to focus her languishing gaze on a doubling cat," while they are given a room; and she leans against a wall, "a tired, pretty girl in the obedient pose of tender victim . . . her tousled head thrown slightly back and slowly turning from side to side, and her eyelids twitching as though she were trying to unravel her excessively thick lashes," as their door is unlocked (*En* 81). Inside the room, the child "limply" tosses her hat on the bed, bumps into the furniture, "[r]eeling with sleepiness," then "softly descend[s] onto his lap," "slowly entwine[s] a somnolent arm" around his neck, "sleepily nudge[s]" something with her foot (*En* 82), "slowly wipe[s] her mouth" with her hand, and collapses her head onto his shoulder—until, finally, "between her eyelids there showed only a narrow, sunset-hued luster, for she was virtually asleep" (*En* 83).[18] Throughout this passage, a series of parallel adverbs—"limply," "softly," "sleepily," "slowly," the last of which appears three times—depict the increasing torpor of the little girl's movements. At the same time, the verbs that express her actions—especially "entwine"—echo the Enchanter's earlier fantasies of manipulating her sleeping form. As the child's lethargy grows, so does the Enchanter's longing to possess her. He even identifies the hotel room's architecture with her sleepiness as he struggles with the windows' shutters, "squeezing tight their eyelike chinks." Aroused by "her drowsiness, her wooziness, her diminishing smile"; by "how defenseless, abandoned, warm she was"; and, of course, by his own thoughts as expressed in this descriptive lullaby, he begins to caress her (*En* 82). A knock at the door interrupts him, however, and he has to deal with a series of farcical mishaps that, as he wryly tells a policeman, are "all the more unacceptable because I am not alone but have a weary little girl with me" (*En* 84). Eventually, the Enchanter finds his way back to the room, where the child is sound asleep, and he is able to enact his fairy-tale fantasy at last.

Entering the room, he finds his enchanted maiden "lying supine" upon "the island of the bed."[19] He notices the "strange" way in which "her enchanted slumber flow[s] evenly past everything"—as if she were Sleeping Beauty, dozing in her castle for one hundred years (*En* 87). Almost immediately, he decides to remove his wristwatch to prolong the moment and fully enjoy "the realm of her repose," "the hour he ha[s] deliriously desired for a full quarter century." He imagines her sleep, then, as a special physical and temporal "realm," like Beauty's castle (*En* 88). Rather than waking his sleeping princess with a kiss, however, the Enchanter wishes to take full advantage of the state of magical timelessness that he thinks will persist as long as she remains unconscious. He forgets that in "Sleeping Beauty" it is the prince himself who breaks the spell.

At first the Enchanter is content merely to look at the girl and catalogue every detail of her slumber. He imagines that he is gazing at a painting—"A price-

18. After drugging Lolita, Humbert assesses her lethargy in similar fashion: her yawns at dinner; her "watertread[ing]" walk from the restaurant; her half-closed eyes in the elevator; and, after he carries her into their hotel room, her "swaying" body, "lolling" head, fluttering eyelids, "the dove-dull, long-drawn tones" of her voice, and the drowsiness with which she raises one foot to fumble at her shoelaces (*AnL* 122–23).

19. This image recalls the setting of the ballet *The Sleeping Beauty* and anticipates "the enchanted island haunted by those nymphets" in *Lolita* (*AnL* 16).

less original: sleeping girl, oil"—and, aware of his own fancifulness, mentally urges her to "Sleep, my precious, don't listen to me" (*En* 88). He examines "those little fissures on her parched lips, and that special crease in the eyelids over the barely joined lashes" (*En* 88). He observes her "strange, sightless little breasts" (*En* 89). He notices each movement that she makes and each "barely audible, somnolent smack of her lips" (*En* 91). He watches as she sighs, "opening her tightly shut navel like an eye, then slowly, with a cooing moan, breathe[s] out, and that was all she needed to glide on in her previous torpor." He finds, however, in yet another voyeuristic afterimage of his earlier fantasies about unseeing eyes and tightly shut eyelike chinks, that his gaze keeps returning to another fold of skin, in particular: "the same suedelike fissure, which somehow seem[s] to come alive under his" glance (*En* 90). The Enchanter is overwhelmed, in fact, by the sight of everything that he only imagined before—by her "visible proximity, the fantastic confrontation permitted by the slumber of this naked girl" (*En* 91). He perceives her sleeping body as a spectacle that he cannot quite touch, as if he were separated from it by glass. Indeed, the fact that it seems to quiver beneath his "prismatic stare," "intricately rippled as if seen through cut glass," while he keeps seeking "the focal point of happiness," recalls the fairy-tale prince gazing at Snow White in her crystal casket (*En* 88).[20]

Staring at the child's unconscious body, the Enchanter does "not know what to undertake, afraid of missing something, of not taking full advantage of the fairy-tale firmness of her sleep" (*En* 90). This phrase refers, of course, to the enchanted slumber of heroines such as Beauty and Snow White, whose suspended state allows them to be gazed at—and, in early versions of "Sleeping Beauty," even touched, kissed, and penetrated—without being awakened. Here, however, the "advantage" of the child's sleep is not that it protects her from harm (as in most tales of enchanted slumber) but that it protects her molester from discovery. The phrase "fairy-tale firmness of her sleep" may also allude to Andersen's "Princess on the Pea"—in which the heroine's sleep is anything but firm—and thus foreshadow the disastrous consequences of the Enchanter's attempt to enchant his stepdaughter. This phrase, then, encapsulates Nabokov's dark, ironic use of enchanted slumber throughout the novella. In *Lolita*, Nabokov uses a virtually identical phrase—"a fastness of sleep"— to describe a similar situation and even develops it into a series of puns and

---

20. This passage also reflects the fact that the Enchanter appears to be a jeweler, "an appraiser of facets and reflections" (*En* 43).

metaphors that conflate the supposed depth of the girl's slumber with the impenetrability of Beauty's enchanted castle (*AnL* 128, 130–32).

Finally, the Enchanter begins to enthrall himself with his imaginary enchantment of his stepdaughter: "[S]tarting little by little to cast his spell, he beg[ins] passing his magic wand above her body, almost touching the skin" (*En* 91). This scene, too, repeats his earlier fancy of "entwin[ing]" himself around her (*En* 35, 62). At the same time, it provides an even more explicit instance of fairy-tale sublimation than did his previous fantasies. Here, the "spell" refers to his masturbation, and the "magic wand" or "enchanted yardstick" (*En* 91)—variants of the slumber-inducing rod of folklore,[21] such as the spindle that puts Beauty to sleep—to his phallus. This passage seems in fact to identify the common folk motif of enchantment not with a little girl's sleep—which in "Snow White," "Sleeping Beauty," and other tales protects the heroine from sexuality until she matures—but with the aphrodisiac effect that a sleeping child produces on a pedophile.

Disenchantment

The Enchanter also subverts the usual ending of such tales. The novella concludes, as most tales of enchantment do, with a breaking of the spell. However, rather than providing the expected disenchantment found in "Snow White" and "Sleeping Beauty"—a rapturous awakening, followed by a royal wedding— Nabokov's novella ends with the sudden, violent, and shameful disruption of the protagonist's solitary fantasy. When the Enchanter finally touches the child's sleeping body, the erotic spell that he has cast on himself—even as he has pretended to enchant her—dissolves into sexual ecstasy. At that very moment, however, he realizes that the little girl is not asleep, unseeing, immobile, and oblivious, as in his fantasies; instead, she is "fully awake," "looking wild-eyed at his rearing nudity," "tearing from his grasp and ... yelling senselessly" (*En* 92).

Desperately, the Enchanter tries to return to the safe, silent realm of his dreams, in which he is the only actor and everything else has "froze[n] still" (*En* 91). In an ironic inversion of the commands he has given the child in his fantasies—that she should remain silent and lie still—he now desperately implores her, "Be quiet, it's nothing bad, it's just a kind of game, it happens

21. Yearsley, *Folklore*, 69.

sometimes, be quiet" (*En* 92). And in a reversal of the fantastic situation he has often imagined—in which his tentacles entwine themselves around her motionless body—he now finds that she has slipped completely out of his grasp. When the Enchanter tries to seize her, in fact, the little girl seems to recede in both space and time as she evades his clutching hands: "[H]e could not catch hold of anything or anyone, she was growing lighter, becoming slippery as a purple-buttocked foundling, with a distorted infant's face, scuttling from the threshold to the crib and crawling backward from the crib into the womb of a tempestuously resurrected mother. 'I'll make you quiet down!' he was shouting (to a spasm, to the dotlike final drop, to nothingness). 'All right, I'll leave, I'll make you—'" (*En* 93). Here, two other repeated elements of his fantasies—the child's amazingly small size in relation to himself, and the notion that time's usual progression has magically stopped—also reappear in exaggerated and grotesque form. Now, the little girl not only appears tiny, but she shrinks before his eyes; time not only stops, it moves backward. Indeed, the final parenthetical sequence in this passage ("spasm ... dotlike final drop ... nothingness") suggests simultaneously both the child's conception—that is, the very last stage in the imagined reversal of her entire physical and chronological development—and the end of his own orgasm.

This scene portrays the Enchanter's disenchantment in terms of spatial reduction, temporal regression, and the reversal of every aspect of his fantasies. It also identifies his disenchantment more literally with the dwindling final seconds of his "oblique," "senseless" ecstasy and the obliteration of whatever feelings of potency it might have given him (*En* 92). As the scene continues, it describes his subsequent actions with even starker images of diminishment, decline, and destruction. Desperate to escape from the situation, he rushes out of the hotel room, locks it behind him, and stands there for a moment, "barefoot and with a cold smear beneath his raincoat," "gradually sinking." By this time, the child's screams have aroused the hotel's staff and other residents—including two old women, one of whom takes charge of the situation and skillfully knocks the key onto the floor—"but in any event, *it was all over*" (*En* 93; emphasis added). As the Enchanter flees, his movements continue to emphasize the same dwindling, downward trajectory. He "run[s] down the sticky steps," past a diminishing series of figures climbing toward him, and into the street, "for *all was over*, and it was imperative, by any stratagem, by any spasm, to get rid of the no-longer-needed, already-looked-at, idiotic world" (*En* 94; emphasis added). Now, indeed, the novella's accelerating rush toward nothingness includes not only a shrinking of space and a regression of time but also the shutting down of consciousness itself. In this passage, for example, the word "spasm" no longer suggests the Enchanter's extinguished ecstasy, or even his imagining of the child's remote conception; instead, it refers to whatever movement or sensation might enable him to bring his life to an end. The Enchanter's desperate need for something to obliterate his awareness of what he has done, "a torrent, a precipice, a railroad track—no matter what, but instantly"—is satisfied by a large truck, rapidly descending the steep street, that is "about to hurtle downward" upon him. If the Enchanter now imagines himself as rapidly shrinking in size and power, then the monstrous truck, "swelling to full growth," "distending the night," parallels and parodies his earlier sense of gigantic and fabulous potency (*En* 94). Hurling himself under the truck and into "this instantaneous cinema of dismemberment," the Enchanter finds himself reduced, still further, to a fragile membrane that the truck "tear[s]," "shred[s]," and "rip[s] to pieces" beneath its wheels until, at last in that very spasm of final sensation that he sought, the truck obliterates his consciousness altogether, even as the narrative itself ends abruptly with these words: "—and the film of life ha[s] burst" (*En* 95). According to the logic of disenchantment, the Enchanter's spell is finally, decisively, and pointedly broken in a manner that befits the spell. That is, just as the Enchanter earlier bewitched himself with his fantasy of "enchanting" the little girl, so he now suffers a version of the very fate that he planned for her when, as Barabtarlo points out, the novella's "muffled yet audible motif of defloration" culminates in the Enchanter's own body being "ravaged, crushed, and violated" beneath the wheels of a passing truck.[22]

"Beauty's Sleep" in Lolita

Tracing the erotic of sleep and the allusions to enchanted slumber in *The Enchanter*—which Nabokov called a "prototype" of *Lolita*[23]—suggests a new way to read his most famous novel. Admittedly, there are significant differences in plot, setting, character, and narration between the two works. Nabokov says that his father considered them "totally distinct" from each other; Alfred Appel, Jr., claims that they have little in common beyond their premise, and that their execution is utterly dissimilar; and Barabtarlo argues that *The Enchanter*

---

22. Barabtarlo, "Those Who Favor Fire," 94–95.
23. Vladimir Nabokov, "On a Book Entitled *Lolita*," 311.

should not be considered merely a precursor to *Lolita*.²⁴ Despite these dissimilarities, however, in each work Nabokov uses tales of enchanted slumber as a model both for his narrative and for his protagonist's erotic daydreams.

Humbert also fantasizes about ogling, kissing, and caressing his stepdaughter while she sleeps. He dreams, in even more sinister detail, of "gorg[ing] the limp nymphet with sleeping pills" during her mother's absence, "administering a powerful sleeping potion to both mother and daughter so as to fondle the latter through the night with perfect impunity," sedating them "so thoroughly that neither sound or touch should rouse them," and spending "forty nights with a frail little sleeper at my throbbing side" (*AnL* 80, 71, 94, 111). He, too, seems to imagine that child-loving will allow him to transcend time altogether. And Humbert, like the Enchanter, expresses these longings in imagery borrowed from tales like "Sleeping Beauty." He pictures his stepdaughter as a "little princess," surrounded by "a bodyguard of roses" or "[i]mprisoned in her crystal sleep" (*AnL* 39, 52, 123); and he imagines himself as a "conjuror," "wily wizard," "incubus," or "fairytale vampire" who can secretly possess her sleeping body (*AnL* 62, 49, 71, 139). Humbert also attempts to enact this scenario by abducting his stepdaughter after her mother's death. He even takes her to a hotel, appropriately called the Enchanted Hunters, that echoes the hotel in *The Enchanter*, from its storybook servants—a "stooping, groaning gnome" in the novella (*En* 81), a "hunchbacked" bellboy and "porcine" clerk in the novel (*AnL* 117)—to the fact that a flower show in town makes finding a room with two beds impossible (*En* 81; *AnL* 118). For Humbert, too, sharing a room with a sleeping child means the opportunity to fulfill his fantasies; he recounts that night, moreover, in terms of enchanted slumber, from his description of himself as "a comic, clumsy, wavering Prince Charming" to the "beautifully colored capsules loaded with Beauty's Sleep" that he offers Lolita (*AnL* 109, 122). Humbert, too, is punished for attempting to make those fairy-tale fantasies come true. The Enchanter dies almost immediately, but Humbert must comprehend the full enormity of what he has done—must in effect undergo his own disenchantment—before his story ends. And end it must, bitterly, tragically, irrevocably, for no matter how much they may dream about it, Nabokov never allows his child-loving protagonists to live happily ever after.

24. Dmitri Nabokov, "On a Book Entitled *The Enchanter*," 125; *AnL* xxxviii; Barabtarlo, "Those Who Favor Fire," 90. In the broader thematic study from which this essay is excerpted I discuss the novella's ending and its relationship to the endings of "A Nursery Tale" and *Lolita* in greater depth.

{ PART II }
THE AMERICAN YEARS

{ 5 }

Suffer the Little Children

ZORAN KUZMANOVICH

In an ideal scholarly world, one would think of presenting papers or writing articles only at the moment in which one's dissatisfaction with the existing knowledge on a subject one holds dear reaches a boiling point. Only then would one stop examining the nature of the gaps and fissures in the existing explanatory paradigms and offer the right kind of question about the failings of the knowledge at hand, as well as the thinnest outline of an answer. We seem to be approaching that moment in the thinking about the reasons that children in Nabokov's fiction are so often dead at the end of the works in which they appear. When one considers in this context the works Nabokov produced during the period that Brian Boyd calls the "American Years," the deaths of Annabel Leigh, Rudy Haze, Lolita and her child, the barber of Kasbeam's son, Lucette, and Hazel Shade come quickly to mind. It is difficult to think of fully drawn children who survive and prosper in Nabokov's works. In fact, other than Nabokov himself in *Speak, Memory,* only three come to mind: Victor, who despite the buffoonery of his biological parents quietly exits the exquisite doom of Pnin's world unharmed, and of course Ada and Van, who survive into the quarrelsome randiness of old age.

The most disturbing death of a child we read about occurs on the pages of the book in which Nabokov boasts of serving "triumphant life sentences" and thundering against "vicious cruelty" (*SL* 528). It is the death of David Krug in *Bend Sinister.* It is David's childhood, torture, and death on which this chapter

---

I am grateful to Hansford Epes, Randy F. Nelson, Alan Michael Parker, Ellen and Drury Pifer, Karl Plank, and Leona Toker for much that I hope is right with this chapter.

will concentrate. I admit that I have not reached the boiling point of dissatisfaction with the current published discussions of David's death, but I am not convinced by them nevertheless. To put it more honestly, if they have convinced me, most of me still does not believe them. What follows, then, is an effort to settle my disagreements as much with myself as with others. But it is always easier to start with others. Even if one agrees with Ellen Pifer that Nabokov's characters are held accountable for the lived quality of their reality, an interpretation I would share in virtually all other contexts, it is difficult to see how David is accountable for the torture and death that become his reality.[1] I find this difficulty replicated in reading the works of other critics to whom I usually go to contextualize the anxieties that *Bend Sinister* generates. Although they propose readings of Krug's fate that are devoutly to be wished for, David's torture seems to evade their usually penetrating gazes. As a result, although critics of *Bend Sinister* often cite Nabokov's explanation that the work was written for the sake of "the pages about David and his father" and for the sake of "Krug's loving heart" (*BS* xiv), the objects of that love—philosophy; Krug's wife, Olga; Hamlet; and his son David—receive unequal critical attention, with philosophy, Hamlet, and Olga consuming about fifty pages for each one devoted to David. In that the critics seemingly reflect Nabokov's own quite disproportionate attention even in his guise as a "mysterious intruder who takes advantage of Krug's dream to convey his peculiar code message" (*BS* xviii). Of course, since the death of Little Nell, the death of children has never been an easy subject to write about—just witness the lame and dumbfounded responses to the schoolyard and cafeteria shootings that have become a commonplace of American education. Yet David's death is so horrifying and depicted in so tragically farcical a fashion that one cannot simply declare, as Julia Bader does, that in this book "death is disinfected of its horror by being rendered as a problem of fictional representation."[2] Far from masking, transforming, or disinfecting death through the often discussed subtle patterning of spatulate shapes, Nabokov seems to shrink from death's horror, stopping short of explicitly depicting the nature of Krug's grief after he first hears about, then sees on film, his frail son being tortured to death. By making Krug mad but cognizant of the fact that "he and his son and his wife and everybody else

1. See Ellen Pifer, *Nabokov and the Novel* (Cambridge, Mass.: Harvard University Press, 1980).

2. Julia Bader, *Crystal Land: Artifice in Nabokov's English Novels* (Berkeley: University of California Press, 1972), 96.

are merely my whims and megrims" (*BS* xiv), Nabokov in essence is asking readers first to imagine fully, then to nullify fully, the logic of Krug's suffering.

But whether Krug is mad or sane, the product of an epiphany or a migraine headache, "the senseless agony of [Krug's] logical fate" (*BS* 233) is to live and die in a world in which his child has been tortured to death. As Richard Rorty claims, "[T]he death of a child is Nabokov's standard example of ultimate pain," an emotional and intellectual horror so disturbing that, when it happens in *Bend Sinister*, Nabokov "does not attempt to portray Krug's pain."[3] When Nabokov—for it is Nabokov, in *propria persona* (witness his letters to the Doubleday editors in *SL* 480-50), not some implied author—bends a beam of pale authorial light to make Krug mad and thus take him to his bosom near the end of *Bend Sinister*, Rorty sees this bending as the act of sparing Krug. If *Bend Sinister* had indeed ended with Krug's madness, Rorty would of course be right that, for Nabokov, children's suffering is monstrous and for their parents, it is undepictable—that is, literally unspeakable. But the novel does depict David's torture at some length, and moreover it does so twice. After Krug goes mad with grief, the novel continues for eight more pages, a continuation about which Rorty really has nothing to say. Critics who do have something to say about the ending, such as Susan Fromberg Schaeffer, must argue that the narrator's powers over Krug's world are illusory in order to see in the moth that bombinates at the narrator's window evidence of the survival and transformation of Olga Krug's "rosy" soul. Schaeffer, convinced that *Bend Sinister* is "the paradigm of the philosophy expressed in Krug's unwritten essay," sees in the book's ending evidence of that philosophy's coming into being.[4] Yet as a reader who has considerable difficulty finding any paradigm, even in many written essays, I am not certain how one divines philosophical paradigms in essays that have not yet been written. But even if such powers of haruspication are simply a gift I was born without, Schaeffer's reading begs a question: If Krug goes to his maker's bosom, and Olga's rosy soul bombinates at the threshold of a better world, what has happened to the next installment of David's "serial soul" in this optimistic vision of the otherworldly contiguities? At the end of *Bend Sinister*, there are no floating pale beams of light; no paintings of fairy-tale forests to step into; no beautiful, fatidic insects

---

3. Richard Rorty, *Contingency, Irony, and Solidarity* (New York: Cambridge University Press, 1989), 155, 163.

4. Susan Fromberg Schaeffer, "*Bend Sinister* and the Novelist as Anthropomorphic Deity," *Centennial Review* 17 (spring 1973): 145.

flying around; no sudden focal shifts; no cosmic synchronization, no mysterious auras or any other intuited or explicit metaphysical hieroglyphs that could readily point one to David Krug's well-being in the hereafter. The "square echo" of a slammed door frames only David's absence. Why is David denied even a hint of transformation or resurrection? In the novel's temporal scheme, the only images of David projected beyond the novel's putative present occur in Krug's vision of David's future:

> He saw him riding a bicycle in between brilliant forsythia shrubs and thin naked birch trees down a path with a "no bicycles" sign. He saw him on the edge of a swimming pool, lying on his stomach, in wet black shorts, one shoulder blade sharply raised, one hand stretched shaking out iridescent water that clogged a toy destroyer. He saw him in one of those fabulous corner stores that have face creams on one side and ice creams on the other, perched there at the bar and craning towards the syrup pumps. He saw him throwing a ball with a special flip of the wrist, unknown in the old country. He saw him as a youth crossing a technicoloured campus. He saw him wearing the curious garb (jockeylike except for the shoes and stockings) used by players in the American ball game. He saw him learning to fly. (*BS* 188)

Krug's vision gleams and glissades with activity; it is a slide show most parents create in their minds in celebratory anticipation of their child's development. Yet the last time we see David in the novel's present, although we see him through Krug's eyes, stillness dominates: "[T]he murdered child had a crimson and gold turban around its head; its face was skillfully painted and powdered: a mauve blanket, exquisitely smooth, came up to its chin" (*BS* 224).

The body of the dead boy, according to Michael Wood, has been turned into "a statue in Kitsch";[5] certainly the change in pronoun from "his" to "its," along with the gaudy colors. suggests that. Moreover, Wood is right when he insists that, "[a]s so often in Nabokov, we have to imagine the worst; to use the specifics he gives us to divine the ones he withholds."[6] But Wood stops short of explaining why the blanket is so exquisitely smooth. Although Nabokov could be referring merely to the fabric of the blanket, and not to the shape it covers, when the blanket's exquisite smoothness is coupled with Nabokov's descriptions of "limb tearing" and "bone breaking" during the "release game,"

---

5. Michael Wood, *The Magician's Doubts: Nabokov and the Risks of Fiction* (Princeton, N.J.: Princeton University Press, 1995), 59.
6. Ibid.

Nabokov is asking us to share Krug's last vision of his child—a child whom Nabokov implies has been torn literally to pieces. I think I understand why even as astute a reader as Wood was not willing or able to share in that vision.

Yet it is precisely this world of "a wrong turn taken by life" (*BS* xii) that Nabokov quite literally enters and does so by his own design, referring to that entrance as a "device not yet attempted in literature" (*SL* 50). This entrance is presumably an invitation to the reader to identify with the author's norms, to enter the book in which Krug's and David's suffering can be made sense of by being punished in a retribution scene that Nabokov describes in this fashion: "[T]he dummies are at last in quite dreadful pain, and pretty Mariette gently bleeds staked and torn by the lust of forty soldiers" (*BS* xiv). If this life sentence is triumphant, it is certainly not coherent, for when it comes to imagining David's last end, the story really enters us while denying us its sense. Even after I close *Bend Sinister* I cannot rid myself of the sickening crunch of a child's broken bones or of the last image of bare-legged, living David staring in shivering, floodlit incomprehension at the group of hooligans who are about to torture him to death. Despite Nabokov's intercession on Krug's behalf, when I consider my imagination of David's fate, I cannot help but feel like those volunteers in Stanley Milgram's obedience experiments at Yale University—volunteers, ordinary people like you and me, who easily consented to inflict on others what they believed were painful, even dangerously painful, electric shocks, all for the sake of what they understood to be scientific necessity.[7] Imagine their reactions on being told that what the experiment measured was their willingness to obey orders to torture and then you will have some notion of why I am troubled not so much by the finality of David's death as by its instrumentality.

Why would Nabokov, the foundation of whose ideal state was based on there being "No torture and no executions" (*SO* 35), imagine in such repulsively suggestive detail the torture of a tiny creature who, after the death of his mother, comes to serve as the only measure of reality for his philosophical but heartbroken father?

> And what agony, thought Krug the thinker, to love so madly a little creature, formed in some mysterious fashion . . . by the fusion of two mysteries, or rather two sets of trillion mysteries each; formed by a fusion which is, at

---

7. See Stanley Milgram, *Obedience to Authority: An Experimental View* (New York: Harper and Row, 1974).

the same time a matter of choice and a matter of chance and a matter of pure enchantment; thus formed and then permitted to accumulate trillions of its own mysteries; the whole suffused with consciousness, which is the only real thing in the universe and the greatest mystery of all. (*BS* 187–88)

Why would Nabokov inflict so much pain on that little creature and his father? Why torture Krug's loving heart? Why torture David, for whom, I repeat, there is no relief in the emotional and metaphysical economy of the book, even though after David's death Krug has a dream in which his efforts to kiss David make him "sink into the heart-rending softness, into the black dazzling depths of a belated but—never mind—eternal caress" (*BS* 232). That dream the narrator simply dismisses as "confused" (*BS* 233), as merely another torture for poor Krug.

Torture occurs when unlimited force is exerted on the physical or psychological being of an individual ostensibly for some public good, but really in order to destroy all resistance within that person, securing either necessary information or that person's public consent to something he or she finds repugnant. The tortured person knows that the torturers know that he knows that there are no limits to the pain that they can inflict on him. For Elaine Scarry, the tortured prisoner's body and mind become the manifest sign of the torturer's power, a manifestness that cannot be obtained in any other way, because it demands the complete unmaking of the tortured person's world.[8] Torture makes sense to the torturers while destroying in the victim of torture not only "commonsense" (of which, in its one-word spelling, Nabokov was rightly suspicious) but also the very fabric of sense-making mechanisms. Thus, just as consciousness is the only real thing in the universe for Krug, the tortured victim's physical or psychological pain becomes the only trustworthy mark of the real for Scarry. Such trustworthiness is by definition a politically encoded one. J. M. Coetzee argues that, through the secrecy in which torture usually takes place and the goal of the torture, which is the shattering of the victim's world, "the state creates the preconditions for the novel to set about its work of representation."[9] Quite simply, one answer to the question why would Nabokov choose to depict the torture of child, is that torture invites novelistic representation. Yet Coetzee is quick to point out that

---

8. Elaine Scarry, *The Body in Pain: The Making and Unmaking of the World* (New York: Oxford University Press, 1985).

9. J. M. Coetzee, "Into the Dark Chamber: The Novelist and South Africa," *New York Times Review of Books*, January 12, 1986, sec. 7, 13.

there is something tawdry about following the state in this way, making its vile mysteries the occasion of fantasy. For the writer the deeper problem is not to allow himself to be impaled on the dilemma proposed by the state, namely, either to ignore its obscenities or else to produce representations of them. The true challenge is how not to play the game by the rules of the state, how to establish one's own authority, how to imagine torture and death on one's own terms.[10]

Oddly enough, Nabokov's original terms for *Bend Sinister* did not include a scene in which David dies of torture. Originally, the sickly boy was simply to die from his sickness. Between March 22, 1944, when he revealed his plan for *Bend Sinister* in a letter to an editor at Doubleday, to mid-May 1946, when he competed the book, Nabokov changed his mind. I would like to be able to claim that he changed his mind because he had found a way to depict death and torture on his own terms, but I cannot. In both Crystalsen's story and in the scenes from the film shown to Krug, David's death and torture are presented precisely on the Ekwillist state's terms—as bumbling but creative cruelty. It is as if Nabokov, for his own ends, had answered positively Ivan's question in Dostoevsky's *The Brothers Karamazov:* "Imagine that you are creating a fabric of human destiny with the object of making men happy in the end, giving them peace and rest at last, but that it was essential to torture to death only one tiny creature ... and to found that edifice on its unavenged tears, would you consent to be the architect under those conditions?"[11]

But even if much of the edifice of *Bend Sinister* rests on David Krug's unavenged tears, we must remember, with Alexander Dolinin and Julian Connolly, that when it comes to Dostoevshchina, Nabokov's ends are always complex. When Ivan Karamazov gives as grounds for his loss of faith the suffering of children, he detaches himself from the Christian scheme of things. And one could argue that by entering the text in a gesture of metafictional self-presentation, Nabokov, too, encourages detachment, giving us the kind of art that can make the perception of hard moral realities bearable. Such an argument would expand evidentiary possibilities if David's torture lent itself to being understood, explicated, and ameliorated. But as a fictional act it defeats our understanding, because we cannot quite find the emotional or moral means

10. Ibid.
11. Fyodor Dostoevsky, *The Brothers Karamazov,* trans. Constance Garnett (New York: Modern Library, 1937), 254.

to encompass it; we cannot get the necessary closure, and, in my case, I cannot even begin to imagine what it would be like to do so. Whatever world or otherworld Nabokov shows to Krug during Krug's "blessed madness," the foundation of such a world cannot become visible through David Krug's tears. If Ivan Karamazov's story is one of faith lost, *Bend Sinister,* despite David's torture, presents itself through Nabokov's preface (and the readings that rely on it) as a story of faith kept.

If one were to ask why such faith-keeping required the torture of David Krug, several answers suggest themselves. I will produce them severally, because I have not eliminated all possibility of my own disagreement with any of them.

First, the least satisfactory answer: Drawing on some of Freud's most difficult and speculative work—in particular, the 1915 essay "Instincts and Their Vicissitudes," Leo Bersani suggest that the typical Western forms of narrative are themselves complicit in a fascinated fixation with expressions of violence and destruction. Central to this argument is the notion that narrative art emphasizes climactic events or moments of violence, thus inviting and gratifying a sexualized admixture of sadistic and masochistic identification on the reader's part.[12] In other words, Bersani's suggestion leads to the following conclusion: In choosing among the alternatives that Coetzee outlines as supplementarity and rivalry to the tyrant state, Nabokov had selected the first. By this light, far from relying on a device never before attempted in literature, Nabokov in fact was relying on one that never fails to work.

The formalist in me double-clutches at this reading, checks sheepishly around the room for withering gazes of the post-formalist, closes his eyes, and reaches desperately for some grand narrative of formal unity as a marker of spiritual redemption and restored moral order. That grand narrative runs something like this: Vicarious participation in torture of the sort Nabokov describes is good for us. As we know from Milgram's experiments, we are not immune to torture; nor are we ever quite beyond the banality of evil-doing. By being forced to imagine the effects of torture on a loving heart, we recognize how being all too human diminishes us all. Against this dark realization, Nabokov pits the power of storytelling and a set of values that has a very large space for the mysterious, the tender, the ineffable, the sacred, and the sur-

---

12. Leo Bersani, *A Future for Astyanax: Character and Desire in Literature* (Boston: Little, Brown, 1976), 9, 300–301.

prising, a space in which one can feel, if not necessarily see, what Seamus Heaney calls "angelic potential, a motion of the soul."[13] After all, as Sergei Davydov reminds us, Nabokov did write that "We are the larvae of the angels" (see chapter 10).

When the formalist in me opens his eyes again and discovers that he has not died of ridicule, he is ready to face up to the grim biographical, historical, and cultural circumstances of the world into which *Bend Sinister* was published. Such a facing up suggests yet another answer. The fact that Nabokov did not originally plan to have David tortured requires us at least to glance at the world beyond the writer's desk. Sometime after outlining *Bend Sinister* but before publishing it, Nabokov learned of his brother Sergey's death in the concentration camp at Neuengamme (*SL* 63). Nabokov's June 15, 1946, letter to his sister Elena suggests that images of children tortured and killed in concentration camps were very much on his mind, "children as amusing and loved as our own," as he put it.[14] Those children had been tortured to death on such a grand scale because they lived in a world in which their annihilation made sense to their executioners. Nabokov's refusal to make of David's torture and death something other than torture and death suggests an awareness of the dangers not merely of the complicity that Coetzee wrote about but also of the explicability best summed by Theodor Adorno's statement, "[T]here is no longer beauty or consolation except in the gaze falling on horror, withstanding it, and in an unalleviated consciousness of negativity holding fast to the possibility of what is better."[15] What is better for Nabokov is the possibility of a world without torture. To keep that possibility alive, Nabokov gives us David Krug, as cute and lovable as any of our children, but a child who happens to end up tortured to death. In the end, such torture cannot make sense in the world of *Bend Sinister* or in any other world. It cannot because it must not.

13. Seamus Heaney, *The Redress of Poetry* (New York: Farrar, Straus, and Giroux, 1995), 192.

14. Vladimir Nabokov, *Perepiska s sestroi* (Ann Arbor: Ardis, 1985), 41.

15. Theodor Adorno, *Minima Moralia: Reflections from Damaged Life*, trans. E. F. N. Jephcott (New York: Schocken Books, 1978), 47, as quoted in Carolyn Forché, ed., *Against Forgetting: Twentieth Century Poetry of Witness* (New York: W. W. Norton, 1992), 41.

{ 6 }

"Signs and Symbols" and Silentology

JOANNA TRZECIAK

"Signs and Symbols" (1948), by far the most studied of Nabokov's short stories, has been analyzed for its symbolism, its metafictional aspect, and more rarely for the links between its metafictional and narrative levels.[1] In its most basic outline, the story concerns an unnamed Russian Jewish émigré couple

---

1. Articles about "Signs and Symbols" include Larry R. Andrews, "Deciphering 'Signs and Symbols,'" in *Nabokov's Fifth Arc: Nabokov and Others on His Life's Work*, ed. J. E. Rivers and C. Nicol (Austin: University of Texas Press, 1982), 139–52; Gennady Barabtarlo, "English Short Stories," in *The Garland Companion to Vladimir Nabokov*, ed. Vladimir E. Alexandrov (New York: Garland, 1995), 101–17; William Carroll, "Nabokov's Signs and Symbols," in *A Book of Things about Vladimir Nabokov*, ed. Carl R. Proffer (Ann Arbor: Ardis, 1974), 203–17; Carol M. Dole, "Innocent Trifles; Or, 'Signs and Symbols,'" *Studies in Short Fiction* 24, no. 3 (1987): 303–5; David Field, "Sacred Dangers: Nabokov's Distorted Reflection in 'Signs and Symbols,'" *Studies in Short Fiction* 25, no. 3 (1988): 285–93; John V. Hagopian, "Decoding Nabokov's 'Signs and Symbols,'" *Studies in Short Fiction* 182 (1981): 115–19; John B. Lane, "A Funny Thing about Nabokov's 'Signs and Symbols,'" *Russian Language Journal* 40 (1986): 147–60; Terry J. Martin, "Ways of Knowing in Nabokov's 'Signs and Symbols,'" *Journal of the Short Story in English* 17 (1991): 75–89; Charles W. Mignon, "A Referential Reading of Nabokov's 'Signs and Symbols,'" *Studies in Short Fiction* 282 (1991): 169–75; J. Morris, "Signs and Symbols and Signs," *The Nabokovian* 32 (1994): 24–28; David H. Richter, "Narrative Entrapment in *Pnin* and 'Signs and Symbols,'" *Papers on Language and Literature* 20, no. 4 (1984): 418–30; Pekka Tammi, "Nabokov's *Symbolic Cards* and Pushkin's 'The Queen of Spades,'" *The Nabokovian* 13 (1984): 31–32; Leona Toker, "'Signs and Symbols' In and Out of Contexts," in *A Small Alpine Form: Studies in Nabokov's Short Fiction*, ed. C. Nicol and G. Barabtarlo (New York: Garland, 1993), 167–80; Mary Tookey, "Nabokov's 'Signs and Symbols,'" *Explicator* 46, no. 2 (1988): 34–36; and Michael Wood, "Consulting the Oracle," *Essays in Criticism* 43, no. 2 (1993): 93–111.

and their birthday visit to their mentally ill son. Because the son has recently attempted suicide, the parents are not permitted to see him. After returning home from their aborted visit, they resolve to bring their son home from the institution. While celebrating their decision over midnight tea, they are interrupted by two consecutive calls to the wrong number, both from the same girl. The story ends with the phone ringing ominously.

The emphasis of most scholars on interpreting the story's symbols in light of its open ending has privileged the symbolic level and perhaps has underemphasized its equally rich literal level. Many have focused on exploring either the hermeneutic or the metafictional implications of the story's ample symbolism in order to derive a meaning for its open ending.[2] Moreover, because of the seductive analogy between the son's referential mania[3] and the reader's quest for symbols, in most studies of this story—those of Leona Toker and John Hagopian being notable exceptions—the emphasis has been placed on the son rather than on his parents.[4] A possible explanation for why readings have tended to focus on the son is the inconspicuousness of the pervasive, mutually acknowledged silences the couple share throughout the story.

An interpretation that offers the promise of a shift in emphasis from the story's symbolism can be found in Michael Wood's *The Magician's Doubts:*

> What seems to me most striking about the story is its immense shadowy background of pain and frightening possibility; not its secret, but its silence. It is full of things not said, fuller than Nabokov's writing often seems; and it may help us to see what's not said elsewhere; to see that even such a talkative, explicit writer has his silences, that his silences may be larger, more eloquent, than we reckoned.[5]

Following up on Wood's insightful and suggestive remark in this chapter, I advance a reading that foregrounds the story's silences, favoring its literal level over its symbolism and metafictional possibilities, with a bias toward the parents and away from the son. I then undertake a reinterpretation of the story's symbolism from the point of view of the silences, attending primarily to the

2. For example, see Andrews, "Deciphering," 139–52.
3. The term "referential mania" comes from the psychiatrist in the story, Hermann Brink.
4. See Toker, "Contexts," and Hagopian, "Decoding."
5. Michael Wood, *The Magician's Doubts: Nabokov and the Risks of Fiction* (London: Chatto and Windus, 1994), 66.

half-said and the unsaid. Such a reading elevates the surface-level narrative to something suggestive of a much larger picture of unspeakable suffering rather than a mere "human-interest story" that serves as a vehicle for Nabokov's metafictional game of narrative entrapment. Once we turn to deciphering the silences, three foci emerge from the narrative details. These are, in order of increasing scope: parental love and the fear of loss; the tragedies of the Holocaust; and the fragility and finitude of life.

To elucidate the themes of parental love, the unspeakability of loss, and the emotional content of silence in "Signs and Symbols," the story will be compared with its 1935 predecessor "Opoveshchenie" ("Breaking the News"), which initiates these themes. Nabokov himself set the stage for such a comparison in a bibliographical note to "Breaking the News" in his 1973 collection of translations *Russian Beauty and Other Stories*, in which he explicitly pointed up the correspondence in theme and milieu between the two stories.[6] As in "Signs and Symbols," the theme of "Breaking the News" is parental love and the unspeakability of loss, and both stories are set on cold spring days in the life of Russian Jewish émigrés. In fact, "Signs and Symbols" can be viewed as a post-Holocaust reprise of "Breaking the News," with the shift in backdrop effecting a change in the character of the silences in the two stories.[7]

The pervasive silence of "Breaking the News" is an unknowing silence. The story's main character, Eugenia Isakovna Mints, is a widowed Russian Jew who has adapted well to life in pre-World War II Berlin. Proud of her coffee, duck-footed, opinionated, eccentric, and gregarious, she is a well-liked member of an extended network of elderly Jewish émigrés. Severely hard of hearing, an impairment she uses to her advantage, she is able to "silence" whomever she wishes with a simple flick of the switch on her hearing aid. Hers is a world steeped in silence, where sounds are not heard but, rather, misattributed to

---

6. Vladimir Nabokov, "Opoveshchenie," in *Sogliadatai* (Paris: Russkia Zapiski, 1938).

7. In the notes to "Breaking the News" in *A Russian Beauty and Other Stories*, Nabokov wrote: "'Breaking the News' appeared under the title 'Opoveshchenie' (Notification) in an émigré periodical around 1935 and was included in my collection *Soglyadatay* (Paris: Russkiya Zapiski, 1938). The milieu and the theme both correspond to those of 'Signs and Symbols,' written ten years later in English." See Vladimir Nabokov, "Symbols and Signs," *New Yorker*, May 15, 1948, 31–33. "Breaking the News" is published in the collections *A Russian Beauty and Other Stories* (New York: McGraw-Hill, 1973) and *The Stories of Vladimir Nabokov* (New York: Vintage International, 1997). "Signs and Symbols" appears in *Nabokov's Dozen* (New York: Doubleday, 1958) and *The Stories of Vladimir Nabokov*. Page citations for both stories are to the Vintage edition.

things (for example, she takes the hum of her blood to be the hum of the town), lending the story a surreal, carnival-like air.⁸ While surprisingly unproblematic and routine for her, her deafness presents a grave problem for those close to her, who pace, "akh," and "tsk" their way through various tribulations as they grapple with how to break the tragedy of her son's death gently.

At the outset of the story, the reader is laconically informed that, unknown to the widow, her son has just died. This gives the reader a narrative advantage prerequisite for the dramatic irony at work throughout the story. At nearly every turn, the widow meets symbols foreboding death, signs to which she is not at all attuned. In a telling instance, she receives a postcard with a loving note from her overworked son that uncannily reflects the manner in which he has fallen to his death: "[I]a po-prezhnemu po gorlo zaniat i po vecheram priamo valius' s nog." In the Nabokovs' 1973 English translation, the irony comes across more strongly: "I continue to be plunged up to the neck in work and when evening comes I literally fall off my feet."⁹ Likewise, to the reader, the gesture of a loving mother checking on her son's broken watch, in for repairs, highlights her blissful ignorance of the harbingers of death that crop up in the course of the day's errands. As she attends to her activities, reveling in the low-level hum of a world to which she is qute well accommodated, the reader anticipates the moment in which not only the news but also the silence will be broken. The silence of her world, which is initially used to somewhat comic effect, comes to signify her tragic obliviousness and ultimately the tragic obliviousness of the Jews in Berlin of 1935.¹⁰

In "Signs and Symbols," which falls under the long shadow cast by the Holocaust, the situation is quite different. The reader is given no epistemic advantage over the characters. The couple learns—along with the reader— of their son's attempted suicide early in the story. The narrative point of view, most closely allied with that of the mother, picks out the details of their day foreboding death. The parents' love for their son and their grief at his attempted suicide inform the pervasive undercurrent of silences.

The silences in which the couple engage are rooted not in obliviousness but in a shared tacit acknowledgment of the depth of suffering their lives have seen

---

8. Hers is a world populated by "rubbery pedestrians, cotton-wool dogs, mute tramcars": Nabokov, "Breaking the News," 392.

9. Ibid., 391.

10. The Russian original does not state the year in which the story is set. Dmitri and Vladimir Nabokov added the year in their translation: See Nabokov, *Russian Beauty*.

and in all likelihood will continue to see. Descriptive details suggest that the transition to the New World has been marked by loss and discomfort—Ellis Island's elisions have clipped the storied rabbinical family name Soloviechik to Solov, and even to Sol.[11] Unlike the émigré widow of "Breaking the News," who is able to indulge in the joys of good food (wonderful bananas, fruit jellies, fresh pastry) in the company of her friends, the elderly Jewish couple of "Signs and Symbols" is reduced to mere subsistence in the New World. Financially dependent on a successful brother from whom they are estranged, the woman is relegated to wearing cheap black dresses and going without makeup, and the man must endure a poorly fitting dental plate.[12] Companions silently sharing soft, pale meals, they quietly struggle with private memories of the past. Some scholars have treated the Jewish couple as oblivious,[13] but such a reading can occur only if the undercurrent of non-verbal communication between the two is taken for obliviousness. While the silences convey mutual acknowledgment of shared pain, it is the narration that gives the reader intimations of what they are silent about.[14] The wife knows her husband's moods, but it is not until late in the story that she learns, along with the reader, that it is the thought of bringing their son home that he has been mulling over.

The reader gleans from the couple's silent activities the extent of their loving preoccupation with their son—the husband's throat clearings (which his wife silently and tacitly understands) and the couple's inability to sleep (the mother stays up sifting through old pictures and the father arises from an unsuccessful attempt at sleep). Contact with their son has been made difficult by his illness—he is at both a physical and a mental remove. Critics have justly

---

11. I was not able to ascertain the degree of Nabokov's familiarity with Jewish religious culture in America and, more specifically, with the distinguished Lithuanian rabbinical family Soloveichik, one of the most prominent rabbinical families in the United States. Literary output of the members of the Soloveichik clan has been exceptionally meager, the result of a family tradition against publishing except under special circumstances: See *Encyclopedia Judaica* (New York: Macmillan, 1973), 15:127–28, s.v. "Soloveichik" (Mordecai Hacohen).

12. Toker closely engages the descriptive details of the story from a different point of view from that presented here: See Toker, "Contexts."

13. Carroll, "Nabokov's Signs and Symbols," 212.

14. A thought-provoking philosophical analysis of acknowledgment can be found in Stanley Cavell, "Knowing and Acknowledging," in *Must We Mean What We Say?* (Cambridge: Cambridge University Press, 1976), 238–66.

treated the childhood onset of the son's referential mania as a mad response to the (instinctively sensed) signs of impending doom preceding the Holocaust.[15] Likewise, his ongoing conviction that he is the semiotic center of the universe is a perversion of all of nature's unidirectional reference to God found in Psalms (especially Psalm 19) and the El Adon prayer. But neither the messages encoded in nature nor the process of decoding are joyous, and the unrelenting need to intercept nature's encryptions becomes such a torturous task that suicide seems the only escape. With distance, the son's torrents of torture "increase in volume and volubility"—hence the parents' desire to bring their son home, hoping that close proximity will ease his suffering. Yet the real tragedy is that the son is ultimately detached (as Leona Toker has pointed out) and thus unable to acknowledge his parents' love or recognize their suffering.[16] The parents' world is marked by prolonged silences. Not only is the son unable to inhabit this space of shared pain, but he is trapped in a solipsistic world without silence, surrounded by the ceaseless drone of malevolent buzzing.

What allow the couple's silences to work so powerfully are the glimpses Nabokov provides into what they are silent about. The reader is left to extrapolate from a half-told personal history to the full-blown tragedy of the Holocaust. As the woman flips through her photographs, we are offered, as a backdrop to an abbreviated history of the son's descent into mental illness, a few snapshots of the family's life in Europe. These photographs, if enlarged and brought into focus, could well be the Russian Jewish émigré world of "Breaking the News" (a German maid and her fat-faced fiancé; a slanting housefront; "an old, fussy, angular, and wild-eyed Aunt Rosa who had lived in a tremulous world of bad news, bankruptcies, train accidents, etc.").[17] Moving toward a more literal reading of this passage—one contrary to some commentators' interpretations—the photograph of Aunt Rosa is not merely one of the story's many omens of the son's successful suicide attempt. Rather, it is above all the last remnant of someone who succumbed, along with "all the people she worried about," to a fate that the old couple escaped.[18]

15. See, for example, Toker, "Contexts," 177.
16. Ibid.
17. Nabokov, "Signs and Symbols," 601.
18. Carroll, "Nabokov's Signs and Symbols," 212. David Richter lists the photo of Aunt Rosa among a series of narrative details that move from inert to ominous once the reader has succumbed to the narrative entrapment of concluding that the son has committed suicide: see Richter, "Narrative Entrapment," 427–28.

The narration of "Signs and Symbols" moves between a point of view closely allied to that of the characters (principally the woman) and third-person omniscience. In the most lyrical passage in the story, the distance between the narrator's point of view and that of the woman is nearly obliterated. This exposes a train of thoughts and images in the woman's mind the likes of which presumably lurk behind her silences elsewhere in the story. Taken together, these thoughts belie what seems to be her worldview. Although much scholarship has focused on interpreting the rich imagery of this passage in light of the symbolism that appears in the rest of the story, I will examine it from the perspective of silence.

> This, and much more, she accepted—for after all living did mean accepting the loss of one joy after another, not even joys in her case—mere possibilities of improvement. She thought of the endless waves of pain that for some reason or other she and her husband had to endure; of the invisible giants hurting her boy in some unimaginable fashion; of the incalculable amount of tenderness contained in the world; of the fate of this tenderness, which is either crushed, or wasted, or transformed into madness; of neglected children humming to themselves in unswept corners; of beautiful weeds that cannot hide from the farmer and helplessly have to watch the shadow of his simian stoop leave mangled flowers in its wake, as the monstrous darkness approaches.[19]

Multiple layers of silence suggest themselves in the language of this passage. First, these thoughts are unspoken—they lie behind the woman's silence and are given voice by the narrator. The train of thought here takes the form of silent protest, perhaps even silent resignation. Second, at least within the narrator's description, these words fall short of their target, an acknowledgment that pain lies somewhere off the coast of the signifiable, yet the words themselves are beautiful and moving in their incapacity.[20] A coherent, articulate discussion of pain would be too monstrous.[21] Finally, the linguistic markers—

---

19. Nabokov, "Signs and Symbols," 601.

20. Carroll interprets the mother's lyrical train of thought at the end of part 2 as indicative of her obliviousness in contrast to her son's hypersensitivity. Although this is true, it misses the point, as Carroll interprets even the images of the mother's own reveries as somehow on a par with the symbols elsewhere in the story: See Carroll, "Nabokov's Signs and Symbols," 208.

21. It is as if by entering discourse, the morally reprehensible begins to leave the realm of the unacceptable and enter the realm of the tenable. Michael Wood discusses the unspeakability of evil in Nabokov's work: See Wood, *Magician's Doubts*, esp. chap. 3.

"this and much more," "endless waves of pain," and "incalculable amount of tenderness"—convey that the pain prompting these thoughts has an unfathomable, unquantifiable aspect.

Because many of the narrative details in "Signs and Symbols" seem to point to one another, much of the critical commentary on the story would have us believe that they constitute an interpretive key that leads to the solution of what appears to be the final riddle—the significance of the third telephone call. This is particularly true of the often and eloquently discussed numerical references.[22] Two assumptions have guided analysis of the symbolism in "Signs and Symbols." The first is that the third call is a puzzle that has an answer. The second is that the function of the symbols is to point the way to that answer. Both assumptions can be rejected. Although there is no denying that, in "Signs and Symbols," these symbols are richly woven into patterns of cross-referencing, it has often been tacitly advanced that the only mode of symbolism at work in the story is foreshadowing and that this Nabokovian technique of narrative entrapment might well lead down a blind alley. This is the so-called metafictional game. This engaging but ultimately fruitless search for an answer to the story's open ending (most critics agree that there is no one answer) suggests that the reader consider an approach other than the interpretive key framework.[23] The story's signs and symbols certainly play many roles, but they may be best understood as coordinates marking out the tragedy of people's lives, not as harbingers of impending doom referencing one specific event.

One is struck by the solitude and remoteness of the old couple's life in "Signs and Symbols." Their world is sparsely populated by other survivors whom they seem to know only barely. This can be gleaned indirectly from how few names are given: the estranged brother Isaac; a woman on the bus who—in characteristically Nabokovian fashion—bears a vague resemblance to Rebecca Borisovna, "whose daughter had married one of the Soloveichiks in Minsk";[24] the overly made-up fellow émigré Mrs. Sol; and the family doctor,

---

22. The couple lives on the third floor in their third country; the story is divided into three sections; three playing cards fall to the floor; there are three phone calls; and so on. The figure of the triad echoes the pattern found in Pushkin's "Queen of Spades," where the plot hangs on numerical references. Alexander Dolinin has pointed out in conversation that any reader who believes that he or she has correctly completed the pattern in "Signs and Symbols" should recall the fate of Hermann in "Queen of Spades."

23. Cf. Richter, "Narrative Entrapment," 418–30.

24. Nabokov, "Signs and Symbols," 599.

Dr. Solov. The couple does not interact with any of these people in the course of the gray day presented in the story. Contrast this with the 1930s Berlin of "Breaking the News," in which a Gogolian cast of characters parades into the story one by one to inform and console the widow: the obese Chernobylski, who must throw his fat face back and out of the way as he fiercely bares his teeth to fasten his collar; Madame Shuf, "a vivacious lady with a somewhat exaggerated make-up";[25] and Miss Osipov, "a tiny creature, almost a dwarf."[26]

When the unnamed couple in "Signs and Symbols" flees Europe for the New World, it is such people who remain and perish. Two emendations in the 1973 English translation of "Opoveshchenie" heighten its historical contrast to "Signs and Symbols." First, in the English translation, Nabokov explicitly sets "Breaking the News" in 1935, the year in which, not coincidentally, the Nuremberg statutes were put in place, severely limiting the freedom of the Jewish population in Germany.[27] Second, Nabokov chooses to render *"umer, umer, umer!"* (lit., "he's dead, he's dead, he's dead!") in the last sentence of "Opoveshchenie" as "dead, dead, dead!" broadening its scope. Through the grave irony of history, the phrase can be taken to apply to all of the Jewish characters in the story. In the world depicted in "Signs and Symbols," their absence is palpable.

Although "Signs and Symbols" has been scrutinized for every possible bearer of symbolic significance, there is one about which little has been said: the ten-jar sampler of fruit jellies that opens and closes the story. Although it is one of the story's most important symbols, it escapes close scrutiny unless attended to from the standpoint of the story's silences. The parents, while trying to navigate their way through their son's interpretive mania, settle on this apparently innocuous gift, yet a closer look reveals symbolic echoes. At the end of the story, the father begins to mouth the names on the labels of the ten fruit jars, stopping, when the phone rings, with crab apple.[28] It has escaped com-

---

25. Nabokov, "Breaking the News," 393.

26. Ibid., 394.

27. Norman Davies, *Europa*, trans. Elzbieta Tabakowska (Krakow: Wydawnictwo Znak, 1999), 1035.

28. Brian Boyd has ascertained that Nabokov was partial to the Gerber's brand of fruit jellies. My research has shown that unlike apricot, grape, beech plum, and quince, crab apple was not one of Gerber's assorted fruit jellies. If one removes crab apple, the names of the jellies in the story—apricot, grape, beech plum, quince—form an anagram. That is, by taking the final letter in each name and reconfiguring the letters, one can create the word "theme": See Dole, "Innocent Trifles," 304–5.

ment that the Linnean polynomial for the crab apple is *Malus pumilla paradisiaca* and that the common Russian name is *raiskoe iabloko* (lit., paradise apple). This apparently innocuous gift echoes the story of Adam and Eve. Within this symbolic paradigm, mouthing the names on the jars seems to be a gesture toward reenacting the first act of naming, while the fruit jars bear a distant, vague resemblance to the forbidden fruit, a symbol of the origin of human suffering.

Conclusion

The narrative and epistemic advantage enjoyed by the reader of "Breaking the News" is withheld from the reader of "Signs and Symbols." Rather than being made privy to the story's hermeneutic fulcrum early in "Signs and Symbols," the reader encounters it only at the end. Even there, it is not a crucial piece of knowledge but its suppression that drives reader response. Because of the open nature of the ending of "Signs and Symbols," the prospect of the son's third suicide attempt echoes *backward* through the story. Of course, all of Nabokov's stories are written for rereaders and re-rereaders, but "Signs and Symbols" is a story that *provokes* rereading by virtue of its ending. The final act of silence, in denying the reader knowledge of what will happen next, is not trivial; nor is it an act of cruelty toward the reader. It is a way of letting the reader know that following the path of signs and symbols leads nowhere. And at the end of the story it is the parents who will "live on" to know the outcome of the third phone call, while the reader will not.

{ 7 }

Reinventing Nabokov
Lyne and Kubrick Parse *Lolita*

ELLEN PIFER

The recent controversy surrounding Adrian Lyne's cinematic adaptation of *Lolita* has focused heavily on the issue of child abuse. Critics engaged in defending the artistic merits of the novel and the ethics of those adapting it to film understandably have tended to ignore its humor. Perhaps for this reason, they have also tended to dismiss Stanley Kubrick's 1962 version of *Lolita*—labeling it a "demonic comedy" or "weirdly distorted film."[1] If Kubrick's film can be faulted for its near-obsession with the novel's high-flown comedy, Lyne's is devoid of humor to a remarkable degree. Where Nabokov generates comedy out of despair and tragedy out of farce, Lyne and Kubrick each develop only one of the novel's dominant chords.

The voiceover technique that Lyne employs, framing the film's action with passages drawn from Humbert's narration, does capture, as Caryn James says, some of the novel's rich "poetry."[2] But its tone never wavers from the elegiac. In the novel, Humbert's narrative voice is anything but monotonous. Rapidly shifting from the high style of pathos to the low style of farce, from rapturous evocation to mocking self-denigration, Humbert's Protean delivery effects the ironic disjunctions and distance that generate comedy. In Lyne's film, it is always the voice of sad-eyed Humbert that we hear; the only relief from his gloom are

---

1. Richard Schickel, "Taking a Peek at *Lolita*: And It's a Shame You Can't See More than That," *Time*, vol. 151, no. 11 (March 23, 1998), 91; Caryn James, "A Movie America Can't See," *Sunday New York Times*, March 15, 1998, sec. 2, 13.

2. James, "A Movie," 13.

the sly smiles that occasionally break over Jeremy Irons's brooding face, as he tenderly surrenders to the spell of his nymphet's youthful exuberance.

Only Dominique Swain's mercurial performance as adolescent Lo—radiating childish insouciance one moment, bratty insolence the next—lights up the screen with touches of humor. Sue Lyon, the nymphet in Kubrick's movie, displays little of that mercurial magic. She is more vamp than vulnerable child, even though she and James Mason never kiss on screen. Lyne's film, by contrast, offers a number of graphic scenes, obligatory in today's Hollywood films. Although the scenes performed by the adolescent Swain's nineteen-year-old body double ended up on the cutting-room floor, Lyne's audiences witness moist, lingering kisses between young Lo and her middle-aged lover. We are also party to flickering expressions of orgasmic release on the child's face—a suggestion never made by the novel, whose narrative centers on the ecstasy Humbert obtains at her expense. As Humbert reluctantly admits to the reader, "Never did she vibrate under my touch" (*Lo* 166). Controverting this sad evidence—that Humbert's relentless caresses only dampen and finally crush the adolescent's budding sexuality—Lyne portrays Swain in various states of arousal. As though anticipating the film audience's shock, however, he enshrouds these scenes in gloom—Humbert's rapture suitably darkened by hellish awareness that he is debauching a child.

The somber atmosphere of Lyne's movie may owe something to the cultural atmosphere of the 1990s. In 1962, when Kubrick's version of *Lolita* was released, the term "sexual abuse," as Elizabeth Kaye observes, had not yet "invaded the vernacular.... No statistics asserted that one in every five women had been sexually abused by her father or stepfather."[3] Not until the late 1980s did the sexual abuse of children become a widely studied and reported phenomenon—the subject of countless tabloid articles and media talk shows, scholarly and professional research. Kubrick's audience had less difficulty viewing Humbert's nympholepsy as bizarre or aberrant; keeping their distance, they could appreciate the film's sardonic comedy.

For readers of Nabokov's novel, the oscillations of Humbert's narrative voice sustain the reader's salutary sense of distance. In the medium of film, such effects prove more difficult, if not impossible, to achieve. The power of the camera lens to engage an audience lies—to some extent, at least—in its tendency to erase from the viewer's awareness the camera's constant manipulation or

---

3. Elizabeth Kaye, "*Lolita* Comes Again," *Esquire*, vol. 127, no. 2 (February 1997), 53.

control, much as conventionally "realistic" novels attempt to give the illusion that all events and situations arise naturally and spontaneously within its pages. Even more than the language of fiction, moving "pictures" create, and largely depend on, the effect of *immediate*—that is, unmediated—reality. In Nabokov's novel, by contrast, nearly every event, scene, and character alludes to, imitates, or obliquely comments on a precursor or set of precursors in the history and tradition of literature. Defining parody as an imitative "confrontation with a prior text or type of text," Thomas Frosch, like most critics of the novel, discovers this technique at work throughout *Lolita*'s narrative. "Parodists," Frosch adds, "use a voice different from their own in such a way as to call attention to themselves.... This sense of displaced recognition, this incongruous simultaneity of closeness and distance, is a primary source of the delight and humor of parody."[4]

In *Lolita: A Screenplay*, which Nabokov wrote at the behest of Kubrick but which the director largely ignored, the novelist attempts to convert these linguistic effects into cinematic ones, introducing two distancing devices at the outset. Nabokov turns the psychiatrist Dr. John Ray, the ostensible "author" of the novel's foreword (and Nabokov's spoof on the confident clinical expert), into a dramatic persona. Seated at his desk, holding the "manuscript" pages of Humbert's memoir in his hand, Ray speaks directly to the camera—introducing the audience to Humbert's European background and pathology (*LoScreen* 2–3, 8–9). At the end of Nabokov's screenplay, after Ray has made several more appearances on camera, the psychiatrist's voice supplies an epilogue to the film's action, which closes with Humbert's farewell visit to Lolita (*LoScreen* 212–13).

Both Kubrick and Lyne eschewed this device, but Kubrick took up Nabokov's second and boldest idea for distancing the audience. The director moved the novel's climactic scene—Humbert's comically grotesque killing of Quilty—from the last pages of the book to the opening shots of the film. In a long parodic sequence, Humbert repeatedly fires shots into Quilty's body as the drunken man, played by Peter Sellers, absurdly refuses to die. As Quilty engages in a Ping-Pong game with his killer, his desperate effort to stall for time is hilariously rendered, while his fear remains palpable. The scene is a

---

4. Thomas R. Frosch, "Parody and Authenticity in *Lolita*," in *Nabokov's Fifth Arc: Nabokov and Others on His Life's Work*, ed. J. E. Rivers and Charles Nicol (Austin: University of Texas Press, 1982), 181.

masterly re-creation, in cinematic terms, of the simultaneous sense of horror and hilarity generated by the novel.

Lyne's film opens after Humbert's murder of Quilty. We see a blood-spattered Humbert driving away from the scene of the crime, the police in hot pursuit. Eliminating the parodic element from the outset, Lyne is careful not to give away Quilty's identity. In subsequent shots, as Humbert recollects several brief encounters with his rival, the camera deliberately avoids conveying an image of Quilty's face. Only in the murder scene that comes at the end of the novel does the audience gain full view of Quilty, played by Frank Langella. Full view, indeed: The audience sees repeated shots of Quilty's naked body as well as of his face. Such visual candor, while faithful to the narrator's description of Quilty as "naked and goatish under his robe," creates an odd effect after all the oblique, carefully restrained shots of Swain's lithe body (*Lo* 299). As we watch Quilty's bathrobe repeatedly flap open, frankly displaying Langella's genitals, we sense the director's exultation at finally having an adult subject—at being able to let go. Liberated from the onerous legal strictures of filming the child, Lyne can have Langella shot in every sense: Quilty's striptease ends as blood spurts from his chest and mouth. The scene comes closer to Grand Guignol than to Nabokov's sinister comedy.

Lyne's rendering of Charlotte's death, by contrast, is straightforward. Having rushed into the street after discovering Humbert's secret diary, which details his desire for her daughter, Charlotte is summarily run over by a passing car. For his purposes, Kubrick invents a comic aftermath to this event—cutting directly from the scene of the accident to the bathroom of the Haze household. Here an exhausted Humbert—badly shaken but secretly rapturous at his sudden, blissful promotion to the rank of Lolita's only apparent parent—sits soaking in the bathtub. As he takes a festive swig from the bottle of Scotch in his hand, the bather looks up to see Charlotte's friends, John and Jean Farlow, gazing at him with concern from the bathroom door. A pistol that, by another twist of fate, happens to be lying nearby confirms the Farlows' worst fears: The inconsolable widower may try to kill himself. Taking his cue from their expressions, tipsy Humbert struggles to assume the sorrowful demeanor of a grieving husband. Now Kubrick's audience watches, amused and entranced, as bathwater and whiskey bottle become supporting props in Humbert's new role—that of a man drowning in sorrow. Created whole cloth from the director's imagination, the scene serves as a brilliant cinematic correlative to the ironic shifts and witty reversals of Humbert's inimitable narrative voice.

The humor of Kubrick's film owes much of its life to what Richard Schickel calls Sellers's "comic malevolence," and Kubrick takes full advantage of the comedian's genius for improvisation.[5] Taking his cue from Nabokov's screenplay, Kubrick has Quilty shadow Humbert (as his sexual proclivities shadow, or darkly duplicate, Humbert's nympholepsy) much earlier in the film than in the novel. With the camera granting Quilty a more explicit, less hallucinatory presence, Kubrick gives Sellers ample opportunity to adopt outlandish guises and disguises. The comedian runs through a gamut of screen stereotypes—from the tough Brando wiseguy to the officious German psychiatrist, whose absurdly thick accent and rigid gestures caricature a host of Hollywood Hitlers and camp doctors. Hilarious as most of these parodies are, it *is* possible to have too much of a good thing.[6] By handing Quilty's screen persona most of the wit, energy, and parodic self-consciousness that Humbert exhibits in the novel, Kubrick leaves his protagonist precious little to do. Only Shelley Winters's brilliant portrayal of Lolita's widowed mother gives Mason the opportunity to rise above wooden passivity.

Some of Mason's best scenes slyly point up the contrast between the fascination that Humbert's European demeanor exerts on adult women and his abysmal indifference to their full-blown charms. Both Mason and Irons do an excellent job of conveying the cultivated Humbertian manner that reduces Lolita's mother to abject worship. When Humbert, in quest of a summer rental, arrives on Charlotte's doorstep, his dark good looks and cultivated accent fire her connubial and cultural ambitions. Applying liberal doses of perfume, pink "champagne," and bad poetry to the task of ensnaring handsome "Hum," Charlotte is ludicrously unaware of the real source of her success. The artful balance Winters strikes between Charlotte Haze's vulgar pretensions and her touching vulnerability is at once funny and poignant. But where Winters is fuzzily helpless, Melanie Griffith is merely harsh, her strident voice and calculating manner eliminating much chance for humor.

After Charlotte's accidental death, Kubrick's film as a whole loses life. The director takes surprisingly little advantage of the way in which Charlotte and

---

5. Schickel, "Peek," 91.

6. According to James Mason, Kubrick "was so besotted with the genius of Peter Sellers that he seemed never to have enough of him": James Mason, *Before I Forget* (London: Hamish Hamilton, 1981), 430, as cited in Brian Boyd, *Vladimir Nabokov: The American Years* (Princeton, N.J.: Princeton University Press, 1991), 464.

Humbert's miscommunications are played out in another key by Humbert and her daughter. As they travel aimlessly across the country, Humbert and Lolita spend countless hours trapped in the same car or motel room, but they cannot bridge the cultural chasm, the sheer moral void that stretches like the Grand Canyon between them. As Humbert is forced to assume the roles of both parent and perverse lover, the novel records his baffled reaction to the exotic habits and eerie vulgarity of American adolescents. Here Lyne's Lolita proves more resonant than Kubrick's—even though she is inches taller (and rounder) than Nabokov's little girl. Manipulating sticky mounds of bubblegum and noisy jawbreakers to needle her nervous captor, Dominique Swain captures to a T Lolita's trite toughness.

Hypnotized by the media, with its "adman visions" and celluloid versions of romance, Lolita has absolute faith—what Humbert calls "celestial trust"—in their false promises. "She it was," he remarks, "to whom ads were dedicated: the ideal consumer, the subject and object of every foul poster" (*Lo* 148, 155). By the same token, Lolita's naive infatuation quickly turns to contempt when Humbert fails to live up to the "cool" Hollywood hero for whom she initially mistook him. "You talk like a book, *Dad*," she remarks with adolescent suspicion (*Lo* 114). Later, after wariness turns to open disgust, she finds other ways to comment on Humbert's "corny" language: "We passed the New Hotel, and she laughed," Humbert says as they drive away from the town of Beardsley. "'A penny for your thoughts,' I said and she stretched out her palm at once" (*Lo* 208).

In his film, Kubrick gets surprisingly little mileage out of the incongruities, funny and sad, generated by the clash between generations, and cultures, that Humbert and Lolita act out. In the novel, moreover, dramatic incongruities provide ironic distance and comic relief for the reader, who might otherwise find their relationship intolerable. As Humbert waits, trembling with anticipation, for Lolita to fall asleep in the hotel bedroom where they spend their first, fated night together, his romantic ardor is abruptly and ludicrously undercut. In an ironic juxtaposition worthy of Flaubert, Nabokov has Humbert suffer an attack of lowly indigestion: The inflamed lover is overcome by heartburn. Nor does the irony escape Paris-born Humbert, who takes time out to quip: "[T]hey call those fries 'French,' *grand Dieu!*" (*Lo* 129). Humbert's bouts with American "French" fries, mounds of "cottage-cheese-crested salads" looming in diners across the land, and a host of other New World phenomena do not win much attention from either director (*Lo* 148).

Although few writers have rendered with Nabokov's visual acuity the fertile absurdities of the American highway, neither film explores this richly comic vein. Targeting the phony and the philistine, Nabokov's novel spoofs mid-century American popular culture—from Lolita's goony movie magazines to Charlotte's worshipful home-decorating manuals, from "progressive" schools and summer camps to preposterous dude ranches. Kubrick's audience gleans only the faintest reflection of this panorama. Satire gets even shorter shrift in Lyne's film, where it would only puncture the intensity of Humbert's melancholy.

Exposing Humbert's desire for the nymphet as a travesty of romantic love, Nabokov's novel opens with an account of the protagonist's Riviera childhood and adolescent romance. Just as Humbert's desire for Lolita rehearses Edgar Allan Poe's love for his young cousin Virginia Clemm—whom the poet married when he was twenty-seven and she was thirteen—so Humbert's dead childhood sweetheart, Annabel Leigh, is parodically named after the poem Poe dedicated to his dead child bride.[7] Even the setting of "Annabel Lee," with its haunting "kingdom by the sea," is parodically reflected in the Riviera idyll that Humbert, at age thirteen, shares with his Annabel—"a lovely child a few months [his] junior" who dies shortly afterwards of "typhus in Corfu" (*Lo* 12–13).

Nabokov's published screenplay mirrors this theme, providing a series of flashbacks that detail his love for twelve-year-old Annabel Leigh (*LoScreen* 5–7). Kubrick, however, banishes all trace of Humbert's personal past, erasing the suggestive connection between Humbert's ardor for certain sylphlike young "maidens," or "nymphets," and the romantic's quest for a lost paradise or Arcadia. Like so many romantic dreamers before him, Humbert is captivated by an ideal image—an impossible and alluring vision. True to his romantic heritage, he claims to perceive in certain rare and bewitching "girl-children" between the ages "of nine and fourteen" the "demoniac" beauty and fatal allure of a "nymphet" (*Lo* 16). True to her romantic origins, the bewitching "nymphet" is an impossible object of desire, the mythic creation and object of Humbert's fertile imagination. In ardent pursuit of his Arcadia, Humbert can possess, in the physical or sexual sense, only the *body* of a child he has

---

7. For the novel's many references to Poe, see *AnL* 328–32. Appel also points out that Virginia Clemm—who died "of a lingering disease in 1847," eleven years after she and Poe married—was the "inspiration for many of his [Poe's] poems": ibid., 357.

imaginatively transformed—or, as he puts it, "safely solipsized"—into the figment of his dreaming mind (*Lo* 60). And that is exactly what he does to the twelve-year-old child Dolores Haze.

Lyne mines this material but ignores the comedy these scenes generate in the novel—as thirteen-year-old Humbert and his adorable Annabel furtively, and futilely, attempt to consummate their love. Sustaining the dominant chord of nostalgic melancholy, Lyne conveys Humbert's adolescent love for Annabel in sepia-tinted images. Stripped of irony, the sequence, which ends with young Humbert's sobbing at the news of Annabel's death, offers Lyne's audience an easy explanation for the adult's lifelong obsession. Translating parody into sentiment, Lyne winds up championing what the novel spoofs: a pop psychologist's account of Humbert's irrepressible desire for nymphets. By clinically "solving" the mystery at the heart of Humbert's longing, Lyne simplifies, and renders less sinister, its dark power. Kubrick's own efforts to make Humbert a more sympathetic character—by transferring most of his predatory cunning and duplicity to Clare Quilty—similarly backfires: It leaves his film with barely a trace of the novel's tragic resonance and moral depth. By reducing the magnitude of Humbert's crime in the viewer's eyes, Kubrick paradoxically creates a work that is often heartless, especially in the attitude it adopts toward the victimized child.

In the novel, Humbert continually reminds the reader that all the eloquent turns and comic twists of his "fancy prose style" are meant to conceal as well as reveal the details of his story (*Lo* 9). Only gradually, and with great difficulty, can he bring himself to expose the truth of the tale he has to tell: that at age thirty-seven he developed a passion for a twelve-year-old child whom he subsequently begged and bribed, cajoled and tyrannized into sexual cohabitation. As he recounts his relationship with Lolita three years after she has run away from him, Humbert slowly allows certain "smothered memories" to come to light (*Lo* 284). As he does so, these recollected scenes gradually define the difference between Humbert's imaginative creation, the "nymphet" Lolita, and the preadolescent Dolly Haze whose childhood he destroyed. Thus, a gap slowly widens in the narrator's rhetoric, exposing the moral abyss that he cannot gloss over.

At the end of his story, Humbert gazes openly into that abyss and pronounces his own sentence: "Unless it can be proven to me ... that in the infinite run it does not matter a jot that a North American girl-child named Dolores Haze had been deprived of her childhood by a maniac, unless this can be proven (and if it can, then life is a joke), I see nothing for the treatment of my misery but the melancholy and very local palliative of articulate art" (*Lo* 283). Only in art can Humbert restore to the child he tyrannized—the child whose "life," as he says, he "broke"—some semblance of her rightful autonomy, which he failed to grant her during their brief life together (*Lo* 279).

Little of Nabokov's resonant theme of remorse and awakened conscience—a theme to which Lyne's film is almost exclusively dedicated—survives in Kubrick's version. True, Kubrick reveals Humbert in an increasingly brutal light, as the abject lover shifts from toady (painting Lolita's toenails) to tyrant (twisting her arm when she defies him). But Sue Lyon, pert and sophisticated, never strikes the audience as possessed of an inner life. All that she has to withhold from Humbert is her plan to escape with Quilty. By making Lolita appear so grown-up, Kubrick may have avoided public censure, but in failing to reveal the child in the nymphet, his film betrays the innocence that public morality and the censor purport to defend.

At one point in the novel, Humbert admits to his readers that Lolita cried "every night" of their early life together (*Lo* 176). In keeping with Lyne's more sensitive rendering of the child's plight, his audience sees and hears Lolita sobbing on several occasions. In Kubrick's film, Lolita cries only once—when Humbert tells her that her mother is dead. But the pretty teenager's tears are quickly dried when Humbert promises to buy her a new hi-fi and records. Kubrick's Lolita remains remarkably untouched, and unchanged, from the moment the audience first sees her at age twelve to her final appearance, years later, as a callous young housewife of seventeen.

When Humbert rediscovers Lolita three years after their separation, she is married to a poor but kindly mechanic, Dick Schiller, whose partial deafness underscores his imperfect knowledge of his young wife's past. To him, Humbert is merely a concerned father who has come to visit and lend financial assistance now that a baby is on the way. In Kubrick's film, it is not only Dick Schiller's view of reality that has been whitewashed; Kubrick's audience is handed a scrubbed-up version of Lolita's dismal existence. Instead of finding pregnant Mrs. Schiller's "rope-veined" hands and "ruined looks" in doleful harmony with her surroundings, Mason meets Lyon in a cozy cabin, where she is briskly ironing a pile of laundry. Her blonde locks neatly circled by a bow, Humbert's erstwhile nymphet is not clad, as Nabokov has it, in a shabby dress and "sloppy felt slippers" but in a spanking new maternity smock (*Lo* 269, 277).

Lyne's film does far more justice to this poignant aspect of the novel. Gazing at Humbert through a pair of plastic-rimmed glasses, frumpy Dominique Swain exhibits no trace of her former gaiety and insouciance. In this touching scene, one of the most moving and effective in Lyne's film, poverty and disarray bespeak the despoilment of a child's life. We also see their effect on Humbert, who holds himself responsible. That Lolita knows next to nothing about him—except that he made tireless use of her body during their years together—only reinforces Humbert's perception that, as he says in the novel, "[S]omething within her [had] been broken by me" (*Lo* 232). Such nuances of emotion are movingly conveyed by Irons; Mason has no chance to attempt effects that lie outside the range of Kubrick's dark comedy.

In contemplating the mutually exclusive achievements of these two ambitious films, one is reminded of F. Scott Fitzgerald's observation, "[T]he test of a first-rate intelligence is the ability to hold two opposed ideas in the mind at the same time, and still retain the ability to function."[8] Whether such daring equipoise can be achieved on screen is debatable; clearly, neither Lyne nor Kubrick has managed it. To witness such a feat—to discover art in the act of defying logic and gravity—we must return to Nabokov's masterpiece.

---

8. F. Scott Fitzgerald, "The Crack-Up [1936]," in *The Crack-Up: With Other Uncollected Pieces, Note-Books and Unpublished Letters*, ed. Edmund Wilson (New York: New Directions, 1956), 69.

{ 8 }

Pale Fire
The *Vanessa atalanta*

BRIAN BOYD

The unexpected evidence advanced in "Shade and Shape in *Pale Fire*"[1] that Shade's spirit seems to shape the Gradus sections of Kinbote's Commentary, that he is somehow safe on the other side of death, immediately prompts another question, a question Shade's poem has in fact raised from the first: What about Hazel, the daughter he loved, whose death forms the anguished centerpiece of "Pale Fire"?[2]

After recounting Hazel's suicide in canto 2, Shade reports early in canto 3 on the Institute of Preparation for the Hereafter (IPH) and the possibility or impossibility of meeting in death those we have loved. Late in canto 4, he announces himself

>   reasonably sure that we survive
> And that my darling somewhere is alive,
> As I am reasonably sure that I
> 980 Shall wake at six tomorrow, on July
> The twenty-second, nineteen fifty-nine.

---

1. Brian Boyd, "Shape and Shade in *Pale Fire*," *Nabokov Studies* 4 (1998): 173–224. That article and this chapter form parts of Brian Boyd, *Nabokov's* Pale Fire: *The Magic of Artistic Discovery* (Princeton, N.J.: Princeton University Press, 1999).

2. References to *Pale Fire* are to the 1989 Vintage International edition, a corrected version (but with the same pagination) of the first edition (New York: Putnam's, 1962). Where the source is not already explicit, citations will be in the form P.xxx, C.xxx (for Poem or Commentary); page numbers are added, if needed, within long notes in the Commentary.

Of course, he does not wake the next day, and that appears to refute his "my darling somewhere is alive." But if we now know that *he* survives, suddenly the question becomes urgent: *Is* Hazel "somewhere . . . alive"?

Of course, that question has been of utmost urgency for Shade himself ever since she died. "I was the shadow of the waxwing slain / By the false azure in the window-pane," he begins his poem, and at dead center he places Hazel's death, triggered when her first blind date recoils:

> After he'd gone the three young people stood
> Before the azure entrance for a while.
> Puddles were neon-barred; and with a smile
> She said she'd be *de trop*, she'd much prefer
> 400 Just going home.

In that red neon bar[3] in the azure reflected in the puddle, Shade shows that even in the waxwing image, with its azure reflection and the implied red streak of the waxwing's wing, he imagines projecting himself beyond death partly in order to see if Hazel is there.

Throughout the poem, Shade's preoccupation continues. Describing his house and garden in canto 1, he writes:

> I had a favorite young shagbark there
> 50 With ample dark jade leaves and a black, spare,
> Vermiculated trunk. The setting sun
> Bronzed the black bark, around which, like undone
> Garlands, the shadows of the foliage fell.
> It is now stout and rough; it has done well.
> White butterflies turn lavender as they
> Pass through its shade where gently seems to sway
> The phantom of my little daughter's swing.

After switching explicitly to the theme of exploring death's abyss in canto 2, he muses there:

> It isn't that we dream too wild a dream:
> The trouble is we do not make it seem
> Sufficiently unlikely; for the most
> 230 We can think up is a domestic ghost.

---

3. Although "neon signs" now loosely refer to many kinds of display lighting, neon itself burns a brilliant orangy red.

In canto 3, he looks at Hazel's recent death in the light of his earlier experience at the IPH:

> That tasteless venture helped me in a way.
> I learnt what to ignore in my survey
> Of death's abyss. And when we lost our child
> I knew there would be nothing: no self-styled
> Spirit would touch a keyboard of dry wood
> 650 To rap out her pet name; no phantom would
> Rise gracefully to welcome you and me
> In the dark garden, near the shagbark tree.

Shade seems agnostic, even dismissive, about the possibility of Hazel's survival as conventional ghost, phantom, shade, but in canto 4 he ends by affirming his sense of harmony between the order of his verse and his universe and his confidence that somewhere she is alive. He looks out to see Sybil's shadow near the shagbark, and the "dark Vanessa with the crimson band . . . its ink-blue wingtips flecked with white" that echoes both the red-streaked wing of the waxwing in his opening line and the white butterfly turning lavender in the shadow of Hazel's shagbark. Summoning together these signs, he affirms design even in what seem the random remains of the day.

At first Shade's affirmations appear to be negated by the terminal interruption of his murder, but then, as we discover, he finds unfolding for him beyond death a deeper order than he expected, a series of radiant surprises about his "fantastically planned, / Richly rhymed life" (P.969–70). If his sudden death appears to negate his trust in cosmic order, only for that negation itself to be negated and lead into a succession of astonishing positives, what then of Hazel? What of his greatest loss in life? Does she not form part of what he discovers in death?

Surely she does. The redoubled urgency of the question almost indicates a positive answer.

Still, we do not know where to find it. But the stress in Shade's poem on the garden, on Hazel's shagbark, on butterflies showing or changing color in the low sun, on shadows and shades and phantoms, becomes more insistent the more we reread. Shade's very negation, as he contemplates her death—

> no phantom would
> Rise gracefully to welcome you and me
> In the dark garden, near the shagbark tree

—itself seems to invite its own refutation. And there is one quite spectacular appearance of a butterfly in the garden that plays in the setting sun on the edge of light and shade just a moment after Shade finishes his poem, a moment before he meets his death.

Even on a first reading of the novel, we enter an aura of mystery in the description of the *Vanessa atalanta* that cavorts exuberantly around Shade just before his death. As the time of composition and the time of narration converge at the end of *Pale Fire,* Shade gazes about him, searching for his wife: "Where are you? In the garden. I can see / Part of your shadow near the shagbark tree" (P.989-90), and watches as

> A dark Vanessa with a crimson band
> Wheels in the low sun, settles on the sand
> And shows its ink-blue wingtips flecked with white.

Immediately after finishing the poem, he walks over with Kinbote, who has the manuscript tucked under his arm, toward the Goldsworth house. Kinbote tells the story:

> One minute before his death, as we were crossing from his demesne to mine and had begun working up between the junipers and ornamental shrubs, a Red Admirable (see note to line 270) came dizzily whirling around us like a colored flame. Once or twice before we had already noticed the same individual, at that same time, on that same spot, where the low sun finding an aperture in the foliage splashed the brown sand with a last radiance while the evening's shade covered the rest of the path. One's eyes could not follow the rapid butterfly in the sunbeams as it flashed and vanished, and flashed again, with an almost frightening imitation of conscious play which now culminated in its settling upon my delighted friend's sleeve. It took off, and we saw it next moment sporting in an ecstasy of frivolous haste around a laurel shrub, every now and then perching on a lacquered leaf and sliding down its grooved middle like a boy down the banisters on his birthday. Then the tide of the shade reached the laurels, and the magnificent, velvet-and-flame creature dissolved in it. (C.993-95, 290)

Even when we first encounter this passage it seems charged with promise or foreboding—in its attribution of conscious intelligence to the butterfly; in its extraordinary effects of color and sun and shade; in the suggestion that the butterfly might be either tugging at Shade's sleeve, warning him not to cross into the Goldsworth garden, or acclaiming his newest and finest poem ("sporting in an ecstasy of frivolous haste around a laurel shrub . . . sliding down its grooved middle like a boy down the banisters"). Alvin Kernan comments that "[a] reader inescapably responds to this butterfly, even as Shade responded to the white fountain, particularly because of its appearance at the moment of death and the verbal associations with 'shade' and the poet's laurels, as a manifestation of some transcendental force in the universe moving in correspondence with human life."[4] That perhaps overstates or overdefines our initial response, but certainly we react with a sense of wonder to something that, given Shade's imminent death, ought to be an omen yet feels anything but ominous.

Nevertheless, where does it lead? Four pages later—and even on a first reading we know that this will happen at any moment—Shade is shot, and the human drama outweighs any incidental butterfly. Yet each time we return to that passage—a little more conscious, too, each time, of the butterfly–shagbark–shade–phantom links within the poem—we feel that same charge renewed. Still it does not lead anywhere.

This should be a familiar situation for us at this point in reading *Pale Fire*. The "pada ata lane . . ." message in the Haunted Barn also carried a charge of promise from the first, even though the promise soon seemed neutralized in a bath of skeptical irony. When we decipher it as Aunt Maud's message warning via Hazel not to let her father "go to Goldsworth's" on the evening he is shot,[5] it still seems to lead nowhere. Now that we have seen the signs of Shade's survival, we know that the message was not an isolated freak. Perhaps we had better return to it.

Although we see little of Hazel, we do see that she is consistently associated with the paranormal: with the poltergeist that disturbs her just after Maud dies and that seems to reflect Maud's personality, and with the "roundlet of pale light" in the Haunted Barn, which we can also discern spells out for Hazel a message from her great-aunt. But to Hazel, both poltergeist and ghostly light seem chilling and disturbing, frustratingly indecisive and meaningless.

4. Alvin Kernan, "Reading Zemblan," in *The Imaginary Library* (Princeton, N.J.: Princeton University Press, 1982), reprinted in Harold Bloom, ed., *Vladimir Nabokov: Modern Critical Views* (New York: Chelsea House, 1987), 121.

5. The message was first deciphered by Robert Martin Adams, *Afterjoyce* (New York: Oxford University Press, 1977), 153. See also Brian Boyd, *Vladimir Nabokov: The American Years* (Princeton, N.J.: Princeton University Press, 1991), 454.

Yet unlike Hazel, we not only can read a message in the light in the barn, a hint of Shade's still distant death, but we should also now be able to detect a curious triple flash in "pada *ATA LAN*e pad no*T* ogo old w*A*r*T ALAN T*her t*A*le feur f*A*r r*A*n*T LANT* t*A*l told" (C.347, 188) of the *atalanta* butterfly that greets Shade just the moment before he does in fact "go to Goldsworth's" and his death.[6] This subliminal threefold insistence seems still stronger and stranger when we notice the stress on threefold repetition in the report on the Haunted Barn: "There are always 'three nights' in fairy tales, and in this sad fairy tale there was a third one too" (C.347, 190). On the third night in the barn, there is no sign whatever of the "pale light," nothing to add to the apparently senseless babble of the "talking light." But on a rereading, we could decipher its direct message. Can we now, on a re-rereading, also make sense of its *atalanta* undertone?

One of the real difficulties of Nabokov's patterns is that they all interconnect, as things do in this complicated and interesting world of ours. Whatever charge of unresolved import we feel in the description of the *Vanessa atalanta*, a charge boosted immeasurably by the *atalanta*'s flashing through Maud's ghostly message, we cannot dissociate the *Vanessa* from Sybil Shade. After explaining how he first fell in love with his wife, John Shade turns to her directly:

Come and be worshiped, come and be caressed,
270 My dark Vanessa, crimson-barred, my blest
My Admirable butterfly!

At the end of the poem, again, Shade looks over at his wife just before catching sight of the *Vanessa* that will greet him a few minutes later and describes it so as to echo the Admirable he described in his appeal to his wife:

Where are you? In the garden. I can see
990 Part of your shadow near the shagbark tree.
Somewhere horseshoes are being tossed. Click. Clunk.
(Leaning against its lamppost like a drunk.)
A dark Vanessa with a crimson band
Wheels in the low sun, settles on the sand
And shows its ink-blue wingtips flecked with white.

6. Gennady Barabtarlo was the first to notice this threefold *"atalanta"* in his *Aerial View: Essays on Nabokov's Art and Metaphysics* (New York: Peter Lang, 1993), 207.

Pale Fire

Although the *Vanessa atalanta* that dances on and around Shade as he walks to his death seems to carry some transcendental charge, Sybil herself is very much alive. In fact, she has just driven off to a dinner meeting of her club before Kinbote comes over to invite Shade back for a drink. So how can that mysterious *Vanessa* be as mysterious as *seems* to be suggested by the timing and description of its last appearance in Kinbote's note and by that covert fairy-tale triple invocation in Maud's ghostly message? If the *Vanessa* evokes Sybil, how can it also fit within, as it seems to, the pattern of references to Hazel, the garden, the shagbark, shade, butterflies changing color in the shadows, phantoms?

To pose the problem that way is almost to prompt the solution.

Shade introduces Hazel abruptly into the poem, just after addressing Sybil as "My dark Vanessa," with the regretful report that, unfortunately for her, Hazel's looks took after not her beautiful mother's beauty but his own short, fat, twisted self:

>   And I love you most
> 290 When with a pensive nod you greet her ghost
>   And hold her first toy on your palm, or look
>   At a postcard from her, found in a book.
>
>   She might have been you, me, or some quaint blend:
>   Nature chose me so as to wrench and rend
>   Your heart and mine . . . .
>
>   . . . . while children of her age
> 310 Were cast as elves and fairies on the stage
>   That *she*'d helped paint for the school pantomime,
>   My gentle girl appeared as Mother Time,
>   A bent charwoman with slop pail and broom,
>   And like a fool I sobbed in the men's room.
>
>   Another winter was scrape-scooped away.
>   The Toothwort White haunted our woods in May.
>   Summer was power-mowed, and autumn, burned.
>   Alas, the dingy cygnet never turned
>   Into a wood duck.

Notice that "with a pensive nod you greet her *ghost*" brings Hazel forward for the first time directly into the poem. The one fleeting reference to her before this had been to "The *phantom* of my little daughter's swing."

But what do we make of the last lines of that quotation? Kinbote explains Shade's sly twist on the Hans Christian Andersen story, his wittily reversing the conventional preference for the swan in favor of the multicolored splendor of the duck: "The wood duck, a richly colored bird, emerald, amethyst, carnelian, with black and white markings, is incomparably more beautiful than the much-overrated swan, a serpentine goose with a dirty neck of yellowish plush and a frogman's black rubber flaps" (C.319).

Kinbote is helpful here, but he is no naturalist. In the preceding note, he is helpless to explain Shade's "The Toothwort White haunted our woods in May":

> Frankly, I am not certain what this means. My dictionary defines "toothwort" as "a kind of cress" and the noun "white" as "any pure white breed of farm animal or a certain genus of lepidoptera." Little help is provided by the variant written in the margin:
>
> > In woods Virginia Whites occurred in May
>
> Folklore characters, perhaps? Fairies? Or cabbage butterflies? (C.316)

The Toothwort White or West Virginia White (*Pieris [Artogeia] virginiensis*)[7] is, in fact, a woodland butterfly whose numbers are dwindling rapidly through loss of its native habitat. Far from being a "cabbage butterfly," as Kinbote vaguely proposes, the Toothwort White for a long time was not distinguished from *Pieris napi*, the Mustard White, which has suffered population loss through competition with the introduced European *Pieris rapae*, the Cabbage White.[8]

After his helpless gloss on the Toothwort White and his helpful one on the dingy cygnet and wood duck, Kinbote has only one more short, four-line note

---

7. At the time Nabokov was most interested in these butterflies, they were still known by the genus name *Pieris;* that has since been revised to *Artogeia*. "Toothwort White," far from being an accepted common name, seems to have been proposed here for the first time by Shade and Nabokov. The lepidopterist Robert Dirig, who tried to propose a new common name because the West Virginia White is not in fact confined to West Virginia, finds Nabokov's proposal superior to his own proposed "Woodland White," because the butterfly's relatives are also named for the plants on which they feed. For example, the Cabbage White feeds on cabbages (sometimes); the Mustard White feeds on mustard plants (usually); and the Toothwort White feeds on toothworts (almost always).

8. Alexander B. Klots, *A Field Guide to the Butterflies of North America, East of the Great Plains* (Boston: Houghton Mifflin, 1951), 201; Robert Michael Pyle, *The Audubon Society Field Guide to North American Butterflies* (New York: Knopf, 1981), 359. Shade's lines accurately reflect the timing of the butterfly's appearance: the adult butterfly lives for only two weeks in late April and early May.

before the note on the Haunted Barn, the note where Hazel is continuously present longer than anywhere else in poem or commentary, the note where the *atalanta* recurs three fairy-tale times in Maud's message.

But the note begins with Kinbote's description of the owner of the barn, Paul Hentzner, with whom Shade had once rambled every other evening, attracted especially by the German farmer's knowledge of plants and animals: "[H]e esteemed Hentzner for knowing 'the names of things'" (C.347, 185). Coming less than a page after Kinbote's failure to identify the Toothwort White, this ought to strike us as a clear Nabokovian directive: We really should identify that butterfly. Shade certainly knows it. Kinbote has earlier complained about the poet's "coquettish way of pointing out with the tip of his cane various curious natural objects" during their sunset rambles: "He never tired of illustrating by means of these examples the extraordinary blend of Canadian Zone and Austral Zone that 'obtained,' as he put it, in that particular spot of Appalachia where at our altitude of about 1,500 feet northern species of birds, insects and plants commingled with southern representatives" (C.238, 168–69). Had Kinbote paid a little more attention, he might have heard about the Toothwort White, which is indeed mostly a Transitional Zone[9] butterfly, like the *Lycaeides melissa samuelis,* the Karner Blue, that Nabokov himself named in 1943 and first saw on the wing in 1950.[10]

---

9. "The Transition Zone is . . . not well marked in itself, but rather a borderline or tension zone where Canadian and Austral zones meet and mingle. . . . A few butterflies found mostly in the Transition Zone are: *Pieris virginiensis,* . . . *Lycaeides melissa samuelis*": Klots, *Field Guide,* 25.

10. Vladimir Nabokov, "The Nearctic Forms of *Lycaeides* Hüb[ner] (Lycaenidae, Lepidoptera)," *Psyche* 50 (1943): 87–99. As Robert Dirig notes, Nabokov later came to think that this was not just a subspecies but a distinct species, "[b]ut he did not live to do the taxonomic work necessary to prove this, and the question remains" open: Robert Dirig, "Nabokov's Blue Snowflakes," *Natural History* 97 (1988): 68–69. The Cornell entomologist John G. Franclemont reports that he collected butterflies with Nabokov in the Ithaca area "on a very few occasions in the spring" in the early 1950s. "He was interested in collecting one of the 'Whites,' *Pieris virginiensis.* One trip that I recall with pleasure was to McLean Bogs in the second week of May; it was an afternoon of delightful weather and discussions, but no white butterflies": John G. Franclemont, "Remembering Nabokov," in *The Achievements of Vladimir Nabokov,* ed. George Gibian and Stephen Jan Parker (Ithaca, N.Y.: Cornell Center for International Studies, 1984), 227–28. A few years later (May 31, 1959), Nabokov wrote to Franclemont: "In April we stayed for a week in the Great Smokies, Tenn., where we had a delightful time with *Pieris virginiensis*": see Brian Boyd and Robert Michael Pyle, eds., *Nabokov's Butterflies* (Boston: Beacon, 2000), 528. Nabokov caught his first *virginiensis* on April 21, 1959.

The Toothwort White is "dusky white with smoky gray-brown scaling"[11] and, like the Mustard White with which it was long confused, "quite shy."[12] The *Vanessa atalanta*, by contrast, is, in the words of the lepidopterist Robert Michael Pyle, "Unmistakable and unforgettable.... [It] will alight on a person's shoulder day after day in a garden.... In midsummer it is not unusual to see them chasing each other."[13] As Kinbote correctly notes, the *atalanta*, or Red Admirable, "is a most frolicsome fly" (C.270).

The Toothwort White "haunted" our woods in May, Shade says, in the couplet before he laments of his daughter that "Alas, the dingy cygnet never turned / Into a wood duck." Kinbote explains that correctly in terms of the wood duck's having incomparably richer colors than the dingy cygnet. But the Toothwort White is also a dingy white, with a visible scaling, and shy—like the "difficult, morose" Hazel, who has psoriasis (P.357, 355).

Hazel took after her father, not her mother. In Shade's reversed fairy tale, Hazel as dingy cygnet *ought* to have turned into the sumptuous dark colors of the wood duck, but alas she does not. But other negatives turn into positives through death.[14] What if this "alas ... never" is also reversed? If Hazel as Toothwort White—dingy, scaly, withdrawn—now reappears in death as a *Vanessa atalanta*, now takes after her mother, not her father, in looks ("My dark Vanessa, ... / My Admirable") and is now transformed in personality from moroseness to exuberance?

If Hazel can inhabit the *atalanta*, that would suddenly explain the singular charge surrounding the butterfly as it greets Shade moments before his death. It would also explain the fairy-tale repetition of the *atalanta* in the message Maud had spelled out for Hazel; add an ironic twist to Kinbote's "Folklore characters, perhaps? Fairies? Or cabbage butterflies?" in the note about the Toothwort White that immediately precedes his gloss on Shade's reversal of the Ugly Duckling fairy tale; and explain the pattern running through the poem associating the garden, shadows, butterflies, and Hazel's shade. That pattern started with white butterflies changing color as they passed into shade near mementos of Hazel:

> White butterflies turn lavender as they
> Pass through its shade where gently seems to sway
> The phantom of my little daughter's swing.

11. Pyle, *Audubon Society Field Guide*, 359.
12. Klots, *Field Guide*, 201.
13. Pyle, *Audubon Society Field Guide*, 628.
14. See Boyd, *Nabokov's* Pale Fire, chaps. 9-13.

Now it seems to end with another butterfly, with a child's slide echoing a child's swing, and with a spectacular deep flush replacing the white:

> It took off, and we saw it next moment sporting in an ecstasy of frivolous haste around a laurel shrub, every now and then perching on a lacquered leaf and sliding down its grooved middle like a boy down the banisters on his birthday. Then the tide of the shade reached the laurels, and the magnificent, velvet-and-flame creature dissolved in it.

When Hazel headed alone to the edge of Dulwich Forest to investigate the Haunted Barn, like the shy Toothwort White that "haunted our woods," she was troubled and sullen. Now she seems transformed from dinginess and depression into the resplendent color and the confident play of the *atalanta* that she animates for the moment. Then, she was difficult, morose, inclined to sit and moan in a monotone; now, she seems not only to take after her mother in appearance, but also to offer the same kind of support her mother gives to Shade's work as she applauds the poem he has just brought to a close.

If one of our senses identifies something correctly, others will back up the first. Following nature's lead, Nabokov lets us confirm the identification of Hazel with the *atalanta* in several ways. There is space here for only one.

The note on the Haunted Barn provides a key to identifying Hazel in the *Vanessa atalanta*. The "talking light" in the barn whose message Hazel records might be explained away by "an ambushed scamp's toy flashlight" or by Hazel's "own imaginative hysteria," but if such explanations fail, as they appear to, then this message in the barn, even on a first reading, seems to brush closer to the supernatural than anything else in the novel. Yet even Hazel, energized in this scene as nowhere else, can draw only a blank conclusion from the message that cannot begin to be to deciphered until we know about Shade's death. Once we do decode the signal, and once we see the *atalanta* within it, the butterfly that greets Shade walking to his death almost demands deeper explanation.

But the note that records this most supernatural scene in the novel also introduces the novel's most dedicated naturalist, Paul Hentzner, whose "knowing 'the names of things'" (C.347, 185) stands as an invitation to find out more about the Toothwort White and hence discover the parallel to Shade's reversal of the fairy tale of the Ugly Duckling.

This long note on the Haunted Barn points us still another way toward Hazel's transformation. It is Hentzner's son who, Shade recalls, once declared, "Here Papa pisses" (C.347, 186). That "pointless" remark at the edge of Dulwich Forest, as I explain elsewhere,[15] suggests that like the modest Pippa of "Pippa Passes" (1843), whom Browning thought up while walking in a wood near Dulwich, the unassuming Hentzner serves as much more of an inspiration to Shade than the Kinbote who pushes on him his tales of Charles II. But it also points to something else.

In part 2 of Browning's poem, the person inspired as Pippa passes by is the sculptor Jules, an admirer and imitator of Antonio Canova. Jules at one point stops reverently before Canova's famous statue of Psyche holding in her hand a butterfly emblematic of her soul.[16] Webster's Second glosses "Psyche" thus: "*Gr. Antiq.* A lovely maiden, the personification of the soul, usually represented with the wings of a butterfly, emblematic of immortality."[17] In "Pippa Passes," a group of jealous artist friends, offended by Jules's high seriousness of purpose, have duped him into falling in love with an unseen woman, supposedly a passionate admirer of his work, through letters that seem to be from her but that they in fact penned themselves. He marries the naive young woman whom his fellow artists have intimidated into playing the admirer and whom they have instructed to disclose the hoax just after the marriage ceremony. But even as the young woman dutifully recites the speech Jules's colleagues have drafted for her, Jules senses that his young bride genuinely feels for him. He hears Pippa sing as she passes, and her song at once prompts him to take a fresh look at his bride—

---

15. In ibid., chap. 6.

16. "Pippa Passes," pt. 1, ll. 364-65, in Robert Browning, *Poems*, ed. John Pettigrew with Thomas J. Collins (Harmondsworth: Penguin, 1981), 1:314. Canova made two versions of the sculpture. The first (1789-92) is now at Ince Blundell Hall, Lancashire; the second (1793-94) is at the Kunsthalle, Bremen: Giuseppe Pavanello, *L'opera completa del Canova* (Milan: Rizzoli, 1976). Two lines from Dante are inscribed on the second version: "[N]on v'accorgete voi che noi siam vermi / nati a formar l'angelica farfalla . . . ?" ("[A]re you not aware that we are worms, born to form the angelic butterfly . . . ?": *Purgatorio* X.124-25, trans. Charles S. Singleton (Princeton, N.J.: Princeton University Press, 1973), 106-7. Canova also made two versions of "Psyche and Cupid" with a butterfly and two versions of the sculpture without.

17. Speaking about his research for his unfinished *Butterflies in Art* project, Nabokov said of the butterfly paintings he was investigating: "That in some cases the butterfly symbolizes something (e.g., Psyche) lies utterly outside my area of interest" (*SO* 168). This was of course in keeping with the purely taxonomic and evolutionary aims of that project and did not prevent him from using the conventional symbolism elsewhere for an entirely different purpose.

> Look at the woman here with the new soul,
> Like my own Psyche,—fresh upon her lips
> Alit, the visionary butterfly,
> Waiting my word to enter and make bright.[18]

—and to determine on a new life with her and a new course for his art.

Browning's poem seems doubly relevant to Hazel: in young Pippa, a woman unseen or overlooked by others but affecting their lives, and in the statue of Psyche and her butterfly, emblem of the immortality of the soul.

When Hazel explored the barn, she could not construe the ghostly light's message, and even later Kinbote, for all his effort, cannot find in it "the least allusion to the poor girl's fate" (C.347, 189). Concluding his note on the Haunted Barn, Kinbote comments, "There are always 'three nights' in fairy tales, and in this sad fairy tale there was a third one too." He dramatizes the imagined scene—rather well, indeed—to show the blank wait of Hazel with her parents that last night. The playlet ends: *"Two minutes pass. Life is hopeless, afterlife heartless. Hazel is heard quietly weeping in the dark. John Shade lights a lantern. Sybil lights a cigarette. Meeting adjourned"* (192). The experiment seems to prove the hopeless gap between even the dim glimmer of hope of an afterlife that the "roundlet of pale light" had suggested and the blank reality of a dark barn. But for us it proves, if we look closely enough, to allude to the "poor girl's fate"—except that we could hardly call Hazel "poor girl" after her astonishing manifestation as the *Vanessa*.

---

18. "Pippa Passes," pt. 2, ll. 288–91, in Browning, *Poems*, 1:323–24.

{ 9 }

Buzzwords and Dorophonemes
How Words Proliferate and Things Decay in *Ada*

CHARLES NICOL

In a television interview in September 1965, Vladimir Nabokov explained that he was working on a new novel called *The Texture of Time*. A year later, he announced a change in plans: "[M]y *Texture of Time*, now almost half-ready, is only the central rose-web of a much ampler and richer novel, entitled *Ada*" (*SO* 91). It turned out to be part 4; in words similar to Nabokov's description of it in the television interview, its next-to-last paragraph is its own self-reflexive summary description: "My aim was to compose a kind of novella in the form of a treatise on the Texture of Time, an investigation of its veily substance, with illustrative metaphors gradually increasing, very gradually building up a logical love story, going from past to present, blossoming as a concrete story, and just as gradually reversing analogies and disintegrating again into bland abstraction" (*Ada* 562–63). The concrete story consists of Van's drive to Mont Roux for a reunion with Ada, their telephone call, their shock at their mutual aging (almost leading to their going separate ways), and their blissfully permanent reunion.

When Van includes his earlier book as the fourth of *Ada*'s five parts, he is following the lead of another Nabokovian author-narrator, Fyodor Godunov-Cherdyntsev, who included his own earlier *Life of Chernyshevski* as the fourth of *The Gift*'s five sections. But what did Nabokov mean when he called this fourth part "the central rose-web of . . . *Ada*"? It is not physically central, coming

I thank Mary Bellino for her generosity in reading this chapter—twice—and identifying a number of problems. Not only have I followed much of her advice, I have also silently added some of her comments (such as the "polyphony" hidden in "polliphone").

almost at the end, with only twenty-three pages of text left to follow. It does take place in 1922, which is roughly the midpoint in the lives of the long-lived Van and Ada, but that does not seem a sufficient explanation. I assume instead that wherever it is physically placed, like Fyodor's biography in *The Gift*, part 4 is the center—or epicenter—of the novel, with all directions leading out from it.

In a paper delivered in 1976 at the Modern Language Association's first Nabokov session (and published in 1982), I identified the telephone call in part 4 as "the climax of *Ada*" and "the most important event of Van's life."[1] Later, Brian Boyd also found that the pattern of *Ada* "reaches its climax at the turning point of the whole novel" in part 4,[2] but in his view this occurs the next morning: Van and Ada see each other on separate balconies "to crown the pattern" of *Ada*. It is surely curious that, in a novel of 589 pages, we found its climax in different places, roughly five pages and fifteen hours apart. The subject in both places is the reunion of Van and Ada after many years; is it important which is the actual climax? I think it is, because the moment during which Van and Ada talk on the telephone not only unites them, it merges Nabokov's ideas for what had been planned as three separate novels. Thus, this most important moment in the lives of Van and Ada is also the pivotal moment in Nabokov's ability to see this novel as a whole—one epiphany for Van Veen and a quite different one for his creator. It explains much about the concept of Antiterra and the time scheme of the novel; indeed, the entire structure of *Ada* dangles from this single long moment like a pendant jewel flashing as it swings through a sudden ray of light. Therefore, after twenty years, I have returned to this critical moment in *Ada*.

To understand the importance of that call, let us go back to the way *Ada* came into being, as Boyd reported it in the first installment of his long-running "Annotations to *Ada*" in *The Nabokovian:*

> In 1959 Nabokov began to work on a project he thought of as "The Texture of Time" and to toy with another to be called something like "Letters from Terra." After numerous diversions and frustrations, he had a flash late in 1965 of what would become the story of Van and Ada, but the novel did not

---

1. Charles Nicol, "*Ada* or Disorder," in *Nabokov's Fifth Arc: Nabokov and Others on His Life's Work*, ed. J. E. Rivers and Charles Nicol (Austin: University of Texas Press, 1982), 238.
2. Brian Boyd, *Vladimir Nabokov: The American Years* (Princeton, N.J.: Princeton University Press, 1991), 556.

surge into life until February 1966, when he saw the specific link between Van and Ada, "The Texture of Time" and "Letters from Terra," and began to compose apace.[3]

That "specific link" can be found in the first interview Nabokov gave after *Ada* was published: "I began working on the Texture-of-Time section some ten years ago, in Ithaca, upstate New York, but only in February, 1966, did the entire novel leap into the kind of existence that can and must be put into words. Its springboard was Ada's telephone call (in what is now the penultimate part of the book)" (*SO* 122).[4] During the discussion at Cornell in 1998, after I delivered the paper that you are now reading, Brian Boyd volunteered some information on this epiphany that he had not included in his biography. At my urging, he has since made this additional material available in *The Nabokovian*:

> On February 16, 1966, the Nabokovs met James Mason and his partner Countess Vivian di Crespi for lunch at the Hotel Trois Couronnes, the grand hotel on the waterfront at Vevey, the next town along the shore of Lake Geneva to the West of Montreux. The following day Nabokov noted in his diary: "New novel has started to flow." ... The setting of the last chapter of Part Three and the goal and endpoint of Part Four of *Ada* is the Hotel Les Trois Cygnes in Mont Roux, a fusion of the Nabokovs' own hotel, the Montreux Palace Hotel (where they stayed in the older, Cygne, wing...), and the similar-looking and similarly-situated... Trois Couronnes in Vevey. Since Ada uses the in-house phone to call up from the lobby area of the Trois Cygnes to Van, already installed upstairs, and since the idea for that crucial call came to Nabokov within a day after the lunch with Mason and Crespi, it seems highly likely that the Nabokovs' call on the in-house phone up to their lunch hosts the previous day from the lobby floor of the Trois Couronnes precipitated the phone call that at last triggered *Ada*.[5]

---

3. Idem, "Annotations to *Ada:* 1. Part 1, Chapter 1," *The Nabokovian* 30 (spring 1993): 9. Boyd has written so extensively on *Ada* that his commentaries overlap, and other scholars—or, at least, this one—may think that he has not covered some aspect of that novel that in fact he has discussed elsewhere.

4. Also cited in Boyd, *American Years*, 509.

5. Idem, "*Ada*'s Springboard," *The Nabokovian* 41 (fall 1998): 26–27. My initial source was Brian Boyd himself, who generously supplied it by e-mail. His *Nabokovian* note also corrects an inadvertently dropped passage from *American Years*, a hiatus that resulted in less emphasis on the telephone call than he had in fact intended.

Thus, it appears likely that an actual in-house telephone call led to the fictional call that, in turn, was the "springboard" for the novel to "leap into a kind of existence." (Of course, after launching us temporarily into the air, springboards often send us into aqueous regions.) But how does that call link "Letters from Terra," "The Texture of Time," and the story of Van and Ada?

The latter two can be conjoined fairly easily by studying a crucial paragraph during the call:

> That telephone voice, by resurrecting the past and linking it up with the present, with the darkening slate-blue mountains beyond the lake, with the spangles of the sun wake dancing through the poplar, formed the centerpiece in his deepest perception of tangible time, the glittering "now" that was the only reality of Time's texture. After the glory of the summit there came the difficult descent. (*Ada* 556)

This moment is clearly the climax of "The Texture of Time." The telephone voice is the centerpiece of a triptych of which the two linked side panels are the spatial vistas of the present and the memorial vistas of the past. Van had already prepared us to look for such a moment: "To give myself time to time I must move my mind in the direction opposite to that in which I am moving.... The conscious construction of one, and the familiar current of the other give us three or four seconds of what can be felt as nowness. This nowness is the only reality we know" (*Ada* 549–50). This telephone moment has more nowness, more reality, than any other moment in Van's life; it is "the glory of the summit" of reality. And if it is indeed the climax of "The Texture of Time," can the climax of the whole novel *Ada* come five pages later?

To see this telephone call as also the climax of the Van and Ada story, we must remember first that their entire story is intended to be encompassed within the essay that constitutes part 4. Second, that the reason for this longest "now" is that it exists "by resurrecting the past and linking it up with the present," like Proust's madeleine dipped in tea. What makes Van's memory flow into the present is the telephone:

> Now it so happened that she had never—never, at least, in adult life—spoken to him by phone; hence the phone had preserved the very essence, the bright vibration, of her vocal cords, the little "leap" in her larynx, the laugh clinging to the contour of the phrase, as if afraid in girlish glee to slip off the quick words it rode.... Goldenly, youthfully, it bubbled with all the melodious characteristics he knew—or better say recollected, at once, in

the sequence they came: that *entrain*, that whelming of quasi-erotic pleasure, that assurance and animation—and, what was especially delightful, the fact that she was utterly and innocently unaware of the modulations entrancing him. (*Ada* 555)

This description of Van simultaneously experiencing both past and present is written in Nabokov's most ecstatic variety of prose; indeed, "the little 'leap' in her larynx, the laugh clinging to the contour of the phrase" must remind us of what is probably the best-known passage in all of Nabokov's fiction, the "tip of the tongue taking a trip" prose poem with which Humbert invokes his muse at the beginning of his narration in *Lolita*. There is nothing at all comparable in the balcony scene five pages later. (Of course, Boyd has his reasons for choosing the balcony scene as the climax, primarily those involving its hidden references to Lucette. Is it possible to consider the whole section, from phone call through period of doubt to balcony scene, as one extended climactic unit, something like Rex's three-step superhumor in *Laughter in the Dark*?)

But what does this telephone call have to do with a book that was "to be called something like 'Letters from Terra'"? I take this last to be not Van's unsatisfactory 1891 novel briefly summarized in *Ada*, but Nabokov's whole concept of Antiterra as the primary setting for the story of Van and Ada. Antiterra is a place different from Terra either historically, as Brian Boyd and Alfred Appel would have it, or psychologically, as Bobbie Ann Mason and I have argued—that is, after living for many years in a world of two, Van and Ada have re-created the past without any referents outside their own memories and perceptions. This re-created world is called both Antiterra and Demonia in the novel, but it might also be called Vaniada or Veen-us, or even Waterworld (like Venus traditionally, one way of being Antiterra).[6] I believe that the entire novel leapt into existence when Nabokov suddenly saw that the telephone, the most important physical object in Van and Ada's relationship and simultaneously the vehicle of the most important example of "Veen's time," could also be the major technological difference between Terra and Antiterra and that this technological difference could also be explained along a parallel track as simply a matter of the characters' solipsistic perception. How the telephone/dorophone defines the Terra/Antiterra distinction is the subject of the remainder of this chapter.

6. Alfred Appel, Jr., "*Ada* Described," in *Triquarterly* 17 (winter 1970): 160–86; Bobbie Ann Mason, *Nabokov's Garden: A Guide to Ada* (Ann Arbor: Ardis, 1974).

Supposedly, telephones existed on Antiterra early in the nineteenth century, long before Alexander Graham Bell invented them on our world. Actually, the term "telephone" was coined in the eighteenth century on our world as well, where it once described devices that predated Bell's invention: "[T]here were sound telephones and steam telephones and musical telephones long before 1876. In Germany the speaking tube was sometimes called the telephone."[7] So in terms of the word "telephone," Antiterra and Terra could have been synonymous prior to the "L disaster." However, for most of *Ada,* telephones do not exist and are replaced by various substitutes, most often by "dorophones." Whatever it is, the L disaster is not itself the banning of electricity, which is merely a political consequence of the unidentified disaster—indeed, we cannot even say with confidence that electricity has been banned, because that word is never mentioned. However, it is odd that in this first mention, the L disaster "had the singular effect of both causing and cursing the notion of 'Terra.'" Boyd has described his puzzlement at this juxtaposition: "Somehow, in some obscure connection with the 'L disaster,' the notion arose in the Antiterra of the novel that there existed somewhere in space a sibling planet called Terra.... How the 'L disaster' causes and curses the notion of 'Terra' is never spelled out."[8] I also find Nabokov's explanation obscure, but I believe that it is a bit of intentional double-talk, the kind of patter one mutters while stuffing a dove in one's top hat behind one's back; sufficient here is that it does reinforce the connection between telephones and Terra. Presumably telephones are found on Terra; dorophones and other substitutes are found on Antiterra.

But this is not true at the novel's central moment. In part 4, Van and Ada clearly use telephones, which somehow existed in 1922. Their appearance is retrospectively explained by the brief fifth part as being the result of government action: "real lammer" was "forbidden again by 1930" (*Ada* 572). However, if Antiterra is not a "sibling planet" but merely a vision of Terra distorted by memory, pain, and desire, then there are two much more acceptable and logical reasons that telephones exist in 1922 and at practically no other time in the book:

> Van's memories are clustered around this tableau like bees around honey; they have distorted external reality by their density, just as a large body in

---

7. Catherine Mackenzie, *Alexander Graham Bell: The Man Who Contracted Space* (Boston: Houghton Mifflin, 1928), 7.
8. Brian Boyd, "Annotations to *Ada*: 3. Part 1, Chapter 3," *The Nabokovian* 32 (spring 1994): 55, 62.

space bends light. Here, then, is the novel's major source of distortion. For instance, the continually destroyed and re-invented telephone of Antiterra makes no sense without Van's further comment on that conversation: "Now, it so happened that she had never—never, at least, in adult life—spoken to him by phone; hence the phone had preserved the very essence, the bright vibration, of her vocal cords, the little 'leap' in her larynx, the laugh clinging to the contour of the phrase, as if afraid in girlish glee to slip off the quick words it rode." In Van's solipsistic universe, the power of that telephone call negates the existence of all other telephonic memories; since there are no previous telephones in Van's memory, no telephones existed before 1922.[9]

There is another, simpler reason for the telephone's appearance in 1922, also depending on the assumption that Van and Ada alter the past as they try to remember it while writing *Ada*. They write the rest of *Ada* from 1957 through 1967, but part 4 was written as it happened, in 1922, and supposedly was published in 1924. Because the shaping power of memory had no opportunity to interfere with immediate perceptions, in that book Van and Ada talked on the telephone rather than on a mental substitute.

Unfortunately, there is one flaw in all this: The telephone also exists at the end of part 3, after Marina (Van's mother) dies. It is used by Lucette on May 31, 1901; is later described as the "official" term; and is mentioned again on October 10, 1905. Thus, according to Van and Ada's history of Antiterra, telephones existed in the mid-nineteenth century, then were banned, became acceptable between 1901 and 1930, then were forbidden again, and had been unbanned again by the time the book was completed. They were replaced by hydraulic dorophones, which Boyd identifies as a comic thread running through *Ada:* "Nabokov reduces the mystery of matter to farce and replays science fiction as parody in the hydraulic systems that replace electricity and especially in the telephones that gurgle and gulp their comic course through the novel."[10]

However, the dorophone is a very suspicious object. One problem with it is that its name is overdetermined, like an object in, Log help us, a Freudian dream. In the novel, all reasons for the dorophone's existence have to do with water:

9. Nicol, "*Ada* or Disorder," 238.
10. Boyd, "Annotations to *Ada:* 3.," 59.

1. A committee banned electricity so that water power had to be substituted.
2. Aqua's madness includes "a morbid sensitivity to the language of tap water" (*Ada* 23). This explanation gets tangled with the first one: "[S]he felt tickled at the thought that she, poor Aqua, had accidentally hit upon such a simple method of recording and transmitting speech, while technologists . . . all over the world were trying to make publicly utile and commercially rewarding . . . hydrodynamic telephones."
3. Most hilarious is what Marina says in French when she picks up the dorophone: "*A l'eau!*" (*Ada* 208). Incidentally, Alexander Graham Bell himself used "Ahoy!"—a nautical, watery term—as a phone greeting.
4. Supposedly the "dor" in "dorophone" is a corruption of "hydro," because the device is water-powered. However, it is also supposed to be traced, like many other things in *Ada,* to the Chateaubriand poem and the Dore river—itself a water-powered object. Most suspicious of all, this is explained in a dream that Van "retrostructed as far as it would go: in it Demon's former valet explained to Van that 'dor' in the name of an adored river equaled the corruption of hydro in 'dorophone'" (*Ada* 248). This is made explicit later: "[H]e still hoped the Ladore dorophone would be in working order before his departure. *Le château que baignait le Dorophone*" (*Ada* 308–309). "Dor" gets into everything in *Ada,* including its title, *Ada or Ardor.* (Terra is not only our world, it is a name for earth; if the "dor" in "dorophone" is supposedly a corruption of "hydro," then possibly Van might also imagine that "telephone" is a corruption of "terraphone," just as he thinks that psychotherapists are called "terrapists.")

There are ways that the terminology of electricity could be confused with the terminology of hydrology. Both electricity and water have currents; indeed, Bell consistently explained that his telephone worked on "undulating current." Further, there are also reasons that an actual telephone could be called a dorophone on Terra, our planet. One, to a Frenchman, would be if it were gold-colored—and apparently most phones in the novel are either brass or bronze. A more complex one is that, because Bell built a house at Bras d'Or, a lakelike extension of the Atlantic Ocean almost entirely surrounded by the hills of Nova Scotia (and surely not by accident mentioned on the first page of *Ada*), one might call Bell's invention, rather desperately, a dorophone.

Another way to justify calling a telephone a dorophone, equally strained but apparently intended to be noticed and noted, occurs during a different phone call. In 1892, Van converses with his typist Polly, who has confused Bergson's *durée* and *dorée* (French not just for gold-colored but also for the European fish John Dory, presumably what Marina wanted to prepare for Demon when she had to substitute wall-eyed pike, "dory" in quotation marks). Thus, because the all-important telephone call in 1922 is Van's "deepest perception of tangible time," his longest Bergsonian *durée*, the confusion between *dor* and *dur* could have spread throughout the book. It is possibly this jump between *durée* and Chateaubriand's Dore river that triggered Nabokov's structural epiphany.

The reason I believe that this last confusion between *dorée* and *durée* was intended to be picked up by the reader is that, during this phone conversation and nowhere else, the phone becomes first a "campophone" in the phrase "the brass campophone buzzed," then a "polliphone" (*Ada* 376). The phone becomes a polliphone because Polly is on the other end of the line, with a likely pun on "polyphony," but why does it become a campophone? Obviously, the root "camp" means "bell," as in campanile, bell tower. And yet we are specifically told that the campophone "buzzed," so it clearly did not have a bell on it. This seems, then, to be a way of saying that in the Manhattan apartment, Van had a phone that Bell invented or that AT&T, "Ma Bell," owned. Words proliferate, and things decay.

What that particular phone conversation tells us about dorophones is not yet exhausted. There is still another way in which a person who is scient in insects—in other words, a person such as Ada—might call a telephone a dorophone: a "dor" is a buzzing insect of various kinds, a meaning doubtless well known to Nabokov. Dor is also used in such compound words as "dor-beetle," a buzzing beetle. Incidentally, in the coded message Ada sends to Van while her busybody sister-in-law Dorothy peers over her shoulder, Ada nicknames Dorothy "Dora," which is old English for bumblebee. The point of all this is that it would be perfectly legitimate for someone like Ada to call a telephone a dorophone because it buzzes. Of course, to make it difficult, Nabokov never describes dorophones as buzzing; he saves that word for the sound of the brass campophone. But the dorophones do make noise, as do other appliances with "doro" in front of them, such as a "dorocene lamp" that is "murmuring" (*Ada* 419). This is why, when the L disaster is first mentioned at the beginning of the third chapter of part 1, Van says that "our sleek little machines,

Faragod bless them, hum again after a fashion" (*Ada* 17). Dorophones can exist on Terra, too.

Still another meaning of "dor" is "mockery." The phone's refusal to have Ada on the other end of the line might be considered a dor by Van. Notice that this possible meaning exists in the original description of Aqua's madness: The tap water starts to echo fragments of conversations, and Aqua is initially pleased to notice "this immediate, sustained, and in her case rather eager and mocking but really quite harmless replay of this or that recent discourse" (*Ada* 23).

The very richness of the etymology of "dorophone" makes it suspect, an infinite series of allusions to an object that may not exist, in contrast to a telephone, which is rare but substantial. As a child, Ada divided life into "ghost things," such as toothaches; "things," which are "the routine stuff of life"; and "real things," which are "infrequent and priceless" (*Ada* 74) and even more rarely come in "towers" and "bridges." By this measure, the telephone call in part 4 is both a tower and a bridge, the most real thing in all of *Ada*. I ask you then to admire this central moment, this telephone call that retains the freshness of Ada's voice, this long stretch of real time during which everything in the novel comes together for both its author (V. Nabokov) and its narrator (V. Veen).

{ PART III }
THE MIRACULOUS AMPHORA

{ 10 }

Metapoetics and Metaphysics
Pushkin and Nabokov, 1799–1899

SERGEI DAVYDOV

Aleksandr Pushkin died without establishing a literary school and without leaving behind a single direct disciple. His poetic message, if it had at all been understood, was soon distorted by foes and friends. Russian literature after the Golden Age took a different course altogether by becoming a tool for the promotion of civic, social, moral, religious, and political causes—a practice that was to numb the aesthetic sensibilities of several generations of Russian readers and critics. The resurrection of Pushkin's legacy came one hundred years after his birth with the advent of the poets of the Silver Age who claimed

The following studies of Nabokov's metaphysics helped to shape the concept of this article: Vladimir E. Alexandrov, *Nabokov's Otherworld* (Princeton, N.J.: Princeton University Press, 1991); Petr Bitsilli, "Vozrozhdenie allegorii," *Sovremennye zapiski* 61 (1936): 191–204; Brian Boyd, "Nabokov's Philosophical World," *Southern Review* 14 (1981): 260–301; Julian W. Connolly, "The Otherworldly in Nabokov's Poetry," *Russian Literature Triquarterly* 24 (1991): 329–39; Sergei Davydov, *"Teksty-matreshki" Vladimira Nabokova* (Munich: Otto Sagner, 1982); D. Barton Johnson, "Vladimir Nabokov's *Solus Rex* and the 'Ultima Thule' Theme," *Slavic Review* 40, no. 4 (1981): 543–56, and *Worlds in Regression* (Ann Arbor: Ardis, 1985); Vladislav Khodasevich, "O Sirine," in idem, *Izbrannaia proza*, ed. N. Berberova (New York: Russica Publishers, 1937), 200–209; Julian Moynahan, "A Russian Preface for Nabokov's *Beheading*," in *Novel* 1 (1967): 12–18; Véra Nabokov, "A Foreword," in *Stikhi* 3–4; Irena Ronen and Omry Ronen, "Diabolically Evocative: An Inquiry into the Meaning of Metaphor," *Slavica Hierosolymitana* 5–6 (1981): 371–86; William W. Rowe, *Nabokov's Spectral Dimension* (Ann Arbor: Ardis, 1981); Leona Toker, *Nabokov: The Mystery of Literary Structure* (Ithaca, N.Y.: Cornell University Press, 1989); Vladimir Varshavskii, *Nezamechennoe pokolenie* (New York: Chekhov House, 1956); and many others whose names had to be omitted due to the lack of space.

Pushkin as "their own" ("*moi Pushkin*") and who perceived their own epoch—their personal lives, loves, and losses—as parallels to Pushkin's.

Perhaps no one at home or in exile made claim to Pushkin's legacy more faithfully than Nabokov. Born one hundred years after Pushkin, Nabokov adopted him as his personal muse and never abandoned that calling. He took Pushkin as his fellow traveler on every one of his literary journeys. Pushkin's presence extends from fleeting allusions to direct quotations (attributed and unattributed), from occasional motifs to entire themes and fully formulated aesthetic concepts. Nabokov liked to endow his favorite characters with a touch of Pushkin, and weighed the "flair, intelligence and talent" of Russian writers and critics on "Pushkin's scales," while exorcising from this sacred domain the "devils," such as the radical nineteenth-century critic Chernyshevsky.[1]

Nabokov's last Russian novel *The Gift*, his most ardent declaration of love for Russian literature, can be seen as a farewell to his twenty-year-long literary career in what he called his "docile Russian tongue." Yet even as an American writer, Nabokov returned to Pushkin as translator and scholar, devoting as many years of his life to *Eugene Onegin* as it took Pushkin to write it. Nabokov's translation, accompanied by three volumes of meticulous commentary, remains the most enduring monument raised to Pushkin on American soil.

Shortly after becoming an American writer, Nabokov translated two of Pushkin's *Little Tragedies,* "Mozart and Salieri" and "A Feast During the Plague."[2] In these philosophical dramas Pushkin experiments with the limits of the genre and probes into metaphysical territory in a manner close to that of Nabokov. Both of these "Little Tragedies" offer an obliging prism through which one can look into Nabokov's own poetics and metaphysics.

"Mozart and Salieri," based on the legend that Salieri poisoned his rival out of jealousy, is a "classical dramatization of the conflict between natural

---

1. See Sergei Davydov, "*The Gift:* Nabokov's Aesthetic Exorcism of Chernyshevskii," *Canadian-American Slavic Studies* 19, no. 3 (1985): 357–74; idem, "Weighing Nabokov's *Gift* on Pushkin's Scales," in Boris Gasparov, Robert P. Hughes, and Irina Paperno, eds., "Special Issue: Cultural Mythologies of Russian Modernism: From the Golden Age to the Silver Age," *California Slavic Studies* 15 (1992): 415–30; Sergei Davydov, "Nabokov and Pushkin," in *The Garland Companion to Vladimir Nabokov,* ed. Vladimir E. Alexandrov (New York: Garland, 1995), 482–96; Monica Greenleaf, "Fathers, Sons and Impostors: Pushkin's Trace in *The Gift,*" *Slavic Review* 53, no. 1 (1994): 140–58.

2. In Vladimir Nabokov, *Three Russian Poets: Translations of Pushkin, Lermontov, Tyutchev* (Norfolk, Conn.: New Directions, 1944).

genius and accomplished mediocrity."³ The theme of an artist's envy of his more gifted rival reappears in a number of Nabokov's novels, in which pairs of unequal talents compete for supremacy and attempt to displace each other. To list some of the most obvious pairs: the cartoonist Rex and the blind Albinus (*Laugh*), the impresario Valentinov and the chess master Luzhin (*Def*), the murderer and writer Hermann and the painter Ardalion (*Des*), the virtuoso executioner M. Pierre and the poet Cincinnatus (*IB*). In *The Gift* the rivals are Fyodor and the more accomplished poet Koncheev, "whose mysteriously growing talent could have been checked only by a ringful of poison in a glass of wine"—a direct allusion to "Mozart and Salieri" (*Gift* 76). On a different level, Fyodor successfully restores Pushkin's poetic legacy, which the radical critic, Chernyshevsky, attempted to obliterate. In *The Real Life of Sebastian Knight*, the younger brother V. loses his writerly contest with Sebastian Knight but triumphs easily over the hackneyed biographer Goodman. In *Lolita*, two artistic monsters, the Old World connoisseur of French literature and the "poshlusty" American playwright, lock horns over a nymphet. In *Pale Fire* the insane commentator attempts to usurp not only the poet's work but even his death.

Like Salieri, the lesser artist often contemplates or actually commits an ethical or aesthetic crime against his rival, for which he will be ultimately punished. In Pushkin's tragedy, Salieri poisons Mozart, but until his death he will be tormented by Mozart's last words that "villainy and genius are two things that don't go together." Nabokov likes to test the validity of this maxim in his works. In Nabokov's universe true "poets do not kill"; rather, they die. But even as victims, the moral victory is theirs, while the villains are punished and their world shattered. Their punishment is often death, but even in the "afterlife" they are reminded by the unforgiving deity of their proper place: "[T]here is a green lane in Paradise where Humbert is permitted to wander at dusk once a year, but Hell shall never parole Hermann" (*Des* 9).

Salieri's foray against Mozart and heaven ("They say there is no justice on the earth. I know there is none in Heaven") evolves in Nabokov's novels into an arcane metaphysical drama. Nabokov models his cosmology as an analogy to poetics. The "anthropomorphic deity," the author, populates the pages of his novels with human-like creatures and endows them with a share of his own artistic and metaphysical intuition. Depending on their shrewdness, some characters begin to suspect the presence of the "deity" outside the novel, and

---

3. E. Wilson, "Introduction," in ibid.

several of them become aware of their inferior existence within the world in which they have to die as soon as the novel comes to its close. Beyond the book's covers, of course, looms the splendid reality, the "eternity" of their creator and their judge.

To write badly is a cardinal sin in Nabokov's universe, and the indignant author castigates those who dared to scribble their "poshlusty" opus inside his sacred text (stories "Lips to Lips," "Admiralty Spire"). Pushkin himself used this stratagem in *Eugene Onegin:* The jealous poet Lensky challenged Onegin to a duel and was killed. On the metapoetic level, the poet lost his duel to a more formidable rival, Pushkin himself, in whose exquisite verse novel Lensky dared to write his "obscure and limp" elegies: "Tak on pisal temno i vialo, Chto romantizmom my zovem (Thus did he write, "obscurely" and "limply" [what we call romanticism—]" (*EO* 1:237). Death is the just punishment for this impudence.

In the novel *Despair,* Hermann kills his double and writes a flawed detective tale about it. The deity rejects both of these sacrificial offerings and informs Hermann that the path to immortality through art is closed to him. Faced with such a prospect, Hermann rebels:

> The nonexistence of God is simple to prove. Impossible to concede, for example, that a serious Jah, all wise and almighty, could employ his time in such inane fashion as playing with manikins.... God does not exist, as neither does our hereafter, that second bogey being as easily disposed of as the first. (*Des* 101)

For this mock-Karamazovian sally the wrathful god *canes* Hermann with a disreputable "stick," drives him to despair, madness and jail, and reminds him that even in Hell there will be no parole.

To make it clear that artistic failure and blasphemy bode lethal consequences for the hero, Nabokov entitles his next novel *Invitation to a Beheading.* A pencil "as long as the life of any man except Cincinnatus'" (*IB* 12) is all Nabokov gives his prisoner with which to face the gallant invitation. In the prison cell a poet is born who attempts to "write off" the edge of death. Cincinnatus even admits that he writes "obscurely and limply, like Pushkin's lyrical duelist" (*IB* 92): "Envious of poets. How wonderful it must be to speed along a page and, right from the page, where only a shadow continues to run, to take off into the blue" (*IB* 194). Thanks to his "criminal intuition," Cincinnatus soon learns to write like that. While acknowledging the supremacy of the script that surrounds his scribbling, Cincinnatus begins to doubt the ontology of that world in which he is to die with Nabokov's last sentence. Only toward the end does Cincinnatus learn the simple and uncanny truth—that he cannot die because he is only a literary character, and that the only mortal being around is the author: "[A]nd it was somehow funny that eventually the author must needs die—and it was funny because the only real, genuinely unquestionable thing here was only death itself, the inevitability of the author's physical death" (*IB* 124). After this revelation, Cincinnatus crosses out his last written word, "death," and mounts the scaffold.

Cincinnatus's startling move catches his author unprepared. He hesitates to execute the smart little fellow whose ingenious art and metaphysical insight are worthy of his creator. With one hand, the demiurge-author beheads the "turpid Gnostic," who declined the invitation and thus brought about the novel's collapse. With his other hand, the author-redeemer rescues his shrewd hero from the novel's debris for having passed the test in metaphysics. The character returns to his creator and earns his share of immortality: "Comme un fou se croit Dieu nous nous croyons mortels" (*IB* epigraph).

As the next title suggests, *The Gift* is a bildungsroman about aesthetic education. To become a poet, Fyodor has to identify the true father figures and purge the impostors.[4] In the course of the novel, Fyodor writes several works, each exceeding its predecessor in merit. Having reached perfect rapport with his progenitors and mentors—his father, Pushkin, and Nabokov—the disciple becomes the curator of their heritage. For his art and faith, Fyodor is rewarded with love, with the return of his father from beyond life and with the novel *The Gift*, which becomes Fyodor's own creation. Fyodor is the only character who is allowed to step out of the pages of a novel onto its cover, to become its author. Fyodor does not die as a result of this metamorphosis into the new installment of his life. On second reading of *The Gift*, Fyodor is already the "deity" beyond the book's covers. Somewhere in this congenial unity of the son and the father, of the inner and the outer text, of the character and his author, and, by implication, of a mortal and his Creator may lie the secret of Nabokov's metaphysics.

A well-known Russian writer, Boris Zaitsev, once said that Nabokov is a writer "who has neither any God, nor perhaps, any Devil."[5] Denis de Rougemont

---

4. Greenleaf, "Fathers."
5. Gleb Struve, *Russkaia literatura v izgnanii* (New York: Chekhov House, 1956), 287.

in his book *The Devil's Share* (quoted by Irena and Omry Ronen in their "diabolically evocative" piece) mentions a story of Jacob Boehme in which Satan, when asked, "Why did you leave Paradise?" answered, "I wanted to became an author."[6] Nabokov once said that "a creative writer must study carefully the works of his rivals, including the Almighty" (*SO* 32). A strong opinion such as this intimates indeed a certain "affinity between the creative impulse and the first disobedience."[7] However, it seems to me that Nabokov steers clear of the "Luciferian temptation." He is no Salieri, grumbling against Heaven for shortchanging him, nor does he shake his fist against his "author," like Hermann. Nabokov is more like his favorite heroes, Cincinnatus and Fyodor, who create "along with," not "against," their creator. In a remarkable 1925 letter to his mother, Nabokov wrote: "I understand how God as he created the world found this a pure, thrilling joy. We are translators of God's creation, his little plagiarists and imitators, we dress up what he wrote, as a charmed commentator sometimes gives an extra grace to a line of genius."[8]

The recurring metaphor of "life as a text" is central to Nabokov's cosmology. In the poem "An Unfinished Draft" (1931), a poet muses that "human days are only / words on a page picked up by you / upon your way (a page ripped out— / where from?)" (*PP* 66-67). In "Ultima Thule," the artist Sineusov claims "that everything—life, patria, April, the sound of spring or that of a dear voice—is but a muddled preface, and that the main text still lies ahead," to which Falter, who claims to possess some ultimate secret, replies: "Skip the preface!" (*Stories* 520-21). In *Pale Fire,* the poet John Shade jots down a "note for further use": "*Man's life as a commentary to abstruse Unfinished poem*" (*PF* ll. 939-40). And in *The Real Life of Sebastian Knight,* the metaphor of "life as a text" gets its most exquisite treatment:

> The answer to all questions of life and death, "the absolute solution" was *written* all over the world he had known: it was like a traveller realising that the wild country he surveys is not an accidental assembly of natural phenomena, but a *page in a book* where mountains and forests, and fields, and rivers are disposed in such a way as to form a coherent *sentence;* the *vowel*

---

6. Denis de Rougemont, *The Devil's Share. An Essay on the Diabolic in Modern Society* (New York: Meridian Books, 1956); 131-32; Ronen and Ronen, "Diabolically," 376.

7. Ronen and Ronen, "Diabolically," 376.

8. Brian Boyd, *Vladimir Nabokov: The Russian Years* (Princeton, N.J.: Princeton University Press, 1990), 245.

of a lake fusing with the *consonant* of a sibilant slope; the windings of a road *writing* its message in a round hand, as clear as that of one's father; trees conversing in dumb-show, making sense to one who has learnt the gestures of their *language*. ... Thus the traveller *spells* the landscape and its sense is disclosed, and likewise, the intricate pattern of human life turns out to be *monogrammatic,* now quite clear to the inner eye disentangling the interwoven *letters*. (*RLSK* 178–9; emphasis added)

If a "page" is a metaphor of earthly life, then what is the "opus" from which it was torn?

Like Tolstoy, Nabokov has the eerie habit of pointing to some "book" at the moment his characters are about to die.[9] But rather than a "book of life," read to the last page, as was the case in Tolstoy, Nabokov's "book" has something to do with the passage to the next realm. It is sometimes written in an arcane tongue or exists only in the mind of the dying man. On the eve of his execution, Cincinnatus reads the novel *Quercus* and begins to laugh about the "inevitability of the author's physical death" (*IB* 124). A volume of Annenskii and Khodasevich are mentioned at the moment of Yasha Chernyshevsky's death (*Gift* 60). (Nabokov considered Khodasevich "the greatest Russian poet that the twentieth century has yet produced" [*Gift* 10]). Yasha's father, just moments before he dies, muses: "Funny that I have thought of death all my life, and if I have lived, I have lived only in the margin of a book I have never been able to read" (*Gift* 323). The last words of the nineteenth-century critic Chernyshevsky were: "A strange business: in this book there is not a single mention of God" (*Gift* 312).[10] A few moments before the greatest Russian poet, Pushkin, died, he asked his friend: "'Raise me; let's go, higher, higher—well, come on!' Then, upon recovering, he continued: 'I had a vision that I was climbing up on top of those books and bookcases with you, up high—and I got dizzy.'"[11]

9. In Tolstoy, such an enigmatic "book" appears at the moment of Anna Karenina's death. "The candle, by the light of which she had been reading that book filled with anxieties, deceptions, grief, and evil, flared up with a brighter light than before, lit up for her all that had before been dark, flickered, began to grow dim, and went out for ever": Leo Tolstoy, *Anna Karenina*, ed. G. Gibian, trans. A. Maude (New York: Norton, 1970), part 7.
10. Iurii Steklov, *N. G. Chernyshevskii: Ego zhizn' i deiatel'nost'*, 2 vols. (Moscow: Gosudarstvennoe izdatel'stvo, 1928), 2:637.
11. V. Veresaev, *Pushkin v zhizni*, 2 vols., 6th ed. (Moscow: Sovetskii pisatel', 1936), 2:425–26; Ernest Simmons, *Pushkin*, 2nd ed. (Gloucester, Mass.: Peter Smith, 1971), 423.

The step from the "page" to the "main text" is a transcendental leap, a metamorphosis, accomplished through something that is akin to death but is not death. "We are the larvae of the angels," Nabokov mused in one of his early metaphysical poems:

> Nay, Being is no murky riddle!
> The moonlit dale is bright with dew
> We *are* the larvae of the angels:
> How sweet to gnaw on tender leaves!
>
> Sprout bristles! Crawl, contort, grow sturdy!
> The more voracious your green course,
> the more like velvet, more like splendor
> the tails of your unfolded wings. (*Stikhi* 105)

Dante used a similar image: "Perceive ye not that we are worms, / born to become angelic butterfly" ("noi siam vermi / nati a formar l'angelica farfalla").[12] Metamorphosis, like mimicry, might be one of the Creator's gifts to His creatures. The entomologist Nabokov is a fierce anti-Darwinist who discards the notion that natural selection alone accounts for the miracles of mimicry. Rather, it was given to the creatures as an artistic gift with which to imitate and celebrate the patterns of His varicolored world (*SM* 125).[13]

If mimicry is an artistic gift, metamorphosis can be a metaphysical one. The transition from egg to larva to pupa, breaking through the coffin-like cocoon to become a magnificent butterfly or moth, does not involve death. In the story "Christmas," the soul of the dead son metamorphoses into a magnificent Indian moth (*Stories* 136), and in *Invitation to a Beheading*, on the eve of the execution, a beautiful moth shows Cincinnatus how to escape death (*IB* 203–4). In his essay "The Art of Literature and Commonsense," Nabokov spells out this conjecture without metaphors, in plain prose:

> That human life is but a first installment of the serial soul and that one's individual secret is not lost in the process of earthly dissolution, becomes something more than an optimistic conjecture, and even more than a matter of religious faith, when we remember that only commonsense rules immortality out. (*LL* 377)

12. Dante, *Purgatory* X, ll. 124–26.
13. Cf. Alexandrov, *Otherworld*, 46.

Thus, the reintegration of the torn-out "page" into the original "volume" may well be the key metaphor for the "installment of the soul" onto some new and higher level of being, while death is only the platform from which one changes trains.

Some of Nabokov's characters, too, suspect "that the horror of death is nothing really, a harmless convulsion—perhaps even healthful for the soul," and that there once lived "sages who rejoiced at death" (*IB* 192). In the last chapter of *The Gift*, Fyodor discovers the ancient sage who gave Nabokov the quibbling epigraph for *Invitation to a Beheading*:

When the French thinker Delalande was asked at somebody's funeral why he did not uncover himself (*ne se découvre pas*), he replied: "I am waiting for death to do it first (*qu'elle se découvre la première*). There is a lack of metaphysical gallantry in this, but death deserves no more. (*Gift* 321–22)

Shortly after *The Gift*, Nabokov translated Pushkin's philosophical tragedy, "A Feast During the Plague," whose heroes display an even greater "lack of metaphysical gallantry."[14] A congregation of young, life-thirsty men and women carouse while facing death point-blank. Wine and merriment is their last bastion against the onslaught of Thanatos. The Dionysian feast held among the corpses releases in the revellers a spontaneous eruption of creative Eros. The singers, dancers, and poets perform under the baton of their Chairman—himself a newborn poet—a highly artistic ritual. Through their exaltation of music, poetry, wine, and lovemaking on the brink of the grave, the revellers seem to have freed themselves from time-honored pieties.

Yet still, the memory of their Christian past lingers. The harlot Mary sings a ballad about her idyllic Scotland, when "our bonny church on Sundays / sas full of young and old" and "our happy children's voices / rang in the noisy school."[15] When the plague came, people mourned their dead and asked God to comfort their souls. For Mary's ancestors the vision of Paradise was attainable and attractive. Jenny, the song's heroine, knows that she will be reunited with her beloved after death. The Chairman acknowledges the Eden-like nature of the past, "the wild paradise of [Mary's] dear land."[16] He, too, knows

---

14. Pushkin's play is a translation of act 1, scene 4, of John Wilson's drama "City of the Plague" (1816). The Chairman's "Hymn to the Plague" is Pushkin's original poem.

15. Nabokov, *Three Russian Poets*, 12.

16. Ibid., 13.

that there *is* an afterlife, for he is haunted by the shades of his late mother and wife. However, for him "who has been torn from a familiar world by some dark vision" their Paradise is lost: "Where am I? Sacred child of light, I see you / above me, on a shore where my wrecked soul / now cannot reach you." In his ecstatic "Hymn to the Plague," the Chairman proposes to his congregation a desperate and devious bid: to fool death by embracing it and thus attain some unprecedented, savage immortality.

...

There's bliss in battle and there's bliss
on the dark edge of an abyss
and in the fury of the main
amid foam-crested death;
in the Arabian hurricane
and in the Plague's light breath.

All, all such mortal dangers fill
a mortal's heart with a deep thrill
of wordless rapture that bespeaks
maybe, immortal life,
—and happy is the man who seeks
and tastes them in his strife.

And so, Dark Queen, we praise thy reign!
Thou callest us, but we remain
unruffled by the chill of death,
clinking our cups, carefree,
drinking a rose-lipped maiden's breath
    full of the Plague, maybe![17]

An old Clergyman interrupts the feast and enjoins the apostates "by the holy wounds / of One Who bled upon the Cross to save us,— / break up your monstrous banquet, if you hope / to meet in heaven the dear souls of all those / you lost on earth."[18] He entreats the Chairman with the sacred memory of his mother and wife, but the Chairman remains unperturbed. He rejects salvation in Christian terms and threatens to curse those who might follow the

---

17. Ibid., 16.
18. Ibid., 17.

priest. The finale is brief: "The Clergyman departs. The feast continues. The Chairman remains plunged in deep meditation."[19]

In the finale of *The Gift*, Fyodor, perhaps anticipating his liberation from the cocoon of the book and the next installment of his "serial soul," as the novel's author, quotes to Zina a curious passage from the cheerfully invented "elegant atheist," Pierre Delalande:

> [T]here was once a man . . . he lived as a true Christian; he did much good, sometimes by word, sometimes by deed, and sometimes by silence; he observed the fasts; he drank the water of mountain valleys; . . . he nurtured the spirit of contemplation and vigilance; he lived a pure, difficult, wise life; but when he sensed the approach of death, instead of thinking about it, instead of tears of repentance and sorrowful partings, instead of monks and notary in black, he invited guests to a feast, acrobats, actors, poets, a crowd of dancing girls, three magicians, jolly Tollenburg students, a traveler from Taprobana [Ceylon], and in the midst of melodious verses, masks and music he drained a goblet of wine and died, with a carefree smile on his face. . . . Magnificent, isn't it? If I have to die one day that's exactly how I'd like it to be. (*Gift* 377)

Nabokov, who was himself baptized into the Christian faith, died without receiving the holy sacraments. He was cremated (a practice discouraged by the Orthodox church) and buried without Christian rites to the tunes of two arias from Puccini's *La Bohème* played by an organ.[20] No Byzantine symbols enhance the bluish marble slate at the Vevey cemetery. It says simply:

VLADIMIR NABOKOV
ECRIVAIN 1899–1977

In 1991, the ashes of Véra Nabokov joined his.

"Che gelida manina . . ."—"Si. Mi chiamano Mimì."

---

19. Ibid., 19.
20. Professor Marina Ledkovsky, a relative of Nabokov's who was present at the ceremony, kindly shared this information with me. She also pointed out the "very Nabokovian" pattern of the date, name, and place—7.7.77, Vladimir Vladimirovich, Vevey. Dmitri Nabokov, who chose the music with his mother, told me that one day his ashes will be added to his parents' urn.

{ 11 }

Nabokov the Pushkinian

IRENA RONEN

In his Paris speech on the one-hundredth anniversary of Aleksandr Pushkin's death, Nabokov spoke about the difficulty of translating Pushkin into French because of the Russian poet's dependence on the French poetic idiom of the eighteenth century: "As a result, when his poetry is translated into French, the reader recognizes ... the French eighteenth century—rose-tinted poetry thorny with epigrams.... This first impression is so wretched, this old mistress so insipid, as to discourage the French right away."[1] As Nabokov proceeded, against the obstacles, with his endeavor to translate Pushkin's poetry into French, he made the following observation: "[E]ach poem I selected found its own special echo in one French poet or another. But I soon understood that Pushkin had nothing to do with this: I was being guided by my personal literary recollections, not by that false French reflection one has the impression of finding in his verse."[2]

It would be fair to say that many years later, Nabokov became able to combine his individual reading of Pushkin with a very exacting scholarly examination of Pushkin's reading in the Western literatures. Nabokov's attitude toward Pushkin, although permanent in essence, gradually grew in depth and complexity. Many factors played a part in shaping his view of Pushkin's biography as a spiritual value and his interpretation of Pushkin's art.

One of the leitmotifs of Nabokov's early poetry, after his escape from Russia but before his hope of an early return had been abandoned, was the anguish

---

1. Vladimir Nabokov, "Pushkin, or the Real and the Plausible," trans. Dmitri Nabokov, *New York Review of Books*, March 31 1988, 41.
2. Ibid., 42.

and glory of exile. The 1920s invited comparison with the 1820s, and in Nabokov's poem "Exile," Pushkin's southern exile was perceived biographically as a possible model for exiles in an alien land:

Я занят странными мечтами
в часы рассветной полутьмы:
что, если б Пушкин был меж нами—
простой изгнанник, как и мы?

Так, удалясь в края чужие,
он вправду был бы обречен
"вздыхать о сумрачной России",
как пожелал однажды он.[3]

[I am occupied with strange reverie / in the hours of daybreak twilight: / what if Pushkin were among us, / just an exile like ourselves? // Then, having withdrawn to alien lands, / he would truly be doomed / "to sigh for somber Russia," / as he had once wished.]

Recollecting his first taste of exile in *Speak, Memory*, Nabokov evoked his stay in Yalta: "I felt all the pangs of exile. There had been the case of Pushkin, of course—Pushkin who had wandered in banishment here, among those naturalized cypresses and laurels—but though some prompting might have come from his elegies, I do not think my exaltation was a pose" (*SM* 244).

In the 1920s and 1930s, Nabokov was among those who, in the spirit of Aleksandr Blok's Pushkin speech of 1921, perceived in Pushkin's heritage the supreme achievement of Russian culture and considered retreat from Pushkin a renunciation of pure and free art in general. Nabokov's final statement in the polemic about the modern appraisal of Pushkin, which continued forcefully in émigré literary circles even after the demise of futurism in Russia, was his novel *The Gift*, a triumphant celebration of Pushkin at the centennial of his death. At the same time, Nabokov commenced his prodigious activities as a mediator between Russian literature and the West by publishing his French lecture about Pushkin in *Nouvelle Revue Française*.

As the exigencies of the literary struggle for Pushkin's aesthetic and ethical values and against the so-called committed art—whether Mayakovskian or Merezhkovskian—receded during the 1940s, when the free Russian literature

3. Vladimir Nabokov, "Izgnanie [1925]," in idem, *Stikhotvoreniia i poemy* (Kharkov: Folio; Moscow: Act, 1997), 398).

in Europe ceased to exist and Nabokov escaped to America, subtle changes and new features began to show in his perception, comprehension, and artistic use of Pushkin's art. In America, the great argument about Pushkin acquired a new and different, inter-literary significance. As Galya Diment has noted, "In an ironic and perfectly Nabokovian twist of destiny, Vladimir Nabokov and Edmund Wilson began and ended their relationship through the agency of the same 'spirit'—that of Aleksandr Pushkin."[4] Indeed, Nabokov's first extensive English translation of Pushkin, "Mozart and Salieri," was published a year after his arrival in the United States.

In the poem "An Evening of Russian Poetry" (1945; *PP* 158–63), the image of Pushkin is associated with travel "on long and lonely roads," which, Nabokov says, in Russian poetry "were always fated / to lead into the silence of exile." The poem ends with the lecturer translating a listener's compliment into Russian:

"How would you say 'delightful talk' in Russian?"
"How would you say 'Good night'?"
 Oh, that would be:
"Bessonnitza, tvoy vzor oonyl i strashen;
lubov moya, otstoopnika prostee."

[Insomnia, your stare is dull and ashen, / my love, forgive me this apostasy.]

"[T]voi vzor oonyl i strashen" is a recognizable echo of the line from "Vospominaniia v Tsarskom Sele" ("Recollections at Tsarskoe Selo," 1814), in which Pushkin evokes the destruction of Moscow in 1812: "Moskva, skol' Russkomu tvoi zrak unylyi strashen! [Moscow, how your doleful visage terrifies a Russian!]." Similarly, Nabokov's "ashen" for "strashen" points at Pushkin's image of Moscow's ashes: "Gde mirt blagoukhal, i lipa trepetala, / Tam nyne ugli, *pepel,* prakh [Where myrtle was redolent and linden quivered, / there are now coals, ashes, and dust]."

One wonders to what extent Nabokov's apology to insomnia and Russian poetry reflected, in March 1945, the pity about which he wrote in his celebrated Russian wartime poem "Kakim by polotnom" (1944):

No matter how the Soviet tinsel glitters
upon the canvas of a battle piece;

---

4. Galya Diment, "Three Russian Poets," in *The Garland Companion to Vladimir Nabokov,* ed. Vladimir E. Alexandrov (New York: Garland, 1995), 709.

no matter how the soul dissolves in pity,
I will not bend. (*PP* 127)

When Nabokov began to write in English, he faced the problem of transplanting to another language and literary tradition his major native source of creative inspiration and the supreme object of his emulation. The Pushkinian subtext sometimes would be introduced in Nabokov's English novels and short stories by means of thematically motivated direct quotations (as in the case of the poem "Brozhu li ia vdol' ulits shumnykh," which fulfills an important plot-building function in *Pnin*), or through such seemingly casual biographical reference as in the story "That in Aleppo Once": "She was much younger than I—not as much younger as was Nathalie of the lovely bare shoulders and long earrings in relation to swarthy Pushkin" (*Stories* 561).

On other occasions, Pushkin is alluded to through purely abstract structural patterns associated with his art—such as the three-way relationship among the author, the eyewitness narrator, and his acquaintance, the protagonist, in *Pnin*. This relationship is modeled in part on *Eugene Onegin* and in part on *Belkin's Tales*, so that the well-known motif of squirrels in *Pnin*, identified at the textual level with the undying presence of Mira Belochkin and, generally, with women in Pnin's life, subtextually may be yet another Pushkinian allusion. So are such "texts within the text" as Pnin's letter to Lisa Wind, which finds its way to the narrator, just as Tatiana's letter became Pushkin's possession and, indeed, scans in part in iambic tetrameter.[5]

In Nabokov's later English works there is a striking proliferation of challenging enigmatic references to names and situations associated with Pushkin's life and art, and even to Pushkin scholarship. In *Look at the Harlequins!* the obvious confusion between Prince Vadim's genealogy and Pushkin's ancestry in Annette Blagovo's garbled reference to the quarrel between Vadim's forefather and either Ivan the Great or Peter the Terrible is an allusion to the line in Pushkin's poem "My Pedigree": "S Petrom moi prashchur ne poladil / I byl za to poveshen im [My grandsire did not hit it off with Peter, / and in result was hanged by him]," as Nabokov rendered these lines in his commentary to *Eugene Onegin* (*EO* 2:33). Annette's subsequent appearances at the literary parties is compared to the poise of Tatiana as Princess N., while the librarian and publisher Oksman appears to be a ligature of two prototypes: Il'ia

---

5. Gennady Barabtarlo, *Phantom of Fact: A Guide to Nabokov's* Pnin (Ann Arbor: Ardis, 1989), 277.

Isidorovich Fondaminsky (Bunakov), the editor of *Sovremennye Zapiski*, and Iulian Grigorievich Oksman, the famous Pushkin scholar.

Beside this, in his new role as educator in a wider and deeper sense than his position as college professor implied, Nabokov took on the role of translator and interpreter of Pushkin for English-speaking audiences, at first by publishing, in 1944, his translations of some of Pushkin's lyric and dramatic poetry. Although the translations were free, they were frequently felicitously faithful in both sound and sense. Eventually, Nabokov created an English-language *Eugene Onegin,* complete with commentaries. (In format, the edition resembled K. R.'s brave experiment with Shakespeare's *Hamlet*—an *en regard* Russian verse translation and two volumes of scholarly commentaries— published in 1899.)

The accompanying text by Nabokov in the Bollingen Series edition of *Eugene Onegin* is a product of supreme intellectual and artistic maturity: The admiration for the artist and man is still there, but the earlier attitude of exalted and exaggerated piety is not. Pushkin's faults are occasionally pointed out using such previously unthinkable terms as "a very poor stanza." A former object of deep veneration, Pushkin's legendary old nurse—the nanny whom Nabokov reverently described in "Izgnanie" ("Exile") as Pushkin's sole confidante ("He will tell everything to her alone")—is now treated with considerable distrust: "The influence of her folk tales upon Pushkin has been enthusiastically and ridiculously exaggerated. It is doubtful that Pushkin ever read *Eugene Onegin* to her, as some commentators and illustrators have believed. In the twenties she ruled the household with a firm hand, terrorized the servant maids and was extremely fond of the bottle" (*EO* 2:452). As Nabokov quotes from the unfinished elegy that Pushkin wrote for his nurse, he ironically admits that translating "*Golubka dryakhlaya moya*" as "My decrepit doveling" would be too much even for a literalist, so that one has to settle for "My dear decrepit friend."

Nabokov is also outspoken in rebuking the pious legends perpetuated by some memorialists, as well as the traditional and Soviet biographers of Pushkin, especially in regard to his linguistic competence: "Like most Russians, Pushkin was a poor linguist: Even the fluent French he had learned as a child lacked personal tang and, judging by his letters, remained throughout his life limited to a brilliant command of eighteenth-century ready-made phrases. When he tried to teach himself English . . . he never went beyond the beginner's stage" (*EO* 2:162).

It should be noted that Nabokov's trenchant—at times, apodictic—critical style bears a strong resemblance to Pushkin's uncompromising literary judgments. Nabokov could express the following opinion: "There are readers who prefer Pushkin's *Scene from Faust* (1825) to the whole of Goethe's *Faust*, in which they distinguish a queer strain of triviality impairing the pounding of its profundities" (*EO* 2:235–36). Pushkin remarked in his notes to *Eugene Onegin:* "The ballets of Mr. Didelot are full of liveliness of fancy and extraordinary charm. One of our romantic writers found in them much more poetry than in the whole of French literature" (*EO* 1:313).

The biographical aspect of Nabokov's commentaries is especially significant as an implied juxtaposition of two historical ages and two great poetic destinies. Nabokov, as has been shown, attributed particular importance to Pushkin's episodes of prolonged exile, as compared with the lot that fell to his own generation. The theme of Pushkin's exile, so important for Nabokov during his European years, is represented somewhat differently in the commentaries to *Eugene Onegin:* The exile that Pushkin had to endure was not as bad as generally believed after all:

> It has become a commonplace with commentators to deplore Pushkin's "exile." Actually, it may be argued that during those six years he wrote more and better than he would, had he remained in St. Petersburg. He was not permitted to return to the capital; this, no doubt, greatly irritated our poet during his years of provincial office and rural seclusion (1820–24, 1824–26). The biographer should not, however, exaggerate the hardships of his banishment. His chief, General Inzov, was a cultured and sympathetic person. Pushkin's vegetation in Kishinev was an easier life than that of many a military man gambling and drinking in the provincial hole where his duty took him and his regiment. His life of fashionable dissipation and romantic adventure in gay, sophisticated Odessa was a very pleasant form of exile indeed, despite his feud with Count Vorontsov. And the quiet of Mihaylovskoe, with the friendly Osipov family at the end of the pinewood ride, was in fact sought out by our poet again very soon after he was permitted to reside where he wished. (*EO* 3:151–52)

With utmost fairness, Nabokov obliquely suggests, polemically in regard to Soviet scholars, that the conditions of Pushkin's life in the south and in Mikhailovskoe were relatively favorable when compared with Soviet punitive measures.

Nabokov's own European "safe exile," as he called it, was, of course, harsher than Pushkin's exile in certain respects, yet we know how desperately Pushkin wished to change his locale for Paris, London, or even Peking. The situation changed when Nabokov came to America, which he did not consider a place of exile—hence, the suggested juxtaposition of Pushkin's twin homelands, Africa and Russia, and of Nabokov's own Russia and America in his Russian and English paraphrases of two often quoted lines from *Eugene Onegin* ("Pod nebom Afriki moei / Vzdykhat' o sumrachnoi Rossii [and sigh, . . . beneath the / sky of my Africa, / for somber Russia]" [*EO* chap. 1, ll. 11–12):

в горах Америки моей вздыхать по северной России. (*Drugie berega* 61)

Beneath the sky
Of my America to sigh
For *one* locality in Russia. (*SM* 73)

Thus, the two lives are consistently examined by Nabokov in search of points of contact. The translator and interpreter unobtrusively but perceptibly enters the text of the commentary with his own critical opinions, tastes, personal biography, and genealogy. Nabokov's affinity with Pushkin, a descendant of a six-hundred-year old Russian noble family, just as Nabokov was; separated from him by exactly one century (1799 and 1899); and linked to him by a network of kinsmen and associates, is manifested in a number of comparable, parallel, or complementary features in their respective biographies. One of these is the border that Pushkin could never cross to escape from, and Nabokov could never cross to return to, his native Russia. This affinity—the affinity of two great writers of two centuries—forcefully prompted Nabokov to include his own reminiscences and opinions in his account of *Eugene Onegin* and the bygone age of Russian life. Pushkin, who never missed the opportunity to emphasize the role of his ancestors in Russian history, would probably have appreciated Nabokov's hypothesis concerning his duel with Ryleev (*EO* 2:426–34), couched in the manner of "The Shot."

Yet the essential and often overlooked attitude of Nabokov toward Pushkin is an apologetic one. In his poem "On Translating *Eugene Onegin*" (1955), this attitude is quite explicit:

What is translation? On a platter
The poet's pale and glaring head,
A parrot's screech, a monkey's chatter,

And profanation of the dead.
The parasites you were so hard on
Are pardoned if I have your pardon,
O, Pushkin, for my stratagem. (*PP* 175)

These lines contain a distinct allusion, by means of an abbreviated quotation and a bilingual pun (if I have your *pardon* < esli budu / Toboi *opravdan*), to Pushkin's epistle to Fedor Glinka (1822):

Пускай судьба определила
Гоненья грозные мне вновь . . .
В моем изгнаньи позабуду
Несправедливость их обид:
Они ничтожны—*если буду*
Тобой оправдан, Аристид. (Emphasis added)

[Even if Fate has allotted me/ A new share of fierce persecutions / . . . / In my exile I shall forget / The injustice of their affronts: / They are of no importance, if I shall be / Absolved by you, Aristides].

Eventually, Pushkin would become rather hard on Fedor Glinka and include him in his epigram "A Collection of Insects" (1829): Vot ** <Glinka>—Bozhiia korovka [Here is ** <Glinka>, a ladybug], which explains Nabokov's blending an entomological theme with the quotation from Pushkin's epistle to Glinka. In fact, the path of the faithful and learned translator is described by Nabokov as an insect's path down the secret stem and its feeding on the root of the original's rose. It needs to be mentioned in this connection that Nabokov's imagery in this stanza ("I grew another stalk and turned / Your stanza patterned on a sonnet / Into my honest roadside prose—/ All thorn, but cousin to your rose") owes a great deal to such poems by Vladislav Khodasevich as "Trudoliubivoiu pcheloi" and, especially, "Peterburg": "I kazhdyi stikh gonia skvoz' prozu, / Vyvikhivaia kazhduiu stroku, / Privil-taki klassicheskuiu rozu / K sovetskomu dichku [And driving every verse through prose, / Pulling every line out of joint / I grafted, after all, a classical rose / To a Soviet wilding]".[6] As a great poet and a Pushkinian, Khodasevich serves here as a model to be emulated and a mediator between his younger contemporary and the heritage of Pushkin.

6. Vladislav Khodasevich, *Stikhotvoreniia* (Leningrad: Sovetskii pisatel', 1989), 155).

Nabokov once summed up his pedagogical principles as follows: "During my years of teaching at Cornell and elsewhere I demanded of my students the passion of science and the patience of poetry" (*SO* 7). This formula is a paraphrase of what he said in "On Translating *Eugene Onegin*":

This is my task—a poet's patience
And scholiastic passion blent.

Nevertheless, he called his Pushkinian efforts, in the same apologetic spirit of self-deprecating humility, "Dove-droppings on your [Pushkin's] monument." There is a lighthearted and ironic biographical side to Nabokov's emotional resignation, suggested by a relevant recollection in his memoirs (*SM* 67). As a young girl, Nabokov's mother met in the Crimea the well-known seascape painer Ayvazovski, who used to talk about how in 1836 he had seen Pushkin at an exhibition of pictures in St. Petersburg—"an ugly little fellow with a tall handsome wife." Nabokov's mother also remembered "the touch nature added from its own palette—the white mark a bird left on the painter's gray top hat" (*SM* 67).

On one occasion, when asked about his life, Nabokov replied: "My own life has been incomparably happier and healthier than that of Genghis Khan, who is said to have fathered the first Nabok" (*SO* 119). Nabokov's life, no doubt, was also incomparably happier than that of Pushkin. It is also obvious that Pushkin was part of Nabokov's happiness. As Nabokov put it in his Pushkin speech in Paris, "to read [Pushkin's] works . . . , without a single exception is one of the glories of earthly life".[7]

Spiritual encounters of literary giants usually bring about extraordinary results in art. One ventures to predict that the great monogram that unites the names of Pushkin and Nabokov will forever be a source of inspiration to Russian literature and a challenge to literary hermeneutics. Of course, in translating *Eugene Onegin* Nabokov took "the geniuses' professional risk" of being misinterpreted ("professional'nyi risk geniev"), as Khodasevich said about Pushkin.[8] Yet from a broad, cross-cultural point of view, Nabokov's Pushkin studies, along with his lectures on Russian literature, his *Song of Igor's Campaign,* and his studies of Gogol and Lermontov, were, to blend Khodasevich's memorable phrase with a line from the draft of Pushkin's "Autumn," "a grafting of the classical rose" to "the virgin forests of youthful America."

7. Nabokov, "Pushkin," 39.
8. Vladislav Khodasevich, *Koleblemyi trenozhnik: Izbrannoe,* ed. V. G. Perel'muter, E. M. Ben', A. V. Naumov, and N. N. Bogomolov (Moscow: Sovetskii pisatel', 1991), 202.

{ 12 }

Nabokov and Tiutchev

CHRISTINE A. RYDEL

To Edmund Wilson's comment that Tiutchev "doesn't have much range ... does he?" Nabokov replied: "Pushkin is a sea, but Tyutchev is a well. Slick but true" (*NWL* 95, 97). Although Nabokov seldom drew from this well, the spirit of Fedor Ivanovich Tiutchev runs through his works. Nabokov tells us that at Cambridge he invited "the poetry of Pushkin and Tyutchev" into his rooms (*SM* 265). Later, when Nabokov taught Russian literature, he always included Tiutchev, especially for "the cool brilliancy of [his] many waters."[1] And in an imagined conversation in *The Gift*, Fyodor Godunov-Cherdyntsev tells the poet Koncheev, "[O]f late it's Tyutchev who shares my night lodgings most often." "A worthy house guest," Koncheev replies (*Gift* 85).

Godunov-Cherdyntsev then recalls their early enthusiasm for the Silver Age poets, among whom Aleksandr Blok figured prominently. As Vladimir Alexandrov notes, "Nabokov's admiration for Blok is clearly reflected in his own verse"; most relevant to a discussion of Tiutchev in Nabokov is the second poem of the pair, "On A. Blok's Death."[2] Here Pushkin, Lermontov, Tiutchev, and Fet welcome Blok as he arrives in the next world. Nabokov assigns to each metaphors that crystallize their most salient trait. Tiutchev, a spring flowing into the mist ("Tiutchev—kliuch, struiashchiisia vo mgle"[3]),

---

1. Brian Boyd, *Vladimir Nabokov: The American Years* (Princeton, N.J.: Princeton University Press, 1991), 12.
2. Vladimir E. Alexandrov, *Nabokov's Otherworld* (Princeton, N.J.: Princeton University Press, 1991), 215–17.
3. Note here the internal rhyme "Tiutch/kliuch" that further identifies the poet with the spring (see *Stikhi* 181–82).

arrives with dew in the air to greet Blok. When Tiutchev sings about the "gleam of ringing waters," he offers a gift of "cool brilliancy" to Blok, the only Silver Age poet who merits a place in paradise.

Unfortunately, Godunov-Cherdyntsev's father, Konstantin Kirillovich, dismisses all contemporary poetry, including Blok's, as rubbish. However, he knows Pushkin "as some people know the liturgy" and loves to declaim "The Prophet" as well as "the incomparable 'Butterfly' by Fet, and Tyutchev's 'Now the dim-blue shadows mingle'" (*Gift* 160–61). The Fet poem would certainly appeal to the lepidopterist, but why Tiutchev's? Probably because of the line: "The moth's unseen flight / is heard in the night air."[4] In addition, the poem's famous line, "I am in everything and everything is in me," would elicit a response from someone who feels most alive when, on expedition, he feels "at one" with nature.

Tiutchev's poem "Summer Evening" moves another of Nabokov's characters at a literary soirée, when Mrs. Luzhin arranges to bring her husband "back to life." Following a long, tortuous disquisition by a journalist, a "plain-looking man who had listened to the whole of the journalist's idea" says, "[A]nd note ... that Tiutchev's night is cool and the stars in it are round and moist and glossy, and not simply bright dots." This man, Petrov, generally spoke little: "His sole function in life was to carry, reverently and with concentration, that which had been entrusted to him, something which it was necessary at all costs to preserve in all its detail and in all its purity" (*Def* 230)—like a line from Tiutchev.

While describing yet another cultural evening in the émigré community, Vadim, the narrator of *Look at the Harlequins!* notes that such events are too trivial to record, except for lines from Tiutchev and the rehabilitated Blok, which were "cited in passing ... and which ornamented sad lives with a sudden cadenza coming from some celestial elsewhere, a glory, a sweetness, the patch of rainbow cast on the wall by a crystal paperweight we cannot locate" (*LATH* 58). Vadim sadly notes that his wife, Iris, who does not understand Russian, misses such moments of beauty.[5]

In "Cloud, Castle, Lake," Tiutchev's lyrics, though mentioned only in passing, ultimately provide a subtext to the narrative. Ostensibly, Nabokov's bru-

---

4. Fedor Ivanovich Tiutchev, *Lirika*, 2 vols. (Moscow: Nauka, 1966), 1:75. My translation.

5. Note that "Iris" means rainbow, not incidentally an element of a typical Tiutchev landscape.

tal story simply relates the plight of a Russian refugee who wins a "pleasure trip" at an émigré charity ball in Berlin. Reluctant at first to accept the prize, Vasili Ivanovich tries to return the ticket, but he eventually finds it simpler to go. He travels for three days (descent into hell?) in the country with an unsavory group, who ultimately beat him after harassing him from the start. The apparent cause of the group's cruelty is Vasili Ivanovich's desire to leave and live in a small inn, where from his window he can see the idyllic scene that originally prompted him to leave his fellow travelers—a happy configuration of cloud, castle, and lake (in Russian, cloud, lake, and tower), a scene common in that part of Europe but extraordinary to the unfortunate Russian. On his return to Berlin, Vasili Ivanovich visits the narrator and relates his adventures.[6]

Critics have long seen this story as something of an epilogue to Nabokov's *Invitation to a Beheading* (1935). Indeed, after the tour group tortures Vasili Ivanovich and forces him back on the train, he wails, "Oh, but this is nothing less than an invitation to a beheading" (*ND* 122–23/ *Ves* 246). As Robert Hughes says, "Vasili Ivanovich . . . is Cincinnatus C. [the hero of *Invitation to a Beheading*] in another guise." The main link between the two characters is their love of nineteenth-century Russian literature, especially the lyrics of the great Romantic poet Tiutchev.[7]

The Tiutchev connection provides an even deeper link between the two works: "Cloud, Castle, Lake" serves as a condensed version of the novel itself. The submerged, camouflaged Tiutchev allusions simultaneously provide an ironic, deeper reading of the story. Gavriel Shapiro quotes a passage from *Invitation to a Beheading* in which Cincinnatus contemplates his inner world of beauty:

> Dreamy, round, and blue, it turns slowly toward me. It is as if you are lying supine, with eyes closed, on an overcast day, and suddenly the gloom stirs under your eyelids, and slowly becomes first a languorous smile, then a warm feeling of contentment, and you know that the sun has come out from behind the clouds. With just such a feeling my world begins: the misty

---

6. Vladimir Nabokov, "Cloud, Castle, Lake," in idem, *Nabokov's Dozen* (Garden City, N.Y.: Anchor Press/Doubleday, 1984), and in *Vesna v Fial'te* (in Russian) (Ann Arbor: Ardis, 1978) (hereafter, *ND* and *Ves*). All page citations are to these editions.

7. Robert P. Hughes, "Notes on the Translation of *Invitation to a Beheading*," in *Nabokov: Criticism, Reminiscences, Translations*, ed. Alfred Appel, Jr., and Charles Newman (Evanston, Ill.: Northwestern University Press, 1970), 289, 292.

air gradually clears, and it is suffused with such radiant, tremulous kindness, and my soul expanses so freely in its native realm. (*IB* 93–94).[8]

Shapiro convincingly argues that this passage evokes several of Tiutchev's lyrics, among them "Uraniia," and "Cache-Cache."[9] However, Cincinnatus's dream world echoes other Tiutchev poems, most significantly, "Vchera v mechtakh obvorozhennykh" (Yesterday in Charmed Dreams, 1836) and "Teni sizye smesilis'" (Blue-gray Shadows Mingle, 1836), not incidentally the favorite Tiutchev poem of Konstantin Kirillovich Godunov-Cherdyntsev, who also disappears into his ideal world.[10]

In "Yesterday in Charmed Dreams," a sunbeam awakens a young girl as she lies on her bed; it also disperses the gloom of night that enters through a window. Certain "clusters" of words, synonyms, and images from Tiutchev's poems find their way into Cincinnatus's dream world. In his vision we have "sonnyi mir" (dream world), "s zakrytymi glazami" (with closed eyes), "temnota pod vekami" (darkness under lids), "v tomnuiu ulybku" ([turns] into a languorous smile), "vyplylo iz-za oblakov solntse" (the sun has come out from behind the clouds), and, farther on, "vot" (lo!/there it is!), "razlita" (suffused), and "kover" (rug). The title of the poem contains the word "mechta," not only a dream, but a daydream, a link to Cincinnatus's longed-for other world. Tiutchev's young woman fell asleep only after the last ray of the moon touched her "languorously lit eyelids" ("Na vezhdakh [old form of 'vekakh'] tomno-ozarennykh"). Later, "a sleepy lock of [her] hair played with an invisible dream" ("sonnyi lokon/Igral s nezrimoiu mechtoi"). The sunbeam also "has run along the darkly glimmering rugs" ("Po temno-brezzhushchim kovram"). In Nabokov, a patterned rug ("uzorchatyi kover" [*ND* 94/*Ves* 99]) appears in a simile about time. Tiutchev repeats "vot" three times in the poem to point out the ways in which the sunbeam—light as smoke, like a snake, and like an unraveling ribbon—touched the young girl's bosom. Nabokov uses "vot" to point to the boundaries of Cincinnatus's dream world, the point beyond which he loses control, where he spots his prey and espies a woman gliding in his direction—not unlike Tiutchev's snakelike manifestations of the sunbeam.

---

8. Gavriel Shapiro, *Delicate Markers: Subtexts in Vladimir Nabokov's* Invitation to a Beheading (New York: Peter Lang, 1998), 135–37.

9. Ibid.

10. Tiutchev, *Lirika*, 1:86–87.

In "Blue-gray Shadows Mingle," the lyrical narrator asks "quiet twilight, sleepy twilight" ("sumrak tikhii, sumrak sonnyi") to pour itself into his soul and implores the darkness, "quiet, languid, and fragrant" ("tikhii, tomnyi, blagovonnyi") to flood and make everything quiet.[11] He tells the darkness: "Fill my feeling to overflowing with the mist of self-forgetfulness.... Let me taste annihilation." Richard Gregg suggests that in this lyric, "the poet is expressing a desire not for death but for a radically transformed *life*"—as does Cincinnatus.[12] "Teni sizye smesilis'" and "Vchera v mechtakh obvorozhennykh" play a significant role in "Cloud, Castle, Lake," as do "Uraniia," "Silentium!" and "Odinochestvo" (Solitude)—poems that Shapiro sees supplying a subtext for *Invitation to a Beheading*.[13] In addition, the word "vezhdy" appears in Tiutchev's "Zedlitz: Byron," which figures in the story. Also, Cincinnatus sees from afar visions of the Tamara Gardens (*IB* 42–43, 76–77) that prefigure Vasili Ivanovich's own ideal Tiutchev landscape. Cincinnatus, too, would like to escape into the valley, but only Vasili Ivanovich will have the chance to experience his own Tiutchev paradise—if only for a brief time.

After entering the empty third-class train car, the group members sit together, but "Vasili Ivanovich, having sat down by himself ... opened a little volume of Tyutchev, whom he had long intended to reread; but he was requested to put the book aside and join the group" (*ND* 115/ *Ves* 237). The English version omits allusions to two Tiutchev poems—"Silentium!" and "Yesterday in Charmed Dreams." The first appears as an untranslatable pun of the most famous line in all of Tiutchev: "Mysl' izrechennaia est' lozh'" (The uttered thought is a lie). In Nabokov, one finds, "My sliz'. Rechennaia est' lozh'"—that is, "We are slime. Spoken is the lie"(*Ves* 237).[14]

The second poem immediately follows only as "the wonderful [line] about the crimson exclamation" ("i divnoe o rumianom vosklitsanii"). Svetlana Pol'skaia mistakenly identifies the "crimson exclamation" as a reference to "Vesennie vody" (Spring Waters). She cites the exclamation "Vesna idet, vesna idet!" (Spring is coming, spring is coming!) and the line "Rumianyi, svetlyi khorovod" (Crimson, light round dance) as the marvelous thing Vasili

---

11. Ibid., 1:75.

12. Richard A. Gregg, *Fedor Tiutchev: The Evolution of a Poet* (New York: Columbia University Press, 1965), 86–87. The translation comes from this work.

13. Shapiro, *Delicate Markers*, 135–39.

14. Ibid., 139; Julian W. Connolly, *Nabokov's Early Fiction: Patterns of Self and Other* (Cambridge: Cambridge University Press, 1992), 256.

Ivanovich wishes to reread.[15] However, this poem simply uses the word "rumianyi" and contains an exclamation, as does "Net, moego k tebe pristrast'ia" (No, I don't have the strength to hide my fondness for you). "Rumianyi" appears in three other poems: "Zedlitz: Byron," "Gerder: Pesn' skandinavskikh voinov" (Herder: Song of Scandinavian Warriors), and "Yesterday in Charmed Dreams." Only the last poem contains the phrase "crimson exclamation" while having any relevance to the story.

> Vdrug zhivotrepetnym siian'em
> Kosnuvshis' persei molodykh,
> Rumianym, gromkim vosklitsan'em
> Raskrylo shelk resnits tvoikh![16]

> [Suddenly with palpitating radiance, / having touched your young bosom (or breasts), / in a loud crimson exclamation, it [the sunbeam] has / opened wide the silk of your lashes.]

"Yesterday in Charmed Dreams" paints a highly erotic picture of a sunbeam awakening a woman. The "crimson exclamation" occurs at a climactic moment, intimating sexual union. As Gregg comments: "And in the final synesthetic image of light breaking across the barriers of flesh we have a symbol for sexual union as old as Zeus' shower of gold."[17]

Even though Nabokov uses the play of light, especially that of the sun, throughout the story, another aspect of the poem emerges in "Cloud, Castle, Lake." On the second day of the trip, the group members settle down to play a perverse game that degrades sexual union rather than celebrates it, as Tiutchev does:

> [T]he women would lie down on the benches they chose, under which the men were already hidden, and when from under one of the benches there would emerge a *ruddy* face with ears, or a big outspread hand, with a skirt-lifting curve of the fingers (which would provoke much squealing), it would be revealed who was paired off with whom. Three times Vasili Ivanovich lay down in filthy darkness, and three times it turned out that there was no

---

15. Svetlana Pol'skaia, "Kommentarii k rasskazu V. Nabokova 'Oblako, ozero, bashnia,'" *Scando-Slavica* 39 (1989): 119–20.
16. Tiutchev, *Lirika*, 1:87.
17. Gregg, *Fedor Tiutchev*, 73. The translated passage is from this work.

one on the bench when he crawled out from under. He was acknowledged the loser and was forced to eat a cigarette butt. (*ND* 119-20/ *Ves* 242-43; emphasis added)

Here the delicate imagery of the poem turns into a ruddy face with ears (in Russian, "krasnaia golova s ushami," a red head with ears) that crawls out—like a snake, but unlike Tiutchev's—and a "big outspread hand, with a skirt-lifting curve of the fingers." Instead of evoking a poetic "crimson exclamation," they produce only squeals. And the poet's "rumianyi"—that is, crimson or blushing—turns into "krasnyi," or red, but ruddy in Nabokov's English version. When the depraved game is over, Vasili Ivanovich, also snakelike, crawls out from under a bench.

Nabokov's transformation of one of Tiutchev's most beautiful and exalted lines into an ugly pun now makes sense. In "Silentium!" Tiutchev explores the theme that, because the world cannot understand one's deepest and most precious thoughts, all expression is useless. Tiutchev tells man

> Live in your inner self alone
> within your soul a world has grown
> the magic of veiled thoughts that might
> be blinded by the outer light
> drowned in the noise of day, unheard ...
> take in their song and speak no word.[18]

Vasili Ivanovich tries to follow Tiutchev's advice, but the group will not let him. Perhaps Vasili Ivanovich hears not Tiutchev's exalted line, but the group's refrain, "My sliz'" (We are slime). This the group members prove to be. At this point, the second half of the impossible pun becomes clear: "izrechennaia est' lozh'," with its wrenched word order, can mean "the lie is what is spoken"—a reversal of Tiutchev's meaning and a characterization of the group; hence, the misquotation. At first, the group members pretend to draw out Vasili Ivanovich in a friendly manner, but all along they want only to make him the butt of their jokes: "They ... all busied themselves with him, at first good-naturedly, then with malevolence" (*ND* 118/ *Ves* 247).

18. In Vladimir Nabokov, *Three Russian Poets: Translations of Pushkin, Lermontov, Tyutchev* (Norfolk, Conn.: New Directions, 1944), 34. The ten Tiutchev poems that Nabokov translated appear most frequently as subtexts of his own works.

But Vasili Ivanovich has endured the group's cruelty even earlier, when everyone was made to sing a song by Schramm, the tour leader. While everyone sings, Vasili Ivanovich simply mouths the words. (An attempt to follow Tiutchev's advice?) Schramm orders the group to be silent but forces Vasili Ivanovich, who can barely pronounce German, to sing alone. Vasili must endure humiliation, which belies the words of the song:

> Stop that worrying and moping,
> Take a knotted stick and rise,
> Come a-tramping in the open
> With the good, the hearty guys!
>
> Tramp your country's grass and stubble,
> With the good, the hearty guys,
> Kill the hermit and his trouble
> And to hell with doubts and sighs!
>
> In a paradise of heather
> Where the field mouse screams and dies,
> Let us march and sweat together
> With the steel and leather guys! (*ND* 117)

A more literal translation of the original shows how the words uttered (or sung) are but a lie, for Vasili Ivanovich's companions in no way resemble the people of the song:

> Bid farewell to empty anxieties,
> Take a thick stick
> And stride along the open road
> Together with kind people.
>
> Along the hills of your native land
> Together with kind people,
> Without unsociable anxieties,
> Without doubts, to hell with them (or the devil take it).
>
> Kilometer after kilometer
> Mi-re-do and do-re-mi,
> Together with the sun, together with the wind,
> Together with kind people. (*Ves* 240)[19]

19. My translation.

The stick of the song comes into play not as a walking aid but as a means of punishment. A member of the group, who once visited Tsaritsyn (Stalingrad), uses a stick to inflict his own brand of torture on Vasili Ivanovich. When Vasili Ivanovich finally returns to the train, "they began to beat him—they beat him a long time, and with a good deal of inventiveness. It occurred to them, among other things, to use a corkscrew on his palms; then on his feet. The post-office clerk, who had been to Russia, fashioned a knout out of a stick and a belt, and began to use it with devilish dexterity. Atta boy! The other men relied more on their iron heels, whereas the women were satisfied to pinch and slap. All had a wonderful time" (*ND* 123/ *Ves* 246–47)

The perversion of the song parallels, though more drastically, Nabokov's transformation of another of Tiutchev's beautiful lyrics into doggerel. The first Russian line of the song parodies the poem "Ital'ianskaia villa" (Italian Villa, 1837), with the command, "Rasprostis' s pustoi trevogi" (Bid farewell to empty [idle] anxieties), rather than Tiutchev's narrative beginning, "I rasprostias' s trevogoiu zhiteiskoi" (And having bid farewell to life's anxieties). The poem describes a beautiful Italian villa, peacefully deserted for centuries, "guarded by a magic dream." But when man enters, evil follows quickly and spoils the natural scene:

> Suddenly all was confusion: a convulsive tremor
> Ran along the cypress branches . . .
> The fountain fell silent—and some sort of strange babble
> As if through sleep, whispered incoherently.
>
> What is it, friend? Could it be that not for nothing
> Has the evil life, that life—alas!—which flowed in us then,
> That evil life, with its turbulent heat,
> Crossed the sacred threshold?[20]

As in "Silentium!" man can destroy the beauty of silence. In the story, the group repeatedly destroys Vasili Ivanovich's quiet enjoyment of the scenes around him.

The anticipation of happiness Vasili experiences on the eve and morning of his departure proves to be unfounded. His insomnia should have been a warning to someone well versed in Tiutchev. "He slept badly . . . [b]ecause he

---

20. Gregg, *Fedor Tiutchev*, 68–69; Tiutchev, *Lirika*, 1:90–91. Nabokov also "degrades" this poem by changing the iambic pentameter of the original into the ditty-like dance beat of trochaic tetrameter.

had to get up unusually early, and hence took along into his dreams the delicate face of the watch ticking on his night table; but mainly because . . . he began to imagine that this trip, thrust upon him by a feminine Fate in a low-cut gown . . . would bring him some wonderful, tremulous happiness. This happiness would have something in common with . . . the excitement aroused in him by Russian lyrical poetry" (*ND* 114/ *Ves* 236).

Many poets have written about insomnia, but Tiutchev's poem contains elements that appear in Vasili Ivanovich's dreams. "Bessonitsa" (Insomnia, 1829)[21] begins with "the monotonous stroke of the clock; the night's wearying tale" ("Chasov odnoobraznyi boi/ Tomitel'naia nochi povest'"). Like Vasili Ivanovich, alone in the world, Tiutchev's night world is orphaned ("osirotelyi"). In the middle of the night, it seems, "our ineluctable fate has struck and we, struggling with all of nature, are hurled back upon ourselves." Of course, Vasili's feminine Fate in a low-cut gown is not Tiutchev's malevolent force; it is probably just the young Russian lady who drew his winning ticket out of the barrel at the charity ball. Once more, the story trivializes Tiutchev. Vasili Ivanovich's night of insomnia diverges from Tiutchev's, though. Whereas Vasili feels a sense of optimism, a promise of happiness, the suffering poet is filled with dread and a sense of foreboding:

> Only from time to time,
> As it performs the sad rite at midnight,
> The funereal voice
> Of metal mourns us.[22]

The prophetic voice of Tiutchev's insomnia, not Vasili Ivanovich's, ultimately predicts the latter's lamentable fate. He finds not happiness on this trip but the oblivion Tiutchev's fate foretells, especially at the end, when the narrator releases him from duty. Here Vasili Ivanovich's version proves to be the lie. The poem predicts a "tomitel'naia povest'"—exactly what "Cloud, Castle, Lake" turns out to be. In addition, "tomitel'naia" echoes the semantic clusters of Cincinnatus's dream world and thus provides another link between novel and story.

Other Tiutchev poems are buried within the text of "Cloud, Castle, Lake," one of which has a particularly menacing air. On the first day of Vasili Ivanovich's trip, "[t]he locomotive, working rapidly with its elbows, hurried

---

21. Tiutchev, *Lirika*, 1:18.
22. Gregg, *Fedor Tiutchev*, 61.

through a pine forest, then—with relief—among fields" (*ND* 116/*Ves* 238). Why with relief? Perhaps the answer comes from Tiutchev's description of a trip he once made from St. Petersburg to Munich:

> Soft sand comes up to our horses' shanks
>   as we ride in the darkening day
> and the shadows of pines have closed their ranks:
>   all is shadow along our way.
> In denser masses the black trees rise.
>   What a comfortless neighborhood!
> Grim night like a beast with a hundred eyes
>   peers out of the underwood.[23]

After Vasili's train reaches the fields, the sun shines again, and the scene, though faintly echoing Tiutchev's imagery, becomes less sinister: not shadows but flowers merge. "The badly pressed shadow of the car sped madly along the grassy bank, where flowers blended ("slivalis") into colored streaks" (*ND* 116/*Ves* 238); Tiutchev's shadows "slilisia," the perfective form of the verb. And whereas Tiutchev's hundred-eyed beast, night, only appears malevolent, Vasili Ivanovich's multi-eyed and multi-limbed monster—the group—really is. They "all gradually melted together, merged together, forming one collective, wobbly, many-handed being, from which one could not escape" (*ND* 118/ *Ves* 241). Vasili Ivanovich initially tries to escape this group by attempting to read Tiutchev in the train; while surrounded by a Tiutchevian landscape, he ironically reads a Russian poet whose most beautiful nature lyrics describe not Russian scenes—which he found barren and hostile—but German scenes, many of which feature clouds, castles, lakes, and even towers.

In Tiutchev's poetry, towers appear twice, castles seven times, clouds twenty-one times, and lakes eleven times. Other landscape features of "Cloud, Castle, Lake" recur frequently in Tiutchev: forest and pine forest ("les" and "sosnovyi les," 16 times), fields ("polia," 15 times), hills ("kholmy," 9 times), the road ("doroga," 9 times), and verdure ("zelen'," 11 times).[24] The poems that

---

23. Nabokov, "Soft Sands Come up to Our Horses' Shanks," in *Three Russian Poets*, 33; Tiutchev, "Pesok sypuchii po koleni . . . ," *Lirika,* 1:38. The notes to the poem (pp. 350–51) provide the source for Tiutchev's hundred-eyed beast: Goethe's "Willkommen und Abschied."

24. The word counts come from Borys Bilokur, *A Concordance to the Russian Poetry of Fedor I. Tiutchev* (Providence, R.I.: Brown University Press, 1975).

combine several elements include: "Zedlitz: Byron" (1827)—castle ("zamok"), lake ("ozero"), the road ("doroga"), and hill ("kholm"); "Odinochestvo" (Solitude, 1822)—cloud ("oblako"), field ("pole"), verdure ("zelen'"), and hills; "Uraniia"—cloud, forest ("les"), and hill; and "Zachem gubit' ..." (Why Destroy ... from *Faust* IV," 1829)—cloud, lake, verdure.

"Uraniia" links "Cloud, Castle, Lake" with *Invitation to a Beheading*, as noted earlier. Tiutchev's rendering from *Faust* (pt. 1, IV–1067-99) asks that idle dejection (Tiutchev: "unynie pustoe"; Goethe: "der Trübsinn"; melancholy or spleen)[25] not destroy the beauty of the hour, a scene that rivals Vasili Ivanovich's with a landscape of mountains, valley, clouds, and lakes. Tiutchev's translation of a fragment from Zedlitz's poem "Totenkränze" (Funeral Wreaths, 1828), memorializes Byron, whose shade now soars over the earth.[26] On reaching the land along the Rhine, Byron sees the same lakes, hills, and castles that captivate Vasili Ivanovich, who, like the English poet, is an exile. Lamartine's "L'isolement" (Tiutchev's "Odinochestvo" [Isolation, 1822]) provides the saddest subtext with its image of the poet as orphan.[27] The lyrical narrator sits pensively in thick shadows and contemplates scenes that flash before his eyes: the beauty of a valley ("doliny krasoty"), the last ray of dawn as it wanders over the dark verdure of the trees ("po temnoi zeleni"), the moon as it rises on a chariot of clouds ("kolesnitsa oblakov"), his fields ("moi [my] polia"). With desiccated heart, he roams the earth like an orphan shade, unwarmed by the sun. He dejectedly looks in vain from hill to hill ("s kholma na kholm") and finds only horrible emptiness. Ultimately, he asks the winds to carry him, an orphan, away.[28] Shapiro shows how Nabokov reverses this poem in *Invitation to a Beheading* when wind and lightning destroy "not Cincinnatus ... but rather the artificial world around him, and liberate him from his spiritual solitude."[29] Vasili Ivanovich, too, finds freedom at the end, but not before he suffers his own isolation. Like the lyrical narrator of Tiutchev's translation, Vasili Ivanovich lives all alone in the world; but unlike

---

25. Tiutchev, *Lirika*, 2:91-93.
26. Ibid., 2:69-75.
27. Ibid., 2:31-33.
28. Gregg notes that the word "orphan" appears nowhere in the original by Lamartine, but that Tiutchev added it for reasons of his own: see Gregg, *Fedor Tiutchev*, 55-56. The state of being orphaned also connects this poem—at least, in Nabokov's story—to the orphaned world of "Bessonitsa."
29. Shapiro, *Delicate Markers*, 137.

him, Vasili finds a paradise on earth after he has wandered "from hill to hill" ("s kholma na kholm").

Enraptured in his youth by Tiutchev's poems, Vasili Ivanovich not surprisingly falls in love with a scene to which he has long been favorably predisposed. He discovers in a Tiutchev landscape "that very happiness of which he had once half-dreamt":

> It was a pure, blue lake, with an unusual expression of its water. In the middle, a large cloud was reflected in its entirety. On the other side, on a hill thickly covered with verdure (and the darker the verdure, the more poetic it is), towered, arising from dactyl to dactyl, an ancient black castle. Of course, there are plenty of such views in Central Europe, but just this one—in the inexpressible and unique harmoniousness of its three principal parts, in its smile, in some mysterious innocence it had ... as something so unique, and so familiar, and so long-promised. (*ND* 120/*Ves* 243)

In his reactions to this scene, Vasili Ivanovich most resembles the poet Tiutchev. Like Vasili Ivanovich, Tiutchev viewed landscapes with the eyes of a tourist; his landscapes "depict scenes from his own world."[30] But more important, Tiutchev brought literary associations to the places he traveled and saw them through the words of poets he had read earlier. The reader of "Cloud, Castle, Lake" gets caught up in a great chain of allusion. One begins to see the world of the story through the filter of Nabokov, who sees it through the eyes of Vasili Ivanovich, who perceives it through recollections of Tiutchev, who describes specific scenes with other poets in mind. But where one might expect such multilayered filtering to make the world of the story distant and hazy, the allusions themselves make it immediate and clear. Nabokov's texts work like Vadim's paperweight (see p. 124): Tiutchev's sounds synesthetically refract through the crystal and spread their colors of glory and sweetness throughout the pages of his works.

---

30. Anatoly Liberman, *On the Heights of Creation: The Lyrics of Fedor Tyutchev* (Greenwich, Conn.: JAI Press, 1993), 152.

{ 13 }

Nabokov's *Nikolai Gogol*
Doing Things in Style

LEONA TOKER

Nabokov's *Nikolai Gogol* (1944) can be seen as belonging to the genre of "literary investigation" (*khudozhestvennoe issledovanie*), along with his "Abram Gannibal," Aleksandr Solzhenitsyn's *Gulag Archipelago: An Essay in Literary Investigation,* and Abram Terz's (Andrei Siniavsky's) "Strolls with Pushkin" and "In the Shadow of Gogol." The main feature of this genre is a special kind of bifunctionality: One of the functions is informational—to present the results of extensive research; the other is aesthetic.[1] The two form a symbiosis, the aesthetic effect compensating for the deficiencies of the informational aggregate. Thus, Terz's essays were composed when he was debarred from the use of libraries for scholarly verification or footnoting of his material; he responded to this liability by writing self-consciously "hyperbolic" prose (*utrirovannaia proza*) replete with Gulag expressions. Solzhenitsyn's work on *The Gulag Archipelago* was hampered by the insufficiency of primary sources; he dealt with this problem by thematizing the "hearsay" phenomenon and dramatizing it through heteroglot procedures. When Nabokov faced a similar problem with "Abram Gannibal," he solved it by self-consciously trans-

---

1. Cf. Jan Mukařovský, *Aesthetic Function, Norm and Value as Social Facts,* trans. Mark E. Suino (Ann Arbor: University of Michigan Slavic Contributions, 1970), 7. Professional novelists can certainly produce scholarly or journalistic texts in which the aesthetic function is not marked. Siniavsky, for example, has brought this distinction into high relief by signing "Strolls with Pushkin" and "In the Shadow of Gogol" with his pen name Abram Terz yet publishing the monograph "The Fallen Leaves of Vasilii Rozanov" under his real name.

forming separate words of the available sources and separate unverifiable facts into literary motifs—that is, into building blocks of an aesthetic structure.[2]

In his work on *Nikolai Gogol,* Nabokov had the opposite difficulty: The materials were ample, but the projected book, part of the New Directions series, was to be of limited length. With the complexity of his attitude toward Gogol,[3] Nabokov had much to say in little space. And perhaps some things were better left unsaid.

"If parallel lines do not meet it is not because meet they cannot, but because they have other things to do," says Nabokov on Gogol's "four-dimensional" prose (*NG* 145).[4] The same metaphor can be applied to some items on Nabokov's own agenda in *Nikolai Gogol,* items that, like much else in that book, he left unspecified. As is well known, Nabokov's literary-critical lectures and essays generally give prominence to those aspects of other writers' work that are, in one way or another, relevant to his own art. In the monograph on Gogol, much of what remains unsaid has left stylistic imprints on the discourse, and the line that Nabokov takes in determining his attitude toward Gogol is an example of this. When the parallel course becomes tiresome and a meeting is not desired, the "other things to do" are a partial convergence and a swerving away.

The style of the monograph bears traces of attempts to maximize the semantic load. The success of this endeavor partly accounts for the aesthetic appeal of the book. Also effective, however, is the diametrically opposite procedure, that of *pleonastic expansion.* Both of these techniques involve an imitation— but only a partial one—of the corresponding features of Gogol's own writing.

Though modern English stylistics privileges muscular prose and does not favor a proliferation of epithets, the first chapters of *Nikolai Gogol* abound in adjectives, as if the author were in a desperate pursuit of some elusive quality of Gogol's world. The dominant stylistic device of the opening pages of the

---

2. See Leona Toker, "Fact and Fiction in Vladimir Nabokov's Biography of Abram Gannibal," *Mosaic* 22 (1989): 43–56.

3. In *Strong Opinions,* Nabokov would explicitly deny an unqualified admiration of Gogol: "I loath Gogol's moralistic slant, I am depressed and puzzled by his utter inability to describe young women, I deplore his obsession with religion" (*SO* 156).

4. Page citations are to the "corrected" 1961 New Directions edition. On the differences among three different versions of the book—the first, 1944/1959; the "corrected," 1961; and the "revised" Weidenfeld and Nicolson edition of 1973—see Robert Bowie, "A Note on Nabokov's Gogol," *The Nabokovian* 16 (spring 1986): 25–30.

monograph is a *synergetic* adjective-plus-noun structure, the meaning of which exceeds the sum of the meanings of its constituents. Additional connotations are produced by alliteration (a device often used by Gogol), as in "*m*orbid *m*elancholy" (*NG* 1), "*f*everish *f*light" (*NG* 13), "*perverse perse*verance" (*NG* 11), and "*mo*nstrous *p*ro*p*e*nsity*" (*NG* 13); by ironic oxymoron, as in "vigorous purging and bloodletting" (*NG* 1), a "fine . . . misjudgment of symptoms" (*NG* 2), and—in a reference to an image from Gogol's poem—a "delightful corpse" (*NG* 9); or through contrast, such as when Gogol's "poor limp body" is held fast by his stout doctor's "hefty assistant" (*NG* 2) and when the self-directed mutterings of a passerby are interpreted as the auditory effect "meant to render the hectic loneliness of a poor man in an opulent crowd" (*NG* 10). Sometimes two or three adjectives fine-tune an image, as in the double spondee of the "queer pale green tint" (*NG* 11) of St. Petersburg's skies contrasting, a page later, with the periphrastic two-feet trochee of the Ukrainian "cloudless cobalt" (*NG* 12). An adverb—usually from a quite different semantic field—may also come in to qualify the adjective, as in "grotesquely rough handling" (*NG* 2) and "diabolically energetic physicians" (*NG* 1).

The monograph opens as follows:

> Nikolai Gogol, the strangest prose-poet Russia ever produced, died Thursday morning, a little before eight, on the fourth of March, eighteen fifty-two, in Moscow. He was almost forty-three years old—a reasonably ripe age for him, considering the ridiculously short span of life generally allotted to other great Russian writers of his miraculous generation. (*NG* 1)

The categorical ring of the superlative "the strangest" conflicts with the sense of bafflement conveyed by describing Gogol as a strange "prose-poet," one who does not fit into cut-and-dried genre distinctions. The information about the day of the week and the hour of the demise ("died Thursday morning") introduces a note of recency, of news about last week's death of a common acquaintance or a celebrity. Yet the touch of familiarity dissolves when Gogol's age of forty-three is treated as "reasonably ripe."[5] This sustained epithet resonates with the "ridiculously short span of life" which was "generally allotted" to Gogol's contemporary poets—the connotation of arbitrariness in "allotted" hinting at the political intrigues behind the fatal duels of Pushkin and Lermontov. The adverb "ridiculously" desentimentalizes the issue and lays to rest whatever expectations the reader may have had of a standard no-warts biog-

---

5. Only later did Nabokov learn that his brother Sergei also must have died at this age.

raphy. It also functions as an auditory gesture, a question mark in the air, echoed, albeit with different overtones, by the unexpected hero-worshiping epithet "miraculous" at the end of the sentence.[6]

The semantic synergy of this and similar moments in *Nikolai Gogol* reproduces the feature for which Koncheev reproaches Fyodor Godunov-Cherdyntsev in *The Gift*—namely, "an excessive trust in words" to smuggle in a "necessary thought," while the "lawful road"—in this case, the discussion of the life expectancy of the "miraculous generation"—is open, and the goods imported are, anyway, "duty-free" (*Gift* 351). But then, not all the goods are duty-free: The venerable Russian tradition of "Aesopian language"[7] is not completely abandoned even in the absence of political censorship.

Indeed, readers sometimes wonder at the paucity of Nabokov's comment on the scenes of the pogrom in Gogol's *Taras Bulba*—one of the issues on which Nabokov's and Gogol's positions diverged so dramatically that comment was practically not needed. Nabokov dismisses *Taras Bulba* as "a melodramatic account of the adventures of quite fictitious cossacks—something like the *Cid* of Corneille and his Spaniards (or Hemingway's Spaniards, for that matter) in a Ukrainian disguise" (*NG* 157–58). He is generally impatient with Gogol's early hits: "When I want a good nightmare I imagine Gogol penning in Little Russian dialect volume after volume of *Dikanka* and *Mirgorod* stuff about ghosts haunting the banks of the Dniepr, burlesque Jews and dashing Cossacks" (*NG* 32). However, the adjective "burlesque," meaning "comically degrading a serious subject," hints at—indeed—the subject's

---

6. The phonetic link between "ridiculously" and "miraculous" resonates, across more than one hundred pages, with the remark that "the difference between the comic side of things, and their cosmic side, depends upon one sibilant" (*NG* 142). Robert Bowie's suggestion that it was out of mischief or "puerile delight" that Nabokov inserted an extra sibilant into the names Pisarev and Veresaev in the first three editions is doubtful: See Robert Bowie, "Nabokov's Influence on Gogol," *Journal of Modern Literature* 13 (1986): 260. The reason for spelling the names with the double *s* may have lain in an experiment in transliteration, because in English a single *s* between two vowels tends to be pronounced as *z*, which was obviously undesirable.

7. The words of Nabokov's Koncheev actually echo the statement that I. S. Aksakov made on the issue: "[T]he writer had become an expert and he managed to pass his view on to the public—like a thief, so to speak, between the lines ... in order to smuggle his thought like contraband past the censor's lookout post—and the thought would tiptoe slowly by, bundled up in double-edged turns of speech!" Quoted in Lev Losev, *On the Beneficence of Censorship: Aesopian Language in Modern Russian Literature* (Munich: Otto Sagner, 1984), 10.

seriousness. For obvious reasons, the issue of Gogol's treatment of Jews was much more inflammatory in 1944 than it is now, but Nabokov smuggled rather more of it into the text than a customs declaration such as "burlesque Jews" would allow.

This is how it seems to work. In the first section, Nabokov suggests that the leeches with which the bloodletting was effected shortly before Gogol's death, "the hideous black clusters of chaetopod worms sucking at his nostrils" (*NG* 5), were for him the types of the very devil that he had tried to exorcise by "a private hunger strike" (*NG* 1). Nabokov goes on to describe the Russian subspecies of the "geographical races" of devils: the Russian "Chort" is a "shrimpy foreigner, a shivering puny green-blooded imp with thin German, Polish, French legs, a sneaking little cad ('*podlenky*') with something inexpressibly repellent ('*gadenky*') about him." Hence, a "cold black caterpillar which chanced to touch the back of [Gogol's] hand as he was plucking some roses in Aksakov's garden sent him shrieking back to the house." Hence also, "In Switzerland, he had quite a field-day knocking the life out of lizards all along the sunny mountain paths.[8] The cane he used for this purpose may be seen in a daguerrotype of him taken in Rome in 1845. It is a very elegant affair" (*NG* 5–7). Recollecting, with some imprecision,[9] the episode of Gogol's killing a hungry black cat in his childhood, the zoologist Nabokov explains that "[t]he arched back of a lean black cat or some harmless reptile with a throbbing throat, or again the slight limbs and slippery eyes of some petty rascal (who indeed was a rascal *because* he was scrawny) provoked Gogol in a special way owing to their 'chort'-like features" (*NG* 6).

The Jews of *Taras Bulba* display most of these features,[10] alongside the stereotypical traits with which they were endowed in Ukrainian popular plays[11]

---

8. In an 1836 letter, Gogol mentions that he was at first bored in Vevey but then got used to it. His occupations there included walks during which he kept "caning the lizards that were running at the sides of the paths": V. V. Veresaev, *Gogol' v zhizni: Sistematicheskii svod podlinnykh svidetel'stv sovremennikov* (Gogol in Life: A Systematic Compilation of True Contemporary Testimonies) (Moscow: Moskovskii rabochii, 1990 [1933]), 201. My translation.

9. Cf. Veresaev, *Gogol' v zhizni*, 42–43.

10. The deal that Taras offers Warsaw Jews for the rescue of his son Ostap from the Poles also strikes some readers as similar to a contract with the devil: See Felix Dreizin, *The Russian Soul and the Jew: Essays in Literary Ethnocriticism* (Boston: University Press of America, 1990), 35.

11. See Gavriel Shapiro, *Nikolai Gogol and the Baroque Cultural Heritage* (University Park: Pennsylvania State University Press, 1993), 50.

and Russian historical romances,[12] prominently including untidiness and grotesque ugliness occasionally relieved by the hackneyed topos of a nymphet Jessica's pretty face.

What Nabokov says about the Freudian implement used against the lizards is not quite accurate: The original cane used near Vevey in 1842 had by 1845 been lost. However that may be, the adverb-plus-adjective structure of the sustained epithet in "a very elegant affair" which concludes section 1 is an ironic gesture, the flourish of an invisible wand, a serpentine question mark in the air. Nabokov then appropriates "that slim ivory-knobbed cane" (*NG* 7) in order to use it as a bridge to section 2, where it appears as the first item in the comments on Gogol's daguerrotype portrait.

In this page-long piece of ekphrasis, the epithetical adjectives are given a new assignment. Though the fingers of Gogol's writing hand are described as "delicately shaped," his lips are "unpleasant," his gaze has "a sunken and slightly 'haunted' expression" (*NG* 7), and if the print "could burst into color we would see the bottle-green tint of that waistcoat flecked with orange and amaranth, with the pleasing addition of minute dark-blue eyespots in between—on the whole resembling the skin of some exotic reptile" (*NG* 8).[13] What the collocation of Nabokov's two sections suggests is that the sickly long-nosed Gogol might occasionally have seen a reptile imp in the mirror. And if that imp was also related to his idea of the Jew, then it remains to recollect Otto Weininger's belief that only those non-Jews who do not find the Jew in themselves are entirely free of antisemitism. Yet Weininger's point is viciously circular: In order to hate the Jew in oneself, one has to be using "the Jew" as a label of something hateful in the first place.

12. See V. V. Gippius, *Gogol*, ed. and trans. Robert A. Maguire (Ann Arbor: Ardis, 1981), 62.

13. The colors must have been taken from the report of a witness by the name of Mikholskii, reproduced in Veresaev, *Gogol' v zhizni*, 427–28. In 1948, Gogol attended a party with a group of Kiev professors sporting a dark-green velvet waistcoat with light-yellow spots next to red flecks and dark-blue eyespots, generally reminiscent of the skin of a frog. On that occasion Gogol was awkward and unsociable. At a certain point Gogol's eyes were attracted by the waistcoat worn by Mikholskii, which was also velvet and had ingenious specks but looked more like a lizard than a frog. On suggesting that he had seen Mikholskii somewhere, perhaps at an inn eating onion soup (the French menu makes one think of Vevey, near Montreux; see n. 8), Gogol went on staring at the waistcoat, then made an abrupt departure. After this episode, one hears no more of the bottle-green waistcoat, only of red or Sunday sky-blue specimens.

Nabokov repeatedly suggests that Gogol's "monstrous propensity for traveling" (*NG* 13) arose from his desire to flee from himself. Eventually, the paranoid fear of the enemy within blended with a revulsion against the hostile environment, the "ominous and monstrous" buzz of public opinion (*NG* 58): The "interest that perfect strangers showed in regard to him seemed alive with dark stratagems and incalculable dangers" (*NG* 59). In parentheses, Nabokov adds, "beautiful word, stratagem—a treasure in a cave,"[14] and then wanders off, pleonastically, into his own future project: "I shall have occasion to speak in quite a different book of a lunatic who constantly felt that all the parts of the landscape and movements of inanimate objects were a complex code of allusion to his own being" (*NG* 59). Several years later, Nabokov would transpose a version of Gogol's "referential mania" on a young Jewish refugee from the Nazi conquest of Europe in "Signs and Symbols."

Section 3 briefly dispenses with Gogol's "uninteresting" boyhood (*NG* 8). The biographical compilation by Veresaev that Nabokov used contains many reminiscences by Gogol's school friends, mainly memories of the tricks Gogol played on schoolmasters, his love of sweetmeats, the eccentric independence of his spirit, his avidity for contemporary literature (of which the school disapproved), his activities as curator of the private pool of books purchased by the pupils, and his devising of paper caps for forefinger and thumb so that the books might not get soiled (for some reason, this invention did not stick). Instead of recycling this material, usually savored in schoolbooks on Gogol,[15] Nabokov describes the young Gogol as "a weakling, a trembling mouse of a boy, with dirty hands and greasy locks, and pus trickling out of his ear. He gorged himself with sticky sweets. His schoolmates avoided touching the books he had been using" (*NG* 8). Most of these details come from the memoir of just one schoolmate, the poet and translator V. I. Liubich-Romanovich,

---

14. On the recent Russian translator's neglect of the word play in this passage, see Gennady Barabtarlo, "Nikolai Gogol: Selected Passages," *The Nabokovian* 19 (fall 1987): 53.

15. One of such didactic books, A. Annenskaia's *N. V. Gogol': Ego zhizn' i proizvedeniia* (N. V. Gogol: His Life and Works) (St. Petersburg: Kolpinskii, 1902), actually starts with the sickly twelve-year-old Gogol being brought to the Nezhin high school. Nabokov's opening his narrative with Gogol's death must be seen in this context, as well (and in the later context of Siniavsky's starting his book on Gogol with the rumor of the writer's premature burial). The copy of Annenskaia's book (duly extolling Taras Bulba's patriotism) held at the National Library in Jerusalem bears the stamp of a private Jewish eight-year school in Lodz. Most of that school's pupils must have perished at approximately the time that Nabokov was working on *Nikolai Gogol*.

who also remembers Gogol deliberately "playing the democrat among us, aristocrat children"[16]—a characterization diametrically opposite to the one Nabokov would receive from former Tenishev schoolmates. On more than one occasion, what Nabokov omits is as telling as what he includes[17]—on the principle of *relevant difference*.

The difference is particularly relevant when it terminates a parallel course. The use of pleonasms is a case in point. Dwelling on Gogol's imagination during his best years, when, having pupated from the negligent schoolboy with dirty hands, Gogol would conjure up throngs of virtual people, characters in search of an author, elicit them from turns of phrase, similes, metaphors, and moods,[18] Nabokov applauds Gogol's "spontaneous generation" (*NG* 83) of multitudes of "homunculi" (*NG* 45–46, 77), "spermatozoids of the brain" (*NG* 50), for no particular purpose ("Fancy is fertile only when it is futile" [*NG* 76]).

Prompted by the inadequacy of most of the existing translations,[19] Nabokov uses a considerable portion of the little space allotted to his text to present the anglophone reader with an approximation of Gogol's own voice—this, as Donald Fanger notes, had not been done by even the best precursor texts.[20] In addition, somewhat like Samuel Johnson, who while discussing tropes in *Lives of the English Poets* actually uses these tropes himself, Nabokov at times deliberately mimics and extends Gogol's trademark technique of pleonasm that so strikingly contrasts with the economy of textual space in the bulk of the monograph.

16. See Veresaev, *Gogol' v zhizni*, 45, 51, 81.

17. The main point of Nabokov's mini-essay on "*poshlost*"—namely, that one of Gogol's major achievements is a versatile exposure of this phenomenon (*NG* 63–74)—can be traced to a passage from Gogol's much despised *Selected Passages from Correspondence with Friends* (trans. Jesse Zeldin [Nashville, Tenn.: Vanderbilt University Press 1969], chap. 18, sec. 3, 103). Interestingly, the same passage deals with Gogol's method of imposing some of his own undeveloped vices on his characters—the imagination-of-the-heart method reminiscent of Nabokov's own.

18. In the worse years, the activeness of his imagination would take Gogol to the brink of madness. He would complain that everything had become unhinged inside him. "For example, I see somebody stumbling; and immediately the imagination seizes upon this and begins to develop it—and everything with most horrible spooks. They torment me so that I cannot sleep, and they sap my strength completely": as quoted in Veresaev, *Gogol' v zhizni*, 448.

19. Nabokov makes an exception of B. G. Guerny's translations of Gogol, which were released while he was working on his monograph.

20. See Donald Fanger, "Nabokov and Gogol," in *The Garland Companion to Vladimir Nabokov*, ed. Vladimir E. Alexandrov (New York: Garland, 1995), 423–24.

The term "pleonasm" (see Nabokov's use of it on *NG* 76) means a redundancy of language; it is derived from the Greek verb *pleonazein,* "to abound," "to be more than enough." Gogol's pleonasms consist of unexpected evocations of images unrelated to the main action otherwise than through an association of ideas, moods, or visual details. At times, the narrative seems to wind into such images oneirically, as when, focusing on the solitary light in the sleeping town, the narrative of Gogol's *Dead Souls* slips into a hypnogogic state and produces the dream image of a lighted room where a lieutenant, poetically exulting in his splendid fifth pair of boots, delays taking them off and going to bed (see *NG* 82–83).[21]

At other times, pleonastic digressions are produced by extended metaphors and similes, as when Gogol (in Nabokov's commented translation) likens the provincial gentlemen at the governor's party to flies that disperse themselves among pieces of sugar:

> The black tailcoats flickered and fluttered, separately and in clusters, this way and that, just as flies flutter over dazzling white chunks of sugar on a hot July day when the old housekeeper [here we are] hacks and divides it into sparkling lumps in front of the open window: all the children [second generation now!] look on as they gather about her, watching with curiosity the movements of her rough hands while the *airy* squadrons of flies that the light *air* ... has raised, fly boldly in, complete mistresses of the premises [or literally: 'full mistresses,' '*polnya khozyaiki,*' which Isabel F. Hapgood in the Crowell edition mistranslates as 'fat housewives'] and, taking advantage of the old woman's purblindness and of the sun troubling her eyes, spread all over the dainty morsels, here separately, there in dense clusters. (*NG* 79; emphasis in Nabokov's text)

As a metonymy, "black tailcoats" points to the vacuousness of the wearers, but the concrete visual image, involving also white shirts, generates another

---

21. Veresaev quotes a memoir of Gogol's stay on the Smirnov estate near Kaluga. "Here, through peeping, it was discovered what Gogol used to do in the morning: lying in bed, he would pick up his boot and attentively examine its heel for a long time": Veresaev, *Gogol' v zhizni,* 452. He also quotes the following remarks of Mrs. Smirnov's brother to the effect that the passionate amateur of boots in *Dead Souls* is inspired by Gogol himself. "His little valise contained little of everything; of clothes and linen it had no more that necessary, but there would be three, and often even four pairs of boots, none of them ever down at the heels. It is quite possible that Gogol too, when alone in his room, would put on a new pair and ... exult in its shape, and afterwards laugh at himself for it": ibid., 455. This invasion of Gogol's privacy is not followed by Nabokov.

black-on-white composition—that of flies on sugar. As the reader is *instructed* to visualize these household pests, the text is carried away by its own buzz, zeroes in on the flies and, on moving away, places them in another densely visualized picture. Not every reader has the quickness to follow the metamorphosis (the vision of the translator responsible for the "fat housewives" must have been dulled by the buzz), but Nabokov, who would perceive the mist (tu*man*) in *Man*ilov (*NG* 103) and hear a boastful rooster (in Russian, a cock cries "coocarecoo") in a *curriculum vitae*, which always "crows and flaps its wings in a style peculiar to the undersigner" (*NG* 119), could evidently not only follow the lead of the text to the utmost detail but also allow the momentum of imagination to swerve into vignettes of his own. He first describes Gogol's technique by way of the kind of extended metaphor that, following Nabokov's own lead (see *BS* 61), S. E. Sweeney calls an "amphiphorical gesture":[22]

> [H]ere, in the simile of the flies, which is a parody of the Homeric rambling comparison, a complete circle is described, and after his complicated and dangerous *somersault, with no net spread under him, as other acrobatic authors have,* Gogol manages to twist back to the initial "separately and in clusters." (*NG* 79; emphasis added)

Then, lest the notion of "stylistic acrobatics" be perceived as a dead metaphor, Nabokov amplifies it with the help of a more unusual feat of showmanship:

> Several years ago during a Rugby game in England I saw the wonderful Obolensky kick the ball away on the run and then changing his mind, plunge forward and catch it back with his hands ... something of this kind of feat is performed by Nikolai Vassilievich. (*NG* 79–80)

The collocation of the pleonastically rambling comparison (rugby) and its opposite, the metaphor of acrobatics that saves Nabokov a lengthy tropological analysis, pits the agenda of condensation against the impulse to extend the play of Gogol's text. Still, things do not work the same way: The extension is less energetic than the original momentum. Moreover, in his "stylistic acrobatics,"

---

22. See Susan Elizabeth Sweeney, "Nabokov's Amphiphorical Gestures," *Studies in Twentieth-Century Literature* 11, no. 2 (1987): 189–211. Cf. Sherry A. Dranch, "Metamorphosis as a Stylistic Device: Surrealist Schemata in Gogolian and Nabokovian Texts," *Language and Style* 17 (1984): 139–48, and Stephen H. Blackwell, comp., "Colloquy on Browning's Door," *The Nabokovian* 34 (spring 1995): 16–25 (esp. Blackwell's and Barabtarlo's comments on pp. 20–21 and 23–24).

Nabokov does use a cerebral safety net that Gogol, as it were, disdains. When the metaphor of acrobatics occurs in *Bend Sinister,* the "safety net," which keeps the performer from a lethal plunge and doubles as a springboard, is provided by mythology: "[M]ythology stretches strong circus nets, lest thought, in its ill-fitting tights, should break its old neck instead of rebouncing with a hep and a hop" (*BS* 61). Mythology is a storehouse of recurrent motifs, and it is by networks of motifs that Nabokov's own pleonasms are protected. Both the somersault and the rugby feat belong, for instance, to the Nabokovian signature motif of roundness, of circles, of vicious circles turning into eggs or ampersands—the motif that, usurping the word of another, incorporates even a wobbly wheel of Chichikov's carriage, idly discussed by two contemplative *muzhiks* in another lengthy quotation from Gogol (*NG* 75).[23]

The metaphor of acrobatics engenders—less spontaneously, perhaps, than in Gogol's text—other images[24] of circus magic, such as the conjurer's patter,

> Beautiful as all this final crescendo [of *Dead Souls*] sounds, it is from the stylistic point of view merely a conjuror's patter enabling an object to disappear, the particular object being—Chichikov. (*NG* 113)

or the vanishing act in Nabokov's satire on Gogol's didactic flop, *Selected Passages from Letters to Friends:*

> County squires are regarded as the agents of God, hard working agents holding shares in paradise and getting more or less substantial commissions in earthly currency. "Gather all your *mouzhiks* and tell them that you make them labor because this is what God intended them to do—not at all because you need money for your pleasures; and at this point take out a banknote and in visual proof of your words burn it before their eyes...."
> The image is pleasing: the squire standing on his porch and demonstrating a crisp, delicately tinted banknote with the deliberate gestures of a professional magician; a Bible is prepared on an innocent-looking table; a boy holds a lighted candle; the audience of bearded peasants gapes in respect-

---

23. Rotundity, as Nabokov shows, is also a recurrent image in *Dead Souls*. What he suppresses, however, is that a case can be made for a meaningful interplay of even Gogol's images and motifs supplied by pleonastic moments.

24. Cf. J. L. Borges's theory that an image in a truly artistic text attracts corresponding images as if by sympathetic magic served by, rather than serving, the plot: J. L. Borges, "Narrative Art and Magic," *Triquarterly* 25 (fall 1972): 209–15.

ful suspense; there is a murmur of awe as the banknote turns into a butterfly of fire; the conjuror lightly and briskly rubs his hands—just the inside of the fingers; then after some patter he opens the Bible and lo, Phoenix-like, the treasure is there.

The censor rather generously left out this passage in the first edition as implying a certain disrespect for the Government by the wanton destruction of state money. (*NG* 126–27)

Nabokov's pleonasms, however, are much more concept-oriented than Gogol's rambling metamorphoses of images.[25] Nabokov praises Gogol's art for "the mysteries of the irrational ... perceived through rational words" (*NG* 55) and implicitly admits the difficulty of matching its gusto.

Commentators on Nabokov's "literary investigation" of Gogol have tended to believe that Nabokov processed "the mottled conglomerate of the actual Gogol" for the sake of "the polished proto-Nabokov he can extract from this recalcitrant ore."[26] If one bears in mind, however, that Gogol's baroque style included the use not only of pleonasms but also of ornate alliterations and experiments with epithets,[27] then Nabokov's trope-rich digressions and his contraband epithets suggest a different project. Nabokov focused on those of Gogol's features that were relevant to his own work, yet while doing so he explored not so much the affinities as the points of difference between the proto-Nabokovian moments in Gogol and the post-Gogolian ones in the style of his own imagination.

---

25. See also Sweeney, "Nabokov's Amphiphorical Gestures," 195–6.

26. Brian Boyd, *Vladimir Nabokov: The American Years* (Princeton, N.J.: Princeton University Press, 1991), 55. Bowie goes even further than this, commenting that the artistic deception in *Nikolai Gogol* involves the magic trick of making Gogol disappear in a work about Gogol: Bowie, "Nabokov's Influence," 255.

27. See Andrei Belyi, "Gogol'," in *Lug zelenyi: Kniga statei* (Green Meadow: A Book of Articles) (New York: Johnson Reprint Corporation, 1967), 117–18.

{ PART IV }
THE GLORIOUS OUTPUT

{ 14 }

The Daedalus–Icarus Theme in Nabokov's Fiction

JULIAN W. CONNOLLY

Readers of Vladimir Nabokov's work recognize that the writer made use of a broad variety of material drawn from classical mythology and Russian folklore when assembling the intricate structures of his fiction. Examples range from some relatively transparent elements, such as the story of Orpheus and Eurydice as a subtext in "The Return of Chorb,"[1] to more complex and diffuse patterns, such as echoes of East Slavic folk beliefs about the *rusalka*, a water sprite often believed to be the spirit of a drowned maiden (perhaps driven to suicide by unrequited love); the latter figures in works as diverse as the poem "L'Inconnue de la Seine" and the novels *Pale Fire* (Hazel Shade) and *Ada* (Lucette).[2] Struck by the fact that Nabokov used the name "Icarus" for automobiles in several novels, from *King, Queen, Knave* to *Look at the Harlequins!*[3] I began to wonder whether elements of the Daedalus–Icarus story

---

1. See, inter alia, Julian W. Connolly, *Nabokov's Early Fiction: Patterns of Self and Other* (Cambridge: Cambridge University Press, 1992), 14–15; Maxim Shrayer, "Decoding Vladimir Nabokov's 'The Return of Chorb,'" *Russian Language Journal* 51, nos. 168–70 (1997): 187–88.

2. For a discussion of the *rusalka* theme in Nabokov's work, see D. Barton Johnson, "'L'Inconnue de la Seine' and Nabokov's Naiads," *Comparative Literature* 44 (1992): 225–48, and Jane Grayson, "*Rusalka* and the Person from Porlock," in *Symbolism and After: Essays on Russian Poetry in Honor of Georgette Donchin*, ed. Arnold McMillin (Worcester: Bristol Classical Papers, 1992), 162–85.

3. Pekka Tammi lists the recurrences of the name "Icarus" in Nabokov's work in *Problems of Nabokov's Poetics: A Narratological Analysis,* Suomalaisen Tiedeakatemian Toimituksia Annales Academiae Scientiarum Fennicae B 231 (Helsinki: Suomalainen Tiedeakatemia, 1985), esp. 352.

might play a similar role in Nabokov's work. This paper represents an initial attempt to investigate that question.

The central features of the Daedalus–Icarus story are well known. Imprisoned by King Minos in the labyrinth in Crete (presumably for aiding Ariadne in her attempts to help Theseus find his way out of the labyrinth after killing the Minotaur), the inventive Daedalus fashioned two sets of artificial wings out of feathers and wax for himself and his son Icarus. Though warned by his father not to fly too close to the sun, Icarus could not resist the joyous feeling that flight afforded him, and he raced ahead of his father, soaring ever higher. Soon his wings began to melt, and he plunged helplessly into the eastern Aegean. Daedalus, having tried and failed to keep up with his son, arrived on the scene too late. Devastated, he could find only traces of the boy's tattered wings floating on the ocean waves.[4]

Nabokov, of course, was well acquainted with this story, and he mentioned it briefly when lecturing to his Cornell students about the character of Stephen Daedalus in James Joyce's *Ulysses* (see *LL* 286). As one looks more closely at the tale, one discerns several elements that might have arrested Nabokov's attention. At its core, the story tells of a father's attempt to save his son's life and of his profound grief at the child's untimely death. This very subject appears as a central theme of Nabokov's art, and it figures prominently at several points over the course of his career, from the early story "Christmas" to his mid-career novel *Bend Sinister* and the complex later novel *Pale Fire*. Yet there are also other elements in the tale that may have sparked the writer's imagination, and these will be considered in the discussion of the texts by Nabokov that seem to reflect the Daedalus–Icarus story.

One can begin by commenting on the choice of the name Icarus (*Ikar* in Russian) for the vehicles owned by a series of protagonists, beginning with the Dreyer couple in *King, Queen, Knave,* and continuing with such figures as Hermann Karlovich in the English-language version of *Despair* and Humbert Humbert in the Russian-language version of *Lolita*. The name seems to hint at the futility of the relevant owners' fantasies of escape from conditions

---

4. This account is based on information provided by Edward Tripp, *The Meridian Handbook of Classical Mythology* (New York: New American Library, 1970), and Sir Paul Harvey, ed. and comp., *The Oxford Companion to Classical Literature* (Oxford: Clarendon Press, 1969).

of emotional (if not physical) confinement or stasis. Thus, Martha Dreyer's hopes that her husband will be killed in a car crash are frustrated when an accident kills not her husband but her chauffeur, while Hermann Karlovich's hopes that the police will believe that he has been killed by a blackmailer are undone when his victim's cane is found in the abandoned Icarus.[5] In both cases, the Icarus car is associated with death and shattered dreams. A similar resonance can be found in the name of the car that carries Nina to her fatal crash in the English version of "Spring in Fialta": The generic "dirty limousine" (*griaznyi limuzin*) of the original becomes a "yellow long-bodied Icarus."[6]

More substantive reflections of the Daedalus–Icarus tale can be discerned in the novel *Invitation to a Beheading*. Several features in this work recall essential aspects of the classical myth. For example, the novel's central character is a man held captive in a labyrinthine prison whose circuitous corridors do not lead the prisoner anywhere except back to his cell (see *IB* 77). The prisoner, Cincinnatus, dreams of escape, and like Daedalus, he has fantasies involving images of flight. "Envious of poets," he writes. "How wonderful it must be to speed along a page and, right from the page, where only a shadow continues to run, *to take off into the blue*" (*IB* 194; emphasis added). Indeed, in childhood, Cincinnatus himself seemed to possess the ability to stride in air, as he recalls in the long written entry in chapter 8. There he writes: "I saw myself, a pink-smocked boy, standing transfixed in mid-air" (*IB* 97). His early experiment in flight is cut short by the horrified indignation of the skeptical crowd.

Several images in the novel echo the theme of potential flight, but they also indicate the difficulty or futility of trying to escape *by means of* flight. Some of these occur in passages that speak of past times when flight was more common than it appears to be at the present moment (see, for example, *IB* 43, 50–51), and one image in particular may point directly to the incident of

---

5. It is worth noting that the name "Icarus" is mentioned several times in the English translation of *Despair* and not once in the Russian original. This frequency may be explained through the phonetic resemblance between the first syllable of the car's name [*ik*] and the name of the object that ruins Hermann's scheme—Felix's "st*ick*" (see *Des* 165, 202–3).

6. Cf. the texts in Vladimir Nabokov, *Vesna v Fial'te* (Ann Arbor: Ardis, 1978), 29, and *Stories* 426.

Icarus's tragic flight and fall. Among the pictures in an old, bound magazine that Cincinnatus peruses early in his confinement, one stands out: "the satiny ripples of the ocean with a two-winged shadow *falling* on it" (*IB* 50; emphasis added).[7] If Cincinnatus is to escape from his prison, he must avoid the disastrous example set by the misguided Icarus.

Cincinnatus does consider other avenues of escape, and one set of fantasies in which he indulges recalls a different part of the story of Daedalus's time on Minos. According to legend, it was Daedalus who gave Ariadne the idea to hand Theseus a skein of thread that would enable him to find his way back out of the labyrinth after slaying the Minotaur. Nabokov introduces an ironic reversal of Ariadne's role into his novel when he allows Cincinnatus to find his own way out of the prison, only to be led by young Emmie back into the prison. The parallel between Ariadne and Emmie is strengthened by the fact that each is the daughter of the man who holds the hero in custody: Ariadne is King Minos's daughter, and Emmie is the daughter of the prison director.

Other motifs that link Cincinnatus's situation with that of Daedalus include Cincinnatus's early career as a craftsman: "[H]e struggled for a long time with intricate trifles and worked on rag dolls for schoolgirls" (*IB* 27). This last detail brings to mind a distinctive component of the Daedalus story that may also have a parodic echo in *Invitation to a Beheading*. King Minos's wife, Pasiphaë, was infatuated with a handsome bull. She commissioned Daedalus to construct a hollow wooden cow covered with hide that she could use to couple with the bull. The result of this strange union was the Minotaur, half-man and

---

7. Just a few pages earlier, Nabokov provides a detailed view of the countryside surrounding the prison as seen from a tower to which Cincinnatus has been led. The carefully crafted presentation of this landscape reminded Robert Alter of the kind of perspective found in a Breughel painting: See Robert Alter, "*Invitation to a Beheading:* Nabokov and the Art of Politics," *Triquarterly* 17 (1970): 49, reprinted in *Nabokov's* Invitation to a Beheading: *A Critical Companion,* ed. Julian W. Connolly (Evanston, Ill.: Northwestern University Press, 1997), 55. Note that one of Breughel's most famous paintings is "Landscape with the Fall of Icarus." What is especially distinctive about this painting is that the figure of Icarus is depicted as only a pair of legs splashing in the sea in the lower right-hand corner of the picture; the ordinary observer would not notice it at first glance. Of course, this is precisely the kind of subtle presentation that one finds in Nabokov's work. (For a nearly contemporaneous treatment of the subject in Breughel's rendition, see W. H. Auden's poem "Musée des Beaux Arts," written in 1938.)

half-beast. It may be no coincidence that Cincinnatus's own wife, Martha, is depicted with an insatiable sexual appetite, and that her two offspring, both illegitimate, are physically marked: "The boy was lame and evil-tempered, the girl dull, obese and nearly blind" (*IB* 31). At one point, the narrator describes Cincinnatus's fear of catching a glimpse of Martha's illicit activities, and this description represents a curious inversion of the Minotaur's figure. At the dinner table, Cincinnatus would be mortally afraid to bend down, "and chance to see the nether half of the monster whose upper half was quite presentable, having the appearance of a young woman and young man visible down to the waist at table ... and whose nether half was a writhing, raging quadruped" (*IB* 64).

Despite the warning implicit in the image of the winged shadow falling into the sea mentioned earlier, Cincinnatus ultimately does escape his wretched confinement, but he does so in a way that reverses the Icarus tragedy. It is not the would-be fugitive's artificial wings that dissolve and fall apart, dooming the fleeing hero; rather, it is the entire, artificial world of the captors themselves that collapses at the end of the novel: "Everything was coming apart. Everything was falling. A spinning wind was picking up and whirling: dust, rags, chips of painted wood, bits of gilded plaster ... and amidst the dust, and the falling things, and the flapping scenery, Cincinnatus made his way in that direction where, to judge by the voices, stood beings akin to him" (*IB* 223).

Although the plot and imagery of *Invitation to a Beheading* center more on the Daedalus aspects of the tale of Daedalus and Icarus than on Icarus or the father–son relationship, it is the latter relationship that comes to the fore in the exquisite short story "Signs and Symbols," written shortly after World War II. In this work, it is not the father (or the father and son together) who is imprisoned in a labyrinth. Rather, the figure in "captivity" is the son alone, and he is being held in a mental institution. Nevertheless, some of the story's most intriguing imagery resonates strongly with elements of the Daedalus–Icarus tale. This is most evident in the account of what seems to be the child's attempt to commit suicide. The doctor describes the boy's attempt as "a masterpiece of inventiveness" (*Stories* 599). The boy was prevented from achieving his goal by a fellow patient who thought "he was learning to fly." The narrator, however, offers a corrective to this view: "What he really wanted to do was to tear a hole in his world and escape." These images, of course, strongly recall Daedalus's and Icarus's attempt to escape the labyrinth through flight.[8]

Yet the story also contains an ominous warning about the potential outcome of such an attempt. On the way to the hospital, the parents observe "under a swaying and dripping tree, a tiny half-dead unfledged bird . . . helplessly twitching in a puddle" (*Stories* 599). This image recalls an image used by Ovid in book 8 of the *Metamorphoses* when describing how Daedalus initiated his son's fatal flight: "Just like a bird that from its lofty nest / Launches a tender fledgling in the air. / . . . / In that fatal apprenticeship, he flapped / His wings and watched the boy flapping behind."[9] The Ovid passage underscores a crucial aspect of the Daedalus–Icarus legend—a father's profound love for his child. This theme lies at the core of the Nabokov story, as well. Although only a few pages long, the story is permeated with images of the father's immense love for his suffering child. In the classical myth, even though Daedalus was a fabulous inventor, he proved unable to save his son from his own folly. The father in Nabokov's story may have fewer inventive tools at his disposal, but his concern for his child is equally poignant. Just before the story comes to its suspended ending, the father moans to his wife: "We must get him out of there quick. Otherwise, we'll be responsible" (*Stories* 602). He then begins sketching plans for safeguarding the life of his child. The story comes to an end, however, before the reader learns whether his plans are ever implemented.[10]

8. The boy's attempt to escape through a window recalls Luzhin's impulse to "drop out of the game" at the end of *The Defense*. Luzhin's final vision of a chessboard, however, may indicate that his attempt to escape the world of chess may not be successful.

9. Ovid, *The Metamorphoses,* trans. A. D. Melville (Oxford: Oxford University Press, 1986), 177. A different avian image in the story may point to another Greek myth. At age six, we are told, the boy drew "wonderful birds with human hands and feet" (*Stories* 601). This mixture of avian and human features reminds one of the Sirens or Seirines, "winged women with bird feet or else birds with women's heads and voices": Tripp, *Meridian Handbook,* 533. The Sirens were associated both with temptation of the living and with death. Nabokov would later tell an interviewer that his pen name, Sirin, was associated with the Sirens. For a detailed discussion of Sirin and its associations, see Gavriel Shapiro, *Delicate Markers: Subtexts in Vladimir Nabokov's* Invitation to a Beheading, Middlebury Studies in Russian Language and Literature 19 (New York: Peter Lang, 1998), 9–29.

10. The ending of the story has generated a sizable debate. Some readers are sure that the ringing phone with which the story concludes is a call from the hospital indicating that the child has succeeded in killing himself. Other readers have argued that the phone

The theme of the father's love for a suffering child recurs in the final text to be considered in light of the Daedalus–Icarus story, *Pale Fire*. The novel contains an explicit reference to Daedalus in a passage from *The Letters of Franklin Lane*, quoted by Charles Kinbote in his commentary to line 810 of Shade's poem. Ruminating on the possibility of life after death, a conversation with Aristotle, and the potential for unraveling the "mystifying maze" of human life, Lane writes: "The Daedalian plan simplified by a look from above—smeared out as it were by the splotch of some thumb that made the whole involuted, boggling thing one beautiful straight line" (*PF* 261). Here, the writer envisions taking a higher perspective on the intricate design created by human life and disclosing its essential sense and direction. Such a perspective, he supposes, might be attained in the world beyond the grave. This vision—of the potential for existence after death and the attainment of a higher perspective and understanding of human experience—reflects a fundamental impulse in the novel *Pale Fire* itself.

Although the excerpt from Franklin Lane's letters is the only direct reference to the Daedalus–Icarus story in *Pale Fire*, several of the novel's essential themes recall that story. For example, like "Signs and Symbols," the novel deals with the core subject of a father's love for his child, and particularly with the pain of the loss of that child. Here, of course, the child is a daughter and not a son, but echoes of the Daedalus–Icarus story are evident nonetheless. Consider, for example, Hazel Shade's death. Although, as noted earlier, her death by drowning may involve elements of the *rusalka* theme, it should be recalled that Icarus's life also ended in the water. What is more, Hazel's death serves as one of the experiences that inspires Shade to write his narrative poem, and the opening lines of this poem suggest the adoption and reworking of central images from the Icarus story:

---

call is once again a "wrong number," or even that the phone call is from an entirely different party. A third group focuses on the indeterminacy or open-endedness of the suspended narration and finds in this either a sign of the author's compassion for the suffering family or a reproach to the reader for falling into the trap of "referential mania." It has even been suggested that the Russian term for the jar of fruit that the father peruses just as the phone rings for the last time—*raiskoe iabloko* ("crab apple" [lit., "the apple of paradise"])—signals an otherwordly turn to the story (the significance of the Russian name was noted by Joanna Trzeciak at the Nabokov Centenary Festival [see chap. 6 in this volume]); one should also note that the "Sirin" is a *raiskaia ptitsa*: See Shapiro, *Delicate Markers*, 15–17.

> I was the shadow of the waxwing slain
> By the false azure in the windowpane;
> I was the smudge of ashen fluff—and I
> Lived on, flew on, in the reflected sky. (*PF* 33)

What one finds here is Shade's ardent dream that the tragic flight of a hapless bird will not end in annihilation but, rather, result in transfiguration and transcendence. Although Shade's poem conveys some uncertainty about the possibility of survival after death (at least in the forms that some traditional belief systems have imagined), it also articulates a hope that transfiguration and preservation are attainable, at the very least in art, if not in life. With his poetry, Shade in essence becomes a new Daedalus.[11] Unlike the Daedalus of old, though, he does not fashion artificial wings that ultimately fail his child. Rather, he creates a new structure—his lyrical poem—that will snatch up the fallen fledgling and allow it to fly forever in the reflected skies of art.

Though Shade himself may have some uncertainty about the potential for survival after death, Nabokov's novel expresses more confidence on this point. Various readings of the work have found evidence that the spirits of several of its dead characters—Aunt Maud, Hazel, and even Shade himself—make their presence felt here and there in the text. One such presence that is particularly significant is the spirit of Hazel, which may animate the *Vanessa atalanta* that Shade observes in his yard as he finishes his poem just moments before his death (see *PF* 69, 290).[12] Butterflies and moths had served as emblems of the immortal spirit of the dead in Nabokov's fiction since the early story "Christmas," and it is worth pointing out that the beauty and grace evoked by images of these natural creatures contrast sharply with the image of erratic and ultimately disastrous flight begun by the incautious Icarus, who was sustained only temporarily by his fragile, man-made wings.

---

11. Charles Kinbote accurately portrays Shade's association with invention when he writes that he observed "Shade perceiving and transforming the world, taking it in and taking it apart, re-combining its elements in the very process of storing them up so as to produce at some unspecified date an organic miracle, a fusion of image and music, a line of verse" (*PF* 27).

12. For a description of the butterfly image and the presence of Hazel's shade, see Brian Boyd, *Nabokov's* Pale Fire: *The Magic of Artistic Discovery* (Princeton, N.J.: Princeton University Press, 1999), 131–41.

One of the organizing principles of *Pale Fire* is counterpoint. Frequently, subjects that are treated with high seriousness and beauty by John Shade in his poem have parodic or degraded counterparts in Kinbote's commentary. This principle can also be observed in relation to the Daedalus–Icarus theme. While Shade writes with great delicacy and emotion about the death by drowning of his beloved daughter, Kinbote also writes about the death of a family member, but in a very different tone. In his commentary to line 71, Kinbote describes the strange death of his father, King Alfin. Alfin, he writes, combined absentmindedness with "a passion for mechanical things, especially for flying apparatuses" (*PF* 103). A special plane was built for him in 1916, and "this was his bird of doom," Kinbote writes. He goes on to recount how Alfin nearly lost control of his plane one day and was just straightening it out when he "flew smack into the scaffolding of a huge hotel which was being constructed in the middle of a coastal heath as if for the special purpose of standing in a king's way" (*PF* 103). With this bizarre incident we encounter a characteristic inversion of John Shade's account of Hazel's death. In Shade's account, it is the child who dies, to be mourned by the surviving parents. In Kinbote's narrative, it is the father who dies, to be survived by a child who was too young to mourn. What is more, this episode provides a parodic inversion of the death of Icarus. Again, it is an adult who dies as a result of an unsuccessful flight, not a child, and the flight comes to an end not because the flier was soaring with youthful impatience and joy but because he was too absentminded to watch where he was going.[13]

It was the intention of this chapter to trace the resonance of the Daedalus–Icarus theme in Nabokov's fiction. As these brief notes have indicated, echoes of the theme can be detected in some of Nabokov's most engaging works. Although Nabokov expressed disdain for heavy-handed reliance on

---

13. A subsequent echo of the Icarus theme in Kinbote's commentary occurs when he describes the seductive lure of suicide. Swiftly dismissing the use of knives or poison, he writes at length about death by falling and, in particular, the sensations one would feel if one were to fall from an airplane: "The ideal drop is from an aircraft, your muscles relaxed, your pilot puzzled, your packed parachute shuffled off, cast off, shrugged off" (*PF* 221). Here the horror and pathos of a fall such as Icarus's is left behind, to be replaced with the sensuous embrace of a plunge into oblivion. (It is worth noting, too, that Kinbote imagines parachuting to safety in America as the final stage of his escape from Zembla. In his fantasy, escape by flight *is* possible.)

classical mythology in contemporary literature (see, e.g., his comments on Joyce's *Ulysses* [*LL* 288]), he was not averse to drawing on elements of myth and folklore to create the elaborate, synthetic constructs for which he is now known. The Daedalus–Icarus tale would have appealed to him because of its treatment of a father's love for his son and its central image of the dramatic, untimely death of the child. Future research may reveal additional permutations of this theme.[14]

14. For example, distant echoes of the theme can be found in *The Gift*, in the section of chapter 5 that depicts Fyodor walking through the Grunewald. This seminal passage touches on two of the basic concerns discussed earlier: the importance of the father–son bond (here, Fyodor and his father, as well as Yasha Chernyshevski and his father), and the untimely death of a son (here, Yasha's suicide). Prefacing the passage is an odd detail— the description of the site where a small airplane had crashed because of the errors of an "overexuberant" pilot who had lost control of his joystick. This suggestion of an unfortunate, modern-day Icarus is followed up later in the passage by another image from the Icarus story—the power of the warm sun. This time, however, the heat of the sun produces a rather different effect. The narrator writes of sunbathing: "The sun bore down. The sun licked me all over with its big, smooth tongue. I gradually felt that I was becoming moltenly transparent, that I was permeated with flame and existed only insofar as it did. As a book is translated into an exotic idiom, so was I translated into sun" (*Gift* 333). He concludes the episode with the comment, "One might dissolve completely that way" (*Gift* 334). As I have argued elsewhere, the sun in this scene represents the workings of creative consciousness: See Connolly, *Nabokov's Early Fiction*, 211–13. When one evaluates this experience in light of Icarus's experience, one realizes that Nabokov may be doing something here that he does constantly in his work: He rewrites and refashions prior texts to create his own artistic fabric. Icarus died because he flew too close to the sun. Fyodor also feels himself on the point of dissolution in the Grunewald scene. At the last minute he pulls back, however, and rather than being absorbed into a higher creative force, he is able to come away from his exposure to this force with a new spirit of autonomous inspiration. Death is abolished; in its place are transcendence and transfiguration.

{ 15 }

Vladimir Nabokov and the Scriblerians

LISA ZUNSHINE

Vladimir Nabokov's short story "Scenes from the Life of a Double Monster" tends to perplex and even disappoint his readers. Susan Sweeney cites a number of critics who wonder what to make of this "uneven, unfinished, and apparently unsuccessful" piece. Brian Boyd describes it as "vividly written [but] plainly missing something, as if a skillful juggler were to throw only one cup and saucer from hand to hand."[1] "Scenes" is frequently remembered in conjunction with Véra Nabokov's unusually negative response to her husband's creative plans: When in the fall of 1950 Nabokov announced to a group of colleagues that he was going to write a novel about the love life of Siamese twins, Véra responded with, "No, you're not!"[2] When Nabokov did write "Scenes"—

I am grateful to Gavriel Shapiro, the editor of this volume, and to the anonymous reviewer at Cornell University Press for their valuable comments on earlier drafts of this chapter.

1. Vladimir Nabokov, "Scenes from the Life of a Double Monster," in *The Stories of Vladimir Nabokov* (New York: Knopf, 1995), 608–14. Page citations are to this edition. Susan Elizabeth Sweeney, "The Small Furious Devil: Memory in 'Scenes from the Life of a Double Monster,'" in *A Small Alpine Form: Studies in Nabokov's Short Fiction*, ed. Charles Nicol and Gennady Barabtarlo (New York: Garland, 1993)," 198; Brian Boyd, *Vladimir Nabokov: The American Years* (Princeton, N.J.: Princeton University Press, 1991), 185).

2. See Boyd, *American Years*, 171; Andrew Field, *VN: The Life and Art of Vladimir Nabokov* (New York: Crown, 1986), 287; Sweeney, "Small Furious Devil," 215; Stacy Schiff, "The Genius and Mrs. Genius," *New Yorker*, February 10, 1997, 44. According to the anonymous reviewer at Cornell University Press, Véra objected to the continuation of the story because Nabokov "apparently intended to have only one Siamese twin . . . be heterosexual, to complicate the narrator's marital plans" (personal communication). This information could add a crucial new dimension to readings of the story. I have not been able to trace its source, however, and so have had to leave it out of the argument presented in this chapter.

a brief, seven-page story, though; not a novel, as he initially intended—it was promptly rejected by the *New Yorker.*

Véra Nabokov's disapproval, the *New Yorker*'s rejection, and critics' puzzlement notwithstanding, "Scenes from the Life of a Double Monster" is in many ways a remarkable story—a unique imaginative foray into the fusing mental processes of two brothers joined together at birth. As this chapter will show, the origins of the story can be traced back to the "Double Mistress" episode in *The Memoirs of the Extraordinary Life, Works, and Adventures of Martinus Scriblerus*, a satire brought forth by the combined efforts of John Arbuthnot, Alexander Pope, Jonathan Swift, John Gay, Thomas Parnell, and Robert Harley, Earl of Oxford, during their off-and-on activity in the so-called Scriblerus Club in 1714–27.[3] By contrasting Nabokov's treatment of the "double monster" theme with that of his eighteenth-century predecessors, one can gain a crucial insight into the imagery and structure of Nabokov's "Scenes."

Nabokov's story opens with Dr. Fricke "stroking" with a "dreamy smile of scientific delectation" the "fleshy cartilaginous band uniting" the twin brothers, Lloyd and Floyd, and asking whether they could recall "the very first time" either or both of them "realized the peculiarity of [their] condition and destiny" (*Stories* 608). Floyd, the first-person narrator of the story, says nothing at the time, but the doctor's question prompts him to remember his and Lloyd's "monstrous infancy" and childhood "atop a fertile hill above the Black Sea on [their] grandfather's farm near Karaz" (*Stories* 608). The word "monstrous" refers, perhaps, not so much to the children's physical shape as to the matter-of-fact cruelty that surrounds them on that farm. The boys' mother is raped by a stranger in a "roadside orchard" and dies shortly after giving birth to them. Their "dusky" aunts take care of the orphaned twins with "ghoulish zest," and as soon as Lloyd and Floyd are old enough to attend to insipid instructions shouted at them from crowds of leering spectators, their grandfather Ahem starts exhibiting them for money. A "worried crook" named Novus marries one of the aunts, not because he loves her—no one bothers about such fine feelings atop this "fertile hill"—but to gain access to the profitable "double monster." Floyd's narrative ends (and so does his and Lloyd's childhood) on the day

---

3. See Charles Kerby-Miller, ed., *The Memoirs of the Extraordinary Life, Works, and Discoveries of Martinus Scriblerus. Written in Collaborations by the Members of Scriblerus Club John Arbuthnot, Alexander Pope, Jonathan Swift, John Gay, Thomas Parnell, and Robert Harley, Earl of Oxford* (New York: Oxford University Press, 1998).

that he and Lloyd try to escape from their covetous relatives and are intercepted by their "uncle" Novus, who kidnaps the twins to start touring them around the country. We do not know how and why Lloyd and Floyd end up in the hands of Dr. Fricke, but his relationship with them recalls some of the abuse that they experienced with Ahem and Novus. The main difference is that, whereas the relatives exploited the children for money, Dr. Fricke is excited (a feeling, in his case, akin to sexual excitement) by having in his possession a rare specimen, a natural subject for scientific monographs.

"Fricke" is, of course, a loaded surname. Because of its overtones of freakishness, it is a development (or, rather, a "prefiguration," as it *opens* the story) of the theme of mental as opposed to physical monstrosity—that is, the dangerous emotional deficiency that allows the anonymous rapists, Ahems, Novuses, and Frickes to objectify and exploit other human beings. "Dr. Fricke" is also a perfunctory jab at Dr. Freud. Finally, it is an allusion to a freakish brainchild of the British Age of Reason—Dr. Martinus Scriblerus—a virtuoso who falls in love with and marries a pair of Siamese twins exhibited at a London raree-show.

It is likely that Nabokov discovered Martinus Scriblerus in the late 1940s. From 1943 to 1948, Nabokov was lecturing three days a week at Wellesley College, where he became friendly with Charles Kerby-Miller, an eighteenth-century scholar who was working on his monumental edition of *Martinus Scriblerus* (eighty-three pages of *The Memoirs* proper, more than three hundred pages of commentary). At the time, Nabokov's own research interests drew him to the eighteenth-century literature: Such authors as Pope, Swift, Richardson, Stern, Radcliffe, and Lewis were on his reading list as he began scouring stacks of "seventeenth-, eighteenth-, and nineteenth-century Russian, French, and English literature in the libraries of Cornell, Harvard, and New York City, ready to seize on the smallest phrase that might recall or elucidate Pushkin."[4] Massive exposure to eighteenth-century literature and his predilection for "aberrations in general, both physical and psychological" accounted for his interest in the material with which Kerby-Miller was working.[5] Kerby-Miller's book was published in 1948; Nabokov's "Scenes from the Life of a Double Monster," written in October 1950, echoes both the "Double Mistress" episode of *The Memoirs* and Kerby-Miller's accompanying commentary.

4. Boyd, *American Years*, 337.
5. Dmitri Nabokov, as quoted in Sweeney, "Small Furious Devil," 197.

In his commentary, Kerby-Miller documents the history of the Scriblerus Club and tracks down hundreds of allusions to ancient myths, works of classical philosophy, and the eighteenth-century literary and political scene contained in *The Memoirs*. He tells the history of Arbuthnot, Pope, Swift, Gay, Parnell, and Harley's getting together in 1714 and deciding to ridicule bad taste in learning and the arts (leaving it to themselves to judge what constituted good and bad taste) by publishing the errors and pretensions of the fictional philosopher Martinus Scriblerus. *The Memoirs'* first eight chapters deal with Martinus's education and transformation into a Critic—that is, someone who "converts every Trifle into a serious thing, either in the way of Life, or in Learning."[6] The second part of *The Memoirs* lists his exploits in philosophy and physics and prepares the ground for the Scriblerians' grand scheme—to publish a number of books presumably written or edited by Martinus and to claim that he was the actual author of several existing works. (One of these was Richard Bentley's 1732 edition of Milton's *Paradise Lost;* Bentley, a prominent classical scholar, was one of the Scriblerians' favorite objects of ridicule). The purpose of such hoax was to

> obscure the already dubious line between authentic and spurious publications until the reading public became bewildered. Thus gullible people could be trapped into accepting absurdities, . . . while the critical and wary would learn to scan every new production in the learned and literary world that seemed in any way ridiculous with a skeptical eye, ready to charge it with being another work by the mysterious Scriblerus.[7]

(Nabokov—the perpetrator of literary hoaxes and the inventor of Vivian Calmbrood and Vasily Shishkov—must have found such a plan deeply congenial.)

Chapter 14 of *The Memoirs* shows Martinus taking a break from his studies and finding himself by the site of a raree-show featuring the pygmy "Negro Prince"; the Man-Tiger; the majestic lion; the spotted leopard; and two "Bohemian sisters, whose common parts of generation had so closely allied them, that Nature seem'd to have conspired with Fortune, that their lives should run in an eternal parallel"—or, plainly speaking, the sisters share a single body from the waist down.[8] Martinus falls in love with one of the twins,

6. Kerby-Miller, *The Memoirs*, 129.
7. Ibid., 29–30.
8. Ibid., 143, 146.

named Lindamira, who eventually agrees to elope with her learned admirer and marry him. Her sister, Indamora, however, is also in love with Martinus and jealous of Lindamira's marital bliss. She takes part in the intrigue orchestrated by the disgruntled freak-show owner (who does not want to lose his profitable double monster to the moronic philosopher) and marries the pygmy Prince.[9] The question of which of the husbands can lay a legitimate claim to Indamora–Lindamira's organ (or organs, as no one knows whether there are two or just one) of procreation has to be decided by the court. After the first round of the legal battle (involving a hilarious exchange between Dr. Leatherhead and Dr. Pennyfeather, respectively the pigmy Prince's and Martinus's attorneys), the court decides that Martinus and his rival should "cohabit with [their] wives, and ... lie in bed each on the side of his own wife." The court urges both husbands to consider that they are "under a stricter Tye than common Brothers-in law, [and hopes] that being, as it were, joint Proprietors of one common Tenement, [they] will so behave as good fellow lodgers ought to do."[10] Such a sentence pleases neither party; Martinus appeals, and after further legal peregrinations, a superior legal body—a "Commission of Delegates"—dissolves both marriages, as "proceeding upon a natural, as well as legal Absurdity."[11] Martinus is heartbroken, and the sisters are returned to the triumphant show owner.

The "Double Mistress" episode was probably added to the manuscript of *The Memoirs* during the first revival of Scriblerian club in 1716–18, when Pope, Gay, and Arbuthnot got together to see whether the adventures of their hero could be turned into a publishable manuscript. Most of the extant "Double Mistress" fragments are in Arbuthnot's handwriting, with revisions and additions by Pope. As Kerby-Miller points out, there seems to have been

---

9. The names Martin, Lindamira, and Indamora go back to a series of plays by John Dryden. *Sir Martin Mar-All* (1667) was a popular farce based in Italian commedia dell'arte and full of tricks and disguises, with the comic star of the Duke's Company, James Nokes, playing the fumbling title character. The 1670 heroic play *The Conquest of Granada* features a sexually aggressive Lyndaraxa, who goads the hot-tempered Abdala to start a revolt against his own brother, the King of Granada. Finally, Indamira is the virtuous bride of the irrationally jealous Aureng-Zebe, an Indian Muslim prince in Dryden's 1675 tragedy *Augeng-Zebe*. For more on these plays, see James Anderson Winn, *John Dryden and His World* (New Haven, Conn.: Yale University Press, 1988).

10. Kerby-Miller, *The Memoirs*, 162.

11. Ibid., 163.

"something like a regular division of labor" between the two, "Arbuthnot sketching out ideas and Pope completing them into finished pieces."[12] In fact, this pattern of collaboration might be one of the reasons that the book was not published until much later. Pope could not always find time to edit the material, even though Arbuthnot was brimming with ideas. *The Memoirs* finally appeared in print in 1741 as part of *The Works of Mr. Alexander Pope,* under the subtitle "Tracts of Martinus Scriblerus and other Miscellaneous Pieces." The "Double Mistress" chapters were dropped as too "vulgar" from the 1751 edition that came out after Pope's death and was prepared by his friend Bishop William Warburton. In the 1797 edition, supervised by Joseph Warton, the chapters were restored, and their humor was characterized as "exquisite" in the preface to the volume. In 1824, the Victorian editors damned the "Double Mistress" episode once more, returning to the mutilated 1751 version of the text, and it was not until 1948 that *The Memoirs* was published in its entirety.

Kerby-Miller painstakingly researched the story of the real twins behind the "Double Mistress" chapters, Helena and Judith, exhibited in London in 1708. The six-year-old girls were advertised in handbills as "one of the greatest Wonders in Nature that ever was seen, being Born with their Backs fastn'd to each other, and [with] the Passages of their Bodies both one way." These children were said to be "very Handsome and Lusty, and Talk three different languages."[13] Swift wrote to one of his friends in 1708 that the "sight of two girls joined together at the back ... causes a great many speculations; and raises abundance of questions in divinity, law, and physic."[14] Later, in their "Double Mistress" chapter, the Scriblerians would revisit some of these "speculations" and "questions" to make fun of metaphysical discourses of the day.

The parallels between Nabokov's "Scenes from the Life of a Double Monster" and the "Double Mistress" episode (including Kerby-Miller's historical commentary) run on several levels, including the details of the twins' appearance and the plot. The boys' "sire" is anonymous, but rumor mentions a "Hungarian peddler" (*Stories* 608); "Helena and Judith were born in Szony, in Hungary."[15] Lloyd and Floyd speak three languages: Turkish, English, and their unspecified mother-tongue (*Stories* 612). Helena and Judith "speak three different languages ... Hungarian or High Dutch, Low Dutch, and French, and

12. Ibid., 61.
13. Ibid., 295.
14. Ibid.
15. Ibid., 294.

[are] learning English."[16] Lloyd and Floyd are "healthy" and "handsome," with "well formed rubbery arms and legs" (*Stories* 609); Helena and Judith are "very handsome, very well shaped in all parts, and [have] beautiful faces."[17] Nabokov's twins' real names, "full of corvine aspirates" (*Stories* 609) have to be changed to glitzy and mutually echoing "Lloyd" and "Floyd"; Helena's and Judith's names emerge in *The Memoirs* as the dramatic soundalikes "Lindamira" and "Indamora." Both sets of twins (Nabokov's and the Scriblerians') try to flee their captivity—Lloyd and Floyd by sneaking to the beach; Lindamira and Indamora by escaping through the window and getting married. Both fail.

A crucial difference between the two narratives concerns the level of emotional and intellectual self-realization of the respective "double monsters." The Scriblerians were not interested in exploring the nuances of their "double mistress's" thoughts and feelings. They turned to the grotesque figure of Indamira–Lindamora to ridicule zealous natural philosophers, antiquarians, litterateurs, critics, free-thinkers, and—if some space was left over—lawyers. By presenting the philosopher as a passionate lover and jealous husband, Arbuthnot and company tapped into a gold vein of ridicule—bawdy jokes with metaphysical twists. The fact that Martinus's enamorata has "a few Heads, Legs, [and] Arms extraordinary" only added to the fun.[18] Although Nabokov borrowed some of the Scriblerians' details, he used them to a very different end: "Scenes" is an attempt to describe a highly unusual mental state by telling a story from the point of view of the "double monster" himself rather than from that of a leering and uncomprehending observer. Consider the following haunting passage:

> When, for example, one of us was about to stoop to possess himself of a pretty daisy and the other, at exactly the same moment, was on the point of stretching up to pluck a ripe fig, individual success depended upon whose movement happened to conform to the current ictus of our current and continuous rhythm, whereupon, with a very brief chorealike shiver, the interrupted gesture of one twin would be swallowed and dissolved in the enriched ripple of the other's completed action. I say "enriched" because the ghost of the unpicked flower somehow seemed to be also there, pulsating between the fingers that closed upon the fruit. (*Stories* 611)

16. Ibid., 296.
17. Ibid.
18. Ibid., 159.

Situated well into the story, this description prompts us to reread the childhood parts of "Scenes" from a very different perspective. If, as Nabokov suggests, every completed action of the children presents a compromise between Lloyd's and Floyd's respective volitions, and each interrupted gesture is never canceled altogether but still "enriches" implicitly the one that has been carried, then Floyd's childhood memories and perceptions should also be considered a product of two competing and compromising mentalities—in spite of Floyd's consistent attempts to represent Lloyd's mental processes as separate and markedly inferior to his own. Unable to comprehend his cognitive limits and dependencies, Floyd emerges as yet another unreliable narrator in Nabokov's gallery of Hermanns, Humberts, and Kinbotes.

Inevitably, both "Scenes from the Life of a Double Monster" and the "Double Mistress" episode grapple with the theme of mental versus physical monstrosity. The Scriblerians portray the poor double Lindamira–Indamora as merely pathetic in her amorous inclinations and reserve the full force of their sarcasm for the formidable intellectual freaks. Physically unexceptional Martinus and Drs. Leatherhead and Pennyfeather are the true monsters of the piece. Something very similar happens in Nabokov's "Scenes." Deformed Lloyd and Floyd are contrasted with a throng of able-bodied emotional freaks—their "ghoulish" relatives and keepers, who compete for the exclusive right to exploit the brothers. The only person who likes the boys and pities them without ulterior motives is a "hysterical" cook on their grandfather's farm—a "mustachioed woman" who one day declares "with an atrocious oath that she would, then and there, slice [them] free by means of a shiny knife" (*Stories* 612) that she suddenly flourishes. Of course, she is instantly "overpowered" (*Stories* 612) by Ahem and Novus and thus contributes to the realignment of the characters along the lines of physical and mental deformity. Situated in the context of freak-show lore, the "mustachioed woman" brings to mind the staple feature of such shows: the bearded lady. Thus, as something of a physiological curiosity herself, the mustachioed woman "likes" Lloyd and Floyd; she sides with them in her own, "hysterical" way and is predictably "overpowered"—just as Lloyd and Floyd always are—by the superior physical force of the true monsters, Ahem and Novus.

Dr. Fricke occupies an important place in the hierarchy of monstrosity in "Scenes," and his reaction to the twins is reminiscent of the behavior of the freakish title character of the Scriblerian satire. Fricke's "dreamy smile of scientific delectation"—his obvious sensual pleasure at having the "monster" at his full scholarly disposal—hark back to the Scriblerians' making fun of the "passion" with which learned men treat their objects of study, living creatures and artifacts alike. When Martinus first sees his "charming Monster," the authors marvel at "how violent, how transporting must that passion prove, where not only the Fire of Youth, but the unquenchable Curiosity of a Philosopher, pitch'd upon the same object!"[19] Kerby-Miller notes that the "passion of the virtuosi for monsters and abnormalities was frequently ridiculed in the late seventeenth and early eighteenth centuries. However, in translating that passion into actual amorousness ... the Scriblerians [opened up] an entirely original vein of humor."[20] Two hundred years later, Nabokov built on the Scriblerians' bawdy conflation of amorous and scientific passion to create his Freud-informed figure of a *passionate* scientist, Dr. Fricke.

By uncovering Dr. Fricke's connection to the Scriblerians' Martinus, we can understand better the closing paragraph of "Scenes" and connect it to the opening episode of the story. At the end of his narrative, Floyd daydreams about "some adventurous stranger" stepping "onto the shore from his boat in the bay" and experiencing "a thrill of *ancient* enchantment [on finding] himself confronted by a gentle mythological monster in a landscape of cypresses and white stones" (*Stories* 614; emphasis added). The imagined "adventurous stranger" worships Lloyd and Floyd and sheds "sweet tears" (*Stories* 614) over them—a seemingly appealing alternative to "that worried crook," uncle Novus, who greets the brothers on the shore, treats them roughly, and kidnaps them. Curiously, the gentle stranger envisioned by Floyd also bears a strong resemblance to Martinus, the tireless admirer of everything strange and "ancient," moved to worship his "charming Monster" of a mistress.[21] Thus, the two characters

19. Ibid., 146–47.
20. Ibid., 305.
21. Ibid., 147. Martinus's predilection for things ancient is part of the Scriblerians' ironic commentary on the late-seventeenth-century conflict between the ancients and the moderns. Everett Zimmerman summarizes the battle of the "'ancients and moderns' in England ... as one between two views of history—that of the humanists, who valued knowledge of the past only insofar as it was intrinsically valuable for the present, and that of the antiquaries, who valued whatever understanding of the past became available no matter how estranged from present concerns": Everett Zimmerman, *The Boundaries of Fiction: History and the Eighteenth-Century British Novel* (Ithaca, N.Y.: Cornell University Press, 1997), 99. For more on the conflict and the role played by the Scriblerians, see Joseph M. Levine, *The Battle of the Books: History and Literature in the Augustan Age* (Ithaca, N.Y.: Cornell University Press, 1991).

who frame the narrative—Dr. Fricke and the adventurous stranger—are really the same figure of a freakish naturalist drawn to "monsters."

The realization that Nabokov's story has a circular structure suggestively complements its traditional readings. Gennady Barabtarlo has argued persuasively that "Scenes" remains "a brightly picturesque piece of an absent whole, sporting magically seamless transitions whose interlinked chain is left dangling at the end."[22] If, as proposed here, the final episode in fact foreshadows the opening one—through its portrayal of a Martinus-like figure of a learned enthusiast—the story turns out to be more tightly structured that is generally thought. Thus, by providing a Scriblerian context for Nabokov's text, one gains a new understanding of the formal framing of "Scenes" along with uncovering its hidden genealogy.

One surprising payoff of situating Nabokov's story next to *The Memoirs* concerns the word "Scenes" in the story's title. It has never received any critical attention, perhaps because it was automatically perceived as a half-hearted authorial admission of the somewhat disjointed nature of the narrative. Once one questions this traditional reading, however, the word "Scenes" emerges as a sign of a cinematic rethinking of conventions of the raree-show and points toward the story's alignment with Nabokov's other pointedly "cinematic" narratives, such as "The Assistant Producer" (*Stories*) and *Laughter in the Dark*.

Vladislav Khodasevich noted once that the "style of life" depicted in the *Laughter in the Dark* is "permeated and poisoned" with the motif of cinema.[23] With certain provisos, this insight also applies to "Scenes." Floyd's beatific vision of a worshiping stranger on the beach points to a sad lopsidedness of Floyd's self-conceptualization: Used to being exhibited and gazed at, he cannot imagine a relationship in which he is not an observed object. Fatally, he seems to gauge his happiness as directly contingent on the personality and reaction of his audience. There are "bad," cruel, insensitive observers who make him miserable (nearly everybody on the farm), and there are "good" observers, such as the fictitious teary-eyed connoisseur of ancient wonders who greets the brothers after their escape (incidentally, one is again reminded of Martinus, into whose loving embrace Lindamira–Indamora falls on fleeing the prison of the raree-show). It is difficult to say whether Floyd himself

---

22. Gennady Barabtarlo, "English Short Stories," in *The Garland Companion to Vladimir Nabokov*, ed. Vladimir E. Alexandrov (New York: Garland, 1995), 112.

23. Vladislav Khodasevich, as quoted in David M. Bethea, "Nabokov and Khodasevich," in Alexandrov, *Garland Companion*, 457.

is aware of the terrible irony of his situation—that is, of the fact that the unappealing Dr. Fricke is the earthly embodiment of Floyd's imagined "good" observer. Most likely, this realization eludes him. In fact, one of the peculiar effects of the story is that, even as Nabokov subtly comments on the dangers of Floyd's willing self-commodification, he draws his readers into the same vicious circle that entraps his hero. At the end of "Scenes," we sigh together with Floyd and wish for a kind, appreciative, admiring stranger borne by the tide and naively envision him as a *positive* alternative to dreadful uncle Novus lying in wait on the shore.

The word "Scenes" in the story's title thus refers to Floyd's reimagining his and Lloyd's childhood as a series of bright cinematic vignettes or sequences— the doctor sequence; the scene of the rape; the first encounter with a normal child; the shiny-knife sequence; the scene of escape; the adventurous-stranger sequence (the stranger is played by the same actor who impersonates Dr. Fricke, sans the Freudian eyeglasses, balding pate, and disciplined beard). Hence, the specific "movie" lingo and the "script-like" style of some of the descriptions, such as this one:

> [The] ardent faces [of our audience] still pursue me in my nightmares, for they come whenever my dream producer needs supers. I see again the gigantic bronze-faced shepherd in multicolored rags, the soldiers from Karaz, the one-eyed hunchbacked Armenian tailor (a monster in his own right), the giggling girls, the sighing old women, the children, the young people in Western clothes—burning eyes, white teeth, black gaping mouths. (*Stories* 612)

Nabokov recasts the Scriblerian raree-show in a modern cinematic mold and focuses on the deforming effects that the ruthless objectification of the "exhibited" human beings has on their psychology. Floyd's tortured narcissism is revealed in his failure to envision any relationship other than that between the observer and the observed and in his attempts to ignore or obliterate the mental presence of his brother. Like Scriblerians before him, Nabokov explores nuances of human fascination with "monsters." Going further than his eighteenth-century predecessors, he enunciates the price paid for this fascination by those in the limelight.

{ 16 }

The Triple Anniversary of World Literature
Goethe, Pushkin, Nabokov

OMRY RONEN

In 1999, bookmen, scholars, and readers—men and women whose lives and characters have been shaped not only by heredity and the array of intersubjective affinities and aversions that is known as social environment but also, and perhaps above all, by the books they have read—celebrated, some with detached admiration, others with impassioned loving gratitude, the anniversary of the birth of Vladimir Nabokov. His art, his books, his attitudes, and his opinions opened a new world for readers to explore and learn from, not only teaching them how to read but also helping the young to choose their field of endeavor or to find moral courage in the face of adversity, injustice, or the petty tyranny of the commonplace, and reassuring them that even Kafka's Gregor Samsa the dung beetle had wings, although he did not know it.

Lev Shestov concluded his parable of the chrysalis and the caterpillars in *Apotheosis of Groundlessness* with the following words: "Those who create it [reality] deserve torture and execution. And there are in the wide world enough jails and voluntary executioners: most books are also jails, and great writers have not infrequently been executioners."[1] At a superficial glance, these words, written in 1905, seem to refer to *Invitation to a Beheading*. But Nabokov, who placed some of his protagonists behind the bars of their mania or in prison states of physical and mental coercion, as well as in the ample enclo-

---

1. Lev Shestov, *Apofeoz bezpochvennosti (Opyt adogmaticheskogo myshleniia)*, repr. ed. (Paris: YMCA-Press, 1971), 72.

sures of their creator's narrative space-time, was not an executioner but a liberator. His motto, however, would have been *Sola arte* rather than Shestov's *Sola fide*. So Adam von Librikov redeems R., and R. helps to freedom his first reader, his copy editor "Hugh Person."

Nabokov's writing—his languages and what they conveyed—was so fascinating and compelling that it surely would not be an exaggeration to say that, for some Russian readers, *The Gift* became a *What Is to Be Done?* of a new age. At the same time, in the West many were persuaded by Nabokov that Russian literature was a land of such loveliness that they should learn Russian in order to reach it.

By achieving a broad linguistic confrontation and an inspired synthesis of several great literary traditions in a twin, yet manifestly whole, body of bilingual writing, unprecedented in the lay verbal art of the Occident, Nabokov became the embodiment of a new, interlingual, transnational literature. That literature, using a coinage out of *Ada,* might be called Amerussian.

This remarkable virtue of Nabokov's art endows with special fatidic significance the concatenation of three anniversaries that readers and historians of literature observed in 1999. August 28, 1999, marked two hundred and fifty years since the birth of Goethe, the creator of the concept of, and the term, *Weltliteratur* (world literature). The expression was first recorded in his conversation with Eckermann on January 31, 1827: "National literature at present means little; the epoch of world literature is imminent, and we all should assist its early advent."[2]

From a number of his subsequent short articles it becomes clear how Goethe envisaged world literature. It certainly was not to be simply a collection of the so-called great books from all over the world. Rather, it would be a great synthesis of national literary achievements attained in practice at what Goethe called a marketplace of spiritual commerce, in which a key part would be played by the translator and the interpreter. In fact, the portents that suggested to Goethe the arrival of the new age were the publication of a French translation of his *Faust* and the appearance of Prosper Mérimée's collection of Illyric folk poetry, *La Guzla,* printed anonymously and ascribed to the folk singer Hyacinthe Maglanovich. (This, of course, did not prevent Goethe from

---

2. Johann Peter Eckermann, *Gespräche mit Goethe in den letzten Jahren seines Leben* (any ed.), entry dated January 31, 1827.

identifying its author as the author of *The Theatre of Clara Gazul* on the strength of the obvious anagram, *Gazul/Guzla*.[3])

As Goethe contemplated relevant literary facts, he arrived at a definition of world literature not as a mechanical accumulation of books, a sum total of various national literatures, but as a system of interliterary and intercultural choices, reflections and refractions: "Only from this can a general world literature finally emerge: from all nations learning about the attitudes of all towards all, and then each will find in another what is acceptable and what is not, what should be emulated and what needs to be shunned";[4] "Any literature begins, in the long run, to be fed up with itself unless it is refreshed by a sympathetic interest from the outside. What natural scientist did not rejoice in the miraculous discoveries made with the help of mirror reflections? Any man learns from his own experience, sometimes unconsciously, the usefulness of mirror reflections in moral life and, having perceived this, realizes how much his vital education owes precisely to such reflections."[5] Clearly, Goethe suggests an analogy: national literatures ought to learn from their reflections in other literatures. From the French translation of his *Faust* he derived an obvious lesson: "Although this dramatic poem was born of a dark element and played out in a motley but fearful setting, nevertheless the French language, which endows everything with joyful lightness, facilitates its contemplation and understanding, makes it considerably more clear and graspable."[6] In a sense, this observation holds true in regard to the effect that Nabokov's translation of *Eugene Onegin* has on Russophone readers: the inherent precision of the English language makes Pushkin's meaning more focused and more accessible.

Goethe's thoughts about world literature were part of his moral preoccupation with a still broader idea, which we, the historians of Slavic literatures, usually associate with a much later prophecy by Dostoevsky in his notorious Pushkin speech. It was the idea of the "generally human," which Goethe developed in his correspondence with Carlyle and in his reviews of Carlyle's works, especially *German Romance*: "It is known that for some time past the efforts

---

3. *Theatre de Clara Gazul, comédienne espagnole* (Paris, 1825). Goethe identified the anagram *Gazul/Guzla,* and Prosper Mérimée as the author of *Guzla,* in the second chapter of his article "Nationelle Dichtkunst" (1828).

4. Johann Wolfgang von Goethe, "Allgemeine Betrachtungen zur Weltliteratur" (1830).

5. Johann Wolfgang von Goethe, "Zur Zeitschrift der französischen Romantiker *Le Globe*," no. 4 (1828).

6. Idem, "*Faust*. Tragedie de Mr de Goethe" (1828).

of the best poets and theoreticians of art of all nations have been directed toward the generally human. The universal gleams and glimmers through the national and the personal in every feature, be it historical, mythological, fabulous, or even simply fictional.... Everything in the literature of an individual nation that can point in this direction should be shared by all.... A true and general tolerance will be attained only if we let individuals and peoples keep their characteristic traits, provided they bear in mind that the distinguishing feature of true merit is that it is universally human."[7]

Such was Goethe's rough blueprint for world literature. Nabokov, who in many respects contributed more than any other writer to its realization, manifested throughout his art mixed feelings toward Goethe: a profound attraction tinged with a streak of equally deep revulsion. Certain master themes (the king of Thule, the Erlking, the fiery death and transformation) that Nabokov inherited from Goethe, as well as his free translation from *West–Eastern Divan* and the entire problem of emulation, parody, caricature, and reconciliation in Nabokov's attitude toward Goethe, are discussed in detail in *Cold Fusion*, a collection of essays on Russian–German literary relations edited by Gennady Barabtarlo.[8] What is pertinent to the matter at hand, to the essential features of world literature as it was understood by Goethe, is Nabokov's characteristic method of blending Goethe's characters and situations with those, for example, of Pushkin (Gretchen and Rusalka) or of letting the moth of "Selige Sehnsucht" escape directly into Tiutchev's "Teni sizye smesilis.'" Neither should it be forgotten that in his first attempt to make Pushkin come alive in a Western literary environment (France, in that instance), Nabokov seems to have consulted Goethe, the first master builder of a poetic bridge between East and West and the first German writer to be widely recognized and admired west of the Rhine. Both the title and the underlying dichotomy of Nabokov's French lecture and essay "Pouchkine ou le vrai et le vraisemblable" ("Pushkin, or the Real and the Plausible" in Dmitri Nabokov's translation[9]) appear to be a tribute to "Über Wahrheit und Wahrscheinlichkeit der Kunstwerke" (published in 1798) by Goethe, who appears in that essay, in the same sentence with

7. Idem, "*German Romance.* Volumes I–IV. Edinburgh, 1827 (by Carlyle)" (1828).
8. Omry Ronen, "Nabokov and Goethe," in *Cold Fusion: Aspects of the German Cultural Presence in Russia*, ed. Gennady Barabtarlo (New York: Berghahn Books, 2000), 241–51.
9. Vladimir Nabokov, "Pushkin, or the Real and the Plausible," trans. Dmitri Nabokov, *New York Review of Books*, March 31, 1988, 38–42.

Byron and Pushkin, as Nabokov confronts the reality of a photograph and the plausibility of a historical illustration—and, eventually, the inner truth of art and the outer verisimilitude of imitation.

That lecture by Nabokov was written for the one-hundredth anniversary of Pushkin's death. The June 6, 1999, was the bicentennial of his birth, and among the many enigmas surrounding Pushkin, there remains the exact nature of his role in world literature.

One side of the problem seems quite clear. In his pithy poetry, drama, and prose, Pushkin condensed, miniaturized, and encapsulated the great Occidental achievement of the ancients and of Dante, Ariosto, Shakespeare, and Goethe, as well as some traditions of the Orient, to implant them in the youngest national verbal art of Europe: literature in the modern Russian language.

Pushkin's contribution in the opposite direction is considerably more difficult to define. As Nabokov put it in his French lecture on Pushkin, "It is always harder for a poet than for a proseman to cross borders." In the nineteenth century, the West had very little knowledge of Russia's most sublime achievement, its poetry. The "Russian age" in European literature was inaugurated by the evocative power of Turgenev's prose and the exotically perceived moral prophecy of Tolstoy and Dostoevsky. Pushkin's reputation in Europe was based on hearsay and frequently doubted; his sole truly outstanding export to world literature, in Goethe's sense, during the nineteenth century was the contribution of his poem *Tsygany*, through the good offices of the same Mérimée, to the theme and character that Mandelstam has called "the youngest European myth": Carmen, the feminine counterpart of Don Juan (it should be noted that the two meet in a poem by Tsvetaeva and in Nabokov's *Ada*).[10] One might say that Pushkin received from Europe its recent lay myth and gave in return an even younger one.

Aside from that, there is the conjectured impact of Pushkin's "Scene from Faust" on the episode of the arrival of the bark in *Faust* II.5, the general popularity of "The Queen of Spades," and Pushkin's profound influence on Slavic literatures, including the Polish response, ranging from Miczkiewicz's magnificent poetic and historical counteraction to Conrad's verbose and com-

---

10. Osip Mandel'shtam, "A. Blok (7 avgusta 21 g.–7 avgusta 22 g.)" (1922). Published again in 1928 under the title "Barsuch'ia nora" ("Badger's Nest"), the title that is generally used in the English translations of this essay. The cycle of poems by Tsvetaeva in which Carmen defeats Don Juan is "Don Zhuan" (1917). The description of the aged Don Juan meeting a little *gitana* and suffering "a premature spasm" can be found in *Ada* 489.

monplace parody of "The Shot." Otherwise, the item in the history of world literature that seems to be especially appropriate as an allegory of Pushkin's reception outside Russia during the first century since his death is the title of the first Japanese translation of *The Captain's Daughter:* "A Diary of the Butterfly Meditating over a Flower's Soul: Astonishing News from Russia."[11]

The reason for this state of affairs is obvious: in poetry, especially lyric poetry, the boundaries of the national language are a greater obstacle than elsewhere, as Naum Berkovsky has rightly observed in his book on the Western reception of Russian literature.[12] However, in the case of Pushkin, even his prose turned out to be too elusive for his foreign readers, notwithstanding Dostoevsky's insistence on Pushkin's universal, all-human understanding and appeal (*vsechelovechnost'*) as a justification of Russia's divine mission to lead "the all-human reunion of all the tribes of the great Aryan family."[13]

Thus, the cause of world literature, as Goethe correctly foresaw when he called the translator "a prophet in his own country," turned out to depend first and foremost on the art of interpreting; the science of philology; the skill, erudition, and taste of the writer who takes up the most responsible duty that a man of letters can think of: the duty of a translator. Pushkin was well aware of this when he wrote in his unfinished essay on Chateaubriand's prose translation of *Paradise Lost* the words that provided Nabokov with an epigraph for his translation of *Eugene Onegin:* "Nowadays—an unheard-of case!—the first of French writers is translating Milton word for word and proclaiming that an interlinear translation would be the summit of his art, had such been possible."[14] In this essay Pushkin actually addressed the problem of Milton's reception in France and his image in the contemporary French fiction and drama, as well as the reception of Chateaubriand's *Essay on English Literature* by some

---

11. The first Japanese version of *The Captain's Daughter* appeared under this title in Tokyo in 1883. In some Russian bibliographies it is listed as "Serdtse tsvetka i dumy babochki. Udivitel'nye vesti iz Rossii" (The Heart of a Flower and the Thoughts of a Butterfly: Amazing News from Russia): See A. S. Pushkin, *Kapitanskaia dochka*, izdanie podgotovil Iu. G. Oksman, "Literaturnye Pamiatniki" (Moscow: Nauka, 1964), 278.

12. Naum Berkovsky, *Mir, sozdavaemyi literaturoi* (Moscow, 1989), 459.

13. F. M. Dostoevsky. "Pushkin (Ocherk)," *Dnevnik pisatelia*, vol. 3 (St. Petersburg, 1880). The quote in Russian reads, "ko vseobshchemu vossoedineniiu so vsemi plemenami velikogo ariiskogo roda": F. M. Dostoevsky, *Sobranie sochinenii*, vol. 10 (Moscow, 1958), 457.

14. A. S. Pushkin. "O Mil'tone i Shatobrianovom perevode 'Poteriannogo raia,'" *Polnoe sobranie sochinenii, Vol. 12: Kritika. Avtobiografiia* (Izdatel'stvo AN SSSR, 1949), 137.

English critics. As such, Pushkin's piece pertained precisely to the realm of world literature as Goethe conceived it.

Pushkin's own art had to wait for another century for such a translator as Chateaubriand aspired to be, and it finally found him in the great artist who returned with interest the riches that Pushkin had received from the West.

The significance of the third great anniversary of world literature, April 23, 1999, is unique even when compared with the other two. A multilingual genius with comparable achievements in two great literatures, Nabokov actually attained the interliterary stature of a world writer envisaged by Goethe and the supranational significance that Dostoevsky had claimed for Pushkin.

Nabokov realized Goethe's ideal in a manifold manner: as an original poet, fiction writer, memoirist, and playwright; as a translator of Russian poetry and prose; and, last but not least, as a scholar and critic. These three aspects of Nabokov's life work are closely interrelated.

Part of what makes Nabokov's prose and poetry an epitome of world literature is the enormous, thematically relevant scope of his breathtakingly vivid writing—his penetration into national characteristics and attitudes; his landscapes, ranging from Lhasa to Texas; his evocations of villages, cities, and towns, whether invented (such as Fialta [Fiume plus Rialto, not only *fialka* plus Yalta] in which one recognizes Abbazia, previously described by only one Russian writer, Chekhov, in his letters and in the story "Ariadna") or real (such as New York, the familiar skyline of which undergoes an eerie change in "Time and Ebb"); his taxonomic precision or tantalizing evasiveness in describing the wealth and variety of nature, from the plants and butterflies of Vermont to the "swarming of hesperozoa in a humid valley on Venus";[15] and his rare, ripe, unforgettable response to "the clamor of the century" in *Glory, Bend Sinister, Pnin, Ada,* "Tyrants Destroyed," "The Assistant Producer," and "Conversation Piece," probably the best dissection of pernicious propaganda ever written. It is not only Nabokov's prose, but also his poetry, that is imbued with motifs that are vitally linked to the essence of world literature. Without taking this into consideration, it is impossible to understand such cryptic pieces as "The Paris Poem," with its theme of Parisian Russian poetry's failed contact with the West and promise of a new, gloriously successful meeting, or "Lines Written in Oregon," and why the Esmeralda of that poem, whether she is a butterfly or Hugo's gypsy dancer, is extolled in German.

15. Vladimir Nabokov, "Time and Ebb" (*Stories* 581).

But there is also another, very specific, metaliterary and metalinguistic aspect of Nabokov's art, which involves images of languages—real languages in contact and invented ones—that usually blend Slavic, Germanic, and (in *Bend Sinister*) Romance elements; images of national literatures, sometimes as perceived by foreign readers; images of literary works in various languages, sometimes invented; evocations of literary styles and individual stylistic manners; nonfictional or fictional characters who are men of letters and, at times, invented parallel figures in different literatures, such as Delalande and German Lande (whose prototype was apparently Grigory Landau, with a slight admixture of Lev Shestov). Because of this metapoetic, actively intertextual, and, at the same time, uniquely vivid, evocative, and persuasive individual style, Nabokov, more than any other writer of this century, is relevant to the idea and the reality of world literature. The fact that he translated, with his son, most of his Russian books into English and *Lolita* into Russian, along with the numerous literary quotations, and passages and entire chapters dealing with literary history in these books, makes the boundary between Nabokov's original fiction and poetry, his translations, and his critical prose quite fluid. This is true particularly because, as Khodasevich has noted, literary devices are characters in Nabokov's books.

The function of Nabokov's translations, literary essays, and scholarship sets them apart from his fiction. As one considers the great corpus of Nabokov's translations, one immediately perceives a single, dominant criterion in Nabokov's choice of texts. He selected those Russian books that had not previously become part of the Occidental body of great writing, the kind of writing that is not merely acknowledged with dutiful respect but actually read as living poetry and prose. Except for the unique medieval masterpiece *Slovo o polku Igoreve*, all of these books belong to what Russian critics call the Golden Age of Russian literature. Pushkin, Lermontov, and Tiutchev were the focus of Nabokov's attention, as was Gogol, of whom Nabokov would translate only some fragments for the purpose of quoting but to whom he devoted an entire monograph.

Through these efforts, Nabokov succeeded in correcting the slant in the Western—especially the Anglo-American—view of nineteenth-century Russian literature, which traditionally had been biased in favor of the "translatable," nonpoetic, verisimilar, voluminous, socially oriented, and frequently didactic art of the great Russian novel in the era of so-called realism. Nabokov's consistent aesthetic criticism of Dostoevsky's artistic faults, which he showed to be as intimately related to the famous Russian prophet's errors of moral judgment as the pitfalls of Chernyshevsky's thought corresponded to the great radical's stylistic blunders, was, among other things, aimed at reducing somewhat the disproportional place Dostoevsky had taken as a minister plenipotentiary of Russia to world literature so as to allow Pushkin to squeeze in.

In the beginning of his career as a translator, unlike during the later stern period of consistent literalism, Nabokov belonged to the so-called Russian school and aimed at conveying the poetic effect rather than the exact substance of Russian lyric poems in his English versions. He did this not only by choosing English poetic equivalents for Russian poetic locutions (that were often quite distant in sense), but also by seeking what might be called cross-cultural substitutes. Thus, in his rendering of Tiutchev's "Uspokoenie," the paronomastic sound reiteration of the thunder god's name, Perun, in the word *pernatye* (the feathered tribe) would be represented anagrammatically by dismembering the phonetic or graphic shape of Perun's Germanic equivalent, Thor, and distributing it among the representatives of two families of birds: *TH-* would go to *th*rush, and *-OR* to *or*iole.

Eventually, Nabokov abandoned such attempts to create equivalent substitutes in English for Russian lyric texts, even though most of his renderings were miracles of erudition, wit, and poetic inspiration. Too much depended on chance in applying such a method, and, moreover, important characteristic features of Russian poetics had to be sacrificed in order to make a translation read as an original English poem would.

Nabokov applied the method of literal faithfulness to his translation of Russia's greatest work of narrative poetry, *Eugene Onegin*, as well as to the many specimens of Pushkin's lyric poetry that he translated in the commentaries. As a result, these translations no longer sounded like traditional English poetry, but began to resemble the prosody and diction of unrhymed and metrically loose modern verse. Russian poetry of the Golden Age became accessible to American readers and began to attract lovers of poetry.

One recurrent object of Nabokov's scholarly and educational interest must also be considered here, because it has to do with a vital process in the evolution of world literature: the metamorphosis that the meaning of original texts undergoes in reception, especially when that reception does not detract from the original by distortion but improves an imperfect work. Nabokov first observed a less general aspect of this phenomenon when he described, in *The Gift*, the reception of Chernyshevsky's novel by "*genial'nyi russkii chitatel'*," the

Russian reader of genius who succeeded in understanding what Chernyshevsky so clumsily had been trying to express.

Nabokov described a more lasting and significant improvement and growth of a literary work that had become part of world literature and penetrated other cultures and other historical periods in *Lectures on Don Quixote:*

> *Don Quixote* is one of those books that are, perhaps, more important in eccentric diffusion than in their own intrinsic value. It is significant that the work was immediately translated abroad.... [T]he good knight thrived and bred through the world, and at last was equally at home everywhere: as a carnival figure at a festival in Bolivia and as the abstract symbol of noble but spineless political aspirations in old Russia.
>
> We are confronted by an interesting phenomenon: a literary hero losing gradually contact with the book that bore him; leaving his fatherland, leaving his creator's desk and roaming space after roaming Spain. In result, Don Quixote is greater today than he was in Cervantes's womb.... We do not laugh at him any longer. His blazon is pity, his banner is beauty. He stands for everything that is gentle, forlorn, pure, unselfish, and gallant. The parody has become a paragon.
>
> Don Quixote has ridden for three hundred and fifty years through the jungles and tundras of human thought—and he has gained in vitality and stature. (*LDQ* 111–12)

As we celebrated Nabokov's one-hundredth anniversary, his books had reached Russia at last; they had also reached a new generation of readers all over the world. At this earnest end of the age, it is time to count our blessings: the gigantic presence of Nabokov is growing with time, not only as Pushkin's true successor in twentieth-century Russian literature, but also as the firstborn of world literature and a paradoxical fulfillment of poor Dostoevsky's prophecy of Russia's gift to the world: a universal man.

{ 17 }

Vladimir Nabokov, Translator of Lewis Carroll's *Alice in Wonderland*

NINA DEMUROVA

Lewis Carroll's *Alice in Wonderland* stands at the very beginning of Vladimir Nabokov's life, at one of those strange reversals of fate that were his lifelong preoccupation. It was one of his earlier books; it was issued in Berlin in 1923 by Gamaiun, one of Berlin's many new Russian publishers, and bore the title *Ania v strane chudes* (Ania in Wonderland). On the front page, next to the publisher's mark—a mythical bird of wisdom—was the name V. Sirin, another wizard bird of the Russian folklore.

Nabokov said that he worked on his translation for "one summer"—it must have been the summer of 1922. During that period, he also published two books of poems—*Gornii put', Grozd'* in 1923 and, a little earlier, in 1922, his translation of Romain Rolland's "Colas Breughnon." In a letter to S. J. Parker many years later, he wrote that he "was commissioned to translate [*Alice*] by the publisher and had not such prior plans," that he was paid about $5, and that "it was easier than Colas Breughnon" (*SL* 519).

No other Russian at the time, perhaps, was by accident of birth and education so well suited for the translation of Carroll's immortal classic and for the evocation of his particular world and spirit. "The kind of Russian family [to which] I belonged," Nabokov wrote later, "a kind now extinct—had, among other virtues, a traditional leaning toward the comfortable products of Anglo-Saxon civilisation" (*SM* 79). He meant not only Pears soap, English toothpaste, and a "bewildering sequence of English nurses and governesses" (*SM* 86), but also English books and the English language itself. In fact, he was "surrounded by England" in those days. He recollected English fairy-tales, tales of the

Knights of the Round Table, Mary Corelli and other sentimental and didactic English authors, and, of course, *Alice in Wonderland,* which he read, he told Parker, in 1906. "In common with many other English children (and I was an English child)," he told A. Appel in 1966, I have been always very fond of Carroll."[1] Perhaps this was so because *Alice* was so different from all those "Soniny prokazy," "Primernye devochki," and "Kanikuly" by Madame de Segur (born Rastopchina); the Russian children's magazine *Zadushevnoe slovo;* and books by many other Russian children's authors of the time that made future writers shudder—an attitude that later he bestowed on some of his characters (see, for example, *Glory*).

Nabokov's translating *Alice* was not completely an accident. Although his life in Berlin was not easy—he had to coach tennis and translate commercial descriptions of some construction cranes—he probably would not have agreed to translate authors of Mary Corelli's type, or had he been obliged to agree, the result would not have been so happy. Although Nabokov said that "spiritual affinities [had] no place" in his concept of literary criticism, a "congenial translator" could create that "*voploshchhenie*" (incarnation, another of Nabokov's words) that alone can be considered a true translation. "[F]idelity to one's author comes first, no matter how bizarre the result," Nabokov wrote in the introduction to his English translation of *Invitation to a Beheading* (*IB* 7–8). That "spiritual affinity" certainly existed between the young Russian émigré who was to become the glory of Russian literature and the modest mathematician from Oxford whose *Alice* books are now read and reread by millions all over the world.

The two authors had much in common beyond their English childhoods. It is not only that both enjoyed chess (Nabokov later spoke of "a very subtle and difficult chess problem" in Carroll's *Through the Looking-Glass* [*SL* 99]), or that both composed crosswords and puzzles. But more important, both were professional scientists (Carroll a mathematician; Nabokov a naturalist) and meditated about such things as "time" and "nothing," "mirror" and "dream." They both had a happy predilection for play (it was not for nothing that Gavriel Shapiro called Nabokov *homo ludens*[2]) and for constructing special worlds with their own rules, and both exalted in alliteration, wordplay, and nonsense.

1. Alfred Appel, Jr., "An Interview with Vladimir Nabokov," *Wisconsin Studies in Contemporary Literature* 8, no. 2 (1967): 132.
2. Gavriel Shapiro, *Delicate Markers: Subtexts in Vladimir Nabokov's* Invitation to a Beheading (New York: Peter Lang, 1998), 212.

Nabokov's translation presented, as Simon Karlinsky says, a "Russified Carroll."³ Critics today tend to condemn Russified translations in toto, saying that they create "absurd Anglicized Russia," show no interest in national "color," and have no respect for the subtleties of the English mentality.⁴ However, viewed in a historical context, the situation is not as simple as that. The early translators of Carroll had to introduce the Russian reader to a most unusual book in which verbal and logical nonsense, all sorts of puns and parodies, played an important role. One could not translate puns or verbal nonsense and wordplay literally; one had to change them, and change them in such a way that the Russian audience understood and enjoyed them. Russifying the English text seemed the only answer, and that was precisely what Nabokov chose to do.

It should also be borne in mind that, at the beginning of the century, the Russians did not know much about England; certainly, they knew much less about it than, say, about France or Germany. English was not widely read or spoken. (Nabokov's family was a notable exception in this respect, as it was in many others.) "To make a book a self-sufficient plaything for Russian children," Brian Boyd writes, "he staged a gleeful raid on the toys and tags of Russian nursery."⁵ The raid started with the Russification of names, which is essential for *Alice* books, because Carroll's choice of a name quite often had a direct bearing on the character's nature and behavior. Nabokov chose the names that were more familiar to the Russian ear; he was also very careful about the social connotations of certain Russian names—especially of their diminutives, where these connotations become even more pronounced.

Nabokov changed the heroine's name from "Alice," which might have sounded cold and remote to a Russian child, to the more familiar and coy *Аня*.⁶

---

3. Simon Karlinsky, "Anya in Wonderland: Nabokov's Russified Lewis Carroll," *Triquarterly* 17 (1970): 310.

4. Etkind directs his criticism toward Poliksena Sergeevna Solovieva; for obvious reasons, he could not write about Nabokov in 1963. One wonders, though, what his verdict would have been. Efim Etkind, *Poeziia i perevod* (Moscow: Sovetskii pisatel', 1963), 347.

5. Brian Boyd, *Vladimir Nabokov: The Russian Years* (Princeton, N.J.: Princeton University Press, 1990), 197.

6. Nabokov may have had another good reason not to call his heroine Alice, for that was the name by which the late Empress Alexandra Fedorovna, wife of Nicholas II, the last Russian czar, was commonly known. Born Princess Alix of Hesse, she changed her name to Alexandra Fedorovna but remained Alix to her family, and Alice to the public. Nabokov may have wanted to avoid using the name of the unfortunate woman, who was murdered by Bolsheviks on the night of July 16–17, 1918.

Alice's friend "Mable," whom she remembers while falling down the rabbit hole, becomes *Ася* and the White Rabbit's housemaid "Mary-Ann" becomes *Маша*. Nabokov also changed details connected with characters' circumstances and all sorts of historical and social realia. In Nabokov's translation, the bright brass plate on the White Rabbit's door reads "Дворянин Кролик Трусиков," and the "dry" passage from the history of England dealing with William the Conqueror and Edwin and Morcar, the earls of Mercia and Northumbria, is replaced with a passage about Владимир Мономах and his elder son, князь Мстислав. Similarly, in chapter 2, when Alice plans to send Christmas presents to her feet, which have suddenly shot almost out of sight, Nabokov invents the following address for her: "Госпоже Правой Ноге Аниной. Город Коврик. Паркетная губерния," in which *Нога* can be taken for the first name and *Анина* for a surname (such as "Hope Саниной"). Bill the Lizard under Nabokov's pen becomes "ящерица Яшка," in which *Яшка* corresponds to his subordinate social status and allows for the play of alliterations for which Nabokov has such a wonderful gift. Listen to the chorus of voices that comments on the events around the White Rabbit's house while Alice is cooped up there:

"Теперь скажи мне, Петька, что это там в окне?"
"Известно, Ваше Благородие, — ручища!" (Он произнес это так: рчище.)
"Ручища? Осёл! Кто когда видел руку такой величины?" . . .
"Где другая лестница?"
"Не лезь, мне было велено одну принести, Яшка прёт с другой."
"Яшка! Тащи её сюда, малый!" . . .
"Стой, привяжи их одну к другой!"
"Да они того . . . не достают до верха."
"Ничего, и так ладно, нечего деликатничать" . . .
"Эй, Яшка, барин говорит, что ты должен спуститься по трубе".

"Now tell me, Pet'ka, what's there in the window?"
"Why, your worship, it's a huge hand." (He pronounced it "hug and.")
"Huge hand? You ass! Whoever saw a hand as huge as that?" . . .
"Where is the other ladder?"
"Give way! I was told to bring just one. Yashka is trotting up with another."
"Yashka! Drag it up here, boy!"
"Hey, put it up against the wall!"

"Stop, bind them together!"
"Look, they isn't ... they doesn't reach to the top!"
"It's OK, don't you worry!"
"Hey, Yashka, the master says, you must go down the chimney."

and so on.[7]

This is a very colorful passage in which the voices speak energetically with a strong low colloquial flavor that surpasses even Carroll's. All those Яшка and Петька, ручища, Яшка прёт, малый contribute to the stylistic expressiveness, as do such words as барин, деликатничать, and ваше благородие.

More difficult for translators are names whose reference frame in the original are not at all known in Russian. For example, the Cheshire Cat (of the phrase "smile like a Cheshire Cat," which itself has different connotations), is a very well-known creature in England. In Nabokov's translation, the Cheshire Cat becomes Масляничный Кот. Nabokov introduces an explanation for this name based on a Russian proverb: "Почему это Ваш кот ухмыляется так?" Alice asks. And the Duchess answers, "Не всегда коту масленица. Моему же коту—всегда. Вот он и ухмыляется." ("Why is your cat grinning so?" Alice asks. And the Duchess answers: "Because it's a Shrovetide cat, that's why.")[8] In some cases, Nabokov coins new names—as in the case of the Mock-Turtle, whom he calls Чепупаха. Чепупаха is a funny nonsense word that, following the principle of portmanteau words, combines черепаху (turtle) with чепуха (rubbish, nonsense). This connects the name directly to puns and other types of wordplay in Nabokov's *Ania v strane chudes*. There is a hilarious cascade of puns that Boyd calls "quadrivial," as opposed to Carroll's "trivial" ones.[9] However this may be, Nabokov obviously revels in the game.

Take, for instance, the passage in the Mock-Turtle's story in which he describes lessons at the bottom of the sea. These are the subjects that he was taught: "Reeling and Writhing, of course, to begin with ... and then the different branches of Arithmetic—Ambition, Distraction, Uglification, and Derision."[10] This is how Nabokov renders it: "'Чему же Вы учились?'—полюбопытствовала Аня. 'Сперва, конечно,—чесать и питать. Затем были

---

7. V. Sirin (Vladimir Nabokov), trans., *Ania v strane chudes* (Ania in Wonderland) (Berlin: Gamaiun, 1923), chap. 4.
8. Ibid., chap. 6.
9. Boyd, *Russian Years*, 198.
10. Lewis Carroll, *Alice in Wonderland*, chap. 9.

четыре правила арифметики: служенье, выметанье, уморженье и пи-ленье.'" And when Аня wonders what "уморженье" may possibly be, the Gryphon argues: "'Крота можно укротить?'—спросил он. 'Да . . . как будто можно',—ответила Аня неуверенно. 'Ну так, значит, и моржа можно уморжить',—продолжал Гриф.—'Если Вы этого непонимаете, Вы просто дурочка.'" The chapter concludes with a funny etymology of the term "lessons." The original text reads: "'And how many hours a day did you do lessons?'—said Alice. . . . 'Ten hours the first day', said the Mock-Turtle, 'nine the next, and so on.' 'What a curious plan!' exclaimed Alice. 'That's the reason they're called lessons,' the Gryphon remarked, 'because they lessen from day to day.'" Nabokov renders the passage this way: "'А сколько в день у вас было уроков?'—спросила Аня. 'У нас были не уроки, а укоры',—ответила Чепупаха.—'Десять укоров первый день, девять—в следующий, и так далее'. 'Какое странное распределенье!'—воскликнула Аня. 'Поэтому они и назывались укорами—укорачивались, понимаете?'—заметил Гриф.". In Russian readers' minds, Nabokov's "укоры" points not only to *укорачиваться* (to grow less), but also to *укор* (rebuke), which, as everyone knows from experience, frequently forms an essential part of the educational process.

Quite often, Nabokov uses ingenious methods to help readers grasp Carroll's implications. For the Russian reader, who would not be familiar with the expressions "Mad as a Hatter" or "Mad as a March Hare," he invents ways to emphasize the lunacy of the two characters. The Hatter complains about his quarrel with Time: "We quarreled last march—just before he went mad, you know—(pointing with his tea-spoon at the March Hare)."[11] In Nabokov's translation, the Hatter says: "Мы с Временем рассорились в прошлом Мартобре, когда этот, знаете, начинал сходить с ума (он указал чайной ложкой на Мартовского Зайца)." "В Мартобре" would have been a very significant pointer for the Russian reader at that time, when the English mythology of lunacy was not at all well known. The pointer refers the reader to Gogol's immortal "Zapiski sumasshedshego," creating a much needed reference frame that supports the text.

The most glorious part of Nabokov's translation is perhaps the parody and verse. Following his Russifying principle. Nabokov chose for his parodies verses that were well known in Russian nurseries. By subtly changing a few words here and there while keeping the rhyme scheme and rhythms intact, he

11. Ibid., chap. 7.

produced wonderfully humorous effect—or what Tynianov called "эффект подмалевки" (background effect) or "оперирование сразу двумя семантическими системами, даваемыми на одном знаке" (simultaneously operating two semantic systems based on one sign).¹² Nabokov chose Pushkin's "Вещий Олег" or "Птичка Божия не знает"; Lermontov's "Казачья колыбельная" and "Бородино"; or the anonymous but well-known "Чижик-пыжик, где ты был?"

Here is just one example in which Nabokov uses for his parody Lermontov's "Казачья колыбельная":

Speak roughly to your little boy
And beat him when he sneezes:
He only does it to annoy,
Because he knows it teases.

    CHORUS (in which the Cook and the baby joined): Wow! Wow! Wow!

I speak severely to my boy,
I beat him when he sneezes;
For he can thoroughly enjoy
The pepper when he pleases!

    CHORUS: Wow! Wow! Wow!

This, of course, is a travesty of the well-known poem, attributed by scholars to different authors,

Speak gently! It is better far
To rule by love than fear;
Speak gently, let no harsh words mar
The good we might do here!

This is how Nabokov renders the parody:

Вой, младенец мой прекрасный,
А чихнешь—побью!
Ты нарочно—это ясно …
Баюшки-баю.

    ХОР: Ау! Ау! Ау! Ау!

12. Iurii Tynianov, *O parodii. Poetika. Istoriia literatury. Kino* (Moscow: Nauka, 1977), 290.

То ты синий, то ты красный,
Бью и снова бью!
Перец любишь ты ужасно,
Баюшки-баю.

   хор: Ау! Ау! Ау! Ау! Ау! Ау!

Sometimes, however, Nabokov is overzealous: His parodies become too strong and too satirical, and he uses imagery that Carroll, a thoroughly Victorian gentleman, might not have approved. To give but one example, this is how Nabokov renders a stanza in "Father William":

Ещё одно позволь мне слово:
Сажаешь ты угря живого
На угреватый нос.
Его подкинешь два-три раза, . . .
Как приобрел ты верность глаза?
Волнующий вопрос.

Nabokov here plays on the Russian word *угорь*, which means both "eel" and "blackhead." In cases such as this, one feels, as Karlinsky puts it, that the translation is the "work of a very young man" and that "it does contain pages not equal in imagination and fidelity to what Nabokov had done in the best and most successful passages."[13]

Nabokov's rendering of Carroll's logical jokes and "nonsenses" are no less successful than his rendering of names and puns, though they are, as Warren Weaver says, especially difficult to translate.[14] Nabokov treats these renderings with the energy and vigor that is characteristic of his style in general.

Nabokov's narrative style is perhaps less formal and reserved than Carroll's, which can be explained not only by personal factors but also by his addressing children exclusively. As a result, Nabokov describes his characters' actions more vigorously: His White Rabbit *семенит*, Alice, *вихрем сорвавшись*, runs after him, while he *улепетывает в темноту*; the daughter of *старой Рачихи* (Nabokov's rendering of Carroll's "old she-lobster" in chap. 3) *огрызается*, the Pigeon *взвизгивает*, and so on.

---

13. Karlinsky, "Anya in Wonderland," 314.
14. Warren Weaver, *Alice in Many Tongues: The Translations of Alice in Wonderland* (Madison: University of Wisconsin Press, 1964), 81.

Other points of interest in Nabokov's translation are worth mentioning. He manages long syntactical constructions successfully. He knew only too well that Russian syntax is much heavier than English syntax: In the introduction to *Invitation to a Beheading*, he wrote that, "[f]or the sake of that clarity which in English seems to require less elaborate electric fixtures than in Russian" (*IB* 8), he cut the long periods—for instance, at the very beginning of the tale—into shorter ones and generally did his best to avoid long Russian words. In a number of cases he tried using literal translations (кальки) of English idioms and phrases, something that he would develop into a special literary device in his later work. Although sometimes such translations are a little clumsy, one cannot deny that they are expressive.

And some aspects of Nabokov's translation are perhaps less successful than one could wish. There is, for instance, much more similarity in Nabokov's "роялем и слоном" than in the Mad Hatter's original riddle ("Why is a raven like a writing-desk?");[15] the young writer had some difficulty choosing between the personal pronouns "ты" and "вы" or assigning gender to the creatures (thus he makes Голубь hatch the eggs). But these are, of course, minor things. One should remember, as Karlinsky suggests, that *Ania v strane chudes* was the work of a very young man who obviously had to hurry to meet a deadline, and that, with very few changes, it would have become one of the best translations of *Alice in Wonderland*.[16]

Nabokov's parodies are very vigorous and have a degree of freedom (which is true of his translations in general) that bespeaks a future master. Strangely enough, the only poem in *Alice in Wonderland* that he did not translate was the lyrical introduction, in which Carroll remembers the golden afternoon on the river, when he told the three Liddell girls the story of "Alice in Wonderland." It is possible that Nabokov found the task too forbidding. In the last stanza of his dedication, Carroll wrote:

> Alice! a childish story take,
>   And with a gentle hand,
> Lay it where Childhood's dreams are twined
>   In Memory's mystic band,
> Like pilgrim's wither'd wreath of flowers
>   Pluck'd in a far-off land.

15. Nabokov, *Ania v strane chudes*; Carroll, *Alice in Wonderland*, chap. 8
16. Karlinsky, "Anya in Wonderland," 314.

Was it impossible for Nabokov to translate this stanza, which may have reminded him of the "сказочносчастливое" (happy as a fairytale) childhood in Russia?

Nabokov's translation, strangely enough, was instrumental in getting him his first university job in the United States. In a letter to his sister Helena, he wrote that, after a number of frustrations, he was "invited to lecture by a certain university enticed by my having once translated 'Alice in Wonderland' into Russian. Then I was invited to Stanford University in California, and here things got a bit easier" (*SL* 60).

What is more important, perhaps, is that echoes of *Alice* reverberate in many of Nabokov's works, both prose and poetic, and form a subtext in more than one. Sometimes this subtext is almost imperceptible; sometimes it is very clear.

{ 18 }

Nabokov on Malraux's *La Condition humaine*
A Franco-Russian Crisscross

JOHN BURT FOSTER, JR.

Writing Edmund Wilson on November 27, 1946, in a letter rightly featured in Terry Quinn's dramatization of *The Nabokov–Wilson Letters,* Nabokov detailed his objections to André Malraux's novel *La Condition humaine.* Readers of the correspondence will sense that this letter marked a key turning point in the two men's friendship, will even suspect that it could have ignited the kind of bitter polemics that erupted over the *Eugene Onegin* translation, only here with a literary work closer to Wilson than to Nabokov. Set in Shanghai amid the 1927 split between the Chinese nationalists and communists, *La Condition humaine* had been serialized in 1933 in the *Nouvelle revue française,* the famous journal that in 1937 would publish one of Nabokov's two French writings, his centennial essay on Pushkin. Malraux's novel went on to win France's prestigious Goncourt Prize and to become well known in the United States under the title *Man's Fate;* Wilson had just warmly recommended it to Nabokov in his letter of November 17: "Have been reading up the early books of Malraux and deciding that he is probably the greatest contemporary writer. Did you ever read *La Condition humaine*? I should be curious to know how you reacted to it" (*NWL* 175).

Nabokov's response, qualified only by the concession that Malraux was "a good kind man, a very decent fellow" (*NWL* 175), was withering.[1] Arranged, dossier fashion, in a list of eleven numbered accusations, his letter ranges from

---

1. See *NWL* 175-77 for the full text. To facilitate presentation of the letter, further citations will be to the numbered items in Nabokov's critique.

complaints (item 3) about Malraux's references to crickets and mosquitoes (luckily he found no moths or butterflies in the novel) to incredulity (item 9) at his chapter titles. But Nabokov mainly focuses on Malraux's allegedly careless style, which he condemns as hopelessly stereotypical, either for using trite sentence rhythms (item 8), or for trying to summarize a complex civilization such as China's with a few well-known local details (item 11), or again for limiting the portrayal of characters to a few obvious speech mannerisms (item 4). Here it seems significant that item 8 connects *La Condition humaine* with Malraux's next novel, *Le Temps du Mépris*,[2] a short, hastily written work that most critics ignore and that the author himself came to regret. In trying to explain why Nabokov should mention, much less have read enough of, this book to form a judgment of it, one notes that it was Malraux's most recent novel in early 1936. At that time, Nabokov had a special interest in contemporary France, having embarked on a two-month reading tour in that country and Belgium and doing his first publishable writing in French, the autobiographical sketch "Mademoiselle O."[3]

In any case, such is Nabokov's indignation with Malraux's stylistic failures that in item 2, where he gathers his rhetorical talents to launch a suitably crushing turn of phrase, he retools a cherished image soon to appear in *Speak, Memory* (*SM* 144–45). The words identifying the train that carried Nabokov to Biarritz as a child undergo a sinister alteration, from the ever so alluring Compagnie Internationale des Wagons-Lits et des Grands Express Européens to the harshly contemptuous "Compagnie Internationale des Grands Clichés." So much for Wilson's advocacy of Malraux. On this occasion, however, Wilson declined battle, replying, "I knew I would get a rise," and tactfully proposing that they return "to the more profitable discussion of Pushkin, Flaubert, Proust, Joyce, etc." (*NWL* 178–79). He did not, however, budge an inch on Malraux, brushing off Nabokov's request for a detailed rebuttal of the eleven accusations with the comment that some "seem to me badly taken, the others of little importance" (*NWL* 178).

This chapter will reply to Nabokov's invitation, not along the lines of Wilson's missing rebuttal, but in the intercultural terms of what I call a "Franco-Russian crisscross." By this phrase I mean the border space between two

2. André Malraux, *Le Temps du Mépris* (*Days of Wrath*) (Paris: Gallimard, 1935).
3. Brian Boyd, *Vladimir Nabokov: The Russian Years* (Princeton, N.J.: Princeton University Press, 1990), 422–26.

national cultures, rife with potential misunderstanding and conflict, that can open when people who are supremely well versed in certain areas of their native cultures also develop a genuine interest in aspects of a second culture. Just as Nabokov combined Russian and French in his studies at Cambridge, so the autodidact Malraux, while making his way in French literary and artistic circles, absorbed the works of Dostoevsky and Tolstoy and for a time followed the Russian Revolution with sympathy. In short, as part of what would look like cosmopolitanism in their home settings, Nabokov and Malraux came to occupy an intermediate, or "hyphenated," position between those two cultures—without, of course, any necessary resemblance between their positions. Thus, Nabokov had little interest in French politics, and Malraux could read Russian literature only in translation. This is what I call the crisscross effect, which cuts against the possibility for some sort of productive Franco-Russian cultural interchange—such as Wilson might have envisioned when he invoked "Pushkin, Flaubert, Proust" to parry controversy over Malraux. Instead, one gets two distinct trajectories—or, in Nabokov's image, trains going in opposite directions; his trips to prewar France on "Grands Express européens" versus Malraux's presumed weakness for a Franco-Soviet world of "Grands Clichés." Nabokov's letter gives his side of this Franco-Russian conflict, but unlike his similar critique of Sartre, we have no record of Malraux's views about Nabokov.[4]

Because Nabokov read *La Condition humaine* in the original (the English version by Haakon Chevalier does not always convey important cultural, psychological, and political nuances), his criticisms of Malraux's style belong on the French side of this cultural border. But his most searching and thought-provoking commentary addresses the other side of the crisscross, for it centers on cultural, historical, and political issues raised by Malraux's treatment of things Russian. Here, to put matters in perspective, it should be noted that the 1920s Shanghai of *La Condition humaine*, somewhat like Berlin of that period in Nabokov's Russian fiction, is a city of displacement, expatriation, and exile. More like Cold War Berlin, however—though with a colonialist slant alongside the clash between communist and nationalist Chinese—it is a divided city, with a French Concession and a British-dominated International

---

4. For Nabokov's critique of Sartre, see D. Barton Johnson, "The Nabokov–Sartre Controversy," *Nabokov Studies* 1 (1994): 69–80. Sartre had harshly reviewed a French translation of Nabokov's novel *Despair* in 1939.

Concession in addition to the Chinese city. As in all of Malraux's novels, moreover, *La Condition humaine*'s cast of characters is strikingly multinational: In addition to the Russians, who, as will be shown, annoyed Nabokov, there are figures with ties to Japan, Germany, Hungary, Belgium, and the United States, as well as to France and China.

This diversity cuts two ways in assessing Nabokov's letter. If one can say that attacking the Russian part of *La Condition humaine* singles out just one facet of a much more ambitious book, one might also reply that major problems with this Russian facet could impugn Malraux's skills in portraying foreign cultures in general. Besides questioning Malraux's mastery of his own culture on the basis of Nabokov's French interests, therefore, Nabokov also draws on his native culture to criticize Malraux's perceptiveness as an observer.

In this spirit, in fact, Nabokov questions not just the Russian side of the novel but also its Chinese and French dimensions. Thus, he suggests (item 11) that Wilson ask "a cultured Chinese about the howlers in *La Condition humaine*" and hints (item 6) at a certain triteness in the businessman Ferral, a major French character. Ferral is a leader in the French Concession and is dismissed by Nabokov as a "capitalisto-individualisto-lotiesque-decobratique Frenchman." Two issues stand out in this hyphenated torrent of criticism. So strong is Nabokov's commitment to uniqueness that even individualism—at least, when it hardens into an -ism—can evoke his scorn, though in fairness it should be added that Malraux was no admirer of dogmatic individualism, either. Pierre Loti was the author of self-consciously exotic novels, some with "Eastern" settings, most notably *Mme Chrysanthème* (1887), which gave Puccini the idea for *Madame Butterfly*. Anticipating the more recent critical analysis of Orientalism as a system of ready-made ideas and clichés, Nabokov implies that Malraux's East is no more authentic than Loti's. Item 10 drives this point home with a rare, admittedly backhanded tribute to Soviet literature, holding that "Pilniak, Lidin, Vsevolod Ivanov, and other . . . writers of the first Soviet decade who loved using Chinese backgrounds . . . did this kind of thing better."

Nabokov's evaluation of the novel's Russian material focuses mainly on Katow, a communist militant in Shanghai who, though somewhat less prominent than his Franco-Japanese comrade Kyo Gisors, is usually considered one of the book's two real heroes. Item 6, however, does raise a brief but very Nabokovian objection to the vagueness of an incidental character, a "Russe de Caucase." Nabokov, in fact, misidentifies this woman as Ferral's mistress, although rumor connects her instead with the police chief in the French Concession.⁵ One might also feel that Malraux's label is not quite as inept as Nabokov implies. In a city of exiles, how precise would most people be in identifying the circumstances of their birth? Still, given the great linguistic, religious, and ethnic diversity of the Caucasus, Nabokov is right to spot a certain hollowness in Malraux's phrase, which clashes with his novel's obvious goal of capturing Shanghai's cultural multiplicity between the wars.

In contrast to this episodic character, Katow is the target of four barbed comments, including (item 5) an elaborate dissection of his name. As elsewhere, Nabokov is amused by the fate of Russian names on entering the Roman alphabet. Why on earth does Katow end in "w," he wonders, speculating that Malraux might have altered "'Schatow' from a German translation (or a French translation employing German transliteration)." Schatow (or Shatov), of course, is a protagonist in Dostoevsky's *Devils* who is killed by a secret political group in an incident modeled on the notorious Nechaev Affair. Although the tragic finale of Malraux's novel highlights Katow's own gruesome death, which involves being thrown alive into the boiler of a steam locomotive, and although Nabokov's *Bend Sinister*, whose arrival at the printer is mentioned in this very letter, builds up to a comparable scene involving the hero's son, Nabokov's comment does not focus on the three writers' shared concern with the atrocious extremes of ideology-driven politics. Instead, Katow's name becomes the pretext for two implied criticisms of Malraux.

Emphasis of the name's closeness to Shatov brings out Malraux's participation in what Nabokov regarded as a misguided French fascination with Dostoevsky: When forced to invent a Russian name, Malraux—it would seem—could think of nothing better than to consult one of his novels. This scenario may seem fanciful, but Nabokov has a point. Much later, in his unorthodox autobiography, Malraux identified himself as a writer with the same motto-like tribute to Dostoevsky, taken from Nietzsche and linking him with Stendhal, that formed the epigraph for André Gide's influential book on Dostoevsky.⁶ But, and here is Nabokov's second barb, Katow should not be

---

5. André Malraux, *La Condition humaine. Romans* (Paris: Pléiade, 1947), 240.
6. André Gide, *Dostoïevski* (Paris: Plon-Nourrit, 1923). The epigraph from Nietzsche is "Dostoevsky was the only psychologist from whom I had anything to learn: he belongs to the happiest windfalls of my life, happier even than the discovery of Stendhal." Malraux makes an equivalent statement in *Le Miroir des limbes. Oeuvres complètes* (Paris: Pléiade, 1996), 3:15.

equated with the victimized Shatov; he is closer to the ruthless Nechaev. "*Kat*," Nabokov first mentions, is an old Russian word "which happens to mean executioner"—or, he adds, perhaps "Sh" makes way for the "K" of Kaliaev, which links Malraux's hero with a famous terrorist, as Simon Karlinsky has explained (*NWL* 178). To understand the self-incriminating force of these word games, which Nabokov gleefully describes as "the vengeance of the word," we need to recall that Katow is, after all, a communist militant.

The issue of communism becomes explicit in item 4, which attacks Katow and his Chinese counterpart Tchen for belonging to a basically Soviet literary tradition of "staunch pig iron strong-silent communists." A related complaint in item 8 inveighs against the "best machine gun-order-of-the-day-*simplicité héroique-qu'il mourut* modern style." Although this daunting tirade does not refer directly to Katow, it could, given previous comments, be read as a dissenting judgment on the locomotive scene, at the end of which Katow gives his ration of cyanide to two prisoners who are terrified at the prospect of being boiled alive, then tries to compose himself to await his fate. The tentativeness of this heroism makes it less simplistic than Nabokov's language suggests, but we cannot, of course, be sure that he had this episode in mind.

Another, more thought-provoking reaction to Katow's politics is found in item 7, which is devoted to a remark he makes about the past: "when I was still a social revolutionary."[7] Nabokov's response to this evolutionary scheme is quick and colorful: "[a]s a frog would say, when I was still a tadpole." He clearly objects to the remark's bland assumption of communist infallibility. He then adds, in effect returning to the Kaliaev allusion in item 5, that Malraux must have needed this detail to account for Katow's "leaning towards terroristic tactics." This point is surprising, for although the Socialist Revolutionary Party did have a terrorist arm, the real terrorist in *La Condition humaine* is not Katow but the Chinese student Tchen. He eventually becomes a suicide bomber, even though Katow intervenes to try to hold him back. Also surprising is Nabokov's omission of another Russian character, Vologin, the Comintern's emissary to China and arguably a more typical Soviet-era communist than Katow. This man, who awakens distrust in Katow's comrade Kyo and who is quick with glib ideological explanations despite his distance from Shanghai, suggests that Malraux himself was troubled by communists' claims to infallibility, even in 1933. By 1934, Malraux would be a fractious foreign

7. Cf. Malraux, *Condition*, 271.

guest at the Congress of Soviet Writers that ratified socialist realism, and in 1946, he was close to Charles de Gaulle and a major critic of the French Communist Party. Significantly, both Katow and Kyo die estranged from the Russian Communist Party as represented by Vologin, making it even harder to accept Nabokov's tendency to see Katow as an orthodox Soviet type.

For possible insight into this one-sidedness, one must return to those socialist-revolutionary tadpoles and communist frogs, who are obvious close relatives of the dictatorial Toad in *Bend Sinister*. Despite the rejection of socialist-revolutionary tactics implied by Nabokov's reference to Kaliaev—in part, if we understand tadpoles to be immature frogs, because those tactics could be read historically as a first step to Bolshevik terror—does the image not also convey Nabokov's indignation at how the communists obliterated their most numerous political rivals, taking frogs now as monstrously transformed tadpoles? Consider the portrait, in *Speak, Memory*, of the village schoolmaster V. M. Zhernosekov. Calling him a "fiery revolutionary,"[8] Nabokov pays tribute to his efforts to improve the health and education of the peasantry. He ends this portrait with the pointed comment that, "[u]nder Lenin's regime, when all non-Communist radicals were ruthlessly persecuted, Zhernosekov was sent to a hard-labor camp" (*SM* 29). Perhaps it was Malraux's apparent ignorance of this alternative history, in which unheralded civic virtue was repaid with gross injustice, that understandably agitated Nabokov and fueled his harsh appraisal of Katow on the basis of one casual comment.

Nabokov's fourth accusation involving Katow actually comes first in his dossier. To readers unfamiliar with *La Condition humaine*, this pair of objections might look like a stylistic quibble, turning on little more than a Russian's privileged experience of winter. "What are those interesting *couvertures*," asks Nabokov, in which the crowd in an unidentified scene are wrapped, and "where the hell has the author seen people sneezing when exposed to frost?" The details to which he refers, however, are not casual ones. In fact, once one realizes that they come from the same passage about Katow's memories of the Russian Civil War,[9] one understands why they are first in Nabokov's dossier. In a moment of sudden recollection with obvious analogies to *Speak, Memory*, to which Nabokov was beginning to turn in earnest as this letter was being written, a scene from Katow's Russian past briefly interrupts the action in

---

8. Boyd confirms that he was a Socialist Revolutionary: see Boyd, *Russian Years*, 58.
9. Cf. Malraux, *Condition*, 231–32.

Shanghai. We learn that while serving in a Red battalion he was captured by White forces near the Lithuanian border. Then, in a maneuver with better-known practitioners several decades later in the same area, the communists were ordered to dig their own graves, take off their clothes, and line up to be shot in the wintry dawn. Because the area had changed hands several times in the war, the inhabitants of a nearby village were forced to watch as an object lesson. These are the people wrapped in bedding in Nabokov's first question, while the ones sneezing in the frost are the nearly naked prisoners awaiting execution. In the subsequent shooting, Katow was merely wounded; he managed to survive among the corpses and was rescued the next day when the village again changed hands.

Obviously, such an incident would be highly charged for someone such as Nabokov, whose father died at the hands of a White faction with a Hitlerian future (*SM* 177) but who also lost a cousin fighting on the White side, and whose family lived in fear of Red offensives in the Crimea in 1918–19. Nabokov's response, one realizes, has been to distance the event by questioning its artistic truth—and, by extension, its possible historical accuracy. To this end, Nabokov invokes the standard of absolute precision that guided his own memory writing. Thus, the generalized French noun "*couvertures*," he in effect contends, is simply too vague to do justice to a group of people routed from their beds, and "sneezing" just does not fit his own experience of freezing weather. Still, despite the anecdote in *Speak, Memory* about his father's attempt to catch cold at an open window (*SM* 174), it seems doubtful that Nabokov ever had the opportunity to test the power of frost to induce sneezing in conditions such as those Malraux describes.

In any case, for Malraux the scene of the sneezing prisoners meant more than just an atrocity story against the Whites. For one thing, he later floats a similar story about the Reds, in which a captured White officer had the stars on his epaulettes nailed to his shoulders.[10] At stake in both incidents is a sudden juxtaposition of the narrated past and the authorial present. When Malraux wrote *La Condition humaine* in the 1930s, harsh anecdotes such as these from the Russian Civil War, irrespective of the side involved, would have struck readers as a premonitory glimpse into the current state of Europe, with its similar ideological hatreds. Several years after Malraux, Marguerite Yourcenar would pursue this linkage between the Russian Civil War and the crises of the 1930s in detail in

10. Ibid., 378.

Le Coup de Grâce (1939), in which an unhappy love story ends when the woman, who has been captured by her erstwhile White lover after joining a Red guerrilla band, demands that he be her executioner. At the time of Wilson's letter, Nabokov had just addressed a related topic in *Bend Sinister,* in which he conflates the two extremes in creating Paduk's imagined "Communazi" dictatorship. One might even say that Nabokov, whose father was arrested by Reds when Lenin seized power, only to be murdered by Whites in Berlin in the troubled years before Hitler's attempted putsch in 1923—and who himself had to flee both the Bolsheviks and the Nazis—had actually *lived* through the violent swirl of conflicting ideologies depicted by Malraux and Yourcenar. Malraux's motives for having Katow recall the Russian Civil War were thus closer to Nabokov's own experience of the postwar years than Nabokov seems to have realized.

In addition, the execution is not simply an atrocity story for Malraux; it is an occasion for showing contrasting complexities of response in the witnesses. On the one hand, there are the villagers who, forced to watch, try to avoid looking, yet their heads keep turning toward the prisoners as if they were "fascinated by horror." On the other hand, the sound of those sneezes, so intensely and incongruously human, seems to shame the machine gunners into delaying their fire, as if wishing, in Malraux's words, that "life could become less indiscreet."[11] In the spirit of Malraux's title, an episode of total war has taken on the aspect of a Pascalian thought experiment about the human condition, here in order to show the potential for complex cross-currents of feeling: unacknowledged sadism among the villagers, an ineffectual solidarity with their victims among the executioners. Or, turning from the memory to the person remembering, we sense that for the survivor-witness Katow, the image of the sneezing prisoners has ended up being more meaningful than the massacre that followed; death does not dominate his psyche, in sharp contrast to the obsessed terrorist Tchen. For Katow, it seems, the "indiscretion" of the sneezes counters the horror of mass execution with an intuition of the preciousness and precariousness of life, something that Malraux may not have *learned* from Tolstoy and Dostoevsky but that their example could certainly have driven home, perhaps by joining Nicholas Levin's tubercular cough in *Anna Karenina* with the story of Dostoevsky's mock execution. This is not the place to develop this interpretation of Malraux's novel. But although there definitely were readers, especially in the 1930s, for whom Malraux epitomized

11. Ibid., 231–32.

what Nabokov dubbed the "machine gun-order-of-the-day-*simplicité héroique-qu'il mourut* modern style," those phrases are clearly inadequate to Katow's memory, despite its machine guns and death.

By and large, therefore, Nabokov's vivid off-the-cuff comments about *La Condition humaine* seem to represent a missed opportunity. Despite its brilliant rhetorical flourishes, despite interesting insights into Nabokov's creative process between *Bend Sinister* and *Speak, Memory,* despite clear signs of his desire to be a scrupulous cultural observer, and despite moving reminders of his turbulent experience of twentieth-century history, the letter does not do justice to potential agreement between the two writers. It tends, in short, to emphasize the crisscross effect at the expense of convergences. The most important convergence for this chapter is the intensity of Nabokov's and Malraux's insight into the crises of the 1930s, but other points are worth exploring, such as their interest in metamorphosis, which is crucial to Malraux's writings on art and which, like mimicry, is a concept that bridges the natural sciences and cultural history.[12] Further parallels would include their similar situations as "children of the twentieth century," born on either side of 1900, and their unusual openness to cultural multiplicity, which is evident in Malraux's global horizons as an art critic and in Nabokov's multilingual authorship.

Nabokov's parting shot to Wilson is itself an ironic emblem of these missed connections. When he accuses Malraux of ignoring the "*shamanstvo* of a book, i.e., that the good writer is first of all an enchanter" (*NWL* 177), his metaphoric allusion to the vital role of the marvelous and irrational in Siberian religion intersects with an unnamed Russian's comments on the same point in Malraux's most recent novel *Les Noyers de l'Altenburg*.[13] Nabokov would have

---

12. On mimicry, see Magdalena Medarić, "Mimikriia kak simvolicheskii obraz mira: na materiale proizvedenii Nabokova i ego sovremennikov," a paper given at the international Nabokov colloquium organized by Nora Bukhs and the Centre de recherches sur les littératures et les civilisations slaves de l'Université de Paris-Sorbonne, November 28–30, 1996. Medarić uses the concept to compare Nabokov with Thomas Mann, a novelist he criticized even more than Malraux.

13. André Malraux, *Les Noyers de l'Altenburg. Oeuvres complètes* (Paris: Pléiade, 1996), 2:638. (*Les Noyers* was first published in Lausanne in 1943 and in Paris in 1948; its English title is *The Walnut Trees of Altenburg.*) *Les Noyers* is "the first installment of *La Lutte avec l'Ange,* written during the war, in some ways even more remarkable" than *La Condition humaine* (*NWL* 178), which Wilson mentioned in his reply to Nabokov on December 1. Malraux's major postwar commitments in French politics and in art criticism forced him to abandon the project.

contested this character's attribution of shamanistic power to Dostoevsky while denying it to Pushkin. Still, the character does praise the novel's hero, Vincent Berger, whose uncanny ability to fascinate others recalls Malraux himself, for the very trait that is Nabokov's criterion for good writing. Berger, for this Russian observer, is at least "*un peu chaman.*"[14]

---

14. Ibid., 639. Berger would in fact become Malraux's nom de guerre once he entered the French resistance.

{ PART V }
THE THRILL OF SCIENCE AND THE PLEASURE OF ART

{ 19 }

Theme in Blue
Vladimir Nabokov's Endangered Butterfly

ROBERT DIRIG

I

Among the gossamer-winged butterflies of the worldwide family Lycaenidae, the Blues are perhaps the loveliest in the gentian hues of their wings, the charm of their habits, and the fascination of their life patterns. Vladimir Nabokov was deeply interested in Blues, and in 1943 he scientifically described the Karner Blue as *Lycaeides melissa samuelis*.[1] Unfortunately, this most famous of Nabokov's butterflies has disappeared from much of its former range during the past half-century; it is now extirpated from Canada and endangered in the United States.[2]

I thank Gavriel Shapiro for encouragement, sharing information, and Russian translation; Brian Boyd for sharing critical details on Nabokov's unpublished correspondence and the manuscript of his book (co-edited with Robert Michael Pyle) *Nabokov's Butterflies;* Vladimir Nabokov for correspondence and inspiration; James P. Cassaro, Pyle, and Dieter E. Zimmer for advising on references; James K. Liebherr for permission to photograph Nabokov's Karner Blue specimens in the Cornell University Insect Collection; Stacy Schiff for assistance in interpreting Nabokov correspondence; the Estate of Vladimir Nabokov for permission to reproduce the letter shown in Fig. 19.6; and Boyd, Cassaro, John F. Cryan, and Lee B. Kass for helpful comments on a draft of this chapter.

1. V. Nabokov, "The Nearctic Forms of *Lycaeides* Hüb. (Lycaenidae, Lepidoptera)," *Psyche* 50 (1943): 97–99.

2. R. A. Layberry, P. W. Hall, and J. D. Lafontaine, *Butterflies of Canada* (Toronto: University of Toronto Press, 1998), 157–58; M. W. Clough, " Endangered and Threatened Wildlife and Plants; Determination of Endangered Status for the Karner Blue Butterfly," *Federal Register*, vol. 57, no. 240 (December 14, 1992), 59236–44.

This chapter examines Nabokov's relationship with the Karner Blue as both a scientist and a literary artist.

Nabokov's fascination with the Karner Blue is not surprising, for millions of them flew in shimmering clouds[3] above a landscape he remembered as "a sandy and flowery little paradise,"[4] but they were found in only a handful of widely separated sites.[5] Nabokov had a special fondness for his tiny blue godchild,[6] although it is not the only butterfly he named.[7]

Freshly emerged Karner Blues are resplendent little animals, with wingspans of about 25 millimeters (Fig. 19.1). The wings of the males are deep bluish-purple above, with narrow black rims and white fringes; females have wider dark borders and orange crescents internally edging the white hindwing fringes. Beneath, the wings of both sexes are pale gray, "with dark dots and tiny orange-rimmed peacock spots[8] along the hindwing margins" (Fig. 19.2),

3. J. A. Lintner, "Calendar of Butterflies for the Year 1869," *New York State Museum Annual Report* 23 (1873): 182, and idem, "Calendar of Butterflies for the Year 1870," *New York State Museum Annual Report* 24 (1872): 163; Robert Dirig, "Historical Notes on Wild Lupine and the Karner Blue Butterfly at the Albany Pine Bush, New York," in *Karner Blue Butterfly: A Symbol of a Vanishing Landscape,* Miscellaneous Publication No. 84-1994, ed. D. A. Andow, R. J. Baker, and C. P. Lane (St. Paul: Minnesota Agricultural Experiment Station, 1994), 30.

4. Vladimir Nabokov to Robert Dirig, letter, April 23, 1975, in *SL* 549–50 (the end of the fifth line on p. 549 should read "Vol. 101, 1949"; see also Fig. 19.6 in this chapter); and Brian Boyd and Robert Michael Pyle, eds., with new translations from Russian by Dmitri Nabokov, *Nabokov's Butterflies: Unpublished and Uncollected Writings* (Boston: Beacon, 2000), 713–14.

5. V. Nabokov, "The Nearctic Members of the Genus *Lycaeides* Hübner (Lycaenidae, Lepidoptera)," *Bulletin of the Museum of Comparative Zoology at Harvard College* 101 (1949): 537–38, summarizes known distribution fifty years ago; Dirig, "Historical Notes," 33, maps complete historical distribution, adding Maine and New Jersey; and Robert Dirig, "A Karner Blue Adventure," *News of the Lepidopterists' Society* 38 (1996): 176, adds Connecticut to known records.

6. Vladimir Nabokov, "Drugie berega [chap. 6]," *Novyi Zhurnal* (New Review) 37 (1954): 118, reprinted in Vladimir Nabokov, *Drugie berega* (New York: Chekhov Publishing House, 1954): 128. For an English translation of this passage, see Gennadi Barabtarlo, *Phantom of Fact: A Guide to Nabokov's* Pnin (Ann Arbor: Ardis, 1989), 209.

7. For a detailed list of all the butterflies named by Nabokov, see Dieter E. Zimmer, *A Guide to Nabokov's Butterflies and Moths* (Hamburg: self-published, 1998), 47–55, and its derivative on the Zembla website (http://www.libraries.psu.edu/iasweb/nabokov/ozemble.htm), and Pyle's list in Boyd and Pyle, *Nabokov's Butterflies,* 751–58.

8. The perfection of this image is enhanced by iridescent coloring of the "spots" and by the butterfly's habit of slowly fanning and displaying its wings like a peacock's tail.

as Nabokov so beautifully portrayed them in *Pnin* (127).⁹ Females are a trifle larger than males and have more extensive orange areas on their wings.

In addition to taking nectar at many species of wildflowers, Karner Blues sometimes gather in large companies to drink and obtain salts on damp earth, a phenomenon known as "puddling."¹⁰ This feeding behavior was also described in *Pnin* (127), when Nabokov wrote: "A score of small butterflies, all of one kind, were settled on a damp patch of sand . . . ; one of Pnin's shed rubbers disturbed some of them and, revealing the celestial hue of their upper surface, they fluttered around like blue snowflakes before settling again."¹¹

The Albany Pine Bush habitat in which Karner Blues live is breathtaking—a vast, savannah-like dunescape draped with a rich millefleurs of flowers and shrubs among graceful, widely spaced pitch pines. On a clear day, the cobalt Helderberg ridge looms in the distance, with the Catskills' high peaks floating on the horizon in faint baby blue (Fig. 19.3).¹²

Central to this green and azure masterpiece is wild lupine (*Lupinus perennis* L.), a gorgeous legume that grows in full clumps, with pretty palmate leaves and spires of blue-and-white blossoms reminiscent of Sweet Peas (Fig. 19.4). Wild lupine is the only plant on which Karner Blue caterpillars can feed and thus is vital to the butterfly's existence. The lupine sprouts in late April from thick underground rhizomes and is in full flower by the time the Blues appear during the third week of May.

The eggs that Karner Blue females lay on lupine plants in spring are turban-shaped, are seven-tenths of a millimeter in diameter, and have a nubbly white shell. A tiny caterpillar hatches a week later and crawls to the underside of a lupine leaflet and begins to feed. After about three weeks of growing, the caterpillar is 1 centimeter long and velvety green, with a dark stripe down its back and lighter stripes along its sides. When ready, it pupates in a sheltered nook, often on the ground. The bright green chrysalis rests for a week, the wings changing

---

9. A letter from Nabokov to Wilson dated February 18, 1957 (*NWL* 307–8) identifies this passage as referring to the Karner Blue.

10. Lintner, "Butterfly Calendar for 1870," 163; Dirig, "Historical Notes," 29.

11. A similar experience is described in *CE* 91 and *SM* 138, referring to a puddling assembly of an unidentified Russian Blue disturbed by young Nabokov near Vyra around July 1910. This does not refer to the Karner Blue, as interpreted by Barabtarlo, *Phantom of Fact*, 209.

12. Diligent conservation efforts by many people and organizations since the early 1970s have resulted in a nature preserve of about 5,600 hectares in this beautiful region.

first to salmon, then violet, just before the butterfly hatches. When the miracle finally happens, a wet, bedraggled adult somersaults out, rights itself, and begins to expand its wings. Fluids pumped from the body swell the wings to full size in about twenty minutes, while the proboscis is readied for feeding. When fully formed and dry, the new Karner Blue will bask in the sun before making its maiden flight (see Fig. 19.4, which illustrates all stages of Karner Blue life history).

This second brood of butterflies appears from mid-July to early August, the hottest period of the year in their pine barrens habitat. The lupines will already have shed their oval brown seeds onto the sand, and their leaves, whitened with powdery mildew, will be dying down for the year. After mating, female Karner Blues of this summer brood lay eggs on lupine seed pods and stalks or on adjacent surfaces. These rest unhatched through the glories of autumn foliage and under an insulating blanket of snow through the winter, until the following April. Then, as lupine sends up fuzzy new leaves through the sand, the eggs finally hatch, reinitiating the Karner Blue's annual pattern of two cycles through all the life stages.

II

With this context for the butterfly, I now provide a brief history of its naming.

Karner Blues were first discovered in the 1860s near London, Ontario, and in the Karner (formerly Center), New York, barrens near Albany,[13] their common name deriving from the latter site.[14] Within a few decades, the butterfly had been reported from widely scattered sandy places in a narrow band from Maine and New York City to Minnesota and Wisconsin.[15]

Lycaena scudderi W. H. Edwards, the first scientific name used for this butterfly, was a tribute to Samuel Hubbard Scudder, a well-known Harvard

---

13. W. Saunders, "Article XI—List of Diurnal Lepidoptera Collected (Unless Otherwise Specified) in the Immediate Vicinity of London, C.W.," *Canadian Naturalist and Geologist* 7 (1862): 132, reported 1861 sightings, apparently the first notice of this butterfly in the nontaxonomic literature. Lintner, "Butterfly Calendar for 1869," 182, reported 1869 observations, the first record from the type locality.

14. The Karner Blue's vernacular name was bestowed by Alexander B. Klots, *A Field Guide to the Butterflies of North America, East of the Great Plains*, Peterson Field Guide Series No. 4 (Boston: Houghton Mifflin, 1951), 48, 160, 176.

15. Nabokov, "Nearctic Members"; Dirig, "Historical Notes" and "Karner Blue Adventure."

lepidopterist.[16] Following the vagaries of nomenclatural interpretation, the butterfly successively had been called *Lycaeides scudderii* and *Rusticus scudderii* by Scudder, and *Plebeius scudderi* by T. A. Chapman, before Nabokov took up the study of this group of Blues soon after his arrival in the United States.[17]

Nabokov was paid to curate the Lepidoptera at Harvard's Museum of Comparative Zoology (MCZ) from 1942 to 1948,[18] and he made his most sustained and important contributions to lepidopterology during this episode. After several years of study that included extremely meticulous observations of wing-scale rows and dissections of male genitalia, Nabokov published three scientific papers on the group in *Psyche*, the journal of the Cambridge (Massachusetts) Entomological Club, and in the MCZ's *Bulletin*.[19] These included his 1943 description of the Karner Blue as the eastern North American subspecies *samuelis* of *Lycaeides melissa*, the Melissa Blue that occurs as several other subspecies throughout western North America.[20] Since the species name *scudderi* could no longer be used for the Karner Blue because it correctly referred to another species,[21] Nabokov, with characteristic style and attention to detail, doubly honored Scudder by giving his first name to the same butterfly that was formerly known by a derivative of his surname.[22] He also selected a male and female among Scudder's specimens from Karner as the

---

16. Alfred Goldsborough Mayor, "Biographical Memoir, Samuel Hubbard Scudder, 1837-1911," *Memoirs of the National Academy of Sciences* 17 (1919): 79-104.

17. Scientific synonymy is summarized in Nabokov, "Nearctic Members," 535-37.

18. Brian Boyd, *Vladimir Nabokov: The American Years* (Princeton, N.J.: Princeton University Press, 1991), 45, 61.

19. Nabokov, "Nearctic Forms" and "Nearctic Members"; V. Nabokov, "Notes on the Morphology of the Genus *Lycaeides* (Lycaenidae, Lepidoptera)," *Psyche* 51 (1944): 104-38.

20. Nabokov, "Nearctic Forms."

21. F. Martin Brown, "The Types of Lycaenid Butterflies Named by William Henry Edwards. Part III. Plebejinae," *Transactions of the American Entomological Society* 96 (1970): 368-70; John H. Masters, "A New Subspecies of *Lycaeides argyrognomon* (Lycaenidae) from the Eastern Canadian Forest Zone," *Journal of the Lepidopterists' Society* 26 (1972): 153.

22. Nabokov to Dirig (see Fig. 19.6); Boyd and Pyle, *Nabokov's Butterflies*, 713-14. Alexander B. Klots suggested the same: "I feel as certain as anyone can about anything Nabokov does that *samuelis* was named for SAMUEL Hubbard Scudder" (Alexander B. Klots to Robert Dirig, letter, March 31, 1975). Nabokov considered the name *samuelis* appropriate for the Karner Blue as early as April 7, 1943, as is evident in a previously unpublished letter to William Comstock: See Boyd and Pyle, *Nabokov's Butterflies*, 276. See also Robert H. Boyle, "An Absence of Wood Nymphs," in *At the Top of Their Game* (New York: Nick Lyons Books, 1983), 125.

types[23] of the taxon, thus defining Karner, New York, as the type locality, or the place from which the butterfly was first described. Because he scientifically named this butterfly, Nabokov's own name is tied to it in perpetuity and properly appears after the genus, species, and subspecies names, thus:

Lycaeides melissa samuelis Nabokov

Nabokov first saw living Karner Blues at Karner on the morning of June 2, 1950, seven years after he had described them, and collected five males that repose in the Cornell University Insect Collection (Fig. 19.5).[24] A few months later, he wrote: "I visit the place every time I happen to drive from Ithaca to Boston (as I do yearly in early June), and can report that, despite local picnickers and the hideous garbage they leave, the lupines and *Lycaeides samuelis* Nab. are still doing as fine under those old gnarled pines along the railroad as they did ninety years ago."[25]

However, as early as 1952 (in the passage just quoted), Nabokov was instead using the name "*Lycaeides samuelis* Nabokov" for the Karner Blue,[26] believing he had erred in considering it a subspecies of the Melissa Blue. He persisted

---

23. A "type" is the first museum specimen of a new species or other taxon that is permanently linked to a formally published description that follows a scientific protocol.

24. Nabokov wrote to Wilson on May 15, 1950, in anticipation of finding the Karner Blue on this trip (*NWL* 246). He reported success in another letter, dated June 3, 1950 (Beinecke Library, Yale University, published in Boyd and Pyle, *Nabokov's Butterflies*, 462; see also *SO* 199). Boyd, *American Years*, 168, 296, and Charles Lee Remington, "Lepidoptera Studies," in *The Garland Companion to Vladimir Nabokov*, ed. Vladimir E. Alexandrov (New York: Garland, 1995), 278, document later visits by Nabokov to Karner—through 1956, at least; also see Nabokov to Dirig (Fig. 19.6). In "Nearctic Members," 540, Nabokov reports searching for Karner Blues at known localities in the Merrimack River valley of New Hampshire in the summer of 1946, but he did not find them.

25. V. Nabokov, "On Some Inaccuracies in Klots' *Field Guide*," *Lepidopterists' News*, vol. 6 (1952), 41. Similar characterizations by Nabokov of the Karner Blue's type locality appear in *NWL* 246; Robert H. Boyle, *The Hudson River: A Natural and Unnatural History* (New York: W. W. Norton, 1969), 34, and ibid., 2nd ed. (1979), 34; Boyle, "Absence of Wood Nymphs," 125. See also Nabokov, *Drugie berega*, 128, and Barabtarlo, *Phantom of Fact*, 209. Nabokov's quotes in Boyle's references were transcribed from a verbal exchange with Boyle (Robert H. Boyle to Robert Dirig, verbal communication, December 1998). Nabokov's letter to Patricia Hunt dated February 6, 1951 suggests that he was unaware of the great biotic richness of this inland pine barrens: see *SL* 113-15; Boyd and Pyle, *Nabokov's Butterflies*, 466-68.

26. Nabokov, "Inaccuracies"; but see his letter to Louis Griewisch from the same year (1952), in which he used the trinomial: Boyd and Pyle, *Nabokov's Butterflies*, 496-97.

Figure 19.1. A male Karner Blue basking on a flower at Karner, the type locality, on July 21, 1996. Photograph copyright © by Robert Dirig.

Figure 19.2. A resting female Karner Blue, showing the "dark dots" and "peacock spots" of the wing undersides, as described by Nabokov in Pnin *(see text); Karner Pine Bush, New York, July 21, 1997. Photograph copyright © by Robert Dirig.*

Figure 19.3. A mid-July view of the Karner Pine Bush, looking south from the summit of a high sand dune. A veneer of short shrubs and herbs covers the dunes amid widely spaced pitch pines. The cobalt Helderberg ridge looms on the horizon, with the Catskills' high peaks in the distance at the upper left corner. Photograph copyright © by Robert Dirig.

Figure 19.4. Wild lupine (caterpillar foodplant) and life history of the Karner Blue (see the self-explanatory caption). Copyright © by Robert Dirig.

Figure 19.5. Male Karner Blue specimens collected at Karner on June 2, 1950, documenting Nabokov's first sighting of his famous blue butterfly (Cornell University Insect Collection). Photograph copyright © by Robert Dirig.

Montreux-Palace Hotel
1820 Montreux, Switzerland

April 23, 1975

Robert Dirig, Esq.
Karner Blue Project
Xerces Society
315 Plant Science Bldg.
Cornell University
Ithaca, N.Y. 14853

Dear Mr. Dirig,

      The story of *Lycaeides samuelis* Nabokov, which I separated in 1943 (Psyche, Vol.I) from the W. American race of another species, now known (after a nomenclatorial readjustment) as *Lycaeides idas scudderi* Edwards, is told in detail in my paper on the genus in the *Bulletin of the Museum of Comparative Zoology, Harvard College, Vol. 101, 1949*. The name I gave it alludes to Scudder's Christian name. When thirty years ago I attempted to classify *samuelis*, I regarded it as a subspecies of *melissa* Edw.on the basis of the length of its falx but now I know better. There are additional structural differences, there are larval differences (which I hope you will find and publish) and there is the crucial fact of *samuelis* and *melissa* not interbreeding at their meeting point which must surely exist already given the inexorable progression of *melissa* from Illinois eastward during the last decades.

      This is why I am delighted by your project of writing about it and the celebrated Pine Barrens which I remember as a sandy and flowery little paradise the last time I visited them when commuting between Cornell and Harvard.

Yours sincerely,

Vladimir Nabokov

Vladimir Nabokov

Figure 19.6. Letter of April 23, 1975, from Vladimir Nabokov to Robert Dirig about the Karner Blue (reproduced by arrangement with the Estate of Vladimir Nabokov). Nabokovians can easily find published transcriptions of Nabokov's correspondence; seeing an actual letter is much less common. This letter was drafted or dictated and signed by Vladimir but typed by Jacqueline Callier, the Nabokovs' secretary at Montreux.

in this view to the end of his life, as is evident from several letters written between 1971 and 1975,[27] although he never published the new status. Several people who have studied *Lycaeides* butterflies in the interim suspect that the Karner Blue is a full species, but the work required to prove this would be very complex and thus far has not been undertaken.[28]

III

In addition to lepidoptery, Nabokov was deeply immersed in his writing and teaching during the years he lived in the United States (1940–59). Because of his expertise with butterflies and moths, it is not surprising that lepidopteral motifs frequently infuse his nonscientific writing. Nabokov's descriptive passage in *Pnin* and a book review, biographical writing, and several letters that mention the Karner Blue have already been cited.[29]

Nabokov's delightful poem "On Discovering a Butterfly" (later retitled "A Discovery") was written on the train between New York and Washington, D.C., on December 6 or 7, 1942, and published in the *New Yorker* the following

27. Véra Nabokov to Roderick Irwin, January 25, 1971, Vladimir Nabokov Archives, Montreux, in Boyd and Pyle, *Nabokov's Butterflies*, 681; Vladimir Nabokov to William Field, May 25, 1972, in *SL* 501 and Boyd and Pyle, *Nabokov's Butterflies*, 693–94; Vladimir Nabokov to Robert Wool, April 18, 1975, in *SL* 547 and Boyd and Pyle, *Nabokov's Butterflies*, 713 (also published as Vladimir Nabokov, "Novelist as Lepidopterist," *New York Times Magazine*, July 27, 1975, sec. 6, 46); Nabokov to Dirig (see Fig. 19.6); Vladimir Nabokov to Alfred Appel, Jr., April 23, 1975, in *SL* 550 and Boyd and Pyle, *Nabokov's Butterflies*, 714.

28. The rationale for this belief is the extreme specialization of the Karner Blue: It is double-brooded; feeds on a single native legume; and occurs in widely dispersed, very local metapopulations in savannah-like landscapes that were naturally maintained by a fire cycle. The Melissa Blue, in contrast, is a generalist; has multiple broods; feeds on several different legumes, including naturalized European species, in various habitats; and differs morphologically. In Nabokov to Dirig (see Fig. 19.6), Nabokov also hinted of "larval differences." A thorough taxonomic revision of North American and Eurasian *Lycaeides* taxa using modern methods not available to Nabokov (DNA and cladistic analysis), and further basic life-history studies and captive breeding, are necessary to resolve this puzzle. Laurence Packer, John S. Taylor, Dolores A. Savignano, Catherine A. Bleser, Cynthia P. Lane, and Laura A. Sommers, "Population Biology of an Endangered Butterfly, *Lycaeides melissa samuelis* (Lepidoptera; Lycaenidae): Genetic Variation, Gene Flow, and Taxonomic Status," *Canadian Journal of Zoology* 76 (1998): 320–29, offers a beginning.

29. See fnn. 4, 6, 9, 22, and 24–27.

May.[30] It distills the imagery of butterfly collecting and study in a unique and masterly fashion and has long been supposed to refer to the Karner Blue.[31] Both the context of its composition and the text's internal details show this to be a misattribution.[32]

Before boarding the train in New York, Nabokov visited the American Museum of Natural History, where he "gasped with delight when he saw the red type label on his Grand Canyon butterfly,"[33] a new satyrid he had recently named *Neonympha dorothea* Nabokov,[34] now known as *Cyllopsis pertepida dorothea* (Nabokov).

Two years before, he had described the Cormion Blue (*Lysandra cormion* Nabokov) from two specimens collected in 1938 in the French Alps; the type series of this taxon is also in the American Museum.[35] The first stanza of this poem is very puzzling as a possible reference to Karner Blues, which always occur in sandy valleys:

I found it in a legendary land
all rocks and lavender and tufted grass,
where it was settled on some sodden sand
hard by the torrent of a mountain pass.

30. Vladimir Nabokov, "On Discovering a Butterfly," *New Yorker*, vol. 19, no. 13 (May 15, 1943), 26, reprinted in Vladimir Nabokov, *Poems* (Garden City: Doubleday, 1959), 15–16, and in *PP* 155–56. This poem has also been set to music by Christopher Berg, "II. A Discovery," *Four Songs on Poems of Vladimir Nabokov for Coloratura Soprano and Piano*, Tender Tender Music, New York (1995), 8–11. Nabokov told Wilson on December 13, 1942, that he "wrote it on the way to Washington": see *NWL* 91 and Boyd, *American Years*, 53. The poem even captures the soothing rhythm of rail travel.

31. Don Rittner, "Karner Blue," *Pine Plains*, vol. 1, nos. 3–4 (December 1977), 9, mentions this poem in a Pine Bush land-conservation context, assuming that it was written about the Karner Blue. Joann Karges, *Nabokov's Lepidoptera: Genres and Genera* (Ann Arbor: Ardis, 1985), 81, lists it among Nabokov's literary references to this butterfly.

32. Other scholars of Nabokov's Lepidoptera have come independently to the same conclusion. See Zimmer, *Guide*, 116–17, and Pyle's introductory essay in Boyd and Pyle, *Nabokov's Butterflies*, 74.

33. Boyd, *American Years*, 53.

34. V. Nabokov, "Some New or Little Known Nearctic *Neonympha*," *Psyche* 49 (1942): 61–80.

35. Idem, "*Lysandra cormion*, A New European Butterfly," *Journal of the New York Entomological Society* 49 (1941): 265–67. See also the photograph and commentary in *SM* facing p. 288, and the color photograph in Brian Boyd and Kurt Johnson, "Nabokov, Scientist," *Natural History*, vol. 108, no. 6 (July–August 1999), 49.

After long pondering, it struck me that the Karner Pine Bush is in a very wide "pass" (the Mohawk River valley) between the Helderbergs and Adirondacks, where there is abundant sand (but no rocks), so by stretching a point the poem might still work with this interpretation.

Its subject is obviously a Blue—

The features it combines mark it as new
to science: shape and shade—the special tinge,
akin to moonlight, tempering its blue,
the dingy underside, the checkered fringe

—and Nabokov was studying *Lycaeides* Blues at Harvard at the time. However, the Cormion Blue has a checkered fringe, whereas that of the Karner Blue is white (see Figs. 19.1 and 19.2). Also, Karner Blues have a pale gray venter that is not really "dingy," and they do not occur in mountainous habitats. The poem's subject may be a composite of several Blues, but it was obviously inspired more directly by *Lysandra cormion* than by *Lycaeides melissa samuelis*.[36]

The technique of dissecting butterfly genitalia and the wonder of microscopic examination and discovery are beautifully portrayed in these lines:

My needles have teased out its sculptured sex;
Corroded tissues could no longer hide
that priceless mote now dimpling the convex
and limpid teardrop on a lighted slide.[37]

Smoothly a screw is turned;[38] out of the mist
two ambered hooks symmetrically slope,[39]

36. Brian Boyd to Robert Dirig, letter, September 22, 1998, shared his translation of a letter (in Russian) from Nabokov to Véra dated December 7, 1942, in which Nabokov mentions studying the genitalia of *Lysandra cormion* on December 6 in New York, just before traveling to Washington, D.C., on the train, "proving beyond doubt" (in Boyd's words) that this poem relates to the Cormion Blue.

37. A lepidopterist dissects male butterfly genitalia out of the "corroded tissues" at the end of the abdomen, after it has been soaked and softened in diluted potassium hydroxide; clears them in oil of cloves; and mounts them (temporarily in a drop of water or permanently in balsam) on a glass microscope slide for study. The "priceless mote" in this instance refers to the minuscule genitalia of the first known Cormion Blue, a unique and irreplaceable type specimen.

38. That it, the focusing knob on a compound microscope.

39. See images of the "ambered hooks" (male genitalia) of *Lycaeides* Blues in Nabokov, "Nearctic Members," plate 1.

or scales like battledores of amethyst[40]
cross the charmed circle of the microscope.[41]

The last three stanzas of this poem are an exquisite rendering of the type concept:

I found it and I named it, being versed
in taxonomic Latin; thus became
godfather to an insect and its first
describer—and I want no other fame.[42]

40. "Battledores of amethyst" is a reference to Nabokov's study of the colored wing scales of Blues, most of which are roughly rectangular and arranged in regular rows, looking much like the woven grid of a battledore (shuttlecock or badminton racket). See the images in Nabokov, "Nearctic Members," plate 2. The use of "battledore" has further subtlety (1) entomologically, to mean the scattered, specialized androconial (scent) "battledore scales" of male lycaenid butterflies that resemble a tennis racket, attached to the wing membrane by the "handle" (see inset figure; see also John Watson, "On the Battledore Scales of Butterflies," *Monthly Microscopical Journal* (August 1, 1869): 73–80, plate 21, which depicts examples that suggest a modern tennis racket, and Nabokov, "Notes on Morphology," 126); (2) in its verbal sense of "to toss back and forth," as when a butterfly specimen's wing is moved while being viewed through a dissecting microscope, such movement implied by use of the verb "cross" in the next line; (3) in the resemblance of this scale type to the rim and handle of a butterfly net, used to sweep at and catch a flying butterfly in much the same way that a racket catches an airborne feathered shuttlecock; and (4) as a possible reference to tennis, a major athletic interest of Nabokov's—the similar motions of this sport and butterfly collecting being rather striking. Robert H. Boyle, who interviewed Vladimir and Véra Nabokov for a *Sports Illustrated* article in 1959, told me that Nabokov actually used terms for tennis swings when he swung his net at butterflies: Boyle to Dirig, verbal communication, December 1998.

A greatly enlarged battledore scale from a male Karner Blue's wing (Samuel Hubbard Scudder, The Butterflies of the Eastern United States and Canada with Special Reference to New England, *vol. 3* [Cambridge, Mass., 1889], pl. 46, fig. 29).

41. A similar image of the microscope's enchanted universe and a description of Nabokov's working setup and routine at the MCZ appear in his letter to his sister Elena Sikorski dated November 26, 1945, in *SL* 58–59 and Boyd and Pyle, *Nabokov's Butterflies*, 386–87.

42. In his boyhood, Nabokov developed an intense desire to find and name a new butterfly species. This seemingly unusual preoccupation in one so young is easily explained by the entomological books available to him in the family library. Some of these dated from the late 1600s and 1700s, when many new species and other forms were being described

Wide open on its pin (though fast asleep),[43]
and safe from creeping relatives and rust,[44]
in the secluded stronghold where we keep
type specimens[45] it will transcend its dust.

Dark pictures,[46] thrones, the stones that pilgrims kiss,
poems that take a thousand years to die
but ape the immortality of this
red label on a little butterfly.[47]

It was a great thrill to see Nabokov's "red labels" on his Karner Blue type specimens at the MCZ while sitting at the same spot he occupied when he had worked at Harvard fifty years before. The specimens had been prepared by Scudder in the Victorian era, and my sense of communion with these two earlier lepidopterists was strong as I studied their juxtaposed handwriting, took notes on the label information, and savored the magic of this rare moment in science.

---

by European taxonomists (*SM* 122–23). The brilliant boy pored over the original descriptions and illustrations of many new species in these compelling books, and his wish was only to follow the model provided by the antique literature at hand. Other well-known entomologists have expressed the same longing. See, for example, William Beebe, *High Jungle* (London: Bodley Head, 1952), 216; Margaret Fountaine, *Love Among the Butterflies, The Travels and Adventures of a Victorian Lady* (New York: Penguin Books, 1980), 91; A. S. Byatt, *Angels and Insects* (London: Chatto and Windus, 1992), 136.

43. That is, in the set position of museum specimens.

44. See Véra Nabokov to Laura Mazza, letter, February 20, 1961, in Boyd and Pyle, *Nabokov's Butterflies*, 547–48, for Nabokov's explanation of "creeping relatives and rust," which is a biblical allusion but also has an entomological meaning. Curators of insect collections must constantly guard against the larvae of clothes moths and dermestid beetles that eat the bodies and wings of dried butterflies. Rusting of the pin is also a danger when specimens are stored in humid places.

45. In the Nabokov letter translated in Boyd to Dirig, September 22, 1998 (see fn. 36), Nabokov also notes that the American Museum's types, including his specimens of *L. cormion* (which had to be fetched before he could study them), had been transferred to an entomological institute fifty miles from New York, perhaps as a safeguard against possible bombing during World War II.

46. Probably galleries of ancestors' portraits, to complement juxtaposed images of other long-enduring things.

47. Red labels are placed on the pins of insect type specimens as an immediate visual cue of their importance, in the same way that red is used for stop signs and valentines.

IV

Attention was first drawn to the disappearance of Karner Blues at the Karner locality in 1973, when extensive educational, political, and scientific efforts were begun to preserve the famous butterfly and its habitat. Since that time, the Karner Blue has been very closely studied throughout its range and is now among the best-known American butterflies—as shown in a 1994 anthology that summarized current knowledge and other scientific publications. The Karner Blue remains a focus of conservation concern, and because of its endangered status, funding has been available to support continuing research. Its disappearance can largely be blamed on physical alteration of its microhabitat in combination with "global warming."[48]

Although much occupied with literary efforts at Montreux after returning to Europe, Nabokov occasionally discussed the Karner Blue in letters to American lepidopterists during the last few years of his life, especially in 1975.[49] On March 21 of that year, an article on endangered butterflies appeared in the *New York Times,* accompanied by a drawing of his *samuelis*.[50] Alfred Appel, Jr.,

---

48. See Robert Dirig and John F. Cryan, *Endangered Pine Bush Lepidoptera, The Fragile Ecology of the Karner Blue and Buck Moth,* rev. ed. (Ithaca, N.Y.: self-published, 1975), and idem, "The Karner Blue Project: January 1973 to December 1976," *Atala* 4 (1976): 22–26; Don Rittner, ed., *Pine Bush: Albany's Last Frontier* (Albany, N.Y.: Pine Bush Historic Preservation Project, 1976); John F. Cryan and Robert Dirig, *The Moths of Autumn* (Albany, N.Y.: Pine Bush Historic Preservation Project, 1977); Michael Lipske, "New York's Pine Bush, Suburbs Sprawl Across the Dunes," *Defenders of Wildlife,* vol. 54, no. 4 (August 1979), 192–99; Robert Dirig, "Nabokov's Blue Snowflakes," *Natural History,* vol. 97, no. 5 (May 1988), 68–69, and idem, "Historical Notes"; Andow et al., *Karner Blue Butterfly*; Ann B. Swengel and Scott R. Swengel, "Factors Affecting Abundance of Adult Karner Blues (*Lycaeides melissa samuelis*) (Lepidoptera: Lycaenidae) in Wisconsin Surveys 1987–95," *Great Lakes Entomologist* 29 (1996): 93–105; Elizabeth P. Nickles, Hassaram Bakhru, Helen T. Ghiradella, and Arthur Haberl, "Elemental Analysis of the Eggshell of the Karner Blue Butterfly (*Lycaeides melissa samuelis*) Using a Nuclear Microprobe," *Nuclear Instruments and Methods in Physics Research* 99 (1995): 387–89; Kurt Johnson, "Vladimir Nabokov and the Lepidopterists' Society: A Centenary Tribute," *News of the Lepidopterists' Society,* vol. 41, no. 2 (summer 1999), 41, 43; Kurt Johnson and Steve Coates, *Nabokov's Blues: The Scientific Odyssey of a Literary Genius* (Cambridge, Mass.: Zoland Books, 1999).

49. See Véra Nabokov to Irwin, January 25, 1971; Nabokov to Field, May 25, 1972; Nabokov to Wool, April 18, 1975; Nabokov to Dirig, April 23, 1975 (Fig. 19.6); and Nabokov to Appel, April 23, 1975.

50. Bayard Webster, "Butterflies to Be First Insects on U.S. Endangered List," *New York Times,* vol. 124 (March 21, 1975), 35, with an ink illustration of a male Karner Blue by

a former Cornell student, mailed this article to him, and a few days later I wrote to ask him why he had called the butterfly *samuelis*.[51] In addition, on March 27, Robert Wool of the *New York Times Magazine* inquired whether Nabokov might write something on butterflies for the publication. On April 18, Nabokov replied to Wool declining a writing commitment, but attaching a brief letter to the editor, which was published in July.[52] On April 23 (his seventy-sixth birthday), he took a break from literary duties to indulge in writing two more letters about his famous Karner Blue, one to Appel thanking him for the clipping, and the other to me (Fig. 19.6). In my letter he detailed his views on its species status and told me that "*samuelis*" had been named for Samuel Scudder. These Karner Blue-related letters have all been published in *SL* and elsewhere.[53] Earlier communications to Wilson, Boyle, and Griewisch that involve the Karner Blue were cited earlier.[54]

Robert Dirig. The same drawing was used in a centenary tribute to Nabokov: see Michael Lopez, "The Karner Blue Muse," *Albany Times-Union* (April 18, 1999), G1.

51. My letter to Nabokov dated March 29, 1975, read in part: "I see your name in the Xerces Society Membership List. In the recent issues of *Atala* and *Wings* [the journal and newsletter, respectively, of the Xerces Society, an organization dedicated to the conservation of invertebrates] you undoubtedly have read of the Karner Blue Project. I have been working on this butterfly for two and one-half years, familiarizing myself with the literature, rearing and photographing it, and corresponding with others who have done so. A week ago a notice was published in the *Federal Register* that this butterfly and forty others have been selected for review by the Office of Endangered Species in Washington, D.C.... At this moment I am heavily involved in a book on the Karner Sand Plains or Pine Bush near Albany, New York. I am contributing the chapter on the Karner Blue and helping with other sections and with the illustrations. The book is being put together as a resource for persons who will wish to develop the area in the near future, and as an appeal for preservation of at least part of the remaining Sand Plains.

"In this book ... I would very much like to tell why the butterfly is now known as *samuelis*—i.e., for whom it was named and why. If you can find the time to write a few lines about your naming of *samuelis* for me, I would be immensely grateful."

The resulting book is Rittner, *Pine Bush*, in which my chapter, "Karner's Famous Blue Butterfly," appears on pp. 197–210. The Karner Blue Project is discussed in Dirig and Cryan, "Karner Blue Project."

52. Nabokov to Wool, in *SL* 547; Boyd and Pyle, *Nabokov's Butterflies*, 713; and *New York Times Magazine*, July 27, 1975, sec. 6, 46.

53. See Véra Nabokov to Irwin, January 25, 1971; Nabokov to Field, May 25, 1972; Nabokov to Wool, April 18, 1975; Nabokov to Dirig, April 23, 1975 (Fig. 19.6); and Nabokov to Appel, April 23, 1975.

54. See Nabokov to Wilson (*NWL* 307–308) and the works cited in fnn. 24–26.

A remarkable fact about Nabokov's interaction with this butterfly is that he undoubtedly knew it as a child. Among the entomological works in the Nabokov family's library at Vyra was Scudder's sumptuously illustrated 1889 classic, *The Butterflies of the Eastern United States and Canada with Special Reference to New England*.[55] One can envision young Vladimir poring over the magnificent lithographs in this book and reading, with breathless interest, Scudder's encyclopedic accounts of species from another continent. Scudder had included full information on his namesake, *Rusticus scudderii,* which the precocious boy could not have failed to note. Throughout his life, Nabokov maintained a deep respect for Scudder based on the impression this work made in his youth.[56] In one of the twentieth century's most symmetrical entomological coincidences, Nabokov landed at the MCZ some thirty years later, where he curated Scudder's butterfly specimens and shortly after renamed the Karner Blue in his honor, designating as holotype the very specimen Scudder had figured in his book. Equally remarkable is the likelihood that, on the day in late April when Nabokov was born in Russia, eggs of the Karner Blue would have been hatching among tender lupine plants at Karner, half a world away.

Six years before he died, Vladimir told his son, while on a butterfly hike, that he had "accomplished what he wished in life and art, and was a truly happy man."[57] His work with Blues must also have brought him great satisfaction, for he expressed to Appel, in 1966, that his "passion for lepidopterological research, in the field, in the laboratory, in the library, [was] ... even more pleasurable than the study and practice of literature."[58]

---

55. See *SM* 122. Samuel Hubbard Scudder, *The Butterflies of the Eastern United States and Canada with Special Reference to New England,* 3 vols. (Cambridge, Mass., 1889), was privately published and initially sold by subscription, but extra copies were later offered for sale in entomological journals. The Nabokov family is not among the subscribers listed on pp. 1957–58, but they easily could have acquired a copy at butterfly stores in Germany during family holidays in Europe or by answering Scudder's advertisements after 1889.

56. Boyle, "Absence of Wood Nymphs," 125.

57. Boyd, *American Years,* 585.

58. Alfred Appel, Jr., "Interview with Vladimir Nabokov," *Wisconsin Studies in Contemporary Literature* 8, no. 2 (spring 1967): 127–52. See also *SO* 78–79 and Boyd and Pyle, *Nabokov's Butterflies,* 641.

{ 20 }

The Evolution of Nabokov's Evolution

JOHN M. KOPPER

"Disintegration or devolution, no less than integration with emergent evolution, has to be reckoned with in the history of natural systems," C. Lloyd Morgan wrote in his 1923 Darwinist treatment of mind, *Emergent Evolution*.[1] While most of his contemporaries were describing extinction and species stability as the only two brakes on evolution, Morgan's evolutionary theory admitted the possibility of an actual retreat in the development of forms. Morgan's thesis contradicts most evolution models of the early twentieth century, which emphasized evolutionary "progress" and glorified the human species as the model of survival. Julian Huxley typifies this vein: "[The] potentialities of the existing human type are so vast that they have not yet nearly been exhausted."[2] Nikolai Fedorov had written decades earlier that our acquisition of immortality was the lone remaining step in evolution. But Morgan's dissenting view demands closer attention, for his notion of a retrogressive "natural system," as he called it, provided an apt philosophical underpinning for the pervasive pessimism shared by many European writers after World War I.

Vladimir Nabokov's Darwinist credentials can be taken as an example. Scientific interest in Darwin had revived at the end of the nineteenth century, thanks largely to the mechanical justification of evolutionary theory offered by the newly publicized work of Gregor Mendel in genetics. An important work in the popularization of evolution was Henri Bergson's 1907 *Creative Evolution*, a text inspired by Herbert Spencer, England's unflagging popularizer

---

1. C. Lloyd Morgan, *Emergent Evolution* (London: Williams and Norgate, 1923), 13.
2. Julian Huxley, *The Stream of Life* (London: Watts, 1926), 49.

of Darwin.³ Nabokov was too young to benefit directly from the Darwin revival, but as Brian Boyd has shown and John Burt Foster has persuasively argued, he was deeply influenced by Bergson, and H. G. Wells was the favorite English writer of his boyhood.⁴ Wells had studied with T. H. Huxley, as eloquent a scientific defender of Darwinist theory as the voluble Spencer was its public philosopher. Thus, through Bergson and Wells, Nabokov received Darwin at second and third hand.

Popular Darwinism at the turn of the twentieth century adhered to at least four propositions. The first was that humankind is still in nature. This, in turn, has two corollaries: (a) the survival of the fittest; and (b) the contingent character of all human institutions. The first of these principles gives us the theoretical impulse behind the novels of Émile Zola and Upton Sinclair, and it persists in the "law of the schoolyard," the jungle code that the Polish author Witold Gombrowicz expounded in his 1937 novel *Ferdydurke*. The second corollary allows one to assume that all social structures, such as the family, marriage, and schools, *may* be interpreted simply as survival mechanisms. In Darwin's theory, these corollaries explain the random success of species, as well as the persistence of outmoded vestiges of former life stages that may actually slow an emergent, dynamic system.⁵ The generation preceding Nabokov subjected all aspects of social organization to an assumption, which Darwin himself scarcely would have tolerated, that "old is *probably* bad." This liberal credo is codified in Spencer's manifesto, "Sociology Is Biology."

Second, Europeans took to heart the idea, first put forward in Darwin's *The Descent of Man* (1871), that humankind possesses an undistinguished primate origin. Two kinds of writing ensued from this new premise: (a) a demythologization of the European aristocracy, which was perceived to have encoded its own bloody origins in a gilded Middle Ages; one might paraphrase, then, that "*history* is biology"; and (b) literary forms of what one could call the "Darwinist gothic," exemplified in many works of Nabokov's cherished Wells, particularly the paradigmatic *Island of Dr. Moreau* (1896) and his novel of social

---

3. Henri Bergson, *L'Évolution créatrice* (*Creative Evolution*) (Paris: F. Alcan, 1907). It was through *Creative Evolution*, incidentally, that Proust found the evolutionary metaphors that he lodged in *The Guermantes Way* (1921), the central volume of *In Search of Lost Time*.

4. Brian Boyd, *Vladimir Nabokov: The Russian Years* (Princeton. N.J.: Princeton University Press, 1990), 294–95; John Burt Foster, Jr., *Nabokov's Art of Memory and European Modernism* (Princeton, N.J.: Princeton University Press, 1993), 82–89.

5. Louis Althusser's revisions of Marxism depend in part on the logic of this argument.

satire, *Tono-Bungay* (1909), in which the optimistic dream of technological evolution ends with a loud crash in egotism, superstition, and the collapse of science. In these works the tug of the past reverses the vector of future time.

Third, Darwinists began questioning whether a species could intervene to ensure—or prevent—its own survival. Theories of survival were not new in Darwin's time. His own work had been partly inspired by T. R. Malthus's *An Essay on the Principle of Population* (1798). But Darwin cast his argument in terms of species survival, the line of thought that served as a source for the utopian constructions of Fedorov and, before that, for the eugenics of both the proto-fascist theorist Houston Stewart Chamberlain and the early Zionist Max Nordau:

> As long as the vital powers of an individual, as of a race, are not wholly consumed, the organism makes efforts actively or passively to adapt itself, by seeking to modify injurious conditions, or by adjusting itself in some way so that conditions impossible to modify should be as little noxious as possible. Degenerates, hysterics, and neurasthenics are not capable of adaptation. Therefore they are fated to disappear.[6]

Fourth, and finally, end-of-the-century writers used received Darwinism to redefine future time. For H. G. Wells, the true abyss of Darwinism was not the "deep time" of the past but the unknowability of the future. Our place between these two immensities fascinated Nabokov:

> When speaking of space we can imagine a live speck in the limitless oneness of space; but there is no analogy in such a concept with our brief life in time, because however brief ... our awareness of being is not a dot in eternity, but a slit, a fissure, a chasm running along the entire breadth of metaphysical time, bisecting it and shining—no matter how narrowly—between the back panel and the fore panel. (*Ada* 314)

Van himself would invent the Darwin-inspired pathology of "chronophobia" (*Ada* 388).

Before inspecting the association of evolutionary theory with Nabokov's art, one must take into account the frequently cited instance in which Nabokov

---

6. Max Nordau, *Degeneration* (New York: D. Appleton, 1895), 540. This edition is translated from the 2nd edition of the German work. I am indebted to D. Barton Johnson for pointing out that Nabokov had read Nordau.

criticized popularized Darwinism. In *Pale Fire,* Charles Kinbote famously declares: "The one who kills is *always* his victim's inferior" (*PF* 234). But this ethical bon mot—which helps one to interpret the endings of *Invitation to a Beheading* and *Bend Sinister* and to understand Nabokov's reaction to his father's murder—swims upstream against the more conventional Darwinisms to which Nabokov in his fictions readily turns. A look at evolutionary theory in *Invitation to a Beheading, Ada,* and *Glory* will show the scope of his views.

Throughout *Invitation to a Beheading,* Nabokov explores the potential meanings of random and spontaneous variation, the mechanism that can produce an unmotivated freak of nature. Recall for a moment the world of *Invitation to a Beheading,* a "future-perfect" land that has paradoxically receded from 1930s technology. Airplanes lie about but are no longer flown. The telegraph operators, cynosures of communication, pass their time celebrating name days, and the town library groups books by length, not content. *Invitation to a Beheading* also abounds in "switchable" characters who move placidly into and out of one another's roles. Thus, the borders of the real are constantly tested and violated. In his examination for sanity, Cincinnatus must imitate "various animals, trades, and maladies" and write a letter to a thunderstorm. The language used to describe this perverse social milieu is strikingly close to Max Nordau's description of a degenerate world:

> If future generations come to find that the march of progress is too rapid for them, they will after a time composedly give it up.... They will suppress the distribution of letters, allow railways to disappear, banish telephones from dwelling-houses, preserving them only, perhaps, for the service of the State, will prefer weekly papers to daily journals ... will simplify the occupations of the day and year, and will grant the nerves some rest again. Thus, adaptation will be effected in any case ... by the renunciation of acquisitions which exact too much from the nervous system.[7]

In *Invitation to a Beheading,* the relentless combination of meaningless propositions and the apparently random speech of the characters leads to a nightmarish version of Darwinist radiation. Superabundance becomes a form of textual pleonasm. The society is filled with words and allows no space in existence that is not mapped by these words. The result is a sort of verbally realized panopticon, where Cincinnatus is jailed by language and watched by

---

7. Ibid., 542.

its bearers. An inevitable symptom of this randomly created disarray is the decay of a sense of plot. With no standards of linguistic discrimination to identify the propriety of propositions, there is nothing to prevent the accumulation of words, no logical terminus to the list of "various animals, trades, and maladies" to be imitated. Projected onto the level of narrative, the reign of random association provides no logical destination for action. A people caught in the toils of this linguistic dementia have nowhere to go, and the time line atrophies. Inspired by Wells, *Invitation to a Beheading*'s future is marked by the deterioration of technology and a regression to what went before. The concepts of future and past that establish the linearity of our experience of time are merged on one another. When time ceases to exist, so does narrative. We have lost Nabokov's "ardis," the arrow of time.

Another way to approach this relationship between time and narrative is through the idea of history—or, to use the word most associated with Nabokov, memory. In an early work, Nietzsche told the following fable or parable:

> Man may well ask the animal: "Why do you just look at me instead of telling me of your happiness?" The animal wants to reply, "Because I always forget immediately what I wanted to say"—but then it forgets even this answer and says nothing. Man is left to wonder.... The animal, totally unhistorical and living within a horizon no larger than a mere point, yet lives with a certain happiness.... The unhistorical resembles an enveloping atmosphere; within its confines alone is life engendered, only to disappear again with the annihilation of this atmosphere.[8]

In *Invitation to a Beheading*, both the behavior of the characters and their attitudes toward history reflect this disordered sense of time's progress. The normal line of human development from child to adult is jumbled, so that on the one hand, the speech and behavior of the adults surrounding Cincinnatus appear frozen at a childish stage, while on the other, the sexual conduct of the jailer's six-year-old daughter Emmie is patently adult. A good example of this chronological retrogression is M'sieur Pierre the executioner's so-called photohoroscope of Emmie (a model of what Clarence Brown has christened the *bédesque*; see chap. 23 in this volume).

---

8. Friedrich Nietzsche, "History in the Service and Disservice of Life," trans. Gary Brown, in *Unmodern Observations,* ed. William Arrowsmith (New Haven, Conn.: Yale University Press, 1990), 88, 91. I have lightly emended Brown's translation.

> Extensively retouched snapshots of Emmie's present face were supplemented by shots of other people—for the sake of costume, furniture and surroundings—so as to create the entire décor and stage properties of her future life.... What appeared to be progressive changes in Emmie's face had been achieved... but one had only to look closer and it became repulsively obvious how trite was this parody of the work of time. The Emmie who was leaving by the stage door in furs, with flowers pressed to her shoulder, had limbs that had never danced. (*IB* 170)

Through montage, M'sieur Pierre surrounds Emmie's cutout photographic image with the dress and furniture characteristic of different ages in a woman's life. Nabokov gives the reader ample grounds to suspect that M'sieur Pierre's horoscope is accurate and that Emmie will grow up to be a child in an adult's body, peer to everyone else in the town. In *Invitation to a Beheading,* the tabula rasa of the newborn child is indistinguishable from the stock of memories, thoughts, and experiences of the adult. Here we find ourselves back at Nietzsche's "beast," but whereas for Nietzsche the animal represented the forgetfulness that allows one to transcend history, for Nabokov the beast is an evolutionary perversion.

The fantastically jumbled evolutionary statements in *Invitation to a Beheading* can be understood better in context of the history of the Russian response to Darwin. In the 1880s, the most outspoken anti-Darwinists in Russia were Nikolai Danilevskii and Nikolai Strakhov. The literary jeremiads of Strakhov culminated in his publication of *The Struggle with the Western World in Our Literature* (1883). In the 1887 issues of *Russkii vestnik,* he continued a personal war against the anti-cultural biases and disquieting philosophy of social anarchy that Darwinists were then reading into the biological sciences. Using a conventionally Slavophile approach, Strakhov linked evolutionary theory to an Occident that had removed God, revelation, and beauty from the drama and uniqueness of human life.

A much more articulate critique of Darwinism was formulated only several decades later. In his *Nomogenesis,* published in Petrograd in 1924, Lev Berg mounted a pointed attack against the fashionably crypto-Hegelian subtexts that many middle-brow Darwinists were then unearthing in the work of their master:

> The struggle for existence is not a progressive, it is a conservative agency: it does not spare the most diverging individuals, exterminating the others;

but, on the contrary, *maintains the standard and restricts variation*. . . . [I]n order to accomplish a *change* the action of natural selection is not sufficient; for that, the alteration of the standard is necessary. . . . Natural selection . . . operates by means of a transformation of the entire mass . . . evolution bears a sweeping character, and is not due to single, accidentally favorable variations. . . . Individual variability is great . . . but *possesses no hereditary value.*[9]

On first reading, it would seem that, in *Invitation to a Beheading*, Nabokov binds himself hand and foot to the Bergian evolutionary hypothesis, interpolating a mock-tragic view of the inevitable fate of a mutant such as Cincinnatus, who "possesses no hereditary value." But in the strange, forked conclusion of *Invitation to a Beheading*, in which Cincinnatus is simultaneously beheaded and allowed omnipotent control of his universe, Nabokov proposes a more positive understanding of the relation of the mortal individual and future time, a connection sealed by the writing process itself. Nabokov's literary closure is announced by a triumph not over, but through, death. If the townspeople represent a virtual world to come that is actually regressing, then liberation from this stagnant dystopian future can come only through the restoration of an arrow of time that acknowledges death. In Nabokov's universe, the only one fit to survive is the one who realizes that no one will survive. When Cincinnatus commits this thought to paper, his text ends. Nabokov thus dismantles Darwin's faith in the survival of hardy, "competitive" forms of life and, at the same time, refuses, for reasons both aesthetic and political, to subject Berg's social unit to anything but scornful parody. In the context of the European novel, which grew largely out of the wedding of comic drama with the prosy, unending adventures of the *picaro*, Nabokov launches the tragic barque of *Invitation to a Beheading* on a largely unmapped sea.

The Darwinist–Bergian debate resurfaces three decades later in Nabokov's *Ada*, where the difficulty the artist Nabokov has in concluding the novel derives directly from his failure to resolve a question at the core of evolutionary theory: the meaning assigned to death. Hence, the troubles the author would encounter if he were to kill off his protagonists, the incestuous Ada and her brother Van. For the comedic rhythm of *Ada* to succeed, the infertile couple

9. Lev Simonovich Berg, *Nomogenesis: or, Evolution Determined by Law*, trans. J. N. Rostovtsow (London: Constable, 1926), 400–1. In conversation, Omry Ronen confirmed the immense influence that Berg's work exerted in Russia during the 1920s.

must outlive the novel, and the promise of survival beyond the text can be guaranteed only if the characters are the authors of that text.

Looking at *Ada*'s eschatology more closely, one sees that incest is an evolutionary crime—as the narrator coyly puts it: "In those times, in this country"—because it interferes with the continuity of human evolution. "If practiced rigidly, incest led to various forms of decline, to the production of cripples, weaklings, 'muted mutates' and, finally, to hopeless sterility. Now *that* smacked of 'crime'" (*Ada* 133). In Nabokov's work, crime invariably serves as a telltale of intellectual distinctiveness and difference. Indeed, a certain judge cited by the narrator endorses crime by rejecting Darwin's ethical reading of incest, for he wishes to protect "one of humanity's main rights—that of enjoying the liberty of its evolution, a liberty no other creature had ever known" (*Ada* 134). In the same discussion of sexuality, Van cites a work on the mating habits of the fly *Serromyia amorata*. The male brings to the female "the juicy leg of a bug" as an offering, and then—in a parenthetical remark not clearly attributable to the entomologist, the narrator, or Van—the reader is informed that this tiny hors d'oeuvre is "the frivolous dead end or subtle beginning of an evolutionary process—*qui le sait*!" (*Ada* 135). "*Qui le sait*," indeed! Cincinnatus, for one, stands at both end and beginning. Between the larva and the metaphorical butterflies that haunt Nabokov's oeuvre stands the fulcrum of Cincinnatus, the opaque cocoon that represents the Janus-faced—or, at the very least, duplicitous—death to which Nabokov persistently refers in his fiction. Elsewhere in *Ada* Nabokov plays with imaginary worlds and creatures that spin in Darwinist orbits: Rattner's "menald world," where the only principle is random variation (*Ada* 416), or Theresa of Terra, swimming inside a test tube "like a micromermaid" and "accidentally thrown away by [the] professor's assistant" (*Ada* 340). Here Nabokov describes the death of an embryonic species such as that which Cincinnatus represents.

These passages seem to bear out the conflict between Darwinists and Berg over deviation and its origins. In response to Darwin's "tychogenesis," or chance evolution, Berg put his own, opposing theory of "nomogenesis," a history of life moved by its own laws. Berg saw Darwin's system as nomic, or lawbound, only in the sense that quantum theory is able to predict a spectrum of change within a vast system. But the quantity of isolatable mutations in the frames of both systems remains negligible. By extrapolation one can see that Darwin's framework promotes exogamy, divergent evolution, chance, and the importance of the individual, while Berg's advances incest, convergence, law, and the action of the mass. Above all other laws Berg places the "choronomic" law: pressure exerted by the environment.

Nabokov's *Glory* appears to present a deviation and a meaningless extinction: the voluntary sacrifice of goodness and the death, offstage, of a naive and unremarkable hero. The steadfast confidant of the innocent Martin is his downstairs college friend Darwin, of the "simian name," as their acquaintance Sonia wryly puts it (*Glory* 68). Darwin shadows Martin throughout the novel. When Martin first attempts to brave the narrow mountain ledge that could lead him either to glory or to extinction, he imagines Darwin looking at him with a mocking smile—and for good reason. The scientist Darwin presides over a universe that does not contain the term "glory" at all. But at the end of the novel, Martin successfully unites his two paths *despite* Darwin. Because he is more fit, Darwin the character survives. By contrast, Nabokov characteristically associates his hero with a meaningless death, whether experienced (as in *Laughter in the Dark, Invitation to a Beheading,* and *The Defense*), witnessed as a traumatic event (*Bend Sinister*), or carried out against another (*Despair*). In the imaginary Zoorland concocted by Sonia and Martin, Sonia passes legislation forbidding caterpillars to pupate (*Glory* 148). Nabokov encrypts in this law a reference to Martin's failure to emerge alive on the other side of the death divide, figured by the Soviet border. When Martin detrains at his chosen station in Provence, he finds accompanying him a crate destined for the Museum of Science (*Glory* 158). As an evolutionary sport, Martin is a prime candidate for inclusion in this museum.

One can now generalize about Nabokov's concept of extinction. In *Invitation, Ada,* and *Glory,* he entertains a variety of deviant evolutionary types, or anomalies, in the succession of species: a Cincinnatus who, in pointed contrast to his wife, cannot reproduce; Ada and Van, the sterile incestuous pair; and Martin, who cannot "pupate" and dies senselessly. The contemporary scholar Marie-Hélène Huet has specifically counterposed the vitality of creativity to the procreative dead end. In her work on teratology, or the study of monstrosity, she writes: "Artistic creation ... can be said to repress superficially the need for the other sex in order to procreate, a repression that will guarantee access to what is termed the *Ideal*."[10] Huet goes on to assume that the (male) artist's image is feminized by this procedure, but Nabokov's examples

---

10. Marie-Hélène Huet, *Monstrous Imagination* (Cambridge, Mass.: Harvard University Press, 1993), 304, n. 11.

suggest that the artist lives in a self-contained sexual universe, impervious to "exogamous" fertilization. The only possible child of art is the ideal. Like David in *Bend Sinister*, the living child is sacrificed.

What place does Nabokov then hold in the larger frame of evolutionary theory since Darwin and in the evolution of plots about evolution? Gillian Beer's study *Darwin's Plots* looks at late-nineteenth-century reactions to Darwin in the novels of George Eliot and Thomas Hardy. For Beer, Darwinist nature is super-fecund, infinite in possibilities. "Deviation, not truth to type, is the creative principle."[11] Beer refers to "dysteleological series of events" and the sense of gaps in time, "undischarged possibilities which do not cease to exist though they are not enacted"—all of which are sensed in Nabokov's fiction, especially in the novels under discussion.[12] In *Beasts of the Modern Imagination*, Margot Norris finds Darwinism emplotted in themes of cultural violence, and she uncovers evolutionist theses expounded by narrators of cultures about to lose their history.[13] We can counterpose the ahistorical existence of Nietzsche's animals with the artist, whose history is inevitably failure.

Against the backdrop of this debate, Nabokov specifically foregrounds two concepts:

1. *Future time is likely to close down.* This is reminiscent of an early position of Darwin's. As Stephen Jay Gould pointed out, Darwin initially rejected the idea that "natural selection ... required organic advance."[14] But in fact this denial raises two possibilities: (a) reverse evolution; and (b) the likelihood that the next species will be our

---

11. Gillian Beer, *Darwin's Plots: Evolutionary Narrative in Darwin, George Eliot, and Nineteenth-Century Fiction* (London: Routledge and Kegan Paul, 1983), 65. Here Nabokov parts company with Berg and returns to Darwin. Berg's claim that evolution is propelled by "transformation of the entire mass" can be assimilated into a Marxist theory of revolution as evolution (Berg, *Nomogenesis*, 400), but Nabokov rejects mass action of any sort for its blind, inertial cruelty. The "conservative agency" represented by Berg's struggle for survival has a place in Nabokov's ethical system, but its place is ironic. What Nabokov's "conservatives" (pro-czarist thugs, moral philistines, and sadistic tyrants) share is their fatal ability to block transformation of the individual consciousness.

12. Ibid., 207.

13. Margot Norris, *Beasts of the Modern Imagination: Darwin, Nietzsche, Kafka, Ernst, and Lawrence* (Baltimore: Johns Hopkins University Press, 1985).

14. Stephen J. Gould, *Wonderful Life: The Burgess Shale and Natural History* (New York: Norton, 1989), 170.

murderers. An example of the former is proposed by Andrei Platonov in the universe of his novel *The Foundation Pit* (1968 [1930]), in which a bear performs mighty feats as a blacksmith and the district's horses are collectivized. An example of the latter would be the people who surround Cincinnatus in *Invitation to a Beheading*.

2. *The species plot of Darwinism is always potentially comic.* But the comedy can be lethal (one thinks of the perverse survival of Margot and Rex at the end of *Laughter in the Dark*). In contrast, the individual's death is not necessarily tragic. It may be absurd, or it may represent a radical transformation or transferral of character into a universe with discrete literary and ethical laws. We recognize the second process at work in Nabokov's creation of a series of moribund heroes, paradoxically *in statu nascendi*. But his fiction as a whole lies on the axis of oscillation between states of absurd cruelty and redemption.

By the 1950s, science had picked up on some of the corners of evolutionary theory imagined by Nabokov, showing that, in the dialogue of two cultures, scientific and literary imagination can take turns holding the lead position. Twenty years after the publication of *Invitation to a Beheading*, biologists discovered examples of paedomorphosis, a developmental stage in which juvenile characteristics are retained by or restored to adults, and of neoteny, an acceleration of sexual development through which the larval body becomes the mature life form, relegating the adult form to a vestigial, or senescent, stage. Nabokov's Emmie (*IB*) and Lolita are neotenous; Cincinnatus is a paedomorph. Only in the cosmologies of theoretical physics, constructed a half-century and more after the texts discussed here—and not through Darwin at all—would science create models in which time would fold in on itself, as it does in *Ada* and *Invitation to a Beheading*.

In this chapter, I have tried merely to describe the space of imagination that joins Darwin and Nabokov. Darwinism in fact offers the explanation for a number of textual effects that we have long identified with early-twentieth-century European literature, specifically modernism. But I will close with the proposal that modernism's "Darwin" might also offer modernism an evolutionary escape from the literary periodizations in which it now seems trapped. As the foil to the postmodern consciousness, modernism now appears almost to be a defensive reaction, a hierarchical and hieratic game that withdraws, through denial of continuous, open discourse, the disturbing contradictions of turn-of-the-century culture, paradoxes—as some would have it—faced much more aggressively by Theodore Dreiser, Maxim Gorky, or Thomas Mann. Edmund Wilson typifies the many readers who criticized Nabokov's work as apolitical and antisocial. Alternatively, modernism is viewed as a movement that, unlike postmodernism, fails to provide strategies for understanding disorder. Those suspicious of the modernist enterprise assert that the task of our age is neither to contain nor to manage the disorder of evolution. It is to adjust to ever evolving cultural and technological systems.

We have come to look on modernism as a momentary hiatus between two periods that celebrated fertility, possibility, and proliferation: the late Victorian and the postmodern. In general, modernism does reject these terms, but it does not replace them with ordered and rigid hierarchies. It looks instead at all of the consequences of randomness: the possibility, for example, of the aberrant gene that *should* lead to an evolutionary leap but actually produces a monster, or the possibility that Julian Huxley and Darwin in his later years were both wrong and that we might be superseded by a species, like the townsfolk in *Invitation to a Beheading,* who are inferior to us. Modernism, then—and Nabokov in particular—entertains the possibility that evolution presents us with an ongoing emergency.

{ 21 }

Toward a Theory of Negative Pattern in Nabokov

STEPHEN H. BLACKWELL

Vladimir Nabokov's fascination with Andrei Belyi's metrical designs in "Lyric Poetry and Experiment" raises the question of how, if at all, these patterns relate to Nabokov's art and method.[1] As he describes Fyodor doing in *The Gift*, on discovering Belyi's method, Nabokov set about attempting to create poems that would reveal the most interesting underlying patterns of unfilled stresses and even, as Brian Boyd has observed, concealed a replica of Ursa Major in his poem "Bol'shaia medveditsa."[2] The essential difference between Nabokov's efforts and Belyi's exemplars is that, through his activity, Nabokov starts with what is in fact a tertiary feature, a side effect, and attempts to reverse the process and make effect precede cause. Such irreverence toward logical sequence should not surprise his readers, but, as he describes, the poetry he produced in this way mostly did not satisfy him. After all, the lovely patterns that Belyi had discovered were in essence the extract of genius, not in themselves a conscious aim of creativity. In other words, the patterns are not of referential or interpretive significance; rather, they represent a hidden, abstract, even mysterious

---

1. Andrei Belyi, "Lyric Poetry and Experiment," in *Selected Essays of Andrey Bely*, ed. and trans. Steven Cassedy (Berkeley: University of California Press, 1985), 222–303. The essay has also been published as "Lirika i eksperiment," in *Simvolizm* (Munich: Wilhelm Fink, 1969), 231–85. That edition is a facsimile of the original, published in Moscow in 1910.

2. Brian Boyd, *Vladimir Nabokov: The Russian Years* (Princeton, N.J.: Princeton University Press, 1990), 149–51. Boyd points out the fundamental connection between this fascination and Nabokov's attraction to subliminal pattern in life and art.

dimension of the poet's creative work. Their uninterpretability—a beauty that seems more akin to nature than to art—certainly must be seen as part of their overall fascination.

Still, Belyi's exercise points to a suggestive yet hidden aspect of artistic language. Consider a poem's scansion: A graphical extract, it is in a sense the shadow of a poem's rhythmic form. But a typical scansion does not make special note of the pattern of unfilled stress points (because these are so common, especially in Russian verse). However, Belyi proved that a rhythm of absence is there to be found, and his designs might be considered the "shadow," background, foil, or negative of a poem's positive rhythmic profile.[3] Hence, the assertion that these designs are a tertiary feature, a shadow's shadow, that attend a poem and subconsciously contribute to its perceived quality. In fact, the designs themselves are certainly the result of chance, stemming from a poet's instinctive ear for rhythmic variety. Thus, the absences or gaps, while forming a key element of the poem's rhythmic texture, can be gathered visually into a coherent unit that might loosely be called the "soul" of a poem. In perceiving the image of absent stresses, one perceives the poem in another dimension, if only metaphorically, with the aid of geometric figures.

The relationship between poem and its Belyian design is suggestive in the context of Nabokov's art and thought, not only in regard to the prominent themes of otherworlds and multidimensionality in his narratives, but also at the more basic level of a human life's individual texture. When Nabokov translates Belyi's concept into human terms, saying, "[H]uman life is not a pulsating heart but the missed heartbeat" (*SO* 186), his metaphor highlights the difference between regular, common-sense perceptions and irregular, occasionally even irrational, realities. It seems that Belyi's "experiment" provoked in Nabokov a sense that art might be perceived in many dimensions simultaneously, and there appears in his works a consistent effort to force the reader precisely into this kind of multilevel perception of the work at hand. As a result, the novels point toward the underside of their own concealed

---

3. The term "negative" is somewhat problematic. One might also use the phrase "patterns of absence." But this term is equally ambiguous, because when a feature is absent in the way discussed here, it is not simply absent but prominently absent. The expected narrative component is negated in a way reminiscent of Cincinnatus's crossing out the word "death" in *Invitation to a Beheading*. By linking up moments of withheld, or negated, information, one opens a new perspective on Nabokov's narrative worlds.

rhythmic texture, their shadow's shadow, in a variety of ways. In this chapter, the discussion will be limited to a few novels: *The Defense, Glory, The Gift*, and, briefly, *Pale Fire*.

An immediate problem arises when attempting to map Belyi's schemes onto Nabokov's novels. Novels, after all, are not lyric poetry (in the sense that Belyi had in mind). However, the basic approach can be transferred. Given that Nabokov was creating lengthy prose narratives, one can identify a variety of ways in which these echo the conventionality of poetry: plot sequence, linguistic traditions, logic, verisimilitude, character roles (protagonist, antagonist), and presence of relevant information, among other features. Each of these establish a set of expectations against which a novel can be gauged.[4] In Nabokov's novels, moments in which traditional flow is interrupted turn out to be prismatic moments that, if used as focal points, offer dramatically unexpected visions of the works.

When considering the poetics of negative patterns, *The Defense* provides a rich starting point. With its thematic, structural, and metaphorical focus tightly determined by the chess theme, its entire world becomes a struggle of negative and positive, of white moves and black countermoves. A complex and beautiful game, chess is also more: It is a model of human competitive existence. Consider for a moment the representational structure of chess: As a physical game, with rules, pieces, board, and two skilled players, chess mimics certain elements of the world of thought and action. This is the game as it is normally conceived and played, from the level of amateur up through that of grandmaster and world champion, each level of achievement paralleling an analogous position in human affairs. Luzhin demonstrates something different. His preference for playing blindfolded, "*v slepuiu*," so that the all-too-physical pieces cannot interfere with his direct experience of "pure chess forces" suggests a quasi-platonic ideal realm in which the mental energies involved in chess interact unsullied by cumbersome matter. Thus, from Luzhin's inverted perspective, the wooden or marble pieces on the board represent the material shadows of the pure forces, while from a mundane viewpoint those forces can be seen as the conceptual shadow of the game itself.

---

4. Boyd contrasts Nabokov with earlier writers based on the unpredictability of his narratives, even within relatively small units like paragraphs: See Boyd, *Russian Years*, 301–2.

Vladimir Alexandrov has productively associated these elements of Luzhin's existence as signs of general body–spirit incompatibility,[5] and this duality also has its part in the positive–negative–double-negative structure suggested here. Alongside Luzhin's inattention to the world's physical details a pattern of absence coexists that highlights his very tenuous connection to the world around him. As all readers have observed, Luzhin has no name or patronymic until the novel's last sentences, at which point both are presented in a genitive denial: "No nikakogo Aleksandra Ivanovicha ne bylo"[6] and "But there was no Aleksandr Ivanovich" (*Def* 256). Less obvious is the fact that the novel's first sentence also marks a denial of first names—"from Monday on he would be Luzhin" (*Def* 15) and, indeed, until the final moment one never hears anyone refer to Luzhin by his first name or any of its diminutives. This namelessness, a sharp contrast with Nabokov's extensively named casts in *Mary, Glory,* and *The Gift,* among others, radiates outward from Luzhin. Thus, several prominent characters in *The Defense* have no names at all: his father (named only in Luzhin's patronymic at his death); his mother; his grandfather; his aunt; his future wife and her parents; the musician (who discovers the chess set); and the first chess opponent (the old man bringing flowers to his aunt). Others (almost exclusively associated with chess) have only last names: Valentinov, Turati, and Luzhin's childhood schoolmates. (Two notable exceptions are the Germans who deliver the comatose Luzhin to his fiancée's house and "little Luzhin," for whom Luzhin unrolls his just discovered roll-up chess set, who is Mit'ka [Dmitri] in the Russian edition and "Ivan" in the English).

This silence prefigures the "nameless existence, intangible substance" announced on Cincinnatus's cell wall in *Invitation to a Beheading* (*IB* 26), and indeed for Luzhin the world is not unlike the collection of shabby stage props cobbled together around Cincinnatus. If "in the beginning was the word," then Luzhin's world is certainly in trouble; his fiancée frequently comments on his clumsy, incorrect use of the Russian language.

Another negative feature presents itself in the gap in narration of Luzhin's life between the day Luzhin hears of his mother's death and the day, sixteen years later, he meets his future wife, an event precipitated by his father's demise. This stretch of time, dominated by his agent and teacher Valentinov, marks the

---

5. Vladimir E. Alexandrov, *Nabokov's Otherworld* (Princeton, N.J.: Princeton University Press, 1991), 58.

6. Vladimir Nabokov, "*Zashchita Luzhina,*" in *Mashen'ka. Zashchita Luzhina. Priglashenie na kazn'. Drugie berega* (Moscow: Khudozhestvennaia literatura, 1988), 238.

period in which the development of Luzhin's human side seems to have been overlooked by "life itself" (*Def* 92). The absent narration of these years reflects again the apparent incompatibility between Luzhin's existence in the world of "chess forces" and the mundane world of human events. Combined with the general namelessness of Luzhin's world when it is eventually described, this gap may lead to the conclusion that Luzhin resides primarily within the ethereal world of pure chess, a notion reinforced by the newlyweds' failure to consummate their marriage. His isolation even in youth suggests that his connection to the physical world is tenuous from the outset, while his more comfortable existence among chess forces reveals his soul's proper place. Rather than a literal embodiment of the gnostic body–spirit opposition, however, the puzzle of Luzhin's existence suggests the uniqueness of his inappropriate existence, as though he, a creature of the negative underworld of pure chess consciousness, has accidentally been born in the world of human beings. Or, to recall again Belyi's designs, it is as if a mute creature for whom those abstract rhythmic shadows are the primary reality accidentally strays into the incomprehensibly clamorous world of words. Luzhin's life, with its overtones of a bewildered journey through unknown territory, recalls vaguely the story "The Dragon" (1924), in which the beast named in the title, after a thousand years in hiding, emerges to snack on the industrial world and then, terrified by a rider in knight's costume advertising cigarettes, retreats to his cave and dies.

If *The Defense*, like the pattern on a chessboard, seems to lend itself naturally to a positive–negative dichotomy, *Glory* may be best viewed as a negative inversion of a traditional heroic tale: It is the story of a young man with no passions, no ambitions, and no particular talents, who does nothing of any special note. And, as Nabokov says, "[N]othing much happens at the very end" (*Glory* xiv). To be sure, Martin Edelweiss dreams big, and for him the contradiction between his romantic imagination and his essentially unremarkable existence is a source of inner torment. But the negative space provided by Martin's story serves as the background for a different type of heroism and the glorification of a new set of values, related but not identical to the ones Martin cherishes.[7]

7. On the fairy-tale element in *Glory*, see Edythe C. Haber, "Nabokov's *Glory* and the Fairy Tale," *Slavic and East European Journal* 21 (1977): 214–24; Charles Nicol, "Why Darwin Slid into a Ditch: An Embedded Text in *Glory*," *The Nabokovian* 37 (1996): 48–52; Leona Toker, *The Mystery of Literary Structures* (Ithaca, N.Y.: Cornell University Press, 1989).

As others have noted, Martin lives in a world dominated by his imagination, his early youth marked by imaginary forays down a path into a painted forest hanging over his bed.[8] The line between the real world and these imaginary adventures is quite hazy, and throughout his life imagination seems to extend into, or to be echoed by, his mundane existence, an ambiguity announced in his descent from the "Indrikov" family, recalling the mythical "indrik-beast." Likewise, Martin's real experiences—the episode with the brigand in the Caucasus, the affair with Alla, his yearnings for Sonia—are extended and revised in his imagination, mingling and merging with other preferred story elements. However, for all his imagination, nothing especially romantic or heroic happens in Martin's life.

In order to think about this puzzle in the right way, it is necessary to consider exactly how Martin's mental world is constituted. In his childhood, his mother read him English tales and legends of chivalric heroism and maidens awaiting rescue, and "it was very hard to stop and lead him to bed, since he would always beg her to read some more" (*Glory* 6), signaling Martin's reluctance to leave those imaginary worlds. Precisely these images define Martin's imaginary heroism as a young man, explaining why his worldly life is so uneventful. Somehow, he has refused to recognize or accept the artificiality of those make-believe worlds, and for him their misty reality is superior to the one he inhabits. Given this refusal, it is strange that Martin is not at all attracted to modern acts of heroism—to war with the Bolsheviks and the glory it might hold. The reason, of course, is that his ideal—as he gradually realizes during the novel—is an aesthetic, not a chivalric, heroism, in sharp contrast to the messy, ugly chaos of twentieth-century civil war. Likewise, Martin cannot win Sonia's heart precisely because she is a gypsy, not a damsel in distress—except on one occasion, which he bungles hopelessly, after her sister's death. Martin misinterprets Sonia's arrival in his bed as an opening to a romantic rescue, not realizing that she is merely reenacting an old ritual she had with her sister.

Thus, Martin lives his life in an imaginative world of aesthetic forms—forms that he internalized as a child but that have very little place in the humdrum existence he leads. In this regard, Martin's conceived exploit into Soviet Russia is especially ingenious, as it merges his aesthetic sense of heroism with an authentic, worldly situation. An act with no obvious purpose, however, Martin's planned journey is essentially nonheroic from a mundane perspective.

---

8. Edythe Haber and Leona Toker have both noted this parallel.

When Zilanov expresses his surprise that Martin might attempt a "high deed" or *podvig*, he is certainly imagining some dramatic motive, such as spying or rescue, akin to those of his counterrevolutionary associates, and not the empty, whimsical reality of Martin's stunt. Martin's is a nonheroic act, a *ne-podvig*, a travesty of heroism. Although Zilanov does not comprehend it, it is precisely this pointlessness that gives the deed value in Martin's aesthetic world.

This non-exploit of Martin's leads to one very peculiar feature of the novel: its non-ending. The inversion of the traditional chivalric tale is complete, because the hero embarks on his quest at the end, rather than returns from it. Boyd has suggested that the absence of the expected narrative describing Martin's trip across the border to his doom implies that, just as the novel is the preface to the undescribed journey, life might be seen as the preface to a richer, transcendent afterlife in which life's text can be revisited in infinite variety.[9] This modified conception of "return" could displace the hero's narrative return, thus restoring the imbalance posed by the open ending. One might revise Boyd's idea somewhat to suggest that the preface is the only text, as it is in this novel, but that its aesthetic form lends it a textural richness that is often overlooked in the course of mundane existence. There is no "sequel," but the preface is far richer than it initially seems. In Martin's case, the fact of his disappearance while realizing an aesthetic ideal casts new light on all of the aesthetic elements of his previously ineffectual life. The mundane details of his death are irrelevant next to the extraordinary sequence of ordinary details his life has comprised; his biography displays not only a pattern of significant moments but also a particular texture based on the regular absence of remarkability. In a way, Martin's existence, like Luzhin's, is incommensurate with the world around him.[10] He, too, is more comfortable in the extract of artistic forms than in the practical world of things and deeds. Thus, by excluding all vestiges of novelistic form, focusing instead on the patterns contained in a seemingly unexceptional life, this non-novel about nothing glorifies the pointless artistry of ordinary existence.[11]

---

9. Boyd, *Russian Years*, 361.

10. Boyd notes the "Chekhovian" nature of the conclusion, alluding to the similar ordinariness of Chekhov's tales: Boyd, *Russian Years*, 358.

11. *Invitation to a Beheading* runs a close second and, if not for space limitations, could easily be included in this discussion. For discussion of some aspects of that work's negative profile, see Brian Thomas Oles, "Silence and the Ineffable in *Invitation to a Beheading*," *Nabokov Studies* 2 (1995): 191–212, and Stephen H. Blackwell, "Reading and Rupture in Nabokov's *Invitation to a Beheading*," *Slavic and East European Journal* 39, no. 1 (1995): 38–53.

Compared with *Glory*, *The Gift*—with its clockwork precision of device, its well-rounded plot, its circles clasped by sonnets—might seem at first far too much of an affirmative artistic gesture to admit any discussion of negativity. However, given its pseudoautobiographical form, it is not surprising that Fyodor also falls prey to Belyi's schemes. *The Gift* celebrates an artist's literary creativity, and more generally Russian literature itself, as Nabokov points out in the English preface to the 1963 translation. But by means of this highly self-conscious, even self-referential, emphasis on literature and literary creation, the novel in effect reifies these, offering them up for metaphorical interpretation. For not only does *The Gift* celebrate and commemorate Russian literature, but it also portrays at great length Fyodor's experience of reading those monuments.

In Nabokov's last Russian novel, the process of reading is more heavily encumbered than nearly anywhere else in his oeuvre.[12] The (at first) unexpected and unannounced shifts between first- and third-person narration and among various narrative perspectives, combined with the unmarked insertion of several fantasies envisioned by Fyodor, each representing a departure from traditional narrative form, constitute their own analogue to Belyian design. Here, the design points toward the inadequacy of the first reading, and one is led to experience the novel's unprecedented concern for the process of its own reception, which therefore, by necessity, becomes a major covert theme and a focal point for Nabokov's artistic attention. In this regard, reading serves in *The Gift* as the "negative" of writing, and as Nabokov said elsewhere, the delights of creative reading correspond exactly to the delights of authorship (*SO* 40–41). The act of reading—the realization of a text in a reader's creative and critical imagination—represents a reflection of the act of writing, although the specific response, the individual reenactment, is ephemeral and independent of the printed text (even as it is partially governed by it). To put this in rather more Nabokovian terms, a novel might be seen as the concrete

---

12. For a variety of perspectives, see Alexander Dolinin, "*The Gift*," in *The Garland Companion to Vladimir Nabokov*, ed. Vladimir E. Alexandrov (New York: Garland, 1995), 135–69; Iu. V. Levin, "Ob osobennostiakh povestvovatel'noi struktury i obraznogo stroia romana V. Nabokova '*Dar*,'" *Russian Literature* 9, no. 2 (1981): 191–229; Pekka Tammi, *Problems of Nabokov's Poetics: A Narratological Analysis* (Helsinki: Academia Scientiarum Fennica, 1985), 80–97, and Stephen H. Blackwell, *Zina's Paradox: The Figured Reader in Nabokov's Gift*, Middlebury Studies in Russian Language and Literature, vol. 23 (New York: Peter Lang, 2000). *Zina's Paradox* contains an overview of the various approaches.

form of an artist's vision and its reading as yet another projected shadow, here analogous to the twice-removed patterns of Belyi's diagrams. After all, no one would argue that Fyodor's reading of Pushkin, in which Pushkin's voice merges with the voice of Fyodor's father, coincides with Pushkin's artistic vision. Yet neither would anyone argue that Fyodor's reading is essentially flawed.

The novel makes use of the reflective relationship among conception, composition, and creative reception in other fundamental ways. The nature of *The Gift*'s representational mode—its fairly realistic evocation of émigré Berlin—combines with its portrayal of an artist's growth ultimately to produce a portrait of its own becoming. As is well known (but certainly not universally affirmed), *The Gift* can be seen as identical to the future novel Fyodor describes to Zina in the last pages.[13] Accepting that premise for the moment (as I generally do), Fyodor's suggestion that he will "re-chew" and render unrecognizable the specific details of his personal autobiography means that the narrative at hand is not a realistic representation of Fyodor's life but, rather, a plausible artistic reconception of it. A reader's perception of the novel, like Fyodor's experience of Pushkin, Godunov-Cherdyntsev, Grum-Grzhymailo, Gogol, and others, constitutes the tertiary shadow of the world hidden behind Fyodor's text. It might be sufficient to suggest that the concluding paragraph's hint toward the novel's rereading points in this direction. But there is another, even more compelling piece of evidence in favor of such an interpretation: a brief sequence of remarks by the first-person narrator in chapter 3 ("[B]ut what would happen if she were now resurrected? I don't know, you should not ask stupid questions" [*Gift* 150]/"[N]e nado sprashivat' glupostei"[14]) suggests an interruption in the tale's narration in which the teller addresses his audience, in this case Zina. On reflection, this moment reminds one of Zina's central role in the novel: She is Fyodor's first reader and audience, and as she did the Chernyshevsky book, she reads and hears Fyodor's works before he publishes them. That is, the reader receives those works by way of her consciousness. Keeping this detail in mind, *The Gift* is best viewed as representing the moment of Zina's creative reading, itself an emanation of Fyodor's artistic activity. This nearly silent shift in the novel's level of representation has a

---

13. Likewise, this problem is made explicit by Shade's line, "Man's life as commentary to abstruse / unfinished poem. Note for further use" (*PF* 67). This metaphor, constituting the core of the novel, is an obvious metaphysical echo of Belyi's results.

14. Vladimir Nabokov, *Dar* (Ann Arbor: Ardis, 1975 [1952]), 169.

subtle effect on its overall form, forcing one to take seriously the diverse nature of an artwork's realizations; this trebling of the text dramatizes the need to approach an artwork from various perspectives, just as Fyodor has encoded multiple points of view into the novel's narrative voice.

Pale Fire represents an extreme development of Nabokov's patterns of light, shadow, and double shadow. A few general remarks should demonstrate suggestive ways in which *Pale Fire* expands on these issues. Like *The Gift*, *Pale Fire* includes a fictitious autobiographical artwork (this time a poem) and a reader of that narrative. However, while Zina's creative reading in *The Gift* is written into the text of the inner artwork, Kinbote's idiosyncratic reading in *Pale Fire* receives a separate manifestation in his preface and copious notes—and these notes, of course, demonstrate a perplexing relationship to John Shade's poem "Pale Fire," a poem that, in Kinbote's conception, should have been inspired by the events his notes describe. The index, as a further culling of the high points in the poem and commentary, is yet another, now tertiary, Kinbotian reflection of the poem. But the novel comprises all of these, and the actual responses to the novel as a whole prove to be the most fascinating element of all. The recent outbreak of Kinbotology (Kinbote-itis?) on the NABOKV-L electronic forum is a particularly amazing demonstration of this uncanny dimension of Nabokov's art.[15] It is clear from reading the rejoinders that the novel sustains several inner possibilities: any one of Shade, Kinbote, or Botkin might have created the novel's artistic portrayal of the others—or they might not have. The ephemeral twinkling between these alternative versions of the novel's form, the possibility of envisioning and then scrutinizing the novel's world under first one, then another, light, creates a new invisible pattern—this time, perhaps, like the shapes in Belyi's diagrams, a pattern that is beyond the author's conscious intentions.

---

15. D. Barton Johnson, ed., NABOKV-L (NABOKV-L@listserv.ucsb.edu), December 1997–February 1998, various participants. Cf. Brian Boyd, *Nabokov's* Pale Fire: *The Magic of Artistic Discovery* (Princeton, N.J.: Princeton University Press, 1999), 296.

{ 22 }

Nabokov and Early Netherlandish Art

GAVRIEL SHAPIRO

This chapter discusses the reasons for Nabokov's fascination with Early Netherlandish art, for which his novel *Pnin* serves as a primary example.

But before that subject is broached, it should be noted that although the significance of literary sources in Nabokov's works is well known and frequently studied, the role of painting has not been sufficiently addressed. Yet painting figures prominently in Nabokov's oeuvre. In his boyhood and early youth, Nabokov entertained the idea of becoming a landscape painter (*SO* 17, 166–67). He received excellent training under the tutelage of several artists, particularly the celebrated Mstislav Dobuzhinsky, to whom Nabokov dedicated a poem, characteristically entitled "Ut pictura poesis" (1926), and whom he later described as "that unique master of the line" (*Stikhi* 181–82; *NG* 154). Even though in time Nabokov came to realize that his vocation was literature, his keen sense of vision and color, and his great interest in and vast knowledge of the fine arts, are all manifest in his belles-lettres.

It is perhaps these sensibilities of his boyhood and early youth toward painting that Nabokov bestowed in his novel *Pnin* (1957) on the fourteen-year-old Victor Wind, a gifted budding artist. At the same time, Nabokov endowed his character with the knowledge of Early Netherlandish art that he most likely acquired at the time of writing the novel. There is little doubt that Nabokov was familiar with *Early Netherlandish Painting*, a monumental study by Erwin Panofsky (1892–1968), the art historian of world renown.[1] It is worth

---

1. Erwin Panofsky, *Early Netherlandish Painting*, 2 vols. (Cambridge, Mass.: Harvard University Press, 1953).

noting some similarities between the lives of these two men who left an indelible mark in the culture of our time: Born in the same decade into highly cultured families, both Nabokov and Panofsky grew up in Europe at the turn of the twentieth century—in Russia and Germany, respectively. Both were professionally highly regarded in their native languages, and for more than a decade they shared Germany as their country of residence. Like Nabokov, "providentially, Panofsky escaped from Nazi Germany unscathed,"[2] emigrated to the United States, joined academe (in his case, Princeton University), and made the English language his primary medium of creative expression.

Panofsky's *Early Netherlandish Painting* appeared in print in 1953, when Nabokov had begun working on *Pnin*. There is a good possibility, however, that Nabokov familiarized himself with Panofsky's ideas on Early Netherlandish art several years before the book's publication. Panofsky's study in question grew out of his Norton lectures, which he delivered while on his 1947–48 sabbatical leave at Harvard. That year, Nabokov still resided in Cambridge, Massachusetts (it was his last year of teaching at Wellesley before joining Cornell), and it is not unlikely that he attended Panofsky's lectures. Nabokov's familiarity with and great appreciation of Panofsky's work are evident in his letter to Edmund Wilson of August 7, 1957, in which he reveals that his "source for understanding *et in Arcadia ego*, meaning 'I (Death) (exist) even in Arcady,' is an excellent essay in Erwin Panofsky's *The Meaning of the Visual Arts*, Anchor Books, New York, 1955" (*NWL* 320).[3]

Let us now turn to the episode in *Pnin*, central to this discussion, which reflects Victor Wind's—and, apparently, his creator's—fascination with Early Netherlandish painting and its artistic achievements:

> In the chrome plating, in the glass of a sun-rimmed headlamp, he [Victor] would see a view of the street and himself comparable to the microcosmic version of a room (with a dorsal view of diminutive people) in that very special and very magical small convex mirror that, half a millennium ago, Van

---

2. William S. Heckscher, "Erwin Panofsky: A Curriculum Vitae," in Erwin Panofsky, *Three Essays on Style*, ed. Irving Lavin (Cambridge, Mass.: MIT Press, 1995), 182.

3. Although in this letter Nabokov provides Wilson with the most recent publication information on this Panofsky essay, he could have familiarized himself with it almost twenty years earlier, when it was initially published: See Erwin Panofsky, "Et in Arcadia ego: On the Conception of Transience in Poussin and Watteau," in *Philosophy and History: Essays Presented to Ernst Cassirer*, ed. Raymond Klibansky and Herbert James Paton (Oxford: Clarendon Press, 1936), 223–54.

Eyck and Petrus Christus and Memling used to paint into their detailed interiors, behind the sour merchant or the domestic Madonna. (*Pnin* 97–98)[4]

In this passage Nabokov singles out Van Eyck, undoubtedly Jan, the most prolific and accomplished among the Van Eyck brothers, Petrus Christus, and Hans Memling. On close examination of this passage, it is possible to identify the specific paintings by these three artists that Nabokov most likely had in mind. In referring to Jan van Eyck, Nabokov alludes, of course, to his *Arnolfini Portrait* (National Gallery, London) as well as to *The Madonna of Canon van der Paele* (Groeninge Museum, Brugge), which is named toward the end of the novel (see the discussion later).[5] In these two paintings, Jan van Eyck portrays, respectively, to quote Nabokov, "the sour merchant" (together with his bride) and "the domestic Madonna." In both of these paintings Van Eyck employs convex surfaces, the mirror and the polished metal of the armor, respectively, which are believed to reflect the artist's own image.[6] In the case of Petrus Christus, Nabokov evidently refers to *Saint Eligius* (Metropolitan Museum of Art, New York), in which this follower and possible student of Van Eyck portrays the saint patron of the goldsmiths' guild in the guise of a goldsmith (another "sour merchant"); he also employs a convex mirror, which reflects two figures reduced in size—or, as Nabokov puts it, "diminutive people." In mentioning Hans Memling, Nabokov alludes in all likelihood to the painter's *Dyptich with the Virgin and Martin van Nieuwenhove* (St. John's Hospital, Brugge). In this dyptich, Memling employs a convex mirror that reflects both the Virgin and the donor, thereby "evidencing" the latter's presence at the scene.[7]

---

4. Cf. Alfred Appel's remarks (*AnL* 360–61).

5. It is noteworthy that in his interview with Alfred Appel conducted in September 1966, Nabokov referred to his fictional world as "*The Artist's Studio* by Van Bock" (*SO* 73). In this phrase, aside from Nabokov's obvious self-reference—the initials of his given and last names in "Van" as well as an anagrammatic allusion to his last name in V*an Bock*—there looms a possible hint to Van Eyck.

6. For this supposition, see, respectively, Erwin Panofsky, "Jan van Eyck's *Arnolfini Portrait*," *Burlington Magazine*, vol. 64 (1934), 117–28; David G. Carter, "Reflections in Armor in the *Canon van der Paele Madonna*," *Art Bulletin* 36 (1954): 60–62; and, most recently, John L. Ward, "Disguised Symbolism as Enactive Symbolism in Van Eyck's Paintings," *Artibus et historiae* 29 (1994): 9–53.

7. Gennady Barabtarlo was the first to identify Van Eyck's *Arnolfini Portrait* and Christus's *Saint Eligius* in this passage: See Gennady Barabtarlo, *Phantom of Fact: A Guide to Nabokov's* Pnin (Ann Arbor: Ardis, 1989), 173.

In the passage from *Pnin* quoted earlier, Nabokov also highlights the three interlocking characteristics of Early Netherlandish art for which he had a strong predilection in his own creative work: attention to detail, fascination with the convex mirror, and authorial presence reflected in such a mirror. As a verbal artist endowed with remarkable visual acuity, Nabokov paid closest attention to details by thoroughly employing in his own creative process that natural convex mirror—the eye. As an accomplished entomologist, Nabokov was mindful that a man-made convex mirror, such as a microscope—which, by the way, was invented in the Netherlands some 175 years after Van Eyck—enhances the perception of objects and enables one to observe their minute, otherwise imperceptible, details. And finally, Nabokov employed the convex mirror, not unlike Van Eyck, as a device for manifesting his authorial presence.

The utmost importance that Nabokov attached to details was already evident in his early story "Draka" ("The Fight," 1925), at the close of which the narrator is musing: "Or perhaps what matters is not the human pain or joy at all but, rather, the play of shadow and light on a live body, the harmony of trifles assembled on this particular day, at this particular moment, in a unique and inimitable way" (*Stories* 146). Many years later, in his Cornell lectures, Nabokov taught his students to "notice and fondle details" (*LL* 1)—"the divine details"[8]—to understand better "the work of art [which] is invariably the creation of a new world" (*LL* 1).

Nabokov credits Dobuzhinsky, his drawing master, with teaching him to be observant of details. Nabokov recalls:

> He [Dobuzhinsky] made me depict from memory, in the greatest possible detail, objects I had certainly seen thousands of times without visualizing them properly: a street lamp, a postbox, the tulip design on the stained glass of our own front door. He tried to teach me to find the geometrical coordinations between the slender twigs of a leafless boulevard tree, a system of visual give-and-takes, requiring a precision of linear expression, which I failed to achieve in my youth, but applied gratefully, in my adult instar, not only to the drawing of butterfly genitalia during my seven years at the Harvard Museum of Comparative Zoology, when immersing myself in the bright wellhole of a microscope to record in India ink this or that new structure; but also, perhaps, to certain camera-lucida needs of literary composition. (*SM* 92)

8. Ross Wetzsteon, "Nabokov as Teacher," *Triquarterly* 17 (1970): 245.

It is unclear, however, whether Nabokov knew while studying with Dobuzhinsky that close attention to detail constitutes an important innovation of Early Netherlandish artists. Even if he did not, he certainly expressed its significance at the time of writing *Pnin*, most likely under the influence of Panofsky's study. In particular, Panofsky attributes to Early Netherlandish artists, especially to Jan van Eyck, that "all-embracing, yet selective, 'naturalism' which distilled for the beholder an untold wealth of visual enchantment from everything created by God or contrived by man."[9] This, one might add, also implies God's creation. Panofsky maintains that "Jan van Eyck's style may be said to symbolize that structure of the universe which had emerged, at his time . . . ; he builds his world out of his pigments as nature builds hers out of primary matter."[10] Following in the footsteps of Early Netherlandish artists and being undoubtedly familiar with their artistic innovations as described by Panofsky, Nabokov was well aware that attention to detail in his fictional universe manifests the presence of "VN"—not Visible Nature as in the paintings of his half-a-millennium predecessors but, rather, its human namesake, "an anthropomorphic deity" (*BS* xii).[11]

Let us now turn to the convex mirror and to its natural variant—the human eye.[12] The primary importance of the sense of vision is known in philosophy, specifically Western, from time immemorial, so much so that this prevailing trend enabled David M. Levin to dub the latter "a philosophy of light, vision, and enlightenment."[13] It is noteworthy that Nicolaus Cusanus (ca. 1400–64), a German theologian and philosopher and a contemporary of

---

9. Panofsky, *Early Netherlandish Painting*, 1:2.

10. Ibid., 1:181.

11. Cf. Nabokov's dubbing Visible Nature "that other V. N." (*SO* 153).

12. For painters' fascination with mirrors—and particularly convex mirrors—see Jan Białostocki, "Man and Mirror in Painting: Reality and Transience," in idem, *The Message of Images: Study in the History of Art* (Vienna: Instituto per le Ricerche di Storia dell'Arte, 1988), 93–107; G. F. Hartlaub, *Zauber des Spiegels: Geschichte und Bedeutung des Spiegels in der Kunst* (Munich: R. Piper, 1951); and Heinrich Schwarz, "The Mirror in Art," *Art Quarterly* 15 (1952): 97–118. The comparison of the natural convex mirror, the eye, and man-made convex surfaces inevitably suggests itself. Thus, Meyer Schapiro characteristically calls the convex mirror in the *Arnolfini Portrait* "the beautiful, luminous, polished eye": See Meyer Schapiro, "'Muscipula Diaboli,' The Symbolism of the Mérode Altarpiece (1945)," in idem, *Late Antique, Early Christian and Mediaeval Art* (New York: George Braziller, 1979), 10.

13. See David M. Levin, *The Philosopher's Gaze* (Berkeley: University of California Press, 1999), 15.

Early Netherlandish artists, in his treatise characteristically entitled *De visione Dei* described God as an infinite Eye.[14]

For Nabokov, furthermore, the primary importance of the eye and man-made convex mirror was prompted, as mentioned earlier, by his aspiration in early youth to become a painter and by his entomological studies.[15] On a more fatidic and whimsical plane, Nabokov was undoubtedly mindful that his surname contained the Russian word "*oko*" (oculus). As can be seen, Ellendea Proffer, who designed the dust jacket for her husband's, Carl Proffer's, *Book of Things about Vladimir Nabokov,* very ingeniously conveyed this notion graphically to the English reader (Fig. 22.1). It is worth noting that the narrator of "Vesna v Fial'te" ("Spring in Fialta," 1936) maintains that he is capable of "open[ing] like an eye, amidst the city on a steep street, taking in everything at once".[16] And the poem "Oko" ("Oculus," 1939) contains a fantasy that "To a single colossal oculus, / without lids, without face, without brow, / without halo of marginal flesh, / man is finally limited now" (*PP* 101).

In addition to assigning to the eye, time and again, such a very telling and prominent role in his fiction, Nabokov employs man-made convex surfaces, examples of which could be already found in his early Russian works. Thus, in the *kursaal* episode of *King, Queen, Knave* (1928), Nabokov's second novel, the febrile Martha observes "glossy blue, red, green balloons bobbed on long strings and each contained the entire ballroom, and the chandeliers, and the tables, and herself" (*KQK* 252).

One of the primary functions that Nabokov assigned to the convex mirror was the manifestation of his authorial presence.[17] Such manifestation is alluded to, for example, in the *kursaal* episode in Martha's observation that the balloons' convex surfaces reflect "the entire ballroom." This "entire ballroom" in

---

14. Pauline Moffitt Watts, *Nicolaus Cusanus: A Fifteenth-Century Vision of Man* (Leiden: E. J. Brill, 1982), 163.

15. On Nabokov the entomologist and on correspondence between his lepidopteral and literary pursuits, see Daniil Aleksandrov, "Nabokov—naturalist i entomolog," in *V. V. Nabokov: pro et contra*, comp. B. V. Averin, M. E. Malikova, and A. A. Dolinin (St. Petersburg: Russkii Khristianskii gumanitarnyi institut, 1997), 429–38.

16. Vladimir Nabokov, *Vesna v Fial'te* (Ann Arbor: Ardis, 1978), 7. The translation of this passage into English is mine. In the English translation, this comparison to the eye is substituted for "all my senses wide open" (see *Stories* 413).

17. For the most recent discussion of authorial self-representation in convex mirror, see Victor I. Stoichita, *The Self-Aware Image: An Insight into Early Modern Meta-Painting* (Cambridge: Cambridge University Press, 1997), 215–21.

Figure 22.1. Ellendea Proffer. Jacket (detail) for Carl Proffer, ed., A Book of Things about Vladimir Nabokov *(Ann Arbor: Ardis, 1974).*

particular includes Martha's dancing partner, Blavdak Vinomori, an anagrammatized representation of Vladimir Nabokov. And toward the end of the *kursaal* episode, and of the chapter, Franz notices "the foreign girl in the blue dress [who] danced with a remarkably handsome man in an old-fashioned dinner jacket" (*KQK* 254). Franz recalls that "they had appeared to him in fleeting glimpses, like a recurrent dream image or a subtle leitmotif—now at the beach, now in a café, now on the promenade. Sometimes the man carried a butterfly net" (*KQK* 254). As to leave no doubt who this couple is, Nabokov paints the verbal portrait of Véra and himself: "The girl had a delicately painted mouth and tender gray-blue eyes, and her fiancé or husband [was] slender, elegantly balding" (*KQK* 254). And in the foreword to the English translation of the novel, Nabokov admits, as he puts it, "the appearances of my wife and me in the last two chapters" for "visits of inspection" (*KQK* viii).

The authorial presence is also suggested by the convex mirror in the passage from *Pnin* cited earlier. It is implied by Victor's seeing himself "in the chrome plating" and by the subsequent mention of Van Eyck. The authorial presence becomes evident, however, toward the end of the novel, in the episode of the protagonist's housewarming party, which contains a description of Jan van Eyck's *Madonna of Canon van der Paele*. Nabokov presents the painting in a somewhat caricatured fashion as an "ample-jowled, fluff-haloed Canon van der Paele, seized by a fit of abstraction in the presence of the puzzled Virgin to whom a super, rigged up as St. George, is directing the good Canon's attention" (*Pnin* 154). The mention of this painting occurs supposedly because Laurence Clements, Pnin's university colleague and former landlord, bears a "striking resemblance" to the Canon (*Pnin* 154). In fact, Nabokov's mention of Jan van Eyck's masterpiece intricately alludes to the authorial presence in the novel. The key to understanding this is not "the good Canon" but, rather, St. George, his saint protector. (One might note in passing that the other saint, St. Donatian, is pointedly absent from the novel's description of the painting.) On close examination of St. George's armor in Van Eyck's painting, one can discern a reflection of a human figure, which is believed to be that of the artist himself. Van Eyck's self-portrait as a reflection in the armor of St. George also implies authorial presence by way of birthday, as Nabokov celebrated his birthday on April 23—or St. George Day.[18] Van Eyck's self-representation could also

---

18. For a more detailed discussion, see Gavriel Shapiro, "Two Notes on *Pnin*," *The Nabokovian* 29 (1992): 36–37.

draw Nabokov's attention as it appears "on the side" (*na boku*) of St. George's armor. Further, by mentioning Van Eyck's painting, Nabokov implies his own authorial presence both chromesthetically and anagrammatically: Van Eyck's vermilion hat and hose and a dark blue mantle in his image, reflected in St. George's armor, could also attract Nabokov, because "V" and "S," the initials of his first name, Vladimir, and of his pen name, Sirin, in the writer's chromesthetic system belong to the red and blue groups, while the Russian rendition of the color combination, red and blue (*krasno-sinii*) anagrammatically suggests Sirin.

The authorial presence is reinforced in this same episode when Joan Clements, Laurence's wife, ostensibly speaks of some unidentified writer who is clearly Nabokov. And Joan's "fetching way . . . of interrupting her sentences, to punctuate a clause or gather new momentum, by deep hawing pants" (*Pnin* 159), is designed to underscore the importance of the pronouncement and to draw the reader's attention to it.[19] As Gennady Barabtarlo has aptly commented, the pronouncement itself sums up "the principal feature of *Pnin*'s composition and of Nabokov's novelistic art in general."[20] Furthermore, the sentence in its English original, "But do**n**'t you thi**n**k—haw—that what he **is** trying to **do**—haw—practically in **a**ll his **n**ovels—haw—is—haw—to express the fantastic recurrence of certain situations?" (*Pnin* 159) contains the anagram of Nabokov's abbreviated first name, surname, and pen name—Vlad. Naboko(v) Sirin.[21] Rendered into Russian as, "A **v**y ne **d**um**a**ete,[22] **ch**to to, chto on pytaetsia sde**la**t' prakti**ch**es**ki v**o **v**sekh svoikh **rom**an**a**kh, eto peredat' **neb**yval**o** **p**ovt**o**renie **o**predelennykh **s**itu**a**tsii," the sentence, once again

---

19. Even Joan's manner of discourse suggests that she acts here as a representative of the author whose own speech—at least, over the phone—is characterized in his own admission, by "hemmings and hawings" (*SO* xv).

20. Barabtarlo, *Phantom of Fact*, 246. Cf. Nabokov's response to Clarence F. Brown's assertion that he is "extremely repetitious": "I do not think I have seen Clarence Brown's essay, but he may have something there. Derivative writers seem versatile because they imitate many others, past and present. Artistic originality has only its own self to copy" (*SO* 95).

21. It is worth noting that Nabokov first employed his pen name of "the Russian years" as Vlad. Sirin. For the history and meaning of Nabokov's nom de plume, see Gavriel Shapiro, *Delicate Markers: Subtexts in Vladimir Nabokov's* Invitation to a Beheading (New York: Peter Lang, 1998), 9–29.

22. Cf. the reverse translation of this phrase in Vladimir Nabokov, *Dar* (Ann Arbor: Ardis, 1975), 327, and in *Gift* 293.

anagrammatically, but this time in the Russian translation, contains the writer's first, patronymic, last, and pen names—Vladimir Vladimirov(i)ch Nabokov Sirin.

In conclusion, as a verbal artist and entomologist, Nabokov attached great importance to detail, for the close scrutiny of which, in both his literary and lepidopteral pursuits, he employed the convex mirror, the eye and the microscope, respectively. Following in the footsteps of Early Netherlandish artists, particularly Jan van Eyck, Nabokov used the convex mirror to manifest his authorial presence. But while Early Netherlandish artists included their image merely reflected in the convex mirror, and not among the painting's main cast,[23] Nabokov manifests his authorial presence, as the deity who rules his fictional universe, in the multitude of diverse ways, of which the convex mirror is but one example.

---

23. As some art historians suggest, Early Netherlandish artists depicted themselves in reflection, not directly, out of humility. For the most recent discussion of this, see Justus Müller Hofstede, "Der Künstler in Humilitas-Gestus. Altniederländische Selbstporträts und ihre Signifikanz im Bildkontext. Jan van Eyck—Dieric Bouts—Hans Memling—Joos van Cleve," in *Autobiographie und Selbstportrait in der Renaissance*, ed. Gunter Schweikhart (Cologne: Walther König, 1998), 39–69.

{ 23 }

Krazy, Ignatz, and Vladimir
Nabokov and the Comic Strip

CLARENCE BROWN

Vladimir Nabokov was a writer of astounding visual acuity: He truly *saw* the world and rendered its shapes and color with unparalleled clarity. Like every great novelist, he attended to the entire range of culture, from the highest, where he and Véra were at home, to the lowest, where many of his characters and even a few of his readers (like me) can sometimes be found.

One of the elements of popular culture that caught and held his attention, from his early childhood to the end of his life, was the comic strip. Just as he knew how to read and write English before he was literate in Russian, so also the first comic strips that he knew were American.

Efforts have been made, however incomplete, to hunt out the many general references to the comic strip, and to specific strips, in Nabokov's work. It is far more interesting to observe the slight traces of sequential pictorial narrative (another way to say comic strip) that crop up in the fabric of his imaginary world, usually as a part of the décor rather than as the foreground action. To avoid clumsy circumlocutions, I have invented a name for this heretofore neglected element in the composition of his fictional world: The word for this "comicstrippishness" is *bédesque,* a term to be explained shortly.

From an early age, Vladimir Nabokov received serious instruction in drawing. The little domestic faculty provided for his education by his parents included at least three teachers whose sole mission was instruction in draftsmanship, the ability to draw being then deemed indispensable to general culture.

During a crucial period of Nabokov's adolescence, his drawing masters included a Mr. Cummings (1907), who was English; a Russian named Yaremich (1910), who evidently was not a success, as Nabokov dismisses him as "impressionist"; and the painter Mstislav Dobuzhinsky (1912–14). Dobuzhinsky, his last teacher, considered Nabokov the worst pupil he had ever had, but Nabokov revered him for his method, which consisted of demanding that the student reproduce from memory things he had seen every day but failed to notice properly. One detects in Dobuzhinsky's pedagogy one of the sources of Nabokov's own later fetish for precise description and his high esteem for those people who do not move through the world in a half-somnolent state but actually see their surroundings.

On the available evidence—the few actual drawings by Nabokov that have survived—one must admit that the drawing masters failed. But Nabokov's medium was not crayon, pastel, ink; his medium was language. And very few modern writers have achieved in words alone the astonishing visual effects that are so commonplace in the pages of Nabokov as to seem after a while routine. Many of the visual effects, being essentially synaesthetic, are unrealizable except in words. This worst of Dobuzhinsky's pupils was, in his natural medium, the Leonardo of modern prose.

I am a professional cartoonist. My comic strips have appeared in London's *Spectator* ("Ollie"), New York City's *Village Voice* ("Hereafter"), and even in the *American Poetry Review* ("Nightshift"), among other periodicals. And I was Cartoon Editor of the old *Saturday Review.* My cartoons appeared in every issue of that magazine during my tenure and in a great many other publications. And, as a professor of comparative literature, I have lectured on the history of the comic strip at Princeton University, always hiding behind the catalogueese of "Pictorial Narrative."

Furthermore, just as I am a reader of Nabokov, he was also a reader of mine: Several times, he drew attention to "Ollie" in the *Spectator,* to which he subscribed. It is hardly necessary to add that, in this intellectual commerce, the trade deficit is all on my side and is immense beyond calculation.

In "Anniversary Notes," Nabokov's reply to those who contributed to the *Triquarterly* tribute to him on his seventieth birthday, he comments learnedly on my Russian poem, then adds an extra little pat on the head: "His cartoons in a British weekly are marvelous" (*SO* 300). Four years later, in a letter to me dated November 11, 1974, Nabokov wrote in part:

> I have always felt a friendly warmth when seeing your articles, or looking at those enchanting "Russian" funnies (some years ago in a London weekly—*ya ne putayu*?) or reading your book on Mandelshtam.

He calls the strip "Russian" because there was a Russian character in it. It means far more to me that he called it "marvelous" and "enchanting."

But, reluctant as I am to quit this cavalcade of self-congratulation, I have probably done enough to declare an interest and establish my credentials.

One part of the visual world surrounding him in childhood that Nabokov seems to have noticed with a precision that would have delighted Dobuzhinsky was precisely the comic strip—again, specifically American.

> Or he would solemnly bring me from America the *Foxy Grandpa* series and *Buster Brown*[1]—a forgotten boy in a reddish suit: if one looked closely, one could see that the color was really a mass of dense red dots. Every episode ended in a tremendous spanking for Buster, which was administered by his wasp-waisted but powerful Ma, who used a slipper, a hairbrush, a brittle umbrella, anything—even the bludgeon of a helpful policeman—and drew puffs of dust from the seat of Buster's pants. Since I had never been spanked, those pictures conveyed to me the impression of strange exotic torture not different from, say, the burying of a popeyed wretch up to his chin in the torrid sand of a desert, as represented in the frontispiece of a Mayne Reid book. (*SM* 69–70)

Any interviewer who needed to get a rise out of Nabokov could do so by asking him about "popular culture." The master would usually supply a fresh disparagement, and this in spite of the fact that he, like all novelists, relied on it helplessly. Humbert also looked over Lolita's shoulder:

> Her eyes would follow the adventures of her favorite strip characters: there was one well-drawn sloppy bobby-soxer, with high cheekbones and angular gestures, that I was not above enjoying myself. (*Lo* 167)[2]

---

1. "Foxy Grandpa" was the creation of Charles E. ("Bunny") Schultze; "Buster Brown" was created by Richard Felton Outcault, whose earlier "Yellow Kid" is often cited as the first American comic strip.

2. This is a clear reference to Harry Haenigson's "Penny."

An element of popular culture that is seldom far beyond the margin of a page by Nabokov is the motion picture. *Laughter in the Dark* (1938) seems to have been conceived as a film and is steeped in film imagery. The close alliance of the film and the comic strip is a topic too familiar to be more than mentioned, but it is worth noting that the villain of *Laughter in the Dark*, Axel Rex, is a cartoonist.

In the Russian original (*Kamera obskura*, 1932), Nabokov described his comic strip. Although this was revised out of the English translation, it is highly relevant to our theme. The strip was entitled "Cheepy" (or "Cheapy"—both occur) and had a guinea pig as the eponymous character. The cartoonist begins his strip as a means of enlisting public sympathy on the side of animals in the fight against vivisection. But it became very popular around the world and turned into a cash cow for its creator, who behaved very much like an up-to-date cartoonist, licensing "Cheepy" dolls and other spinoff products and suing anyone who infringed his copyright.

In her book about the changes that Nabokov's books underwent on their way from Russian into other languages, Jane Grayson speculates very plausibly that "Cheepy" was cut because it made the cartoonist too sympathetic a character.[3] I personally endorse the idea that comic-strip artists are already so unlikely to be villains that no further good qualities can safely be imputed to them.

It is perhaps worth mentioning that the title itself, *Laughter in the Dark*, for all its suggestiveness of *amor fati*, is also precisely descriptive of an audience in a darkened moviehouse watching Betty Boop or Felix the Cat.

Even without the comic strip "Cheepy," however, *Laughter in the Dark* remains saturated with cartoon images in the decor. There are moments when the background seems as much drawn as written: "He sat with her on the balcony high above the blue streets with the wires and chimneys drawn in Indian ink across the sunset" (*Laugh* 19).

In America, the motionless pictures of the comic strip and the motion picture of the cinema developed in the intimately incestuous cross-breeding that could only delight the author of *Ada*. This is perhaps why, In his fine book about Nabokov and the film, *Nabokov's Dark Cinema*,[4] Alfred Appel instinctively includes a section detailing most of the overt references to comic strips

---

3. Jane Grayson, *Nabokov Translated* (Oxford: Oxford University Press, 1977), 40.
4. Alfred Appel, Jr., *Nabokov's Dark Cinema* (New York: Oxford University Press, 1974).

in Nabokov's work. This book, together with the notes in *The Annotated Lolita,* catalogues most of the actual strips to which Nabokov refers.

In several interviews with his former Cornell professor, Appel continues to develop this theme. Reading the comics page of the *International Herald Tribune,* Nabokov wonders aloud whether Dennis the Menace might not be illegitimate, so little does he resemble either of his parents. At that time, Hank Ketcham, creator of Dennis, was living in Switzerland not far from Nabokov and might have been consulted on this point, though I have no evidence that he ever was. We learn that Nabokov did in fact write a letter to the editor of the paper complaining about plot inconsistencies in the strip "Rex Morgan M.D."[5]

Here are two instances of explicit, although very obscure, references to actual comic strips that seem to have eluded Appel. In *Pale Fire* (*PF* 167) the phrase "the Hercules springing forth from a neurotic child's weak frame" is a verbal replica of the famous comic strip advertising the Charles Atlas bodybuilding course, an ad that has become a part of popular mythology: the ninety-eight–pound weakling who is humiliated before his girl when a bully on the beach kicks sand in his face. After successfully studying the Atlas method, the neurotic child, now a Hercules, returns and beats the bully to a pulp.

Far more obscure, and still a puzzle to me, is the reference in *Pale Fire* to tiger tea. The homosexual Charles the Beloved has married Disa, Duchess of Payn, and is having a hard time—or, rather, a soft time—trying to make love to her:

> He farced himself with aphrodisiacs, but the anterior characters of her unfortunate sex kept fatally putting him off. One night when he tried tiger tea, . . . hopes rose high. (*PF* 208)

The interesting phrase here is "tiger tea." It comes from the greatest of all American comic strips, George Herriman's immortal "Krazy Kat." There were few long-running episodes in "Krazy Kat," but the one that started in June 1936 ran for months. Tiger tea was brewed from a powerful catnip dropped into Coconino County by Joe Stork. It turned the normally placid and equable Krazy into "a poiminint tidal wave in a notion of dynamite."[6] Tiger tea gives

---

5. Ibid., 31.
6. "Krazy Kat" (June 24, 1936), in George Herriman, *Krazy Kat* (New York: Madison Square Garden Press, 1969), 94.

extraordinary courage to meek creatures. Even the worm turns on the early bird, and the elephant frightens the mouse. Did the fame of Tiger tea last until Nabokov arrived in America four years later? Given the tenacity of popular catchphrases once they have lodged in the public mind, that does not seem impossible.

But these overt references to actual, dimly remembered, or imaginary comic strips, although interesting as an index of Nabokov's fondness for one small corner of popular culture, in the end are no more useful than all mechanical compilations.

I needed a word that conveyed the sense of "comicstrippishness" but that would be less clumsy, a word that conveyed something like the soul or essence of the comic strip. Just as the boy Luzhin, long before he has so much as seen a chess board, glimpses presentiments of chess in "the wayward frolics of geometric lines" (*Def* 36) and even in jigsaw puzzles, so it seems to me that there can be comic strips *in posse*.

Chess is essentially an abstract play of force and counterforce constrained within a rigidly measured grid of relationships; as such, it is quite independent of its material incarnation in patterned board and pieces. Similarly, the procedures of pictorial narrative, the left-to-right movement of figures against a ground and in sequential frames, can be adumbrated in verbal patterns. That, at least, is what I was attempted to name when I came up with the term "*bédesque*."

The French call a comic strip "*la bande dessinée*," or popularly "*la BD*." My coinage *bédesque* has passed the test of satisfying the linguistic intuition of native speakers. I tried *bédesque* on Alain Besançon, the writer and political philosopher, who was on an opportune visit to Princeton. He first countered with *bédique* but then decided that he liked *bédesque* better.

I intend by *bédesque* a certain recurrent motif in Nabokov's imagination, an evanescent little visual theme that has been almost unobserved by readers or critics. It is anything other than obtrusive, but it forms for me one of the indelible signatures of Nabokov's fictional universe.

Before looking at the *bédesque* it might perhaps be logical to begin with caricature, since in art history that long preceded anything that could be called a comic strip. But caricature is everywhere in Nabokov. In *The Real Life of Sebastian Knight*, time itself is caricatured on a clockface: "the waxed moustache of ten minutes to two" (*RLSK* 9). The clock face is perhaps a natural for this sort of thing: "I hate to see the stunned look on the face of a clock that has stopped, she said" (*LATH* 47). Such touches are commonplace, but they are caricature, not the *bédesque,* for the true comic strip is caricature plus action, character, text, and frame.

Here is a first example, and I have deliberately chosen, as a sort of challenge, one that might be initially unconvincing. At one point in *Pale Fire,* reference must be made to the most common of root vegetables. This is accomplished in the sentence: "Every one of these meals was built around some vegetable that I subjected to as many exquisite metamorphoses as Parmentier had his pet tuber undergo" (*PF* 230).

To refer to an ordinary potato by the elaborate periphrasis of calling it Parmentier's pet tuber is already caricatural. To continue by putting this animated comestible through its various "exquisite metamorphoses" is to approach the sequential narrative of the comic strip. Such obliquity flatters the reader by assuming his knowledge of the great culinary genius and his historical association with a particular vegetable. But it does more than flatter or amuse the reader. It also invites the reader to *see,* however many floors beneath the limen of awareness, a burlesque image of Parmentier taking his pet (Spud) out on a leash for walkies. One is perhaps meant to think of mad Gérard de Nerval out for a stroll with his pet lobster on a ribbon. I doubt that many readers seasoned in the ways of Nabokov do in fact pay it much conscious attention. To see the metamorphoses (*pommes purees, pommes frites,* etc.) in a series of linked frames would point to a morbid excess of imagination.

That, however, is surely the point. It is not until one's notice is forced on it that one sees in the phrase the possibility of a tiny germ of drama, with the dramatis personae named and an incipient argument, the relationship between them, sketched in:

Parmentier, a great chef of Paris
Tuber, pet to Parmentier

Here is another example, from *Bend Sinister:* "*The car vanished while the square echo of its slammed door was still suspended in mid-air like an empty picture frame of ebony*" (*BS* 60). The typical synaesthesia of "square echo," in which a sound presents itself to the eye as a geometrical figure, is feasible only in poetry, where saying is believing, or in the comic strip and its cinematic cousin, the animated film.

Again from *Bend Sinister:*

> Ember hesitated, then dialled fluently. The line was engaged. That sequence of small bar-shaped hoots was like the long vertical row of superimposed I's in an index by first lines to a verse anthology. I am a lake. I am a tongue. I am a spirit. (*BS* 31)

The synaesthetic turn is like that of the square echo of the slammed door, but now Nabokov explicates his figure in terms of printing technology. In any case, the sequence of small bar-shaped hoots is quintessentially *bédesque*. The comic strip, being mute, with no access to the ear, has no choice: *All* sound must be conveyed to the eye by graphic means. Over its century and a half of existence, the comic strip has evolved an immense armamentarium of visual shorthand to represent sound. When Krazy Kat threw the brick, her missive of love, at the head of Ignatz Mouse, the brick always went "ZIP!" through the air and "POW!" on contact. On those extremely rare occasions when Herriman, who did not like to fiddle with anything so radically perfect as his basic plot, had the brick collide with another head, it made a different sound.

Nabokov was no less fastidious in this matter. Notice that his is a specifically European busy signal—that sequence of small bar-shaped hoots—not American, the dull intermittent buzz of Ma Bell.

We are not done with sequential images in this brief passage, however, for all those *incipits* beginning with the first-person singular that follow one another across Ember's mental screen as he waits with the receiver to his ear constitute a sort of pictorial narrative very like that of recent comic-strip experiments in surrealism such as those of the French artist Maurice Rosy.[7] The images are more than a little erotic, complete with post-orgasmic dreaming and ending with something like Molly Bloom's breathless assent: I will. I will. I will. I will ... The full sequence is:

> I am a lake. I am a tongue. I am a spirit. I am fevered. I am not covetous. I am the Dark Cavalier. I am the torch. I arise. I ask. I blow. I bring. I cannot change. I cannot look. I climb the hill. I come. I dream. I envy. I found. I heard. I intended an Ode. I know. I love. I must not grieve, my love. I never. I pant. I remember. I saw thee once. I travelled. I wandered. I will. I will. I will. I will.

7. "Histoires martiennes," in *Les chefs-d'oeuvres de la bande dessinée. Anthologie Planète*, ed. Louis Pauwels (Paris: Les éditions Planète), 424–25.

Another failed telephone call occurs in chapter 7 of *Pnin* and prompts what, for me, is one of the most breathtaking of synaesthetic images. A telephone number is dialed. At the other end of the line, a hand lifts the receiver, but no one speaks. A writer with duller sensory apparatus than Nabokov's might have written that there was silence, but Nabokov knows what acoustic engineers know—namely, that an empty room in which there is no source of noise has its own sound. Nabokov writes that, when the receiver was lifted, a "sonic vista" opened up. This image, made of the very words referring to hearing and vision, must be the locus classicus of synaesthesia.

Nabokov himself encourages one to search for the *bédesque*. If you happen not to notice it, he will reluctantly point it out. It is immensely significant that in one of the rare places where he commented on his own style, he used a specifically comic-strip metaphor: When he concluded that no reader had detected his allusion in *Speak, Memory*, he felt obliged to lay it bare in a later foreword: "[A]nd none discovered the name of a great cartoonist and a tribute to him in the last sentence of section 2, Chapter Eleven. It is most embarrassing for a writer to have to point out such things himself" (*SM* 15). The sentence in question begins: "The ranks of words I reviewed were again *so glow*ing, with their puffed-out little chests and trim uniforms" (*SM* 219; emphasis added). Stretched across the gap in the phrase "*so glow*ing" is the last name of Otto Soglow, the cartoonist who created "The Little King" and who contributed regularly to the *New Yorker*. The words treated with amused retrospective affection by the older writer are those of a youthful poem. In *ranks*, they are *reviewed*, as they strut by in parade formation to be admired by their own author. As far as I know, this is the only instance of the *bédesque* that also refers to an actual comic strip.

The Defense contains a few caricatural creatures in the perpetual wrap-around comic strip of Nabokov's narrative décor. Few readers probably notice them—and, indeed, it might be argued that the creatures would obtrude irritatingly if they were more prominent.

> The frost, incidentally, was extraordinary.... The helpless mercury, under the influence of its surroundings, fell ever lower and lower. And even the polar bears in the zoo found that the management had overdone it. (*Def* 205)

What is going on in the foreground, the proper focus of the reader's attention, is distinctly less than cheerful. Luzhin is thinking about his father's graphically rendered grave—"the depressing waste patch and the cemetery wind"

(*Def* 205). But the polar bears are comic characters in an incipient little pictorial narrative, most of which one has to supply. So is the mercury in the thermometer, whose decline is to be blamed on a demoralizing environment. There is something inherently funny (and inherently *bédesque*) about the pathetic fallacy and anthropomorphized nature, anyway, but these momentary elements of the scene have an irresistible life. Though this life evaporates at once, it does not do so before one subliminally sees the polar bear shrugging his shoulder and making a wry face at his companion when the management's telephone persists in being busy (emitting, perhaps, bar-shaped hoots) or unanswered. One no sooner recalls the high hopes that everyone had for the mercury when it was young, before it fell in with that ruinous ne'er-do-well, the nemesis of so many promising careers, the ambient air, than one forgets it to return to the foreground plight of Grandmaster Luzhin.

These elements of the decor come from the works, but the reason they are in the works, of course, is that they were first in Nabokov's habitual way of thinking. For one finds the *bédesque* in the interviews, too. The interviews belong to the oeuvre, to be sure, because he disliked speaking "off the Nabocuff," as he incorrigibly put it, and always wrote out his answers. Asked by an interviewer to characterize his memory, Nabokov replied:

> I am an ardent memoirist with a rotten memory; a drozy king's absent-minded remembrancer. With absolute lucidity I recall landscapes, gestures,

Figure 23.1. "Emmie's Drawing," IB 61-62 and drawn by Clarence Brown. "A child's hand, undoubtedly Emmie's, had drawn a set of pictures, forming (as it had seemed to Cincinnatus yesterday) a coherent narrative, a promise, a sample of fantasy. First there was a horizontal line—that is, this stone floor; on it was a rudimentary chair somewhat like an insect, and above was a grating made of six squares. Then came the same picture but with the addition of a full moon, the corners of its mouth drooping sourly beyond the grating. Next a stool composed of three strokes with an eyeless (hence, sleeping) jailer on it and, on the floor, a ring with six keys. Then the same key ring, only a little larger, with a hand, extremely pentadactyl and in a short sleeve, reaching for it. Here it begins to get interesting. The door is ajar in the next drawing, and beyond it something looking like a bird's spur—all that is visible of the fleeing prisoner. Then he himself, with commas on his head instead of hair, in a dark little robe, represented to the best of the artist's ability by an isosceles triangle; he is being led by a little girl: prong-like legs, wavy skirt, parallel lines of hair. Then the same again, only in the form of a plan: a square for the cell, an angled line for the corridor, with a dotted line indicating the route and an accordionlike staircase at the end. And finally the epilogue: the dark tower, above it a pleased moon, with the corners of its mouth curling upward."

intonations, a million sensuous details, but *names and numbers topple into oblivion with absurd abandon like little blind men in file from a pier.*[8]

Pause for a moment to consider this figure. It has the streak of cruelty that is inherent in all caricature (and, to the exasperation of many critics, in Nabokov's imagination): "Absurd abandon" seems a heartless characterization of the stumbling of the blind. But this sequential bit of slapstick must be understood as the benign violence of the early comic strip, hopelessly incorrect politically, in which "visual impairment" meant getting poked in the eye with an umbrella.

If the examples presented so far seem much too reliant on the reader's role as accomplice in lettering the balloons and filling in the background of Nabokov's *bédesque,* here, from *Pale Fire,* are sequential frames of a virtual comic strip whose violence leaves very little to the imagination:

King Alfin the Vague, you will recall, was an aviator. He has just executed a tricky aerial maneuver in his trim little aeroplane. Here is his comic strip demise, explicitly presented frame by frame:

> At the last moment, King Alfin managed to straighten out his machine and was again master of gravity when, immediately afterwards, he flew smack into the scaffolding of a huge hotel which was being constructed in the middle of a coastal heath as if for the special purpose of standing in a king's way. The glossy prints of the enlarged photographs depicting the entire catastrophe were discovered one day by eight-year-old Charles Xavier in the drawer of a secretary bookcase. In some of these ghastly pictures one could make out the shoulders and leathern casque of the strangely unconcerned aviator, and in the penultimate one of the series, just before the white-blurred shattering crash, one distinctly saw him raise one arm in triumph and reassurance. (*PF* 103–4)

I have saved for last what I consider the only genuine and unmistakable comic strip in the pages of Nabokov: little Emmie's perfidious drawing in *Invitation to a Beheading* (*IB* 61–62), which seems to hold out to Cincinnatus a plan of escape (Fig. 23.1). Emmie drew it, appropriately, on a blank page in a catalogue of books. It is merely one of the included works in this extremely bookish book, which never tires of flaunting its bookishness. Another is the photo-

---

8. Alfred Appel, *Novel* (spring 1971), 214.

horoscope, one of those bastard comic strips in which actual photographs are fitted out with the characteristic speech balloons of the comic strip.

The drawing itself does not appear, of course, but the description of it is so meticulously explicit that my frame-by-frame forgery of Emmie's work was ... well ... child's play. In any case, it is the one place in Nabokov in which the merely *bédesque* has evolved into its imago form, a full-fledged *bande dessinée*.

Like all comic strips—perhaps like all art, but certainly like all speakers at the conventions of learned societies—it promises more than it can possibly deliver.

{ AFTERWORD }

Nabokov Studies
The State of the Art Revisited

STEPHEN JAN PARKER

As a Cornellian who spent nine years on the beautiful Ithaca, New York, campus, it is a special pleasure for me to take part in the festivities surrounding the Cornell Nabokov Centenary Festival. The classes I took at Cornell with Vladimir Nabokov in 1958 helped to determine the course of my professional life: I was poised at a moment of choice between immunogenetic research and literary studies, and Nabokov proved the difference, as it were. I remained at Cornell for my graduate work, eventually becoming the first recipient of a Ph.D. in Russian literature from the university.

That link between Cornell and Nabokov and me continued in 1984 when George Gibian, my doctoral mentor, and I edited the volume *The Achievements of Vladimir Nabokov*,[1] which presented the materials from the first Nabokov Festival held at Cornell in 1983. In the introduction to that volume we noted how fitting it was for Cornell to serve as host of the first commemoration of Nabokov's achievements and that the first festival was a true celebration of the writer, translator, critic, teacher, and friend—replete with laughter, warmth, and insights. The second Cornell festival, which signals the opening of worldwide centennial activities, will be no less a celebration.

Remarks delivered in September 1998 at the opening session of the Cornell Nabokov Centenary Festival.

1. George Gibian and Stephen Jan Parker, eds., *The Achievements of Vladimir Nabokov: Essays, Studies, Reminiscences, and Stories* (Ithaca, N.Y.: Center for International Studies, Cornell University, 1984).

My role at that first festival was to take a look at the state of Nabokov studies, using a frame suggested by René Wellek that considered scholarship, criticism, influence, and reputation. When I was invited to participate in the 1998 festival, it seemed natural to take another look at Nabokov studies, fifteen years later. What I failed to recognize when I proposed the topic was the impossibility of doing it justice in a short presentation. Nabokov studies today bear no resemblance to Nabokov studies a mere fifteen years ago. There has been an explosion of information and sources, criticism and commentary in the United States and around the world. Fifteen years ago, there was a fledgling American Nabokov Society with a biannual newsletter and a handful of members. Today there is an International Nabokov Society in the United States, another in Russia, and others in such distant places as Japan and South Korea.

Fifteen years ago, there were few of the resources needed for patient scholarship. There was no authoritative bibliography of Nabokov's works; access to his works was incomplete; there was no access to his manuscripts and papers; there was only one volume of correspondence, *The Nabokov-Wilson Letters* (*NWL*); reconstituted lectures from one of his courses and several separate lectures; and biographical information was already highly suspect.

Now the resources are much, much greater. Michael Juliar has provided the indispensable, voluminous *Descriptive Bibliography* of Nabokov's works, with a subsequent update.[2] Through the efforts of Dmitri Nabokov and the Nabokov estate, more of Nabokov's fiction and nonfiction has become available—a volume of plays; a complete collected stories (some published for the first time); the unpublished novella *The Enchanter;* Nabokov's correspondence with his sister in Russian; and a significant segment of the correspondence in English.[3]

Also thanks to the Nabokov estate—following Brian Boyd's careful work on the organization and catalogue—the Montreux archives found a welcome home in 1991 in the Berg Collection of the New York Public Library, offering scholars a wealth of primary material. According to Steven Crook, who is in

---

2. Michael Juliar, *Vladimir Nabokov: A Descriptive Bibliography* (New York: Garland, 1986).

3. Vladimir Nabokov, *The Man from the USSR and Other Plays,* trans. Dmitri Nabokov (New York: Harcourt Brace Jovanovich/Bruccoli Clark, 1984); idem, *The Stories of Vladimir Nabokov,* trans. Dmitri Nabokov (New York: Alfred A. Knopf, 1995); idem, *The Enchanter,* trans. Dmitri Nabokov (New York: Putnam's), 1986; idem, *Perepiska s sestroi* (Ann Arbor: Ardis, 1984); Dmitri Nabokov and Matthew Bruccoli, eds., *Vladimir Nabokov: Selected Letters 1940-1977* (New York: Harcourt Brace Jovanovich, 1989).

charge of the collection, the Nabokov archive has had extensive regular use by scholars from around the world since it opened to the public in 1993, and is today one of the most heavily used collections at the Berg.

Boyd's definitive biography has now relegated Andrew Field's misguided, slipshod work to the proverbial dustbin. Boyd's elucidation of Nabokov's life through fact and work—echoing Nabokov's ideal combination of science and art—has established *The Russian Years* and *The American Years* as the bedrock for all subsequent Nabokov study.[4]

The critical bibliography is now continuously updated on D. Barton Johnson's NABOKV-L e-mail server, in Dieter Zimmer's running bibliography housed at Jeff Edmunds's exceptional Zembla website, and in the annual bibliographies of *The Nabokovian*.[5]

There are still lacunae in the resources, however. In English we have an updated, readily available, nearly complete edition of Nabokov's works, thanks to Vintage International and New American Library. Only recently have the standard works become available in the Russian language, however, with the publication (Saint Petersburg: Symposium, 1997–2000) of two five-volume sets, one containing the works of Nabokov's American period, the other his Russian works. A substantial collection of translations of Nabokov's Russian poems is in preparation, and another volume of lectures is possible. Another volume of correspondence may be published, as well. Material pertaining to Nabokov's lepidopterological interests, including his unfinished history of the butterfly in art and unpublished sections from a continuation of *The Gift*, is nearing completion under the co-editorship of Brian Boyd and Robert Pyle, with the participation and assistance of Dmitri Nabokov.[6] And perhaps there will eventually be a glimpse of at least parts of *The Original of Laura*, Nabokov's last, uncompleted novel. (Her fate is yet to be decided.)

---

4. Brian Boyd, *Vladimir Nabokov: The Russian Years* (Princeton, N.J.: Princeton University Press, 1990); idem, *Vladimir Nabokov: The American Years* (Princeton, N.J.: Princeton University Press, 1991).

5. NABOKV-L list group (NABOKV-L@uscbvm.ucsb.edu); Zembla, website of the International Vladimir Nabokov Society, ed. Jeff Edmunds (University Libraries, Pennsylvania State University), available from http://www.libraries.psu.edu/iasweb/nabokov/zembla.htm; *The Nabokovian*, ed. Stephen Jan Parker (Lawrence: University of Kansas, 1978–).

6. Brian Boyd and Robert Michael Pyle, eds., *Nabokov's Butterflies: Unpublished and Uncollected Writings* (Boston: Beacon, 2000).

It would also be helpful to have a reissued and fully updated version of Juliar's bibliography and, eventually, a selectively annotated critical bibliography picking up from where Sam Schuman's bibliography left off in 1976.[7] And in the year 2027, the restricted Nabokov materials in the Library of Congress will become available to the public.

Much of this work will depend directly on Dmitri Nabokov. May Providence grant him the necessary time and energy and allow him the opportunity to complete his memoirs of his father and mother, which are also in progress.

In 1983, it was easy to look back at the first fifteen years of Nabokov criticism in the United States from the starting point of Page Stegner's *Escape into Aesthetics,* the first published book on Nabokov, and Andrew Field's *Nabokov: His Life in Art.*[8] At that time, about twenty volumes related to Nabokov were in print, and one could easily point to the most important articles and reviews that had appeared. A Nabokov scholar had control of the literature: There were overview introductions to the full range of Nabokov's novels by Donald Morton, G. M. Hyde, and L. L. Lee.[9] There were treatments of a select group of novels by Douglas Fowler, Julia Bader, Dabney Stuart, Ellen Pifer, Lucy Maddox, and David Packman, with different focuses—a reductivist formula, structural features, the centrality of moral concerns, parody, aesthetics, reflexivity.[10] A small group of volumes, by Carl Proffer; Alfred Appel, Jr.; Bobbie Ann Mason; and Alexander Nakhimovsky and Slava Paperno, concentrated on a single novel.[11] There were also several excellent anthologies of criticism; a few

---

7. Samuel Schuman, *Vladimir Nabokov: A Reference Guide* (Boston: G. K. Hall, 1979).

8. Page Stegner, *Escape into Aesthetics: The Art of Vladimir Nabokov* (New York: Dial Press, 1966); Andrew Field, *Nabokov: His Life in Art* (Boston: Little, Brown, 1967).

9. Donald Morton, *Vladimir Nabokov* (New York: Ungar, 1978); G. M. Hyde, *Nabokov: America's Russian Novelist* (London: Marion Boyars, 1977); L. L. Lee, *Vladimir Nabokov* (Boston: Twayne, 1976).

10. Douglas Fowler, *Reading Nabokov* (Ithaca, N.Y.: Cornell University Press, 1974); Julia Bader, *Crystal Land: Artifice in Nabokov's English Novels* (Berkeley: University of California Press, 1972); Dabney Stuart, *Nabokov: The Dimensions of Parody* (Baton Rouge: Louisiana State University Press, 1978); Ellen Pifer, *Nabokov and the Novel* (Cambridge, Mass.: Harvard University Press, 1980); Lucy Maddox, *Nabokov's Novels in English* (Athens: University of Georgia Press, 1983); David Packman, *Vladimir Nabokov: The Structure of Literary Desire* (Columbia: University of Missouri Press, 1982).

11. Carl R. Proffer, *Keys to* Lolita (Bloomington: Indiana University Press, 1968); Alfred Appel, Jr., ed., *The Annotated* Lolita (New York: McGraw-Hill, 1970); Bobbie Ann Mason, *Nabokov's Garden: A Guide to* Ada (Ann Arbor: Ardis, 1974); A. Nakhimovsky and S. Paperno, eds., *An English–Russian Dictionary of Nabokov's* Lolita (Ann Arbor: Ardis, 1982).

special editions of journals on Nabokov; a very few works published in other languages—notably, Maurice Couturier's post-structuralist study and Sergei Davydov's *"Teksty-matreshki"*;[12] and several volumes that do not fall into any easy category, such as Appel's study of Nabokov and the cinema, Jane Grayson's study of Nabokov's English and Russian translations, and Proffer's *Book of Things about Vladimir Nabokov*.[13]

Now, Nabokov criticism has burgeoned into a vigorous growth industry, not only in terms of books, but also in hundreds and hundreds of articles, chapters, essays, notes, and reviews in various languages—not to mention the new electronic dimension of inquiry and shared information on the Internet. Whereas in 1983 only twenty volumes or so related to Nabokov, today there are more than 130 volumes (counting doctoral dissertations), with others on the way. In compiling the annual Nabokov bibliography for the past fifteen years for *The Nabokovian*, I have listed an average of one hundred fifty citations per year. Although the bibliography now has approximately two thousand citations, it is by no means complete, as I am constantly reminded by *The Nabokovian*'s readers. I have not read all of this literature—I doubt that anyone has. Because of this profusion, Nabokov criticism cannot be said to be developing along clear lines of inquiry and discourse. The sheer quantity and richness of his writings have attracted the varying interests of persons in a broad range of disciplines and professions, and each has made a contribution in disparate venues.

If I simply follow along the lines of my review of fifteen years ago, I would note the following. There have been a few more general introductions to Nabokov's writings, by David Rampton, Tony Sharpe, and myself; another has been announced in England by Neil Cornwell; and a study of Nabokov's early Russian prose has been released.[14] A general volume on Nabokov is now

12. Maurice Couturier, *Nabokov* (Lausanne: L'Age d'homme, 1979); Sergei Davydov, *"Teksty-matreshki" Vladimira Nabokova* (Munich: Otto Sagner, 1982).

13. Alfred Appel, Jr., *Nabokov's Dark Cinema* (New York: Oxford University Press, 1974); Jane Grayson, *Nabokov Translated: A Comparison of Nabokov's Russian and English Prose* (Oxford: Oxford University Press, 1977); Carl R. Proffer, ed., *A Book of Things about Vladimir Nabokov* (Ann Arbor: Ardis, 1974).

14. David Rampton, *Vladimir Nabokov: A Critical Study of the Novels* (Cambridge: Cambridge University Press, 1984); Tony Sharpe, *Vladimir Nabokov* (London: Edward Arnold, 1991); Stephen Jan Parker, *Understanding Vladimir Nabokov* (Columbia: University of South Carolina Press, 1987); Neil Cornwell, *Vladimir Nabokov* (Plymouth, U.K.: Northcote House, 1999); Julian W. Connolly, *Nabokov's Early Fiction: Patterns of Self and Other* (Cambridge: Cambridge University Press, 1992).

available in all of the author series, including Twayne and Cambridge. Special journal issues have been devoted to Nabokov not only in North America—*Modern Fiction Studies, Canadian-American Slavic Studies, Russian Literature Triquarterly*—but also abroad, notably in France, in *Delta, Cycnos,* and *Europe*.[15] Another general anthology of criticism was edited by Harold Bloom, and a useful anthology of book reviews was edited by Norman Page.[16] Most notably, there is what accurately has been termed a "Nabokov encyclopedia": *The Garland Companion to Vladimir Nabokov,* edited by Vladimir Alexandrov.[17] This eight-hundred page collection of seventy-two articles by forty-two authors is an indispensable volume for everyone interested in Nabokov's life and works.

In this vast galaxy of Nabokov commentary, only five of his seventeen novels thus far have attracted what might be called constellation volumes. *Lolita* naturally has attracted the most. Fifteen years ago, we had Proffer's *Keys to Lolita;* Appel's *Annotated Lolita;* and Paperno and Nakhimovsky's *Lolita Dictionary.* To these have been added Appel's thoroughly updated and revised *Annotated Lolita (AnL,* 1991); Lance Olsen's *Janus Text,* a useful overview of the novel; Richard Corliss's volume on Lolita in film; Maurice Couturier's book on the Lolita myth, and Bloom's volume of previously published essays.[18] In 1983, *Ada* had Bobbie Ann Mason's garden guide; today, there is also Brian Boyd's *Place of Consciousness*.[19] Next to come is Boyd's full annotation of the novel, if its serialization in *The Nabokovian* is ever completed. Newly gathered

---

15. Charles Ross, ed., "Special Nabokov Issue," *Modern Fiction Studies* 25 (fall 1979); D. Barton Johnson, ed., "Nabokov Issue," *Canadian–American Slavic Studies* (fall 1985); idem, "Vladimir Nabokov Issue," *Russian Literature Triquarterly* 24 (1991); Maurice Couturier, ed., "Nabokov Issue," *Delta* (Montpelier, France) (1983); idem, "Nabokov: Autobiography, Biography and Fiction," *Cycnos* (Nice, France) (1993); Christine Raguet-Bouvart, ed., "Vladimir Nabokov Issue," *Europe* (Paris) (March 1995).

16. Harold Bloom, ed., *Vladimir Nabokov: Modern Critical Views* (New York: Chelsea House, 1987); Norman Page, ed., *Nabokov: The Critical Heritage* (London: Routledge and Kegan Paul, 1982).

17. Vladimir E. Alexandrov, ed., *The Garland Companion to Vladimir Nabokov* (New York: Garland, 1995).

18. Lance Olsen, Lolita*: A Janus Text* (New York: Twayne, 1996); Richard Corliss, *Lolita* (London: British Film Institute, 1994); Maurice Couturier, ed., *Lolita* (Paris: Autremont, 1998); Harold Bloom, ed., *Vladimir Nabokov's* Lolita (New York: Chelsea House, 1987).

19. Bobbie Ann Mason, *Nabokov's Garden: A Guide to* Ada (Ann Arbor: Ardis, 1974); Brian Boyd, *Nabokov's* Ada*: The Place of Consciousness* (Ann Arbor: Ardis, 1985).

around *Invitation to a Beheading* are Julian Connolly's critical companion to the novel, highlighting four alternative readings of the text, and Gavriel Shapiro's *Delicate Markers,* a study of the novel's subtexts.[20] There are two companion volumes to *Pnin:* Gene Barabtarlo's outstanding guide to the novel and Galya Diment's fascinating *Pniniad.*[21] *Pale Fire* has Priscilla Meyer's provocative *Look What the Sailor Has Hidden* and a new interpretation by Boyd, and *The Gift* has Stephen Blackwell's *Zina's Paradox.*[22]

Given such development, it is not a stretch to imagine that some of the other twelve novels will also eventually attract their own volumes. There are no monographs yet on Nabokov's poetry or drama, but a series of volumes is dedicated to Nabokov's short stories—Marina Naumann's study of the early Russian stories; Charles Nicol and Gene Barabtarlo's anthology, *A Small Alpine Form;* and Maxim Shrayer's *The World of Nabokov's Stories.*[23]

One of the most important new directions in criticism over the past decade has been the interest in the nature and significance of otherworldliness (*potustoronnost'*) in Nabokov's fictions, as first identified by Véra Nabokov, then explored in works such as Alexandrov's *Nabokov's Otherworld* and Boyd's exegeses of Nabokov's writings in the two-volume biography.[24]

Among other new directions, there appears to be a strong urge to position Nabokov. For instance, at the beginning of the 1990s Russia rediscovered not only Nabokov but also the émigré polemics of the 1920s and 1930s. In their

---

20. Julian W. Connolly, ed., Invitation to a Beheading: *A Critical Companion* (Evanston, Ill.: Northwestern University Press, 1997); Gavriel Shapiro, *Delicate Markers: Subtexts in Vladimir Nabokov's* Invitation to a Beheading (New York: Peter Lang, 1998).

21. Gennady Barabtarlo, *Phantom of Fact: A Guide to Nabokov's* Pnin (Ann Arbor: Ardis, 1989); Galya Diment, *Pniniad: Vladimir Nabokov and Marc Szeftel* (Seattle: University of Washington Press, 1997).

22. Priscilla Meyer, *Find What the Sailor Has Hidden: Vladimir Nabokov's* Pale Fire (Middletown, Conn.: Wesleyan University Press, 1988); Brian Boyd, *Nabokov's* Pale Fire: *The Magic of Artistic Discovery* (Princeton, N.J.: Princeton University Press, 1999); Stephen H. Blackwell, *Zina's Paradox: The Figured Reader in Nabokov's* Gift (New York: Peter Lang, 2000).

23. Marina Naumann, *Blue Evenings in Berlin: Nabokov's Short Stories of the 1920s* (New York: New York University Press, 1978); Charles Nicol and Gennady Barabtarlo, eds., *A Small Alpine Form: Studies in Nabokov's Short Fiction* (New York: Garland, 1993); Maxim D. Shrayer, *The World of Nabokov's Stories* (Austin: University of Texas Press, 1999).

24. Vladimir E. Alexandrov, *Nabokov's Otherworld* (Princeton, N.J.: Princeton University Press, 1991); Boyd, *American Years* and *Russian Years.*

publications, Russian commentators have picked up where émigré polemics left off. As Alexei Zverev so astutely explains in his essay in the *Garland Companion*, Russia remains preoccupied with the question "whether Nabokov was a Russian patriot and whether it was possible to regard him as organically linked to the Russian tradition." Zverev concludes: "Nabokov remains above all a bone of contention in today's debates which are in essence not about the meaning of Nabokov, and not even about literature, but about liberation from ideological and aesthetic dogmas."[25] Beyond this, a problem for critics in Russia (that is, aside from the limited number of truly bilingual English–Russian scholars) is that Russian scholars have until recently lacked the essential tools for scholarship on Nabokov.

This is not to say that no worthwhile critical writings are emanating from Russia. The recent volume *V. V. Nabokov: Pro and Contra* includes not only translations of Nabokov's writings, but also an excellent collection of articles by Slavists from around the world and sections of commentary and bibliographical information that exhibit the best scholarly qualities of the finest Russian Academy editions.[26]

The desire to position Nabokov is not only a Russian phenomenon. There seems to be almost a ubiquitous need to position him in a tradition, in a cultural context, in a movement, or in regard to specific literary affinities. Is Nabokov a modernist, a postmodernist, a post-postmodernist, or none of the above? Is he a metafictionist? Who influenced him? With whom does he share affinities? These questions are addressed in much of the recent criticism, and they certainly point to continuing critical work. I have in mind John Burt Foster's *Art of Memory and European Modernism* and the French conference on Nabokov and modernism–postmodernism.[27] I am also thinking of Geoffrey Green's *Freud and Nabokov;* Leona Toker's *The Mystery of Literary Structures;* a study of Nabokov and Milan Kundera;[28] and the numerous separate

---

25. Alexei Zverev, "Literary Return to Russia," in Alexandrov, *Garland Companion,* 296.

26. B. V. Averin, M. E. Malikova, and A. A. Dolinin, comps., *V. V. Nabokov: pro et contra* (St. Petersburg: Russkii Khristianskii gumanitarnyi institut, 1997).

27. John Burt Foster, Jr., *Nabokov's Art of Memory and European Modernism* (Princeton, N.J.: Princeton University Press, 1993).

28. Leona Toker, *Nabokov: The Mystery of Literary Structures* (Ithaca, N.Y.: Cornell University Press, 1989); Hana Pichova, *The Art of Memory in Exile: Vladimir Nabokov and Milan Kundera* (Carbondale: Southern Illinois University Press, 2002).

sections in the *Garland Companion* on Nabokov and Belyi, Bergson, Blok, Chateaubriand, Chekhov, Dostoevsky, Flaubert, Gogol, Joyce, Kafka, Poe, Proust, Pushkin, Turgenev, Updike, and Tolstoy.

I can imagine Nabokov gently smiling at all this commotion. After all, we know what he thought about tags and -isms and influences. In the classroom, Gogol's *Dead Souls* was not representative of the natural school; Belyi's *Petersburg* was not a symbolist novel; and *Madame Bovary* was but a fairy tale. But Nabokov was, of course, interested in the literary genealogy of a given text.

There will be other anthologies and other special journal issues; there will be ongoing studies of the novels individually and in groups; there will be studies of Nabokov's poetry and perhaps his theatrical writings; and there will be books devoted to literary affinities and literary and cultural positioning.

Nabokov's influence remains difficult to measure, and I will not do so, except to note that if one judges by the information disseminated over the Internet, there is an ever increasing number of cited comments from a variety of artists, mostly in the form of expressions of admiration and affirmations of influence. And, of course, the question of influence overlaps with the question of reputation. And I think it is safe to say that Nabokov's reputation has never been higher, judging by recent best-book polls. For instance, in the endpiece of the *New York Times Book Review* of August 23, 1998, Edmund Morris, a member of the Modern Library selection board, wrote:

> We ended up with an aggregate of 404 novels, with *Lolita* at no. 1 and *The Color Purple* by Alice Walker, in the position commonly euphemized as last but not least. Those two rankings seemed to me about right, if only because I had just finished reading *Lolita* for the eighth time and was, as usual, in a state of deep despair over the impossibility of ever writing a sentence that could compare with any of the flashing, floating lines that Nabokov released with such lepidopteral prodigality.

One need simply look at the events that are scheduled around the world in the centennial year—in New York, Connecticut, London, Cambridge, Paris, Lausanne, Montreux, Munich, Berlin, Petersburg, and Moscow—to understand Nabokov's pre-eminent stature.

I will close by recognizing some of the people who are most responsible for the development of Nabokov studies, all of whom share an uncommon devotion to things Nabokov.

First, of course, is Dmitri Nabokov. As an unusually gifted translator, he has worked tirelessly to bring his father's texts—prose, poetry, drama, and nonfiction—to the reading public. As guardian of his father's heritage, he has worked equally tirelessly to promote and assist Nabokov studies around the world. And as a son, he has defended his parents energetically from those who would impugn and malign.

Brian Boyd is our Nabokov authority, and Vladimir Nabokov is fortunate to have him as his biographer and explicator. Through the brilliance of his erudition and exegesis, it is Boyd who best teaches us to understand the joy that emanates from Nabokov's art.

I can think of no one who has more citations in the critical bibliography than D. Barton Johnson. His book *Worlds in Regression* serves as a model of encyclopedic knowledge and perceptive close reading.[29] He has worked ceaselessly for the Nabokov Society and for the creation of a fellowship of Nabokovians. It is he who created *Nabokov Studies,* ably edited and published by Zoran Kuzmanovich. And it is he who created the NABOKV-L e-mail network, which brings Nabokovphiles from around the world into daily contact—where questions are raised and answered; dialogues are engaged; news is circulated; and a certain amount of nonsense is tolerated.

This engagement with the electronic age is also greatly furthered by Edmunds's prodigious work at Zembla, which has become an indispensable source for Nabokov scholars and enthusiasts and remains the prime website among a growing number of such sites.

Another most noteworthy Nabokovphile is Gennady Barabtarlo, former editor of the "Annotations" section of *The Nabokovian;* compiler of the *Nabokovian* indexes; officer of the society; author of numerous critical works, including the guide to *Pnin* and a volume of essays on Nabokov's art and metaphysics;[30] and, not least, the translator, with Véra Nabokov, of the Russian edition of *Pnin.*

The officers of the Nabokov Society have done selfless work since the organization's inception twenty years ago: Julian Connolly; Galya Diment; John Burt Foster, Jr.; Charles Nicol; Ellen Pifer; Phyllis Roth; Sam Schuman; and

---

29. D. Barton Johnson, *Worlds in Regression: Some Novels of Vladimir Nabokov* (Ann Arbor: Ardis, 1984).

30. Gennady Barabtarlo, *Aerial Views: Essays on Nabokov's Art and Metaphysics* (New York: Peter Lang, 1993).

Susan Sweeney. Each is an outstanding Nabokov scholar and each has worked selflessly to promote Nabokov studies.

And last, two preeminent European Nabokovphiles: Maurice Couturier, the doyen of Nabokov studies in Europe who has published several books on Nabokov and hosted two international conferences at the Université de Nice, and Dieter Zimmer, who compiled the first bibliography of Nabokov's works, wrote *Les Papillons de Nabokov*,[31] has edited the complete works of Nabokov in German, and maintains the on-line bibliography of Nabokov criticism.

All of these people remain at the forefront of Nabokov studies, and it is they who will guarantee its continued growth.

---

31. Dieter E. Zimmer, *Les Papillons de Nabokov* (Lausanne: Musee cantonal de Zoologie, 1994).

{ POSTSCRIPT }

On Returning to Ithaca

DMITRI NABOKOV

As I stand here before you, ladies and gentlemen, I have a cozy sense of *déjà vécu*, for it was in just such a convivial aura that I recall the Nabokov Festival of 1983, guided by the expert hand of George Gibian, at which one of my many pleasures was rooming at the "White House" with Maestro Borges.

Gavriel Shapiro's organizational hand was untried when he embarked on this project, with whose foretaste he had lived lovingly for some ten years. It is to his eternal credit that he developed posthaste from the rigorous academic with whom I had the pleasure of appearing at the Sorbonne two years ago into an extraordinary "detail man." And without detail, a famous writer has said, art cannot exist. His attention has verged on the telepathic. Besides plunging me into a Jacuzzi of luxury at the Cornell super-Statler, he has, at every turn, foreseen and resolved potential troubles and trifles, from pressing engagements to pressing a suit.

As for me, among the things that have changed of late are my girth and roll center, which would make it impossible to scale the faces and chimneys of my mountaineering days, or the façade of Harvard's Memorial Hall, which I once did, although not, as one well-meaning embellisher has affirmed, while Father was lecturing inside on *Don Quixote* ("Quicksote"—his pronunciation). The same friendly Shakespearean academic, whose views Father respected, suggested it was not a good idea for a son to attend or audit his father's courses. Father passed the advice on to me, and I complied, which was a mistake. But

Editor's note: This is an abbreviated version of the keynote address that Dmitri Nabokov delivered at the Cornell Nabokov Centenary Festival in September 1998.

I do have a fond and vivid recollection of the classes I did nevertheless visit, and those were mostly right here at Cornell.

Apocrypha abounds, from the inane to the insane, and most of us have heard much of it—that Father was a narcissistic alcoholic who died of cancer (modest portions of red, bronchitis); that Mother was a harpy who, inter alia, entered Ithaca book shops to upstage *Zhivago* window displays with *Lolitas*—but the Véra Nabokov record will soon be set straight, perhaps to the chagrin of those to whom a miserable connubium is prerequisite for an artist—in what promises to be a splendid biography of Mother by Stacy Schiff, who is getting to know my mother almost as well as I do, and will, I hope, forgive me for citing what could hardly have been said better. I quote:

> Resentment of Mrs. Nabokov accumulated in equal proportion to the mystique. Who was this "Grey Eagle" in the classroom, the students wondered, while the faculty—very much aware that Nabokov had no Ph.D., no graduate students, no freshmen, and, by the mid-fifties, enviably high enrollments—chafed at the husband-and-wife routine. When Nabokov was being considered for a job elsewhere, . . . an ex-colleague discouraged the idea: don't bother hiring him; *she* does all the work. Nabokov did nothing to check this kind of sniping. He told his students that Ph.D. stood for "Department of Philistines." . . . His colleagues were jealous of the enrollments, mystified by the butterfly net, astounded by the loyalty of the wife. In this last, they echoed the sentiments of Edmund Wilson, who hated her exam administering and her general devotion. Other writers' wives were asked point-blank why they could not be more like Véra, who was held up as the gold standard, the International Champion in the Wife-of-Writer Competition. . . .
>
> Véra Nabokov was a striking woman, white-haired and alabaster-skinned, thin and fine-boned. The discrepancy between the hair and the young face was particularly dramatic. She was "mnemogenic," as Nabokov wrote of Clare in *The Real Life of Sebastian Knight* [who, I interject, is an excellent refutation of the charge that Nabokov created no sympathetic female characters; Zina Merz is another]—"subtly endowed with the gift of being remembered." And that is where the trouble begins. According to the faculty and the students at Cornell, she was luminous, regal, elegance personified, "the most beautiful middle-aged woman I have ever set eyes on"; [or else] she was a waif, [or] dowdy, [or] half-starved, [or] the Wicked Witch of the West. To those same students and faculty emeriti went the

obvious question: what was Mrs. Nabokov doing in her husband's classroom, lecture after lecture? The answers come prefaced with the reminder that it was Nabokov who termed rumor the poetry of truth:

- Mrs. Nabokov was there to remind us we were in the presence of greatness, and should not abuse that privilege with our inattention.
- Nabokov had a heart condition, and she was at hand with a phial of medicine to jump up at a moment's notice.
- That wasn't his wife, that was his mother.
- Nabokov was allergic to chalk dust—and because he didn't like his handwriting.
- To shoo away the coeds [this before the publication of *Lolita*].
- Because she was his encyclopedia, if he ever forgot anything. [This is perhaps a bit closer to the truth.]
- Because he had no idea what was going to come out of his mouth—and no memory of it after it did—so she had to write it all down so that he would remember what to ask on the exams.
- He was blind, and she was the Seeing Eye dog, which explained why they always arrived arm in arm. [Mother would have liked this one.]
- We all knew that she was a ventriloquist.
- She had a gun in her purse, and was there to defend him.[1]

To a loving and observant son, Mother was of course even more, ineffably more, than the most sensitive biographer can say—self-taught literary assistant who sacrificed a jewel case of talents for what both adoration and objectivity dictated, but, most of all, utterly human and humane and maternal. I remember her distaste for the superficial, the approximate, and her insistence that I explain comprehensibly, with diagrams, how an automobile differential or an early binary system worked. Yet she was not only superbly precise of mind, but tenderness personified, to deserving man or beast. When I lay in the deliberately darkened isolation of a burn unit and she could barely see me from her wheelchair under an ineffective outdoor infrared heater, she exclaimed, "Look what's going on behind you!" for the Swiss TV was running a program

---

1. Extracted from Stacy Schiff's *Véra (Mrs. Vladimir Nabokov)* (New York: Random House, 1999).

on animals, a love and cause of her life. In Ithaca she did a lot of things, including learning how to drive under the guidance of a colorful gentleman named Jacoby—both teacher and dealer—who sold us our first car, a slightly limping, mouse-gray prewar Plymouth that took me to boarding school. She shopped, she typed, she knew exactly to what bone-manipulator to take me when I threw out my sacroiliac playing tennis. She had enjoyed target-shooting in her youth, as well as riding and stunt-flying, but she carried no gun to class and had attempted no political assassinations. The Browning .38 for which we had traded a rickety old revolver of mine at an Ithaca gun shop reposed, unused, in a drawer. It now hangs in its holster by my bed, loaded for pears, mad biographers, and other demented souls.

One bit of nonsense—well meant, but exactly the kind of human-interest hogwash that Nabokov detested—caught my eye last week. A 1992 mini-tribute to VN from a coastal college that I feared might be slated for republication quoted a long-ago student as follows:

> [The professor wore] dirty tennis shoes with holes and no socks [and] a shabby jacket with patches and ill-matched trousers, an outfit borrowed from fellow émigré Mikhail Karpovich, a history professor at Harvard.

Sorry, Palo Alto—we may have been émigrés, but we were not proto-beatniks. And anyone familiar with Nabokov's tall, gaunt figure of the 1940s and Karpovich's roly-poly shape would have a real belly-laugh at the thought of their exchanging clothes. Perhaps another story got mixed in here—a true one about the tailcoat that kind but misguided friend Sergei Rachmaninov gave Nabokov for his debut at that summer session. The tailcoat remained unused, while Rachmaninov's gift to me of my first radio—an oval, beige Philco portable—was cherished for years.

I quote ibidem:

> I don't recall taking any notes.... [I]t would have been rather like scribbling... while Michelangelo talked about how he designed and painted.... I don't recall that he lectured in any conventional sense of the term.... The author read from his own works, which were often autobiographical, and "smacked of life."

This source gentleman's adoration is truly touching, but mnemosyne has misspoken again. Father lectured, that distant summer, on Russian drama and other matters from meticulously prepared texts, which exist to this day in my archive. These particular lectures are largely unpublished, but the fact that Father spoke from manuscript rather than "off the Nabocuff," as some would have liked, has made it possible to publish precious Cornell and Harvard lectures that would have been lost, and has, in the process, allowed me to make up for having missed the live performance.

Other award-winning tripe abound. I have already bestowed my personal booby prizes on the likes of the British ecclesiastical journalist Oddie, who ascribes the evils of our—quote—permission society to jazz, the Beatles, *Playboy,* and *Lolita;* critics Valium Val and born-again Bernie; various U.S. Hatches and Podhoretzes who would throw out the babies of art with the messy bathwater of the media; the non-reading virtue-leaguers striving to protect the babies who remain on board, free to watch the grizzliest of dismemberments; the squabbles of Jerry Springer's transvestites, and the possible impeachment of a president for the consequences of bedding what I guess he considered a peach; negligee-photographed scholar Pia Pera—"pear" in Italian—who rips off much of *Lolita* in an attempt at some earnest statement "from the girl's viewpoint," allowing her sleazy Italian publisher to proclaim as much via a belly-band on her book that implies a nexus with Adrian Lyne's totally extraneous fine new film. And besides the legislators who would have the Internet red-flag the word "breast" wherever it is not complemented by "cancer," there are, on the fence's fruitful other side, many frac-tail riders besides Pera who, it seems, can think of nothing new to write about, but whom one ignores unless they cross into the actionable zones of plagiarism and infringement.

We have worse: the infamous biographer Nosik, whom I shall belabor, sticking to my guns and noses ad nosikum. Fortunately, he will soon be supplanted, on the needy Russian scene, at least, by Brian Boyd.

And still worse: a gentleman named Begley, who, in a proposed introduction to *Speak, Memory,* accused the author of *Bend Sinister, Invitation to a Beheading, Tyrants Destroyed,* and "Cloud, Castle, Lake" of being scandalously soft on Hitler. The introduction did not appear.

But let us recall happier things:

> Wonderful Morris Bishop, a truly cosmopolitan man and scholar, who brought Nabokov to Cornell.
> The congeries of sabbatical houses that we rented in Ithaca, each with its personal charms, from horseshoes to basement workshops to a

- splendid cannonball of unknown origin that I dug up in the Hansteens' garden, somehow related in my memory to the expression "Go over like a lead balloon" that, freshly learned, made me roll with laughter during a tennis game with Gordon Sutherland, son of the eminent Cornell law professor and family friend.
- Countless games with Father at the same Cascadilla courts, and even skiing with him, one particularly wintry winter, on the slope of what was then called the University Library.
- The general cocoon of love and well-being and encouragement in which both my parents always enveloped me, whatever the locus—and I was not always an easy son.
- Doctor Asher, our old-world family physician and his sons, who introduced me to the joys of private flying.
- My model-airplane motors that had prophetically tormented our neighbors long before, during school-vacation days spent in Ithaca.
- Watching *The Honeymooners* together on one of the sabbatical TVs, bisected by a perpetual black stripe, or Alfred Hitchcock episodes that presaged a collaboration with Hitchcock that was almost to happen some years later.
- The whole charming aura of Ithaca, where I spent relatively little time because of my studies elsewhere, but which retains far more than its share of space under the subtitle "Happy Time and Place, with Parents."

My father is enjoying some wonderful presents as his one-hundredth birthday approaches:

- The first film based on a work of his that, I am convinced, he would have truly enjoyed.
- Many splendid editions in many tongues, from Vintage to Penguin to Adelphi to Rowohlt to Anagrama to imminent Pléiade to the Library of America, the American Pléiade.
- Adoration, if rather anarchic and often piratical, among a people for which he felt, as he left Europe, that he would never write again.
- That nation's spontaneous project of making the Nabokovs a prototype for restitution, in this case the restitution of the setting for his childhood. And were not language and childhood two of his three great losses?

- The various lists—the BBC's great men of the century, the 100-Book affairs, where he would have been happy to march behind Joyce, whatever the selection process.
- A subtle feeling that he and Joyce are indeed marching together into the pantheon as the great English-language writers of our time, without benefit of Nobels or U.S. citizens' postage-stamp committees.
- The marvelous celebrations planned worldwide for his birthday, some organized by established Nabokovians, others by brilliant newcomers who have materialized like dei ex machina when they were most needed.
- The fact that these celebrations start out here at Cornell, a university he dearly loved, even at moments when he felt sick of teaching in general, for its splendid setting and the academic freedom it accorded him.

For that I thank, from the warmest cockles of a Nabokovian heart, President Rawlings, Professor Shapiro and his cohorts and colleagues, dear friend Bill Buckley, who had to dash off after Thursday night's thespian foray, Terry Quinn who prepared it—and all of you, many of whom I already knew in person, others who have become faces rather than Internet digits and letters on sites that have touchingly hung out signs saying, "Gone to Ithaca," to commemorate Vladimir Nabokov, as well as all those whose presentations I have yet to enjoy.

Now, two final, more personal thoughts.

I don't know how many of you were able to attend my brief reading yesterday from my translation of an unpublished continuation of *The Gift*. What I would have gone on to read, had not a final slice of time inexorably consumed itself, was what the protagonist's father invents: a thunderingly new classification system for the animal world that was, in a way, prophetic. For only now are Vladimir Nabokov's own new concepts of classification being acknowledged by the entomological word—in part, thanks to the specimens preserved at the Cornell Museum—and newly recognized variants being named after characters in his books.

Finally, finally:

While the basic furnishings of Ithaca have not changed much—the hills, the lake, the splendid waterfalls—thank God some of the superstructure *is* different. Had time stood still in every way—the old friends, the brown buses, the period cars we meet in the new *Lolita,* details of streets and buildings, the differently garbed populace, *The Honeymooners* and the Hitchcock—that would have been too poignant for tears, for only Véra and Vladimir Nabokov would be missing.

{ ABOUT THE CONTRIBUTORS }

Vladimir E. Alexandrov is Professor of Russian Literature at Yale University. He is the editor of *The Garland Companion to Vladimir Nabokov* (1995) and the author of *Andrei Bely: The Major Symbolist Fiction* (1986), *Nabokov's Otherworld* (1991; Russian translation, 1999; Chinese translation, forthcoming), and articles on literary and cultural theory and on Russian writers from the eighteenth to the twentieth century. He is completing a book tentatively titled "Mapping Anna Karenina, or The Plurality and Limits of Interpretation."

Stephen H. Blackwell is Associate Professor of Russian at the University of Tennessee. He is the author of *Zina's Paradox: The Figured Reader in Nabokov's* Gift (2000) and co-editor of *In Other Words: Essays in Honor of Vadim Liapunov* (forthcoming).

Brian Boyd, University Distinguished Professor, Department of English, University of Auckland, is best known as the author of the prize-winning *Vladimir Nabokov: The Russian Years* (1990) and *Vladimir Nabokov: The American Years* (1991). Among his other books are *Nabokov's* Ada: *The Place of Consciousness* (1985; 2nd ed. 2001), *Nabokov's* Pale Fire: *The Magic of Artistic Discovery* (1999), and six volumes of Nabokov he has edited or introduced. He has published on Renaissance drama; on American, English, Irish, New Zealand, and Russian fiction; on children's fiction; and on evolution and literary theory. Among his current research projects are a biography of the philosopher Karl Popper, an evolutionary and cognitive account of fiction, and a critical book on Shakespeare.

Clarence Brown attended Duke University, the Army Language School (Russian), the University of Michigan (linguistics), and Harvard University (Russian literature), then taught at Princeton University until his retirement in 1999. His study of Osip Mandelstam won the Phi Beta Kappa Gauss Award for Criticism. He was cartoon editor of the *Saturday Review* in the 1970s. Vladimir Nabokov thought that Brown's birthday poem to him resembled the work of Lomonosov but atoned for this by praising his comic strip, "Ollie," then running in London's *Spectator*. Brown lives in Seattle and continues to write the newspaper column "Ink Soup."

Julian W. Connolly is Professor of Slavic Languages and Literatures at the University of Virginia. He is the author of

Ivan Bunin (1982), *Nabokov's Early Fiction: Patterns of Self and Other* (1992), and *The Intimate Stranger: Meetings with the Devil in Nineteenth-Century Russian Literature* (2001). He has edited two volumes of criticism, *Nabokov's* Invitation to a Beheading: *A Course Companion* (1997) and *Nabokov and His Fiction: New Perspectives* (1999); he has also written more than fifty articles on nineteenth- and twentieth-century Russian literature.

Nina Demurova has taught at Moscow State University, Moscow State Pedagogical University, and is currently Professor at the University of Rusian Academy of Education. She has written on English and American literature and translated a number of English and American authors. Her best-known translations are *Alice's Adventures in Wonderland* and *Through the Looking Glass* by Lewis Carroll; her book *Lewis Carroll: Life and Work* was published by Nauka, The Russian Academy of Sciences publishing house, and was a popular success. In 2000, she received the International Board of Books for Young People Certificate of Honor for Translation.

Robert Dirig has been interested in Nabokov's work on the Karner Blue since 1973 and is an authority on this endangered butterfly. He studied entomology and natural-history education at Cornell University, has worked with Northeastern North American butterflies and moths for forty years, and is employed as a botanical curator at the Cornell University Herbaria.

Sergei Davydov teaches Russian Literature at Middlebury College, Vermont. He holds a Ph.D. degree from Yale University and is the author of numerous studies on Pushkin, Dostoevsky, Nabokov, and literary theory. He is the author of *"Teksty-matreshki" Vladimira Nabokova* (1982) and is working on another book about Pushkin's political and religious thought.

John Burt Foster, Jr. is Professor of English and Cultural Studies at George Mason University and a former president of the International Nabokov Society. In addition to publishing widely in nineteenth- and twentieth-century literature and thought, he is the author of *Nabokov's Art of Memory and European Modernism* and of numerous articles on Nabokov in cross-cultural perspective. Recent essays include "Poshlust, Culture Criticism, Adorno and Malraux," in *Nabokov and His Fiction: New Perspectives* and "Transnational Authorship on the German–Slavic Border: The Examples of Nietzsche and Nabokov," in *Cold Fusion: Aspects of the German Cultural Presence in Russia.*

D. Barton Johnson, Professor Emeritus at the University of California at Santa Barbara, is a quondam two-time president of the International Vladimir Nabokov Society. He is the author of *Worlds in Regression: Some Novels of Vladimir Nabokov* and has written many articles on Nabokov and other Russian modernists. He is the founding editor of the journal *Nabokov Studies* and of NABOKV-L, the Nabokov electronic discussion forum.

Marina Kanevskaya is Assistant Professor of Russian Language and Literature at the University of Montana. She trained as a critic and literary historian at Moscow State University (1973–79), and received a Ph.D. from Indiana University in 1997. She is the author of *N. K. Mikhailovsky's Criticism of Dostoevsky: The Cruel Critic* (2001). She has researched nineteenth- and twentieth-century trends in Russian literature.

John M. Kopper is Professor of Russian and Chair of Comparative Literature at Dartmouth College, New Hampshire. He is co-editor, with Lenore Grenoble, of *Essays in the Art and Theory of Translation* (1997) and has published numerous articles on Nabokov and Andrei Belyi, as well as Gogol, Tolstoy, Leskov, Boris Poplavsky, Shakespeare, and Mary Austin.

Zoran Kuzmanovich teaches literature and film at Davidson College; he writes on the relations among arts, ethics, and politics. Since 1996 he has served as the editor of *Nabokov Studies*.

Dmitri Nabokov was born in Berlin and came to the United States as a young child with his parents. He graduated from Harvard University, served in the U.S. Army, and began the vocal studies that led him to become an opera and concert performer (as a basso) around the world. He has translated most of his father's Russian short stories and plays and many of his novels into English. He is currently preparing an anthology in English of his father's poetry.

Charles Nicol is Professor of English at Indiana State University. He has been publishing on Nabokov since 1967. Elected first president of the International Vladimir Nabokov Society some twenty years ago, he is now serving a second term. Formerly "Annotations and Queries" editor for *The Nabokovian*, he recently won the journal's "Nabokov Prose-alike" contest. He also edited *Nabokov's Fifth Arc: Nabokov and Others on His Life's Work* with J. E. Rivers, and *A Small Alpine Form: Studies in Nabokov's Short Fiction* with Gennady Barabtarlo. He has written on various subjects for *The Atlantic, Harper's,* and the *New York Times Book Review*.

Stephen Jan Parker is Professor of Russian Literature at the University of Kansas. He is the author of *Understanding Vladimir Nabokov;* co-editor with George Gibian of *The Achievements of Vladimir Nabokov;* founder, editor, and publisher of *The Nabokovian;* and co-founder of the Vladimir Nabokov Society.

Ellen Pifer, Professor of English and Comparative Literature at the University of Delaware, has written extensively on modern and contemporary fiction. She is, most recently, the author of *Demon or Doll: Images of the Child in Contemporary Writing and Culture* (2000) and editor of *Vladimir Nabokov's* Lolita: *A Casebook* (forthcoming, 2003). Her previous books include *Nabokov and the Novel, Saul Bellow against the Grain,* and *Critical Essays on John Fowles.* She has been Visiting Professor at the University of California, Berkeley, and the University of Lyon, France, where she held a Fulbright award.

Irena Ronen is an independent scholar. She holds degrees from the Hebrew University of Jerusalem and the University of Michigan in theater studies and Slavic languages and literatures. She is the author of a book on the structure of Pushkin's *Boris Godunov* (1997) and of articles on Batiushkov, Gogol, Pushkin, Nabokov, and Khodasevich.

Omry Ronen is the author of *An Approach to Mandel'stam* (1983), *The*

Fallacy of the Silver Age (1997), *Serebrianyi vek kak vymysel i umysel* (2000), and *Poetika Osipa Mandel'shtama: Izbrannye stat'i* (2002), as well of as several scores of articles on Russian literature and poetics.

Christine A. Rydel is Professor of Russian at Grand Valley State University, Michigan. She has published on a variety of topics, especially Russian Romanticism, Fedor Ivanovich Tiutchev, Bella Akhmadulina, and H. G. Wells in Russia; has served on the editorial board of the journal *Russian Literature Triquarterly;* and has edited four volumes in the series Dictionary of Literary Biography. She is also the author of the forthcoming *A Nabokov Who's Who.*

Gavriel Shapiro is Professor of Russian Literature at Cornell University. Shapiro is the author of *Nikolai Gogol and the Baroque Cultural Heritage* (1993) and *Delicate Markers: Subtexts in Vladimir Nabokov's* Invitation to a Beheading (1998). He has also published numerous articles on nineteenth- and twentieth-century Russian literature and culture. He is currently working on a book tentatively titled "Nabokov and the Pictorial."

Susan Elizabeth Sweeney is Associate Professor of English at Holy Cross College and a past president of the International Vladimir Nabokov Society. She has published about two dozen articles and notes on Nabokov; the most recent, " Looking at Harlequins: Nabokov, the World of Art, and the Ballets Russes," appears in the collection *Nabokov's World: Reading Nabokov* (2002). A specialist in postmodernist fiction, she also studies revisions of such popular genres as mysteries, romances, ghost stories, and folk tales, and recently coedited the volume *Detecting Texts: The Metaphysical Detective Story from Poe to Postmodernism* (1999). "The Enchanter and the Beauties of Sleeping" is part of a larger project on Nabokov's allusions to fairy tales in fictions about pedophilia.

Leona Toker is Professor in the English Department of the Hebrew University of Jerusalem. She is the author of *Nabokov: The Mystery of Literary Structures* (1989), *Eloquent Reticence: Withholding Information in Fictional Narrative* (1993), *Return from the Archipelago: Narratives of Gulag Survivors* (2000), and of articles on English, American, and Russian writers. She is the editor of *Commitment in Reflection: Essays in Literature and Moral Philosophy* (1994) and co-editor of *Rereading Texts/Rethinking Critical Presuppositions: Essays in Honour of H. M. Daleski* (1996).

Joanna Trzeciak teaches at Reed College. Her areas of specialization are Nabokov as self-translating author and translation theory. Her translations of Wisława Szymborska have appeared in the *New Yorker,* the *Times Literary Supplement, Harper's* magazine, the *Atlantic Monthly,* and other periodicals. Her collection of Szymborska's poetry in translation, *Miracle Fair,* was awarded the 2001 Heldt Translation Prize.

Lisa Zunshine is Assistant Professor of English at the University of Kentucky. She is the editor of *Nabokov at the Limits: Redrawing Critical Boundaries* and the author of essays on eighteenth-century literature and culture in *Poetics Today, Eighteenth-Century: Theory and Interpretation,* and *Philosophy and Literature.*